SHAKESPEARE:

Modern Essays in Criticism

SHAKESPEARE:
Modern Essays in Criticism

EDITED BY

LEONARD F. DEAN

UNIVERSITY OF CONNECTICUT

A GALAXY BOOK

NEW YORK   *Oxford University Press*   1961

PREFACE

THE PURPOSE of this volume is to bring together some of the good modern essays on Shakespeare, as many as could be reprinted in a single volume at a reasonable price. I looked for essays offering a fresh and thoughtful interpretation of the plays; and I had in mind the general reader as well as the student, teacher, and critic. The plan was to include a few general essays, at least one on each of the major plays, and as far as possible several essays on a play or group of plays in order to represent contrasting or complementary critical views.

It turned out that almost all of the essays finally selected and available for reprinting had been written rather recently. It is likely, therefore, that this volume has some value as a sampling of contemporary Shakespearian criticism, even though no effort has been made to represent systematically whatever schools of criticism may exist. Good literary criticism is to some extent a creative act, a lucky thing which cannot quite be explained by circumstances; but luck takes different forms at different times and places, and perhaps it is not surprising or altogether accidental that many of the essays in this volume reflect contemporary interest in poetic language, the aesthetics of drama, the Elizabethan theater, and Renaissance modes of thought. Furthermore, critics are sensible people who find it dull to do over again what has already been well done, and this fact, too, helps to account for recent emphasis on patterns of imagery, the structure of ironic drama, and other topics somewhat neglected by earlier critics.

I am indebted to students and colleagues with whom I have

discussed Shakespearian criticism. They have helped to test my judgment and have put me on the track of good things which I might otherwise have missed. I am chiefly indebted, of course, to the authors and publishers of the essays reprinted here; without their co-operation the book could not have been made. I regret that it was impossible for various reasons to include many fine essays. Shakespearian criticism has flourished in our time, and a single volume cannot do justice to it all.

LEONARD F. DEAN

Storrs, Connecticut
January 1957

CONTENTS

ALFRED HARBAGE · Shakespeare's Audience: Modern Appraisals · 3

ALAN S. DOWNER · The Life of Our Design: The Function of Imagery in the Poetic Drama · 19

HARLEY GRANVILLE-BARKER · *The Merchant of Venice* · 37

CAROLINE F. E. SPURGEON · The Imagery of *Romeo and Juliet* · 72

NORTHROP FRYE · The Argument of Comedy · 79

E. K. CHAMBERS · *A Midsummer Night's Dream* · 90

M. C. BRADBROOK · *Much Ado About Nothing* · 97

HAROLD JENKINS · *As You Like It* · 108

JOSEPH H. SUMMERS · The Masks of *Twelfth Night* · 128

E. M. W. TILLYARD · *Richard II* · 138

LEONARD F. DEAN · *Richard II:* The State and the Image of the Theater · 159

C. L. BARBER · Saturnalia in the Henriad · 169

D. A. TRAVERSI · *Henry V* · 192

BRENTS STIRLING · "Or else were this a savage spectacle" · 204

ROY WALKER · *Hamlet:* The Opening Scene · 216

W. H. CLEMEN · The Imagery of *Hamlet* · 222

MAYNARD MACK · The World of *Hamlet* · 237

S. L. BETHEL · *Troilus and Cressida* · 258

HAROLD S. WILSON · Action and Symbol in *Measure for Measure* and *The Tempest* · 267

ELMER EDGAR STOLL · Source and Motive in *Macbeth* and *Othello* · 282

ROBERT B. HEILMAN · Wit and Witchcraft: An Approach to *Othello* · 294

ARTHUR SEWELL · Tragedy and the "Kingdom of Ends" · 311

JOHN F. DANBY · The Fool and Handy-Dandy · 333

MARK VAN DOREN · *Antony and Cleopatra* · 345

OSCAR JAMES CAMPBELL · *Coriolanus* · 360

G. WILSON KNIGHT · "Great Creating Nature": An Essay on *The Winter's Tale* · 378

THEODORE SPENCER · Shakespeare and the Nature of Man: *The Tempest* · 411

EDWARD HUBLER · The Economy of the Closed Heart · 417

SHAKESPEARE:

Modern Essays in Criticism

Alfred Harbage

SHAKESPEARE'S AUDIENCE:
MODERN APPRAISALS

. . . . Shakespeare like Falstaff is the cause that wit is in other men, and the most brilliant criticism in English has been provoked by Shakespeare's plays. But the least brilliant of this criticism is, I believe, that which relates the plays to their audience. It is usually incidental; and it is often careless, cynical, or marked by an incredible condescension. The Elizabethan stratum of humanity is divested of mystery, its common sense assessed at the rate of some early treatise on physiology, its perceptive range simplified to "two levels of intelligence," while whole battalions of our former fellow mortals are dismissed with placid allusions to "groundlings" or "a motley crew." At the safe remove of three centuries the nature of a generation collectively has even been deduced from a heap of nutshells. Sometimes distance lends courage also to the idealist, and the Globe is filled with mute inglorious Shakespeares, but normally we hear the voice of derision and disdain. Not all of the critical attitudes toward the audience are uncongenial, but none of them need be taken on faith.

We are familiar with the tendency in others (and ourselves) to apply colors recklessly to any part of a canvas depicting the lusty age of Elizabeth. Enthusiastic brushwork transforms human beings into Elizabethans. A brief description of Shakespeare's audience by Brander Matthews contains the following phrases: "suberabundant energy," "soaring imagination," "puffed with pride," "reckless daredevil," "sensuous and sensual," "furi-

ous in hate and love," "avid of swift sensation," "primitive savagery of manners," "violently passionate," "frankly brutal." [1] The
portrait is exhilarating but conducive at last to sober reflection.
Were Shakespeare's contemporaries truly such galvanic creatures?
Imagine, if you will, some London carter plodding beside his
oxen on the road to Hackney, some London housewife sewing
a fine seam, some London mason patiently, skillfully pointing the
stones of Bridge Gate at Is. 4d. a long, long day. Imagine entering some Bread Street shop in 1601, fixing the proprietor with
your eye, and saying: "You are puffed with pride, a reckless
daredevil, furious in hate and love, violently passionate, and
frankly brutal." Would he not reply with pardonable dismay:
"Who? Me!" Nothing we can discover from examining their
daily routine, their frugal expense accounts, and their quiet and
sensible letters suggests that Elizabethans, individually or collectively, were vastly different from us. Their nature cannot be
deduced from the defeat of the Armada or the public hangings in
Tyburn. We ourselves live in a spectacular age, without being
individually spectacular.

The kinship we feel with the old playgoers, those of us who
love their drama, must not be confined to the upper classes, no
matter what our own social allegiances or aspirations may be.
I have previously quoted the statement that while Heywood
wrote for apprentices and shopkeepers, Shakespeare "kept in his
mind's eye the approval of the lordly patrons of Blackfriars."
The writer, I suspect, would indignantly repudiate the implications of the statement if put in bald terms—the fine things in
Elizabethan drama were written for the fine people, for lords.
So prevalent is the notion that one is apt to countenance it
through sheer inadvertence; the cloven hoof flashes out in half
the Shakespearean criticism being written. Inadvertence can
scarcely be the explanation for the following: "The movie seems
to be quite as capable of proceeding on two levels as the Elizabethan tragedy: poetry and psychology for the gentlemen's galleries, action and blood for the pit." [2] The writer is a careful
investigator in a modern field, repeating something evidently conceived to be a critical truism. But if we are to confuse social with
spiritual distinction, we may as well subscribe at once to the
belief that Shakespeare's plays were written by the Earl of

Oxford, or Southampton, or Rutland, or whoever the current candidate may be.

Misconceptions are prevalent concerning the intellectual and artistic attainments of the Elizabethan nobleman. One suspects that he is often patterned in the image of Sir Philip Sidney and the Earl of Southampton, the latter generously endowed with the qualities found in the literary works dedicated to him. It is true that the English Renaissance brought forth lords, knights, and gentlemen with literary gifts, in greater number, perhaps, than any comparable span of years, but it was a great age and the law of averages was operating. It is doubtful if the proportion of the genteel classes displaying such gifts, creative or appreciative, was higher than that of the literate ungenteel. That the nobility could produce a Sidney is the less remarkable in view of the ability of the middle classes to produce a Spenser and a Milton. Marlowe and Shakespeare illustrate the remarkable efficaciousness of extraction from workers in leather. Many men of high birth still looked with disdain upon anything so clerkly as literature, while many others, including nominal patrons of now famous dramatic companies, displayed simply a depressing indifference. The Elizabethan great world from the queen down, let the truth be told, was mean to its poets and dramatists.

As we read Sir Edmund Chambers's fine volumes on the Elizabethan stage, we come first to the queen, then to the royal household, then to the Revels Office, until by this magnificent route we arrive at the theatres and the acting companies. All is relevant and all is revealing, but, unless we are wary, we may gather the impression that the drama of the age was an appendage of the court. An equally valid approach to the stage would be a chronicle of London taverns and of enterprisers before James Burbage. Sir Edmund writes:

> It will be manifest, in the course of the present treatise, that the palace was the point of vantage from which the stage won its way, against the linked opposition of an alienated pulpit and an alienated municipality, to an ultimate entrenchment of economic independence.[3]

Let us not forget the spadesmen who dug that entrenchment, the anonymous thousands who dropped their pennies in the gatherer's box: these were the true patrons of Elizabethan drama. The queen, the Privy Council, and the (bribed) officials of the Revels Office sponsored a working arrangement whereby one minor means of her majesty's "solace" could be maintained at the public expense. It was quite unconsciously that the court performed its great service to art: poetry like Protestantism entered the palace through a postern gate.

Sir Edmund continues:

> On the literary side, the milieu of the Court had its profound effect in helping to determine the character of the Elizabethan play as a psychological hybrid, in which the romance and erudition, dear to the bower and the library, interact at every turn with the robust popular elements of farce and melodrama.

But the specifications of the habitué of bower and library had to be modified by something other than farce and melodrama before great drama could result. The appearance of its qualities of greatness awaited that "ultimate entrenchment in economic independence" provided by the populace of London. The names of great lords had been associated with acting companies for generations before plays show signs of poetic or other artistic worth. The drama was as popular at court before the eighties as after, and, for all we know otherwise, *Herpetulus the Blue Knight and Perobia* was as cordially received there in 1574 as *King Lear* in 1606. No great Elizabethan play was written by a sojourner in the great world, and, so far as we know, such plays appealed no more to that world than to the public at large. In fact, the highborn as a class showed a preference for pageantry and pedantry, for pastoral and mask, and the body of drama they ultimately created for themselves was, above all else, fantastic. The bane upon Renaissance drama in Italy was its failure to escape from the palace and the library. Elizabeth and James permitted Shakespeare to write, but there was another kind of permission not within the royal gift—permission to write as he did.

In one sense Elizabethan drama was lordly indeed, or kingly: a throne was the one indispensable piece of theatrical property. Thoughts flew upward, and the multitude had to be treated to displays of majesty. Playwrights shared this taste for grandeur, and the fine people in their audience must have been stimulating. Noble auditors, like command performances, would have given a cachet to dramatic activity. The lordly ones were still lordly; their functions were not all deputized: they were lawgivers and leaders in battle. They were personally imposing, so clad and attended as to give visible token of their power and affluence. They were distinguishable and on view—we may owe them something for that. Playwrights would have been conscious of their presence, and ambition and vanity are great releasers of energy.

It is even conceivable that some playwrights then, like some critics now, assumed the minds of lordly patrons to be as elegantly furnished as their bodies and for them, especially, hung out their "richest words as polisht jewels." But it is hard to believe that we owe the poetry and psychology of the drama to the accident of the writers' having been dazzled. Shakespeare knew an Osric when he saw one, and he knew that Osrics were more plentiful than Sidneys. *Hamlet* itself would not have been written for such courtiers as it portrays. Assuming among the writers a willingness to let the "candied tongue lick absurd pomp," would poetry and psychology have resulted? or satire, "wantonness," pomposity itself? We do not know as we read what sad jest may have been designed to tickle the Earl of Rutland, or what lovely song to charm the groundlings. "Why should the poor be flattered?" to ask Hamlet's question. Because in Shakespeare's theatre there were so many of them.

This is not to imply that poetry and psychology were wasted upon the "gentlemen's galleries." The patrician was as capable of rising above his class as the plebeian. It is only to insist, with weariness, that mentality should not be measured in terms of caste. If we substitute the word "taste" for "mentality," we must reckon with what has been deduced as to the essential "unity of taste" among all castes, and among playwrights and playgoers together, in Elizabethan times.[4] To assume that action and bloodshed (or farce and wordplay) were intended exclusively for the pit is simply not feasible. The disparate elements in the drama— the bloodshed and sweeping action on the one hand and poetry and psychology on the other—are explainable on a sounder principle than that of dual appeal to social levels in the audience.

The disparity may result from nothing more than a theatrical heightening of the actual contrast in life—between the constantly observable crudity of human action and refinement of human thought. Elizabethan drama is not the only great literature where the contrast is glaringly reflected. The soul stirrings of Achilles, kin of the gods, were necessarily infinite, but what he actually did was sulk in his tent or slay Trojans. The balance between the tendency to action and the tendency to reflection is more apt to be disturbed in favor of reflection among modern critical readers of Shakespeare than among Elizabethan playgoers (or human beings generally), so that the action of the plays is apt to seem intrusive. Naturally we wish to think of the nobility as sharing our tastes: we invite only the best people to join our club.

Sometimes Shakespeare's spectators are graded not according to a social hierarchy in his day but an intellectual hierarchy in ours. The "judicious" spectator is newly invoked, and he is endowed with the ability to discern in the play esoteric meanings not intended for the audience as a whole; in default of either his or the playwright's having left a commentary, the modern critic supplies it. Spectacular results can be achieved by this method, and, strangely enough, the most spectacular of all has been achieved by one of the most meticulous of scholars. W. W. Greg distinguishes between the "bulk" or "generality" of Shakespeare's audience and the "humaner minds" and argues that the playwright wrote two meanings into *Hamlet*: the "humaner minds" perceived that Claudius was no murderer and the Ghost's accusations were "a mere figment of Hamlet's brain." Greg presents this theory with earnestness and skill; then later he defends it, although he has "never discovered" whether he believes in it himself.[5] These are baffling tactics. If one were to describe a newly found quarto of the play with a title page bearing an unknown printer's device, stipulating that what appeared to be the device might be after all only the stain of a crushed roach, Greg's indignation can be imagined.

Evidently it is only with the "unknowable," with the meaning of the book rather than with the book as a physical fact, that we may take liberties. Whether Greg believes in his theory is immaterial; he certainly believes in the two levels of intelligence and in the "judicious" spectator. Yet his theory has demonstrated once and for all the slippery nature of this person: we never know when we have him in hand. Originally, he was the occult friend of the playwright; he now serves the critic in a like capacity. So far as the meaning of *Hamlet* is concerned, Adams, Schücking, Granville-Barker, W. W. Lawrence,[6] and presumably most others are content to stand with the "bulk" of the audience. But even if Greg had only a single opponent, J. Dover Wilson let us say, we should have to recognize that among the "humaner minds" in the audience, some were more human than others, and we should have to postulate not two levels of intelligence but three at least —Greg's, Wilson's, and the "generality's."

W. W. Lawrence has said that Shakespeare "provided for the more intellectual spectators something which the groundlings, with their imperfect mentality and defective education, could not perceive, but this was an extension of the simple meaning of his play, and not at variance with it." [7] With the main bearing of this statement, one must certainly agree. It is unfortunate, however, that perfection of mentality and adequacy of education seem still to be measured in ratio to distance from the ground. Are we not too facile in our generalizations about the education and mentality of the penny playgoers? It seems probable that the rank and file were more literate in the sixteenth century than in the eighteenth. In view of the profusion of schools,[8] of the tendency of the trade guilds to make literacy a qualification even for entrance into apprenticeship,[9] and of the manifest interest in self-instruction, we must revise any impressions we may ever have had that London workmen were "nine-tenths illiterate." In a period of eight months during the single year 1585, the publishers disposed of ten thousand copies of their reading primer, *The A B C and Little Catechism.*[10] Using this book, women at their wheels and men at their looms taught, for a pittance, the children of other workers how to read. In the opinion of the one who has most carefully investigated the subject, the people of London constituted "by no means an illiterate society." [11] It would be impossible to prove that more than a fraction even of the groundlings in Shakespeare's audience had no passport to books.

The groundlings, nevertheless, like the audience in general, did not read much: books, candles, and daylight leisure were all hard to come by. The great majority of men and women were "ignorant." But we must ask whether ignorance was so crippling in the time of Shakespeare as it is today. There were, without doubt, more unlighted chambers in the mind of the average spectator than in our own, and creatures of darkness found a dwelling there, but we are likely to overestimate the degree of this benightedness. Miss Doran, in her excellent attempt to discover the Elizabethan attitude toward the ghost in *Hamlet*, has mentioned the "lack of relevance between fact and theory" [12] in Renaissance science. Cannot one say, without casuistry, that when theory is fallacious, the ignorant benefit by their enforced reliance upon observable fact? The burned child who shuns the fire has been an inductive philosopher for ages. It was the learned ones who needed Bacon's recommendations. Edward Topsell was more "learned" about beasts than other Englishmen in 1607. But observe his earnest belief in the existence of the unicorn and his contempt for ignorant unbelievers:

> the vulgar sort of infidell people which scarcely beleeue any hearbe but such as they see in their owne Gardens, or any beast but such as in their own flocks, or any knowledge but such as in their own braines, or any birds which are not hatched in their own Nests.[13]

We must score one for the "vulgar." Topsell was relying upon authority, the rank and file upon experience. We must not decide upon the attitudes and beliefs held by the rank and file of Elizabethans through reading their authorities. We must not assume that credulity, concerning unicorns, satyrs, or even ghosts and demons, was then the especial mark of the uncultivated as it is now.

J. Dover Wilson is quite assured in his pronouncements on what Shakespeare's audience believed about various things.[14] It would be folly to ignore the erudition and analysis of so talented a writer. Inquiry into contemporary point of view is the current fashion in Shakespearean criticism, and a wholesome one, but we must look twice at all the conclusions. The difficulty is that we cannot consult the spectators at the Globe and make sure they had read the right books. If a critic quotes selected passages from selected works to prove what the audience thought upon selected topics, we are likely to witness only a sinister alliance between the pedantry of two ages. The following passage, I believe, does not aid in demonstrating that Hamlet was a man of action and would be so regarded by Shakespeare's audience:

> Perhaps most significant is the statement by the illustrious French physician Laurentius, whose works were read throughout Western Europe: "The melancholike are accounted as most fit to undertake matters of weightie charge and high attempt. Aristotle in his Problemes sayeth that the melancholike are most wittie and ingenious. . . ." If then ability to transact important business was one result assigned to the melancholy temperament, this temperament could hardly have been looked upon as causing morbid inaction. Why then did Shakespeare make Hamlet melancholy? [15]

There is always the possibility that both Shakespeare and his audience had formed an opinion about melancholy otherwise than by reading Laurentius.

An amusing revelation of the practical responses of the audience is offered by the fate of *The Faithful Shepherdess*. Fletcher complained that the audience, noting that the characters were shepherds, but "missing whitsun ales, creame, wasiel & morrisdances, began to be angry." [16] In a word, they wanted the shepherds to behave like shepherds. To them it meant nothing that the play obeyed, in Chapman's words of praise, "the holy lawes of homely pastorall." Unlike Chapman, they were ignorant of such laws. We see the force in operation again in *The Knight of the Burning Pestle*. When Merrythought in the play says, "Never trust a Tailor that does not sing at his work; his mind is of nothing but filching," the Grocer's wife in the audience comments, "Mark this George, 'tis worth noting: Godfrey my Tailor, you know never sings, and he had fourteen yards to make this gown; and I'll be sworn, Mistress Penistone the Draper's Wife had one made with twelve." [17] Here is dramatic criticism in its purest form.

The most invidious modern charge against Shakespeare's audience is that it was primitive, brutal, in some way spiritually debased. It is not infrequently made. In mild form the charge appears in the following passage forming part of an otherwise closely reasoned treatise on the acting time of Elizabethan plays:

Would this audience, composed largely of illiterate Londoners, be able without excess of mental and physical fatigue, to concentrate its undivided attention for three hours without a break upon such an enthralling melodrama as *Richard III* or such a soul-stirring tragedy as *Othello*? Could such primitive beings pay out the nervous energy needed to endure three hours of imaginative exaltation? The very rapidity of the actors' utterance must have imposed a tiresome strain upon untrained minds, toiling in vain to keep pace with speeches not half understood.[18]

The atmosphere created is suggestive of the Old Stone Age; evolutionary processes seem to have been marvelously accelerated since Shakespeare's day. We may be dealing here only with indiscretion of speech. Such cannot be said of the following, included in the most recent study of Shakespeare's audience, and inspired by the putting out of Gloucester's eyes and by other "horrors" in the plays:

What these horrors enable us to do is accurately to measure the sensibility of the audience and to gauge their imaginative reaction. On that evidence we have no choice but to rate both low. This deduction is, of course, amply borne out by our knowledge of the time. A strong vein of brutality and an insensitiveness to physical suffering were part and parcel of the mentality of the Elizabethan audience.

Miss Byrne's summing up presents the "psychological picture" of "an audience primitive and undeveloped imaginatively." [19]

The most furious assault upon the audience on the grounds of spiritual and moral depravity was made by Robert Bridges:

Shakespeare should not be put into the hands of the young without the warning that the foolish things in his plays are for the foolish, the filthy for the filthy, and the brutal for the brutal; and that, if out of veneration for his genius we are led to admire or even tolerate such things, we may be thereby not conforming ourselves to him, but only degrading ourselves to the level of his audience, and learning contamination from those wretched beings who can never be forgiven their share in preventing the greatest poet and dramatist of the world from being the best artist.[20]

A. C. Bradley, the poet laureate's good and even deferential friend, could not let these words pass wholly unrebuked, although in the traditional manner of scholars, he placed the disagreeable matter in a footnote and almost in Latin.[21] Bridges's essay as a whole scarcely invites refutation. The details considered "filthy," "foolish," and "brutal" are of a type to be found also in nondramatic works such as few members of the popular audiences could have afforded to buy. The words themselves are too harsh. To share Bridges's attitude toward the audience, we must share his view that Falstaff was at last bidden a "triumphant farewell" by a creator recoiling in moral disgust; we must be willing to exchange Falstaff as he is for Falstaff as Bridges would have him. There is an obvious risk in endorsing a conception of the audience based upon such details of the plays as "most offend the simple taste" of a particular critic, no matter how eminent he may be; fortunately, scolding the audience is an alternative to excising the plays.

That our "knowledge of the time," as Miss Byrne maintains, establishes the presumption of "a strong vein of brutality and an insensitiveness to physical suffering" is a courageous assertion, placing a tremendous burden upon our knowledge of the time. Miss Byrne is identifying Elizabethans with certain of their institutions. We must consent, presumably, to be identified with certain of ours. The children once harnessed to coal carts in the tunnels of English mines should send us seeking brutality in the poetry of Coleridge and Wordsworth. If we do not find it, perhaps we should wonder how these poets could have been so brutally aloof. It is easy to cast stones. Children are harnessed no more, but evils still are permitted to exist. It would be an indiscretion of taste to mention some of these evils, since we have become so sensitive, so ingenious in evading the spectacle of suffering, so convinced of the ethical superiority of looking the other way.

Each age has its own brutalities. The Elizabethans were forced to live more intimately with theirs, and they acceded to the conditions of their existence. Shakespeare's auditors look at Talbot spattered with stage blood; but as they look, they weep. Throngs gather to see the felons hanged at Tyburn, but "the criminals' friends come and draw them down by their feet, that they may die all the sooner." [22] Is this brutality or tenderness? Animals are baited and whipped in the pits, but voices are raised in protest and the sport is declining.[23] Beneath its "callouses" human nature must have been the same in Shakespeare's day as in ours. The range of feeling must have been the same. People are still compounded of heaven and earth: kind fathers are harsh creditors, decent folk exchange ribaldries, and ruffians rescue puppies. We need to know more about human impulses in all ages before we grow rash about the Elizabethans. We need to distinguish between what is fundamental in human nature and what is superficial adjustment to environment. Perhaps the whole range of impulses was more operative in the less comfortable age of Shakespeare and more apt to impress itself upon art. It is more accurate to say that the audience expected and accepted brutality than that they demanded and enjoyed it. There is a manifest injustice in charging Shakespeare's audience with brutality because of the putting out of Gloucester's eyes, unless we credit it with an exquisite tenderness because of Lear's words over the body of Cordelia.

Among the hosts of books about Shakespeare's plays, some are ignorant and foolish; one can always make a Roman holiday by quoting such books. I have avoided doing so, at the cost of comic relief. The only alternative has involved a certain injustice; one never represents fairly the views of responsible writers by quoting a few vulnerable statements. I have not pretended to evaluate in their entirety the essays I have quoted, but to illustrate from them some of the commoner attitudes toward Shakespeare's audience. That these attitudes may be mistaken is illustrated by opposing counsel. The treatment by Thorndike, although deficient in proof and perhaps mistaken in details, strikes me as essentially true.[24] Bradley, although almost in wonder, affirmed that "the audience had not only imagination and the power to sink its soul in the essence of drama. It had something else of scarcely less import for Shakespeare, the love of poetry." [25] Elmer E. Stoll, in his most recent utterance, rejects the judicious few:

by ear the audience through lifelong attendance responded to the niceties of the different art in the Forum and the Athenian and London theatres. The technique as such they did not understand; but the ideas, sentiments, and morals, the language and situations, were not above their heads, and to what they heard they were accustomed, attuned.[26]

Felix E. Schelling holds no brief for lordly patrons:

The drama of Shakespeare and his immediate fellows spoke to men by right of their manhood, not by virtue of their gentility. It stirred in its appeal the depths of a large and generous humanity.[27]

And Charles J. Sisson points out that most of those qualities with which Beaumont mockingly endowed his citizen-grocer—patriotism, personal pride, love of romance, and the rest—can, in the "spectateur représentatif," scarcely be considered undesirable.[28]

The "representative spectator" may be as much an abstraction as the "typical man," but conveniences must sometimes be used. We may say in the present case, quite apart from Beaumont's satirical use of them as the spectators in The Knight of the Burning Pestle, that a grocer, his wife, and their young apprentice form as acceptable an epitome of Shakespeare's audience as any the facts will warrant us to choose. If Shakespeare did not write to please such a little cockney family as this, he did not write to please his audience. But if he did so write, then there must be some correspondence in quality between the plays and our sample three—the grocer, his wife, and their young apprentice.

Reflection may reduce our amazement. That the potentialities of the human mind are unaffected by time, place, and social position is sound biology, and we may safely presume that our little group possessed human minds. We may even presume that they possessed the right kind of minds. We find them in the theatre separated from many of their neighbors—the stolid, the material, the bigoted, the folk of predominately animal appetite. That they had read few books is no stigma upon them. The modern correspondence between the reading habit and active mentality is a product of new folkways. Even complete illiteracy, when not the product of incapacity or indifference, but of mere conformity, may be consonant with the highest intelligence, sometimes even with heightened powers of memory and observation.

The minds of our spectators have been sharpened by urban life. The cockney as a type has seldom been accused of stupidity. In 1601 London is growing rapidly, teeming with life and variegated activity. As like as not our little group are first generation Londoners, as stimulated and knowledgeable as modern New Yorkers lately transplanted from their prairie homes. In any case, in the crowded London of 1601 alertness is a condition of survival.

They are easy in the company of the audible arts. Music, preaching, speechmaking, storytelling, disputation—these have been available even when food and warmth have not. There is lacking the tremendous range of diversions and distractions to be devised by later centuries, but there is always the spectacle of humanity, the balm of melody, the marvel of words. The theatres have been standing a lifetime, offering an education in literature and history. Wide vistas have been opened to the mind and have furnished it with powers of association. The unlearned have been taught "the knowledge of many famous histories" and few playgoers are "of that weake capacity that cannot discourse of any notable things." [29]

The factor above all else that we must reckon with in assessing the quality of our sample spectators is the almost incalculable effect of interest upon understanding. We have all been amazed at the proficiency of small boys in analyzing batting averages and of certain of their elders, dense in every other way, in moving easily through technical labyrinths concerning their business. Let us assume that our three spectators are intensely interested in plays. Of course, our instincts may still instruct us that no one out of a London shop could possibly have appreciated Hamlet— just as no one out of a Stratford shop could possibly have written it.

NOTES

1. In *Shakspere as a Playwright*, pp. 294-312.
2. Thorp, *America at the Movies*, p. 23.
3. *Elizabethan Stage*, I, 3.

4. See Bradley, "Shakespeare's Theatre and Audience," *Oxford Lectures on Poetry;* and, especially, Sisson, *Le Goût public et le théâtre élisabéthain,* Chapter III (Unité du goût public).

5. "Hamlet's Hallucination," *Modern Language Review,* XII (1917), 393-421; "Re-Enter Ghost: a Reply to Mr. J. Dover Wilson, *ibid.,* XIV (1919), 353-69; "What Happens in 'Hamlet,'" *ibid.,* XXXI (1936), 145-54.

6. For a review of the controversy and a restatement of his own sound position, see Lawrence, "Hamlet and the Mouse-Trap," *PMLA,* LIV (1939), 709-35.

7. *Shakespeare's Problem Comedies,* p. 15.

8. Knights, "Education and the Drama in the Age of Shakespeare," *Criterion,* XI (1931-32), 599-625. Most of the spectators at the Globe "were likely to have received an education of the Grammar school type" (p. 607), i.e., such as Shakespeare himself had received.

9. Dunlop, *English Apprenticeship and Child Labour,* pp. 45, 136.

10. Plant, *English Book Trade,* p. 40.

11. Adamson, "The Extent of Literacy in England in the Fifteenth and Sixteenth Centuries: Notes and Conjectures," *Library,* Ser. IV, X (1929), 163-93.

12. "On Elizabethan Credulity," *Journal of the History of Ideas,* I (1940), 166.

13. *The Historie of Foure-Footed Beastes* (1607), quoted in *ibid.,* p. 166.

14. *What Happens in Hamlet, passim.*

15. Draper, *The Hamlet of Shakespeare's Audience,* pp. 177-8. I question the premise of the concluding statement in the book: "Shakespeare's audience was an audience of men, and Shakespeare's Hamlet was a man's Hamlet."

16. To the Reader.

17. Act II, Scene i.

18. Hart, "The Time Allotted for Representation of Elizabethan and Jacobean Plays," *Review of English Studies,* VIII (1932), 412.

19. Byrne, "Shakespeare's Audience," in Shakespeare Association, *A Series of Papers on Shakespeare and the Theatre,* pp. 200, 215.

20. "On the Influence of the Audience," *The Works of William Shakespeare* (Shakespeare Head Press ed.), x, 334.

21. *Oxford Lectures on Poetry.* He is "not always repelled" by the things condemned in Mr. Bridges's "very interesting and original contribution" and suggests "reasons for at least diminishing the proportion of defect attributable to a conscious sacrifice of art to the tastes of the audience" (p. 367, note 4).

22. *Thomas Platter's Travels in England, 1599,* p. 174.

23. Bearbaiting and bullbaiting were cruel, but they were enjoyed not as cruelty but as sport. There were a conflict of forces and sharing of risks. The activity was more lethal to the dogs than to the bulls, and even the men who whipped the bears took serious risks. Baiting was sometimes for "her Majesty's disport," and interest in it was not a matter of class distinction. Not the "brutal" element but the "sporting" element was attracted. The attitude toward animals, shared by Shakespeare himself, was still strictly utilitarian.

24. *Shakespeare's Theater,* pp. 404-31.

25. *Oxford Lectures on Poetry,* p. 392.

26. "Poetry and the Passions: an Aftermath," *PMLA,* LV (1940), 982-3.

27. *Elizabethan Drama,* I, xxxviii.

28. *Le Goût public et le théâtre élisabéthain,* pp. 52-65.

29. Heywood, *Apology for Actors* (1612), Shakespeare Society Publications, No. III, pp. 52-3.

Alan S. Downer

THE LIFE OF OUR DESIGN:
THE FUNCTION OF
IMAGERY IN THE POETIC DRAMA

Why, there you touch'd the life of our design.
(Troilus and Cressida, II, ii, 194.)

IN DISCUSSING poetic drama one has to begin with a number of
negative generalizations: there is no such thing; there once was
such a thing; it is a lost art, though not necessarily a dead one.
Perhaps it is dormant because it has been defined as if it were a
joining of two elements, poetry and drama, when actually it is
only one: poetic drama. That is, it will not be resurrected by a
poet, like Byron or Stephen Phillips, writing a play, or by a playwright, like Sheridan Knowles or Maxwell Anderson, trying to
write a poem. Poetic drama must be written by dramatic poets.
If the truism is chiastic, truth yet lies in the figure.

But if the definition of poetic drama is schismatic, so too is its
criticism and analysis. In Miss Bradby's fascinating and infuriat-
ing little anthology of *Shakespeare Criticism*, 1919-1935, the
critical lines are drawn: on the one side is the Shakespeare-as-a-
dramatist brigade commanded by Granville-Barker and J. Isaacs;
on the other, Shakespeare-as-a-poet, better equipped and manned,
and officered by Spurgeon and Murry and G. Wilson Knight. The
strange thing about this general confrontation of critical armies
is that although the roll is taken on each side, and all are present

From *The Hudson Review*, Vol. II, No. 2, Summer 1949, pp. 242-
60. Copyright 1949 by The Hudson Review, Inc. Reprinted by permission of the publisher and author.

and as fully armed as possible, no attempt seems to be made to join battle. Mr. Barker will occasionally take issue in a footnote with Professor Bradley, and a junior officer like Eric Bentley speak a few ill-mannered words about the enemy, but nothing conclusive ever happens. Not a shot is fired, not an attempt is made to storm the barricades, or on the other hand to sign a treaty of friendship and mutual aid. It is as if each side felt that something too precious to risk might be involved in either engagement or compromise. As a consequence, both sides are impoverished, and the neutrals uneasily trade with both at once in a state of utter uncertainty. Yet Union is possible with Honor and without Compromise; and it could stem from a recognition of the true nature of poetic drama.

The drama is a unique form of expression in that it employs living actors to tell its story; its other aspects—setting, characters, dialogue, action and theme—it shares with other forms of communication. But the fact that the dramatist is not dealing with characters merely, but with three-dimensional persons is paralleled by the fact that he is not dealing with a setting verbally described but three-dimensionally realized, with action that actually occurs in time and space, with dialogue which is spoken by human voices for the human ear: so many tools, so many tribulations. One of the very real problems of the dramatist is just this, that he, unlike the poet, must deal with the thingness of things; to him a mossy stone must be a mossy stone and a ship tossed on an ocean a ship tossed on an ocean, not a synonym for *peace* or *turmoil*. But the point is, surely, that for the poetic dramatist the stone is more than a stone without ever losing its stoniness, and the tempest may be a highly symbolic one without losing its reality. So, although the drama in general makes considerable use of physical objects—"props"—to tell its story, the higher drama transmutes the physical prop into a symbol, gaining richer meaning without expansion. The poetic drama relates the dramatic symbol to the poetic image, intensifying the unity of the work, and gaining still greater richness without greater bulk, compression being the ever-present necessity of the form.

It is my present purpose to examine the function of imagery in poetic drama, the language of poetry, and its relation to the essentially dramatic devices which might be similarly named the language of props, the language of setting, and the language of action. In the interests of communication I have chosen most of my illustrations from Shakespeare.

The more perceptive of the poetic critics have recognized the existence of this dramatic language, if they have refused to see its true relation to the verbal. Coleridge, for example: "Shakespeare as a poet was providing in images a substitute for that visual language which in his dramatic works he got from his actors." The definition of action as visual language is so illuminating that one wonders why Coleridge did not see by its flash the limitation of the earlier portion of his statement.

In the same chapter of the *Biographia Literaria* he gives the cue to most of his successors: the poetic power, he declares, consists in part of "reducing multitude into unity of effect, and modifying a series of thoughts by some one predominant thought or feeling." In particular this inspired Caroline Spurgeon in her counting and analysis of Shakespeare's images to determine, where possible, the "iterative images" of the plays. Using *image* broadly to cover every kind of simile and metaphor, she produced a documented and be-graphed volume which is the happy hunting ground of the anti-theatrical critics. Miss Spurgeon, however, felt that the results of her study could be used as a more general tonic. In her estimation the iterative image is a revelation of the writer's personality, temperament and quality of mind, and it throws fresh light on individual plays by serving as Background and Undertone, raising and sustaining emotion, providing atmosphere, and emphasizing a theme. It reminds one of the old patent medicines which cured everything from sterility to toothache. From her analysis, for instance, Miss Spurgeon concludes that Shakespeare was more sensitive to the horror of bad odors than to the allure of fragrant ones, and to the loathsomeness of bad cooking than to appreciation of delicate and good, presumably because he had "more opportunity of experiencing the one than the other." There is no other evidence that Miss Spurgeon had a sense of humor.

On the other hand, her extended discussion of the martlet image in *Macbeth* very nearly penetrates to the heart of Shakespeare's dramatic technique. The martlet is a foolish bird and Banquo notices him on Macbeth's castle:

> no jutty, frieze,
> Buttress, nor coign of vantage, but this bird
> Hath made his bed and procreant cradle.

Martlet was a slang word for dupe, like the word gull; that is, a metaphor. But in the *Macbeth* scene the bird is imagined to be present as part of the "setting," and therefore becomes, not a poetic image, but a dramatic symbol, of the "guest who is to be 'fooled.'" Into dramatic symbolism, even when it is so intimately linked with the poetic imagery of the play, Miss Spurgeon will not go. She is, for instance, rather annoyed at the gardener's scene in *Richard II* because "no human gardeners ever discoursed like these," though she recognizes its importance in, as she says, "gathering up, focussing and pictorially presenting," the leading theme of the play.

The other school of modern interpretation of Shakespeare is perhaps best represented by Granville-Barker's essay on *King Lear,* in which he restores the play to the stage and demonstrates that it is essentially theatrical. "The whole scheme and method of its writing is a contrivance for its effective acting. The contrast and reconciliation of grandeur and simplicity, this setting of vision in terms of actuality, this inarticulate passion which breaks now and again into memorable phrases—does not even the seeming failure of expression give us a sense of the helplessness of humanity pitted against higher powers? All the magnificent art of this is directed to one end; the play's acting in a theater." The reactions to this kind of statement are violent and equally dogmatic—mere theatricalism, declared one reviewer.

It is surely too late to go around saying that *King Lear* is not adapted to theatrical representation. Is it not also too late to declare that poetic drama cannot reveal its meaning and depth and implications on the stage as fully as any other work of art in its own medium?

In seeing Shakespeare on the modern stage, we take immediate pleasure in the story and a secondary pleasure in the characterization. But certain critical writers have suggested that there is a third and more important pleasure—the meaning as interpreted by the interplay of images. Since we are reasonably deaf to spoken poetry, it would seem that this is a pleasure re-

served, as the critics suggest, for the study. Aside from the fact
that this makes Shakespeare look a little foolish, like a composer
who writes a quartet to be performed by a one-armed violinist,
is it true? I believe that it is not; that Shakespeare, if he began
as two characters, the Poet and the Playwright, managed to unite
them somehow as the Poetic Dramatist; if he began by using the
language of action *and* the language of poetry he soon learned
to use the language of *imagery in action* which is the major characteristic of poetic drama.

Perhaps the theatricalist and the reader of poetry can find common ground in a consideration of dramatic symbolism. At any
rate, in this subject there is less excuse for the automatic or
reflex sneer at the other's expense, since symbolism is as basic to
drama as imagery is to poetry.

Symbolism grows naturally out of the materials of the drama.
The successful unravelling of the plot dilemma in a Greek tragedy
or a Roman comedy frequently depended upon the manipulation
of some physical object, some prop, a piece of cloth, a footprint,
a birthmark, a chest. In the more intricate popular drama of the
last century, a cache of gold, a missent letter, a list of conspirators
might be the mainspring of the action. In such plays, however,
one tires very quickly of the mere ingenuity by which the even-
tual discovery of the gold, or arrival of the letter is held off.

It was a considerable step up the ladder of dramatic interest
and intensity in the nineteenth century when Ibsen discovered
that the game of "pistol-pistol-who's-got-the-pistol" could not
only make a fascinating plot but could suggest the relation of the
action to some aspect of the experience of the audience. When
Hedda Gabler produces a case of pistols at the beginning of her
play, it is basic dramatic economy that she should give one to
Lövborg to commit suicide with, and use the other to put an end
to her own wretched life. Further, it is nicely ironic. But when
the point is carefully made that these pistols are her sole material heritage from General Gabler, a parallel avenue of suggestion
is opened. She has inherited her personal characteristics from the
old general, and the pistols are symbols, not only of the spiritual
heritage but of the order which shaped it—the empty, decadent
life of the military caste. At the end of the play it is clear that
Hedda's environment and heredity shaped all her actions, drove

her to urge Lövborg's suicide and finally caused her own death. The pistols are not merely the means of the action, but the meaning of the action.

Lest it be objected that such an interpretation of a dramatic symbol stems from the study rather than the stage, a current example may be added. One of the earliest and sturdiest of the successes of the 1947-48 season on Broadway was William Wister Haines's *Command Decision*. There is no pretense about this play: it is a tightly constructed, efficient product, intended for the open market. Yet despite its employment of stereotypes, conventions, and elements of melodrama, the audience is caught up in the movement of the play: we who have usually been asked to worry only about the problems of the doughboy and GI Joe, are suddenly emotionally involved in the problems of majors and brigadier-generals, hitherto satirized or portrayed as villains.

The action takes place in a Nissen hut, headquarters of an airforce command in England. The setting is narrow: the back wall, only a few feet from the footlights, is papered with a huge geodetic survey map of Western Europe. Throughout most of the performance, this map is covered, the curtains being withdrawn only when it is necessary to explain current operations. At such times the audience sees the major target cities to be destroyed and the pitifully short arc of fighter cover. The decision, which the title reflects, is whether the destruction of the targets warrants the certain loss of American soldiers.

These soldiers, whose lives are at stake, and who would be the main concern of the conventional war play or film, we never see. We see only the men whose responsibility it is to send them out and who are popularly supposed to die in bed. Yet humanity is never remote. The whole world of the action is brought into the Nissen hut; each revelation of the map creates increasing tension. At its first showing, it is merely expository: this is where we must operate. At its second, it begins to become symbolic: this is the awful dilemma which presses upon the leading character. Finally, it symbolizes the underlying meaning of the play; the desperate nature of any decision for any man under competing pressures. The map as symbol enables the audience to participate in the emotional tension of the play, serves as a unifying force, and reveals the deeper significance of what might all too easily have been a routine piece of theatrical journalism. It is, further, the best kind of dramatic symbol in that it is never obtrusive, being equally germane to the action and the theme.

It may very well be that Mr. Haines stumbled upon this dramatic symbol quite unconsciously. There is nothing in his work as a novelist to indicate that he is particularly concerned with form in that medium. His experience in Hollywood working with a medium which deals largely and conventionally in visual symbols may have led him unawares to the device. The point is that the device is there for the use of the most prosaic dramatist and it serves to enrich his work by requiring the mechanical aspects of the play to do double duty.

This "language of props" is equivalent to the simpler uses of imagery in poetry, but it can become highly complex in the poetic drama. For the sake of familiarity, if for no other reason, one turns to Shakespeare for illustration. Since it is, however, somewhat unfair to the authors of both works to juxtapose *Richard II* and *Command Decision,* a contemporary of Shakespeare's may be used as bridge and buffer. The simpler uses of dramatic symbolism in the poetic drama are clearly exhibited in the first part of Marlowe's *Tamburlaine.* The Scythian tyrant is obsessed with the idea of power as symbolized in the "sweet fruition of an earthly crown." It is not surprising that the crown—a commonplace symbol, wholly apart from its use in the drama—figures largely in the action.

In the first scene, Cosroe is crowned emperor. In the second act, foolish Mycetes rushes on stage seeking to hide his crown in a simple hole. Tamburlaine overtakes him:

> *Tam.* Is this your crown? (*Taking it*)
> *Myc.* Ay, didst thou ever see a fairer? (*Relinquishing it*)
> *Tam.* (*Ironically*) You will not sell it, will you?
> *Myc.* Such another word and I will have thee executed.
>   Come, give it me!
> *Tam.* No, I took it prisoner.
> *Myc.* You lie; I gave it you.
> *Tam.* Then, 'tis mine.
> *Myc.* No, I mean I let you keep it.

> *Tam.* Well, I mean you shall have it again.
>   Here, take it for a while: I lend it thee,
>   Till I may see thee hemmed with armed men;
>   Then shalt thou see me pull it from thy head:
>   Thou art no match for mighty Tamburlaine.

Later, as Cosroe dies, Tamburlaine puts on his crown; a banquet of crowns is introduced; and the play ends with the triumphant crowning of Zenocrate. Throughout all this action, the symbol remains as simple as possible—verbalized, the crown stands for "perfect bliss" and "sole felicity," its

> virtues carry with it life and death;
> To ask and have, command and be obeyed.

The crown is the symbol of the king's rank, the ruler's god-like power.

The crown which is handled so dramatically in the deposition scene of *Richard II* is, to be sure, the symbol of the king's rank. But it is not simply the sole felicity in which Tamburlaine displayed such interest. It is the symbol of the condition of England, as in the words of Gaunt:

> A thousand flatterers sit within thy crown
> Whose compass is no bigger than thy head;
> And yet, incaged in so small a verge,
> The waste is no whit lesser than thy land.

And Northumberland proposes to "redeem from broking pawn the blemish'd crown." Further, it is the symbol of Richard as actor:

> within the hollow crown
> That rounds the mortal temples of a king
> Keeps death his court; and there the antic sits,
> Scoffing his state and grinning at his pomp;
> Allowing him a breath, a little scene,
> To monarchize. . . .

It is a symbol of that "divinity doth hedge a king":

> For every man that Bolingbroke hath press'd
> To lift shrewd steel against our golden crown

> God for his Richard hath in heavenly pay
> A glorious angel. . . .

The divinity which the crown symbolizes is strengthened by
a second image, the king as the sun:

> knowst thou not
> That when the searching eye of heaven is hid
> Behind the globe, that lights the lower world,
> Then thieves and robbers range abroad unseen. . . .
> But when from under this terrestrial ball
> He fires the proud tops of the Eastern pines. . . .
> Then murthers, treasons and detested sins,
> The cloak of night being pluck'd from off their backs,
> Stand bare and naked, trembling at themselves?
> So when this thief, this traitor Bolingbroke,
> Who all this while hath revell'd in the night
> Whilst we were wand'ring in th'Antipodes,
> Shall see us rising in our throne, the East,
> His treasons will sit blushing in his face,
> Not able to endure the sight of day,
> But self-affrighted tremble at his sin.

The image is extended and explicit. Even the dullest in the audience must have been impressed by it. At any rate, Bolingbroke
is not slow to seize upon it:

> See, see, King Richard doth himself appear,
> As doth the blushing discontented sun
> From out the fiery portal of the east. . . .

At this moment (III, 3) Richard is standing upon the walls of
Flint Castle, which is to say the upper stage, and Bolingbroke is
on the ground. At the end of the scene in response to his opponent's demands, Richard descends to the main stage, with still
another reference to the sun image:

> Down, down I come like glist'ring Phaeton,
> Wanting the manage of unruly jades. . . .

He sees himself no longer as king, but an unsuccessful pretender
to the title.

The climax of the action of the play, in which the complexity of the image is finally revealed, is the deposition of Richard. In the drama, the whole Parliament is assembled, with the lords and bishops of England providing not only a larger audience for the display of Richard's theatrical talents, but a more impressive background for the action. When the great moment comes, Richard makes the most of it, in a scene which should be compared with Tamburlaine's taking and returning of Mycetes' crown.

> Give me the crown. Here, cousin, seize the crown.
> (*As Bolingbroke hesitates*) Here, cousin,
> (*A pause; Bolingbroke steps to him, and Richard holds the crown between them*)
>   on this side my hand, and on that side yours.
> Now is this golden crown like a deep well
> That owes two empty buckets,

and so on. How carefully Shakespeare has pointed the action here; not simply a passing of the crown from one hand to the other, but a tableau, and an extended simile to illustrate it. So the visual symbolic exchange of the crown, to quote Miss Spurgeon's words on another matter, "gathers up, focusses and pictorially presents" the downfall of a man whose nature was ill-suited to kingship, and who has to some extent come to realize the fact.

There are striking uses of this "language of props," the realization of the verbal image in dramatic terms, in later Shakespearean tragedy. For example, in *Macbeth* Miss Spurgeon found repeated iteration in the dialogue of the idea of ill-fitting clothes. Mr. Cleanth Brooks has related the image somewhat more closely to the play by seeing it as an interpretation of Macbeth's position as usurper: he is uncomfortable in garments not his own. Actually, the image suggests disguise. Macbeth is an unhappy hypocrite who declares before the murder of Duncan, "False face must hide what the false heart doth know," and before the murder of Banquo, "We must . . . make our faces vizards to our hearts, disguising what they are."

But the image is more than a mere verbal one. It is *realized*, made visual in the action of the play.

The first four scenes are various moments during and after a battle. In them, Macbeth will naturally be wearing his warrior's costume, his armor, as much a symbol of his nature and achievements as is Duncan's crown. When he defeats Norway, for instance, he is "lapped in proof," but when Ross and Angus greet him as Thane of Cawdor, he protests, "Why do you dress me in borrowed robes?" The image continues, verbally, as Banquo observes, half-jesting,

> New honors come upon him
> Like our strange garments, cleave not to their mold
> But with the aid of use.

Under pressure from his wife, however, he resolves to seize the kingship, to cover his warrior's garments and the golden opinions that went with them with the clothing that was properly Duncan's. The murder is committed with constant reference in the dialogue to the clothing image (skilfully interpreted by Mr. Brooks) and the scene as marked in the Folio ends with the flight of Macbeth and his Lady from the crime as she urges him to

> Get on thy nightgown, lest occasion call us
> And show us to be watchers.

When next Macbeth enters he is wearing his dressing gown, and if the actor is wise it will be such a gown as calls attention to itself, for at this point the change in costume, the disguising of the armor, dramatizes both the change in Macbeth's nature and the iterated poetic image. From now until nearly the end of the play, Macbeth is cowardly, melancholic, suspicious, and unhappy; the reverse of all the qualities that had made him the admired warrior of the early scenes. He cannot buckle his distempered cause within the belt of rule; and Macduff's fear is prophetic, "Adieu, lest our old robes sit easier than our new," prophetic not only for the unhappy Scots, but for Macbeth himself.

One of the achievements of this highly skilful play is the maintaining of interest in, if not sympathy for, the central figure; assassin, evil governor, usurper, and murderer. Shakespeare maintains this interest not merely by portraying Macbeth as a man in the control of wyrd, or too susceptible to uxorial suggestion, but,

I think, by making us constantly aware of the armor—the honest
warrior's nature—under the loosely hanging robes of a regicide.
Until Act II, scene 3, Macbeth is quite possibly dressed as a warrior. From that point, until Act V, scene 3, he is dressed in his
borrowed robes. But in the latter scene, with his wife eliminated
as a motivating force, and with the English army moving against
him, he begins to resume some of his former virtues: his courage
returns, his forthrightness, his manliness. "Give me my armor,"
he cries, and in a lively passage with the Doctor, he makes grim
jests about the power of medicine as Seyton helps him into his
warrior's dress. He is all impatience to be back at the business he
understands as he does not understand government:

> *Macbeth.*
>> Give me my armour.
>
> *Seyton.*
>> 'Tis not needed yet.
>
> *Macbeth.*
>> Give me my armour.
>> Send out moe horses, skirr the country round;
>> Hang those that talk of fear. Give me mine
>>   armour. . . .
>> Throw physic to the dogs, I'll none of it!—
>> Come put mine armour on. Give me my staff.—
>> Seyton, send out.—Doctor, the thanes fly from
>>   me.—
>> Come, sir, despatch.—If thou couldst, doctor,
>>   cast
>> The water of my land, find her disease,
>> And purge it to a sound and pristine health,
>> I would applaud thee to the very echo,
>> That should applaud again.—Pull't off, I say.—

The tragic fall of this good man is dramatically underlined in
his attempts to resume his old way of life. His infirmity of purpose
cannot be more strongly presented than in his donning and doff-
ing of the armor, and his bragging exit, with the equally revealing order:

> Bring it after me!

This is not an isolated, but only a more complex use of costume as symbol in poetic drama. For subtlety it might be contrasted with the costume changes of Tamburlaine, who, appearing first in his shepherd's weeds, casts them off contemptuously at his first triumph:

> Lie here ye weeds that I disdain to wear!
> This complete armour and this curtle axe
> Are adjuncts more beseeming Tamburlaine;

and who later wears in sequence white, scarlet, and black armor to indicate the stiffening of his attitude towards his victims. This is a simple dramatic device. In *Macbeth* the costume change is related to the iterated image to make concrete Macbeth's state of mind, and related also to the larger problem, the power of evil to corrupt absolutely, with which the play is concerned.

Without insisting too strongly on this kind of relation of image and symbol to clothe the idea of the play in reality, a few familiar instances may make the process clearer. *Hamlet,* for example, establishes in its opening scene, with the ghost, and the references to decay and unwholesomeness, what Mr. Knight calls "the embassy of death." The hand of death is upon the play from the very start and references to it are constantly reiterated. However, it is death of a particular sort, not just Hamlet's musings upon the possibilities of suicide. Hamlet speaks of the sun breeding "maggots in a dead dog," the king compares his nephew to a foul disease, and describes his subjects as "muddied, Thick and unwholesome in their thoughts and whispers." The idea is repeated over and over in the play which has been made explicit at the very start, "Something is rotten in the state of Denmark."

But if we have missed it through insensitivity, Shakespeare presents his symbol of the state of Denmark dramatically, in terms of the theater, before our eyes: *Enter two clowns,* who discourse learnedly of death and suicide and toss skulls and bones about the stage remarking on the pocky corpses they now must deal with; "Faith, if 'a be not rotten before 'a die," catches up the very word Marcellus had used earlier to describe the condition of the state.

It is this same kind of symbolism that Miss Spurgeon noticed with some surprise in the Gardener's scene of *Richard II,* in which the "leading theme . . . (is) gathered up, focussed, and pictorially presented." As she points out, this could hardly be missed by any careful reader. The lines of the play are larded with images of nature gone awry, the ugly clouds flying in the fair and crystal sky, the flourishing branch cracked and hacked down, and the summer leaves faded; there is a fearful tempest, a flood tide;

> The bay trees in our country all are withered,
> And meteors fright the fixed stars of heaven;
> The pale-faced moon looks bloody on the earth. . . . ;

an unseasonable stormy day causes rivers to flood. But where the other characters of the play refer to the disordered political conditions in England in terms of unkempt nature, the Gardener reverses them by comparing the task of ordering his garden to the task of the governor of a commonwealth.

> O what pity it is
> That he had not so trimm'd and dress'd his land
> As we this garden!

Miss Spurgeon declares the scene to have been "deliberately inserted at the cost of any likeness to nature, for no human gardeners ever discoursed like these." To demand verisimilitude in what is obviously a poetic device is to apply to Shakespeare the standards of David Belasco. Probably even the most theatrical of theatricalists would be willing to grant the rightness and the effectiveness of the device, for it does realize dramatically and visually in terms of character and action the theme of the play. On reconsideration it may seem over-deliberate, super-imposed, introducing as it does two totally new characters for the sole purpose of the device, but Shakespeare had not yet learned dramatic economy. In *Hamlet*, the gravediggers belong to the plot as well as to the imagery.

The repeated pictures of natural conditions in *Richard II* introduce a second important function of the image in Elizabethan poetic drama. We are all convinced, I suppose, that the dramatist was forced to work without the benefit or encumbrance

of representational scenery, and that the formal nature of the
background of the Globe is the excuse for so many of those

> Barkloughly Castle call they this at hand

speeches, and such more extended and always (on the modern
stage) intrusive passages in which we are informed,

> The grey-eyed morn smiles on the frowning night,
> Check'ring the Eastern clouds with streaks of light,

together with other meteorological data. But perhaps the Elizabethan playwright was more fortunate than his cabined, cribbed
and confined successor. Not only could he shift his scene at will,
or indeed not bother with a "scene" at all, but he could in his
images create a world for his action more complete than any producer could provide, and uniquely adapted to the needs of both
his play and his theme.

In *Richard*, for example, the action transpires not before
painted seacoasts and cardboard castles, but in an envelope
which is at once scenic and emotional. The cumulative effect of
the nature images is not merely to suggest the political condition
of England, but the kind of world in which such a conflict as
that between Bolingbroke and Richard could take place. The
device is not very skillfully used, perhaps, for *Richard* is close to
being an apprentice play. In the later works, the setting as an
emotional envelope is more artfully handled.

Lear is a case in point and a particularly striking contrast to
Richard. Instead of giving magnitude to his action (as in the
other tragedies) by relating the struggles of the protagonist to
affairs of state, in England, Rome, or Denmark, Shakespeare
creates a world of his own, a special world of King Lear, and
he creates it by means of imagery.

It is the worst of all possible worlds. The animals which in-
habit it are dragons, curs, rats, geese, kites, wolves, vultures,
tigers. It is a world of disease, of plagues, carbuncles, boils.
Whatever happens in this world happens in the most violent
manner, wrenched, beaten, pierced, stung, scourged, flayed,
gashed, scalded, tortured, broken on the rack. All this has been
noted before by Miss Spurgeon and others. The world of Lear
is a world of torment, a world unfriendly to man. In such a world

the events of the play are entirely natural, possible, logical. The imagery, better than any possible stage setting, provides a background for the action, enriching the language of the play and serving to unify its execution.

For what, strangely enough, does not seem to have been commented on is the realization of this metaphorical world in the action of the play, in the tempest which runs through its center and in the torturing and blinding of Gloucester. Both scenes have come in for critical attack as incapable of presentation or too horrible for effective use. But it is clear that both are as essential to the play's action as to its theme, and that the blinding of Gloucester—detailed as it is—is made as horrible as possible for a purpose. If we experience an emotion of disgust, or terror, it is because both elements are present, not simply in the action, but in the world of the play. It is the dramatization of the image which makes the meaning of the play evident. If Richard's crown is the "language of props," Lear's tempest is the "language of setting."

The most difficult of the dramatist's devices to appreciate in the study is his primary device, the "language of action." Our modern playwrights are at some pains to render the action clear in extended stage directions, separated from the dialogue by italics and parentheses. Now Shakespeare resorts to a stage direction only rarely, most of the movement in his plays being implicit in the poetry. The significance of this lies less in the freedom of interpretation permitted the actor than in the indication of a further unity between the devices of poetry and the theater in the poetic drama.

For a simple and clear instance of this we may again turn to *Richard II*. The plot of this play, the conflict between Richard and Bolingbroke, might be diagrammed by tracing the letter X and letting the downward stroke stand for the king, the upward for the usurper, and the point of crossing the deposition scene. It is curious to note how the dominance of first the king and then the usurper is symbolized in their positions on the stage as well as in the imagery and the plot line. For three acts, Richard is in the ascendant. Whatever Bolingbroke's activities, Richard maintains his position as king. This is indeed symbolized by his appearance "on the walls" of Flint Castle, while Bolingbroke and his followers remain below. His descent to Bolingbroke's level is accompanied by a punning speech:

> Base court, where kings grow base,
> To come at traitors' calls and do them grace;

but his recognition of the true state of affairs is indicated as Bolingbroke kneels and Richard raises him up. In the deposition scene the shift in positions is completed, and verbalized by Richard in a final allusion to the sun image:

> O that I were a mockery king of snow,
> Standing before the sun of Bolingbroke
> To melt myself away in water drops.

It is a sign of the maturing artist that as his skill increases in each of the dramatic forms he elects to try, Shakespeare relies more and more upon the essentially dramatic materials available to him, the actors, their movements and physical relationships. In the most perfect of the histories, for instance, *1 Henry IV*, he has involved himself in a highly complex plot, the handling of which is a constant source of wonder and admiration. Ostensibly, Shakespeare is relating the events of a portion of the reign of Henry IV, a revolt engineered by the Percy family, and the waywardness of the Prince of Wales. But the two problems confronting the king are brought into significant relationship to one another, and the facts of history are made to serve the purposes of art. The subject of the play is not English history, but the general education of princes. Events have been so modified that the play actually confronts two ways of life—Hotspur's and Falstaff's—and presents the dilemma of Hal in choosing between them. Although a good deal of ink has been spilled over the character of Falstaff, and a number of romantic female tears over Percy, Shakespeare's intention is clear from his manipulation of the characters in a crucial scene. In Act V, Scene 4, Douglas enters, challenges Henry IV, they fight and, "the King being in danger, enter Prince of Wales." One must perhaps visualize the scene in the Elizabethan theater—a broad platform projecting into the audience with entrance doors on each side at the rear. Douglas and the Prince fight, and "Douglas flieth" through one of the doors. As the King goes to join his troops, enter, through the opposite door, Hotspur. The two youths exchange challenges; "They fight."

> *Enter Falstaff.*
> *Falstaff.* Well said, Hal! to it, Hal! Nay you shall find no
>   boy's play here, I can tell you.
> *Enter Douglas. He fighteth with Falstaff, who falls down*
> *as if he were dead. (Exit Douglas.) The Prince killeth*
> *Percy.*

Percy dies, still prating romantically of his honor and his proud titles which now accrue to Hal; Hal speaks his eulogy and turns from the body to go to the nearest door. But on his way, "He spieth Falstaff on the ground." As in *Richard II* the positions of the characters in the scene are symbolic. Hal has, seemingly, been presented with a choice between the way of life represented by Hotspur and the way of life represented by Falstaff. And here they are, two (apparent) corpses on the ground, one on either side of him. The choice is to make, and he chooses—neither. Having bid farewell to Percy, he now bids farewell to Jack, confirming the promise of his first soliloquy and anticipating the rejection of Falstaff at the end of Part II.

Significant illustrations of this "language of action" could be chosen from nearly any of the plays. Indeed, nearly all the most familiar, most memorable scenes involve some kind of symbolic action. Not merely in tragedy, with Lear buffeted by the tempest, or Hamlet leaping into the grave of Ophelia, but in comedy, with Titania fondly caressing the hairy snout of ass-headed Bottom, or Feste torturing Malvolio into a realization of his humanity. The very essence of the tragic idea of *Hamlet* and *Lear* and the comic idea of *A Midsummer Night's Dream* and *Twelfth Night* is contained in those moments of action. This is not to say that the poetry is superfluous. These are further instances of the complete welding of the elements of poetry and the elements of theater which constitute successful poetic drama.

Harley Granville-Barker

THE MERCHANT OF VENICE

The Merchant of Venice is a fairy tale. There is no more reality in Shylock's bond and the Lord of Belmont's will than in Jack and the Beanstalk.

Shakespeare, it is true, did not leave the fables as he found them. This would not have done; things that pass muster on the printed page may become quite incredible when acted by human beings, and the unlikelier the story, the likelier must the mechanism of its acting be made. Besides, when his own creative impulse was quickened, he could not help giving life to a character; he could no more help it than the sun can help shining. So Shylock is real, while his story remains fabulous; and Portia and Bassanio become human, though, truly, they never quite emerge from the enchanted thicket of fancy into the common light of day. Aesthetic logic may demand that a story and its characters should move consistently upon one plane or another, be it fantastic or real. But Shakespeare's practical business, once he had chosen these two stories for his play, was simply so to charge them with humanity that they did not betray belief in the human beings presenting them, yet not so uncompromisingly that the stories themselves became ridiculous.

What the producer of the play must first set himself to ascertain is the way in which he did this, the nice course that—by reason or instinct—he steered. Find it and follow it, and there need be no running on the rocks. But logic may land us anywhere. It can turn Bassanio into a heartless adventurer. Test the

From *Prefaces to Shakespeare*, by H. Granville-Barker, 1946, 1947. Copyright by the Princeton University Press, 1946, 1947. Reprinted by permission of the publisher.

clock of the action by Greenwich time, it will either be going too fast or too slow. And as to Portia's disguise and Bellario's law, would the village policeman be taken in by either? But the actor will find that he simply cannot play Bassanio as a humbug, for Shakespeare does not mean him to. Portias and Nerissas have been eclipsed by wigs and spectacles. This is senseless tom-foolery; but how make a wiseacre producer see that if he does not already know? And if, while Shylock stands with his knife ready and Antonio with his bared breast, the wise young judge lifting a magical finger between them, we sit questioning Bellario's law —why, no one concerned, actors or audience, is for this fairyland, that is clear.

The Merchant of Venice is the simplest of plays, so long as we do not bedevil it with sophistries. Further, it is—for what it is!— as smoothly and completely successful, its means being as well fitted to its end, as anything Shakespeare wrote. He was happy in his choice of the Portia story; his verse, which has lost glitter to gain a mellower beauty and an easier flow, is now well attuned to such romance. The story of Shylock's bond is good contrast and complement both; and he can now project character upon the stage, uncompromising and complete. Yet this Shylock does not overwhelm the play, as at a later birth he might well have done—it is a near thing, though! Lastly, Shakespeare is now enough of the skilled playwright to be able to adjust and blend the two themes with fruitful economy.

THE CONSTRUCTION OF THE PLAY
THE PROBLEM OF "DOUBLE-TIME"

This blending of the themes would, to a modern playwright, have been the main difficulty. The two stories do not naturally march together. The forfeiture of the bond must be a matter of months; with time not only of the essence of the contract, but of the dramatic effect. But the tale of the caskets cannot be enlarged, its substance is too fragile; and a very moderate charge of emo-tion would explode its pretty hollowness altogether. Critics have credited Shakespeare with nice calculation and amazing subtlety in his compassing of the time-difficulty. Daniel gives us one analysis, Halpin another, Eccles a third, and Furness finds the

play as good a peg for the famous Double Time theory as Wilson,
its inventor, found Othello. All very ingenious; but is the ingenuity Shakespeare's or their own? [1] For him dramatic time was
a naturally elastic affair. (It still is, though less so, for the modern
playwright, whose half-hour act may commonly suggest the passing of an hour or two; this also is Double Time.) Shakespeare
seems to think of it quite simply in terms of effect, as he thought
of dramatic space, moving his characters hither and thither without considering the compassing of yards or miles. The one freedom will imply and enhance the other. The dramatist working
for the "realistic" stage must settle definitely where his characters
are to be and keep them there till he chooses to change the
scenery. Shakespeare need not; and, in fact, he never insists upon
place at all, unless it suits him to; and then only to the extent that
suits him.[2] In this play, for instance, where we find Shylock and
Antonio will be Venice, but whereabouts in Venice is usually no
matter; when it is—at Shylock's door or in court before the Duke
—it will be made clear enough to us. And where Portia is, is Belmont. He treats time—and the more easily—with a like freedom,
and a like aim. Three months suits for the bond; but once he has
pouched the money Bassanio must be off to Belmont, and his
calendar, attuned to his mood, at once starts to run by hours
only. The wind serves, and he sails that very night, and there is
no delay at Belmont. Portia would detain him some month or
two before he ventures; and what could be more convenient for
a Shakespeare bent on synchronizing the two stories? For that
matter, he could have placed Belmont a few hundred miles off,
and let the coming and going eke out the time. Did the problem
as a whole ever even occur to him? If it did, he dismissed it as of
no consequence. What he does is to set each story going according to its nature; then he punctuates them, so to speak, for effect.
By the clock they are not even consistent in themselves, far less
with each other. But we should pay just the sort of attention to
these months, days or hours that we do, in another connection, to
the commas and semicolons elucidating a sentence. They give us,
and are meant to, simply a *sense* of time and its exactions. It is
the more easily done because our own sense of time in daily life
is far from consistent. Time flies when we are happy, and drags
in anxiety, as poets never tire of reminding us. Shakespeare's own

reflections on the phenomenon run to half a column of the con-
cordance, and he turns it quite naturally to dramatic account.

THE TRUE PROBLEM

How to blend two such disparate themes into a dramatically
organic whole; that was his real problem. The stories, linked in
the first scene, will, of themselves, soon part company. Shakespeare has to run them neck and neck till he is ready to join
them again in the scene of the trial. But the difficulty is less that
they will not match each other by the clock than that their whole
gait so differs, their very nature. How is the flimsy theme of the
caskets to be kept in countenance beside its grimly powerful
rival? You cannot, as we said, elaborate the story, or charge it
with emotion; that would invite disaster. Imagine a Portia seriously alarmed by the prospect of an Aragon or a Morocco for
husband. What sort of barrier, on the other hand, would the
caskets be to a flesh-and-blood hero and heroine fallen in love?
Would a Romeo or Rosalind give a snap of the finger for them?
As it is, the very sight of Bassanio prompts Portia to rebellion;
and Shakespeare can only allow his lovers a few lines of talk
together, and that in company, dare only color the fairy tale
with a rhetorically passionate phrase or so before the choice is
made and the caskets can be forgotten—as they are!—altogether.
Nor does anything in the play show the artist's supreme tact in
knowing what *not* to do better than this?

But you cannot neglect the Portia story either, or our interest
in her may cool. Besides, this antiphony of high romance and
rasping hate enhances the effect of both. A contrasting of subjects, scene by scene, is a trick (in no depreciatory sense) of
Shakespeare's earliest stagecraft, and he never lost his liking for
it.[3] Then if the casket-theme cannot be neglected, but cannot be
elaborated, it must somehow be drawn out, its peculiar character
sustained, its interest husbanded while its consummation is
delayed.

Shakespeare goes straightforwardly enough to work. He puts
just as little as may be into Portia's first scene; but for the one
sounding of Bassanio's name there would be only the inevitable
tale of the caskets told in tripping prose and the conventional

joking upon the suitors. Portia and Nerissa, however, seen for
the first time in the flesh, give it sufficient life, and that "Bassanio"
one vivid spark more. Later, in due course, come Morocco's
choice of the gold casket and Aragon's of the silver. We remark
that Morocco is allotted two scenes instead of one. The reason
is, probably, that Shakespeare has now enriched himself with the
Lorenzo-Jessica story (not to mention the episode of the Gobbos,
father and son), and, with this extra weight in the Venetian scale
of the action, is put to it to maintain the balance. He could, of
course, finish with both Morocco and Aragon earlier and give
Bassanio two scenes instead of one.[4] And if a romantic hero could
not well wait till after dinner to make his choice, as Morocco
does, Solanio's arrival with the ill news of Antonio could easily
have been kept for the later scene. But this will not do either—
most characteristically will not do for Shakespeare. He has held
his lovers apart, since the air of the Belmont of the caskets is too
rarefied for flesh and blood to breathe. And Portia herself has
been spellbound; we have only had jaunty little Nerissa to
prophesy that love (by the pious prevision of the late lord)
would somehow find out the way.[5] But once he brings them together Bassanio must break the spell. It is the story of the sleeping beauty and the prince in another kind; a legitimate and traditional outcome. And once Shakespeare himself has broken free
of the fairy tale and brought these two to life (for Bassanio as
well has been till now a little bloodless) it is not in him to let
them lapse from the scene unproved, and to the full. The long
restraint has left him impatient, and he must, here and now,
have his dramatic fling. We need not credit—or discredit him, if
you like—with much calculation of the problem. It was common
prudence both to keep Belmont as constantly in our view as
Venice, and the emancipating Bassanio clear of it for as long as
possible. And he is now in the middle of his play, rather past it,
ready to link his two stories together again. He worked forth-
rightly; that is written plain over most of his work. Though he
might now find that he had here material for two scenes, he
would not return in his tracks, telescope Aragon and Morocco—
and take, in fact, all the sort of trouble we, who are his critics,
must take to explain what a much more compact job he could
have made of it! Besides, here is his chance to uplift the two

as hero and heroine, and he will not dissipate its effectiveness.

For Bassanio, as we said, has been till now only little less bound than Portia in the fetters of a fairy tale; and later, Shylock and the bond will condemn him to protesting helplessness, and the affair of the rings to be merrily befooled.[6] The wonder indeed is, considering the rather poor figure—painfully poor by the gospel according to Samuel Smiles—the coercion of the story makes him cut, that throughout he measures up so well to the stature of sympathetic hero. Shakespeare contrives it in two ways. He endows him with very noble verse; and, whenever he can, throws into strong relief the Bassanio of his own uncovenanted imagination. He does. this here. The fantasy of the caskets brought to its due crisis, charged with an emotion which blows it for a finish into thin air, he shows us Bassanio, his heart's desire won, agonized with grief and remorse at the news of Antonio's danger. Such moments do test a man and show him for what he is; and this one, set in bright light and made the scene's turning point, counts for more in the effect the character makes on us than all the gentlemanly graces of his conventional equipment. Unless the actor is much at fault, we shall hear the keynote to the true Bassanio struck in the quiet simplicity—such contrast to his rhetoric over the caskets, even though this was less mere rhetoric than Morocco's and Aragon's—of the speech which begins

> O sweet Portia,
> Here are a few of the unpleasant'st words
> That ever blotted paper! . . .
> Rating myself at nothing, you shall see
> How much I was a braggart. When I told you
> My state was nothing, I should then have told you
> That I was worse than nothing; for indeed
> I have engaged myself to a dear friend,
> Engaged my friend to his mere enemy,
> To feed my means. . . .

Here speaks Shakespeare's Bassanio; and it is by this, and all that will belong to it, that he is meant to live in our minds.

Producer and actors must look carefully into the way by which in this scene the method that has served for the casket story is

resolved into something better fitted to the theme of the bond
(dominant from the beginning of the play, and now to absorb
and transform the dedicated Portia and her fortunes). It is a
change—though we must not insist on the contrast more than
Shakespeare does—from dramatic convention to dramatic life.
From the beginning the pulse of the scene beats more strongly;
and Portia's

> I pray you, tarry: pause a day or two
> Before you hazard; for in choosing wrong,
> I lose your company; therefore forbear awhile. . . .

is not only deeper in feeling (there has been little or nothing to
rouse her till now; she has had to be the picture of a Portia,
hardly more, with a spice of wit to help her through), but how
much simpler in expression! When Bassanio turns to those obses-
sing caskets she must lapse again for a space into fancies of his
swan-like end, her eye the watery deathbed for him, into talk
about Hercules and Alcides (borrowed, one fears, from Morocco),
about Dardanian wives and the like—even as he will be conventionally sententious over his choice. But note how, within the
convention, preparing an escape from it, emotion is roused and
sustained. With the rhetoric of Portia's

> Go, Hercules!
> Live thou, I live: with much, much more dismay
> I view the fight, than thou that mak'st the fray.

for a springboard, the song and its music are to stir us,

> *whilst Bassanio comments on the caskets to himself.*

So (let the actor remember) when he does at last speak, the emotional ascent will have been half climbed for him already. And
while he pays his tribute of trope and maxim, Portia, Nerissa
and the rest watch him in silence, at full strain of attention, and
help to keep us, too, intent. The speech itself sweeps unhindered
to its height, and the pause while the casket is unlocked is filled
and enriched by the intensity of Portia's

> How all the other passions fleet to air . . .

most cunningly contrived in meaning and melody, with its emphasis on "despair" and "ecstasy" and "excess," to hold us upwrought. The fairy tale is finally incarnate in the fantastic word-painting of the portrait and the reading of the scroll. Then, with a most delicate declension to reality, Bassanio comes to face her as in a more actual world, and the curtains can be drawn upon the caskets for the last time. Observe that not for a moment has Shakespeare played his fabulous story false. He takes his theater too seriously to go spoiling an illusion he has created. He consummates it, and turns the figures of it to fresh purpose, and they seem to suffer no change.

Throughout the scene—throughout the play, and the larger part of all Elizabethan drama for that matter—effects must be valued very much in terms of music. And, with the far adventuring of his playwriting hardly begun, Shakespeare's verse is already fairly flawless, and its maneuvering from mood to mood masterly, if still simple. We have the royal humility of the speech in which Portia yields herself (Bassanio slips back to his metaphors for a moment after this); then, for contrast, the little interlude of Gratiano and Nerissa, with the tripping monosyllables of Gratiano's

> I wish you all the joy that you can wish;
> For I am sure you can wish none from me. . . .

to mark the pace and the tone of it. Then follows the arrival of Antonio's messenger with Lorenzo and Jessica; done in plain, easy-moving verse that will not discount the distressed silence in which he reads the letter, nor the quiet candor of his confession to Portia. Now comes another crescendo—two voices added to strengthen it—leading up to her generous, wide-eyed

>   What sum owes he the Jew?
> *Bassanio.*
>   For me, three thousand ducats.
> *Portia.*
>   What, no more!
>   Pay him six thousand, and deface the bond;
>   Double six thousand, and then treble that. . . .

which itself drops to the gentleness of

> Since you are dear bought I will love you dear.

Then, to strengthen the scene's ending, we have the austere prose of Antonio's letter, chilling us to misgiving. And since—in stage practice, and with the prevailing key of the play's writing to consider—this will not do for an actual finish, there is a last modulation into the brisk coda of

> Since I have your good leave to go away,
> I will make haste: but till I come again,
> No bed shall e'er be guilty of my stay,
> Nor rest be interposer 'twixt us twain.

Lorenzo and Jessica make another link (though their relation to Belmont is pretty arbitrary) between the two stories. This, however, is but the secondary use of them. There must be a sense of time passing in Venice while the bond matures, yet we must have continuous action there, too, while the ritual at Belmont goes its measured way; so, as there can be little for Shylock and Antonio to do but wait, this third, minor theme is interposed. It brings fresh impetus to the action as well as new matter; and it shows us—very usefully—another and more human side of Shylock. Shakespeare does not scheme it out overcarefully. The masking and the elopement and the coming and going they involve are rather inconveniently crowded together (the pleasant episode of the Gobbos may have stolen a little necessary space); and one chapter of the story—for were we perhaps to have seen Shylock at supper with Bassanio, Lorenzo and the rest while the disguised Jessica waited on them?—was possibly crowded out altogether.

Once the fugitives, with some disregard of likelihood, have been brought to Belmont, Gobbo in attendance, Shakespeare turns them to account quite shamelessly. They play a mighty poor scene to give Portia and Nerissa time to disguise themselves as doctor and clerk.[7] They will have to play another while doctor and clerk change to Portia and Nerissa again; but for that, as if in compensation, they are to be dowered with the loveliest lines in the play.[8] With the junction of the themes in the trial-scene the constructive problem is, of course, solved. Shylock disappearing, the rest is simple.

SHAKESPEARE'S VENICE

If Lorenzo and Jessica and a little poetry and the consort of
music, which no well-regulated great household of his time
would be without, are Shakespeare's resources (he had no other;
and what better should we ask?) for the painting of the star-
lit garden of Belmont at the play's end, for its beginning he must
show us Venice. He troubles with no verbal scene-painting here;
throughout the first scene the very word is but spoken twice, and
quite casually. We might be anywhere in the city, or out of it,
even. Thereafter we hear of the Rialto, of a gondola, of the
common ferry and suchlike incidentals; but of the picturesque
environment to which modern staging has accustomed us there
is no suggestion at all. Yet he does present a Venice that lived
in the Elizabethan mind, and it is the Venice of his dramatic
needs; a city of royal merchants trading to the gorgeous East, of
Jews in their gaberdines (as rare a sight, remember, as to us a
Chinese mandarin is, walking the London streets today), and of
splendid gentlemen rustling in silks. To the lucky young English-
man who could hope to travel there Venice stood for culture and
manners and the luxury of civilization; and this—without one
word of description—is how Shakespeare pictures it.

We are used nowadays to see the play begun by the entry of
a depressed, sober-suited, middle-aged man and two skipping
youths, who make their way with a sort of desperate merriment
through such lines as the producer's blue pencil has left them,
vanish shamefacedly, reappear at intervals to speak the remnant
of another speech or two, and slip at last unregarded into
oblivion. These are Solanio and Salarino, cursed by actors as the
two worst bores in the whole Shakespearean canon; not except-
ing, even, those other twin brethren in nonentity, Rosencrantz
and Guildenstern.[9] As characters, Shakespeare has certainly not
been at much pains wtih them; they could exchange speeches
and no one would be the wiser, and they move about at everybody's convenience but their own. But they have their use, and
it is an important one; realize it, and there may be some credit
in fulfilling it. They are there to paint Venice for us, the Venice
of the magnificent young man. Bassanio embodies it also; but

there are other calls on him, and he will be off to Belmont soon.
So do Gratiano and Lorenzo; but they will be gone too. Solanio
and Salarino will not fail us; they hoist this flag at the play's
beginning and keep it bravely flying for as long as need be.
When Salarino, for a beginning, addresses Antonio with

> There, where your argosies with portly sail,
> Like signiors and rich burghers on the flood,
> Or, as it were, the pageants of the sea,
> Do overpeer the petty traffickers,
> That curt'sy to them, do them reverence
> As they fly by them with their woven wings.

—there should be no skipping merriment in this.

They are argosies themselves, these magnificent young men, of
high-flowing speech; pageants to overpeer the callow English
ruffians, to whom they are here displayed. The talk passes from
spices and silks into fine classical phrases; and with what elaborate, dignified dandyism it ends!

Enter Bassanio, Lorenzo and Gratiano.

Solanio.
> Here comes Bassanio, your most noble kinsman,
> Gratiano, and Lorenzo. Fare you well;
> We leave you now with better company

Salarino.
> I would have stayed till I had made you merry,
> If worthier friends had not prevented me.

Antonio.
> Your worth is very dear in my regard.
> I take it, your own business calls on you,
> And you embrace the occasion to depart.

Salarino.
> Good-morrow, my good lords.

Bassanio.
> Good signiors both, when shall we laugh? Say,
>   when?
> You grow exceeding strange: Must it be so?

Salarino.
> We'll make our leisures to attend on yours.

No apologetic gabbling here: but such a polish, polish as might have satisfied Mr. Turveydrop. Solanio—if one could distinguish between them—might cut the finer figure of the two. When the Masque is in question:

> 'Tis vile [he says], unless it may be quaintly ordered,
> And better, in my mind, not undertook.

Salarino has a cultured young gentleman's turn for classical allusion. He ranges happily from two-headed Janus and Nestor to Venus' pigeons.

But it is, as we said, when Bassanio and Gratiano and Lorenzo with his Jessica have departed, that the use these two are to the play becomes plainest. They give us the first news of Antonio's losses, and hearsay, filtering through them, keeps the disaster conveniently vague. If we saw the blow fall on Antonio, the far more dramatic scene in which Shylock is thrown from depth to heights and from heights to depth as ill news and this good news strike upon him would be left at a discount. In this scene they are most useful (if they are not made mere targets for a star actor to shoot at). For here again is Venice, in the contrast between sordid Shylock and Tubal and our magnificent young gentlemen, superfine still of speech and manner, but not above a little Jew-baiting. They sustain that theme—and it must be sustained—till it can be fully and finally orchestrated in the trial-scene. It is a simple stagecraft which thus employs them, and their vacuity as characters inclines us to forget this, their very real utility. Forgetting it, Shakespeare's histrionic Venice is too often forgotten also.

THE CHARACTERS, AND THE CRISIS OF THE ACTION

None of the minor characters does much more than illustrate the story; at best, they illuminate with a little lively detail their own passage through it. Not the Duke, nor Morocco, Aragon, Tubal, Lorenzo, Jessica, nor the Gobbos, nor Nerissa, had much being in Shakespeare's mind, we feel, apart from the scenes they played, and the use they were to him. It is as futile, that is to say, to discuss Jessica's excuses for gilding herself with ducats when she elopes as it is to work out her itinerary via Genoa to Belmont; we might as well start writing the life-story of Mistress Margery Gobbo.

PORTIA

Shakespeare can do little enough with Portia while she is still the slave of the caskets; incidentally, the actress must resist the temptation to try and do more. She has this picture of an enchanted princess to present, verse and prose to speak perfectly, and she had better be content with that. But we feel, nevertheless (and in this, very discreetly, she may at once encourage us), that here, pent up and primed for escape, is one of that eminent succession of candid and fearless souls: Rosaline, Helena, Beatrice, Rosalind—they embodied an ideal lodged for long in Shakespeare's imagination; he gave it expression whenever he could. Once he can set his Portia free to be herself, he quickly makes up for lost time. He has need to; for from the moment of that revealing

> You see me, Lord Bassanio, where I stand. . . .

not half the play's life is left her, and during a good part of this she must pose as the young doctor of Rome whose name is Balthasar. He does not very deliberately develop her character; he seems by now to know too much about her to need to do that. He reveals it to us mainly in little things, and lets us feel its whole happy virtue in the melody of her speech. This it is that casts its spell upon the strict court of Venice. The

> Shed thou no blood. . . .

is an effective trick. But

> The quality of mercy is not strained;
> It droppeth as the gentle rain from heaven
> Upon the place beneath. . . .

with its continuing beauty, gives the true Portia. To the very end she expands in her fine freedom, growing in authority and dignity, fresh touches of humor enlightening her, new traits of graciousness showing. She is a great lady in her perfect simplicity, in her ready tact (see how she keeps her guest Antonio free from the mock quarrel about the rings), and in her quite unconscious self-sufficiency (she jokes without embarrassment about taking the mythical Balthasar to her bed, but she snubs Gratiano the next minute for talking of cuckoldry, even as she snubbed Nerissa for a very mild indelicacy—she is fond of Nerissa, but no forward waiting-women for her!). Yet she is no more than a girl.

Here is an effect that we are always apt to miss in the acting of Shakespeare today. It is not the actress's fault that she cannot be what her predecessor, the boy-Portia, was; and she brings us compensation for losses which should leave us—if she will mitigate the losses as far as she can—gainers on the whole. But the constant play made in the Comedies upon the contrast between womanly passion or wisdom and its very virginal enshrining gives a delicacy and humor to these figures of romance which the limited resources of the boy left vivid, which the ampler endowment of the woman too often obscures. This is no paradox, but the obvious result of a practical artistry making the most of its materials. Portia does not abide in this dichotomy as fully as, for instance, Rosalind and Viola do; but Shakespeare turns it to account with her in half a hundred little ways, and to blur the effect of them is to rob her of much distinction.

The very first line she speaks, the

> By my troth, Nerissa, my little body is aweary of this
> great world.

is likely to come from the mature actress robbed of half its point. This will not matter so much. But couple that "little body" with her self-surrender to Bassanio as

> an unlessoned girl, unschooled, unpractised;
> Happy in this, she is not yet so old
> But she may learn . . .

and with the mischief that hides behind the formal courtesies of the welcome to Aragon and Morocco, with the innocence of the amazed

> What no more!
> Pay him six thousand and deface the bond . . .

with the pretty sententiousness of her talk of herself, her

> I never did repent of doing good,
> Nor shall not now . . .

followed by the artless

> This comes too near the praising of myself . . .

and the figure built up for us of the heiress and great lady of
Belmont is seen to be a mere child, too, who lives remote in her
enchanted world. Set beside this the Portia of resource and command, who sends Bassanio posthaste to his friend, and beside
that the schoolgirl laughing with Nerissa over the trick they are
to play their new lords and masters. Know them all for one
Portia, a wise and gallant spirit so virginally enshrined; and we
see to what profit Shakespeare turned his disabilities. There is,
in this play, a twofold artistry in the achievement. Unlikelihood
of plot is redeemed by veracity of character; while the artifice of
the medium, the verse and its convention, and the stylized acting of boy as woman, re-reconciles us to the fantasy of the plot.

But a boy-Portia's advantage was chiefly manifest, of course, in
the scene of the trial; and here in particular the actress of today
must see that she lessens it no more than she need. The curious
process of what we may call the "double negative," by which an
Elizabethan audience first admitted a boy as a girl and then
enjoyed the pretense that the girl was a boy, is obsolete for us;
make-believe being the game, there was probably some pleasure
just in this complication of it. This beside, there was the direct
dramatic effect, which the boy made supremely well in his own
person, of the wise young judge, the Daniel come to judgment.
Shylock (and Shakespeare) plucks the allusion from the popular
story of Susanna; but there may be some happy confusion, perhaps, with that other Daniel who was among ". . . the children
of Israel, of the king's seede and of the Prince's: Springaldes
without any blemish, but well-favoured, studious in all wisdome,
skillful for knowledge, able to utter knowledge, and such as have
livelinesse in them, that they might stand in the king's palace. . . ." For this is the very figure we should see. Here is the
strict court of Venice, like enough to any law court, from East
to West, from Shakespeare's time to now, in that it will seem

to the stranger there very dry and discouraging, airless, lifeless. Age and incredulity preside; and if passion and life do enter, they must play upon muted strings. The fiercely passionate Shylock is anomaly enough in such surroundings. Then comes this youth, as brisk and businesslike as you please, and stands before the judges' bench, alert, athletic, modest, confident. He is life incarnate and destined to victory; and such a victory is the fitting climax to a fairy tale. So the Portia that will—as most Portias do —lapse into feminine softness and pitch the whole scene in the key of the speech on mercy, and that in a key of sentiment, damns the scene and herself and the speech, all three. This amazing youth has the ear of the court at once; but he'll only hold it by strict attention to business. Then, suddenly, out of this, comes the famous appeal, and catches us and the court unaware, catches us by the throat, enkindles us. In this lies the effect. Prepare for it, or make the beauty of it overbeautiful (all the more now, because it is famous and hackneyed) and it becomes a dose of soothing syrup.

This, be it further remembered, is not the scene's top note; conflict and crisis are to come. They are brought about simply and directly; the mechanical trick of the "No jot of blood" that is to resolve them asks nothing else. Shakespeare keeps the medium of the verse as simple; it flows on with hardly a broken line. The conflict is between Portia and Shylock. Bassanio's agony, Antonio's stoic resignation cannot be given great play; the artifice of the story will not even now sustain crosscurrents of human passion. But the constraint of the business of a court accounts well enough for their quiescence (the actors need do nothing to discount it) and the few notes that are struck from them suffice. The action must sweep ahead and no chance be given us to question its likelihood. Even when all is over the Duke departs with not much more comment upon this amazing case than an invitation to the learned young doctor to come to dinner, and Antonio and his friends are as casual about it and almost as calm. There is tactful skill in this. Shylock has gone, that fairy tale is done with; the less we look back upon it, the sooner we come to fresh comedy again the better.

Throughout the scene a Portia must, of course, by no smallest sign betray to us—as well betray it to Bassanio—that she is other than she now seems. No difficulty here, as we said, for Shakespeare's Portia, or his audience either. There was no wondering as he faced the judges why they never saw this was a woman (since very obviously he now wasn't) nor why Bassanio did not know his wife a yard off. The liquid sentences of the Mercy speech were no betrayal, nor did the brusque aside of a young lawyer, intent upon his brief—

> Your wife would give you little thanks for that,
> If she were by to hear you make the offer.

—lose its quite casual humor. All this straightforwardness the modern actress must, as far as she can, restore.

ANTONIO, GRATIANO AND OTHERS

In these early plays character does not as a rule outrun the requirements of the plot. Shakespeare is content enough with the decorative, the sententious, the rhetorical, in his casual Venetians, in Aragon and Morocco; with the conventional in Launcelot, who is the stage clown—the juggler with words, neat, agile, resourceful and occasionally familiar with the audience, as a clown and a juggler should be—under a thin disguise of character; with old Gobbo for a minute or two's incidental fun; with the pure utility of Tubal.

Antonio is flesh and blood. He is the passive figure of the story's demand; but Shakespeare refines this in the selflessness that can send Bassanio to Belmont and be happy in a friend's happiness, in the indifference to life that lets him oppose patience to his enemy's fury; and he makes him more convincingly this sort of man by making him just a little self-conscious too.

> In sooth, I know not why I am so sad. . . .

If he does not, it is not for want of thinking about it. He takes a sad pleasure in saying that he is

> a tainted wether of the flock,
> Meetest for death . . .

But there is a redeeming ironic humor in

> You cannot better be employed, Bassanio,
> Then to live still and write mine epitaph.

He is sufficiently set forth, and there is conveyed in him a better dignity than mere words give. [10]

Nerissa is echoing merriment; not much more.

Shakespeare may have had half a mind to make something a little out of the way of Gratiano. He starts him with a temperament and a witty speech; but by the play's end we have not had much more from him than the "infinite deal of nothing" of Bassanio's gibe, rattling stuff, bouncing the play along, but revealing no latent Gratiano. It all makes a good enough pattern of this sort of man, who will be a useful foil to Bassanio, and can be paired off for symmetry with Portia's foil, Nerissa; and the play needed no more. But there is enough of him, and enough talk about him, for one to feel that he missed by only a little the touch of magic that would have made something more of him and added him to the list of those that survive the lowering of the lights and the theater's emptying. There is a moment while he waits to take his share in Jessica's abduction, and sits reflecting:

> All things that are,
> Are with more spirit chased than enjoyed.
> How like a yonker or a prodigal,
> The scarfed bark puts from her native bay,
> Hugg'd and embraced by the strumpet wind!
> How like a prodigal doth she return;
> With over-weather'd ribs, and ragged sails,
> Torn, rent and beggared by the strumpet wind!

Harsh enough similes for such an occasion! Is this another side to the agreeable rattle? Does the man who exclaims

> Let me play the fool!
> With mirth and laughter let old wrinkles come. . . .

find life in fact rather bitter to his taste? But one must beware of reading subtleties into Shakespeare. If such a Gratiano was ever shadowed in his mind, he made no solid substance of him.

Bassanio we have spoken of; play the part straightforwardly and it will come right.

SHYLOCK

There remains Shylock. He steps into the play, actual and individual from his first word on, and well might in his strength (we come to feel) have broken the pinchbeck of his origin to bits, had a later Shakespeare had the handling of him. As it is, his actuality is not weakened by the fantasy of the bond, as is Portia's by her caskets. For one thing, our credulity is not strained till the time comes for its maturing, and by then—if ever—the play and its acting will have captured us. For another, the law and its ways are normally so uncanny to a layman that the strict court of an exotic Venice might give even stranger judgments than this and only confirm us in our belief that once litigation begins almost anything may happen. Despite the borrowed story, this Shylock is essentially Shakespeare's own. But if he is not a puppet, neither is he a stalking-horse; he is no more a mere means to exemplifying the Semitic problem than is Othello to the raising of the color question. "I am a Jew." "Haply, for I am black. . . ." Here we have—and in Shylock's case far more acutely and completely—the *circumstances* of the dramatic conflict; but at the heart of it are men; and we may surmise, indeed, that from a maturer Shakespeare we should have had, as with Othello, much more of the man, and so rather less of the alien and his griefs. However that may be, he steps now into the play, individual and imaginatively full-grown, and the scene of his talk with Bassanio and Antonio is masterly exposition.

The dry taciturnity of his

> Three thousand ducats; well?

(the lure of that thrice-echoed "Well"!) and the cold dissecting of the business in hand are made colder, drier yet by contrast with the happy sound of Portia's laughter dying in our ears as he begins to speak. And for what a helpless innocent Bassanio shows beside him; overanxious, touchy, overcivil! Shylock takes his time; and suddenly we see him peering, myopic, beneath his

brows. Who can the newcomer be? And the quick brain answers
beneath the question's cover: They must need the money badly
if Antonio himself comes seeking me. Off goes Bassanio to greet
his friend; and Shylock in a long aside can discharge his obligations to the plot.[11] These eleven lines are worth comment. In
them is all the motive power for drama that the story, as Shakespeare found it, provides; and he throws this, with careless opu-
lence, into a single aside. Then he returns to the upbuilding of
his Shylock.

Note the next turn the scene takes. From the snuffling depre-
ciation of his present store, for his own wonted fawning on these
Christian clients, Shylock unexpectedly rises to the dignities of

> When Jacob grazed his uncle Laban's sheep . . .

And with this the larger issue opens out between Gentile and
Jew, united and divided by the scripture they revere, and held
from their business by this tale from it—of flocks and herds and
the ancient East. Here is another Shylock; and Antonio may well
stare, and answer back with some respect—though he recovers
contempt for the alien creature quickly enough. But with what
added force the accusation comes:

> Signior Antonio, many a time and oft
> In the Rialto you have rated me. . . .
> You called me misbeliever, cut-throat dog,
> And spit upon my Jewish gaberdine. . . .

The two Venetians see the Ghetto denizen again, and only hear
the bondman's whine. But to us there is now all Jewry couched
and threatening there, an ageless force behind it. They may
make light of the money bond, but we shall not.

Shakespeare keeps character within the bounds of story with
great tact; but such a character as this that has surged in his
imagination asks more than such a story to feed on. Hence,
partly at least, the new theme of Jessica and her flight, which
will give Shylock another and more instant grudge to satisfy. It
is developed with strict economy. Twenty-one lines are allowed
to Jessica and Launcelot, another twenty or so to her lover and
their plans; then, in a scene not sixty long, Shylock and his household are enshrined. As an example of dramatic thrift alone this

is worth remark. The parting with Launcelot: he has a niggard liking for the fellow, is even hurt a little by his leaving, touched in pride, too, and shows it childishly.

> Thou shalt not gormandize
> As thou hast done with me. . . .

But he can at least pretend that he parts with him willingly and makes some profit by it. The parting with Jessica, which we of the audience know to be a parting indeed; that constant calling her by name, which tells us of the lonely man! He has looked to her for everything, has tasked her hard, no doubt; he is her jailer, yet he trusts her, and loves her in his extortionate way. Uneasy stranger that he is within these Venetian gates; the puritan, who, in a wastrel world, will abide by law and prophets! So full a picture of the man does the short scene give that it seems hardly possible we see no more of him than this between the making of the bond and the climacteric outbreak of passion upon Jessica's loss and the news of Antonio's ruin.[12]

References to him abound; Shylock can never be long out of our minds. But how deliberate is the thrift of opportunity we may judge by our being shown the first effect of the loss on him only through the ever-useful eyes of Salarino and Solanio. This is politic, however, from other points of view. Look where the scene in question falls, between Morocco's choice of his casket and Aragon's. Here or hereabouts some such scene must come, for the progress of the Antonio and Shylock story cannot be neglected. But conceive the effect of such a tragic outcry as Shylock's own,

> So strange, outrageous, and so variable . . .

—of such strong dramatic meat sandwiched between pleasant conventional rhetoric. How much of the credibility of the casket story would survive the association, with how much patience should we return to it? But Salarino and Solanio tone down tragedy to a good piece of gossip, as it becomes young men of the world to do. We avoid an emotional danger zone; and, for the moment at least, that other danger of an inconvenient sympathy with "the dog Jew." When Shylock's outbreak of anguish does come, the play is nearer to its climax, Bassanio's choice is about to free Portia's story from its unreality, and his savage certainty of revenge upon Antonio will now depress the sympathetic balance against him.

But, considering the story's bounds, what a full-statured figure we already have! Compare the conventional aside, the statement of the theme, in the earlier scene, the bald

> I hate him for he is a Christian. . . .

with the deluge of molten passion which descends upon the devoted Solanio and Salarino, obliterating their tart humor; compare the theme, that is to say, with its development, mere story with character, and measure in the comparison Shakespeare's growing dramatic power.

In tone and temper and method as well this scene breaks away from all that has gone before. The very start in prose, the brisk

> Now, what news on the Rialto?

even, perhaps, Solanio's apology for former

> slips of prolixity or crossing the plain highway of talk . . .

seem to tell us that Shakespeare is now asserting the rights of his own imagination, means, at any rate, to let this chief creature of it, his Shylock, off the leash. And verily he does.

The scene's method repays study. No whirling storm of fury is asked for; this is not the play's crisis, but preparation for it still. Shylock is wrapped in resentful sorrow, telling over his wrong for the thousandth time. Note the repetition of thought and phrase. And how much more sinister this sight of him with the wound festering than if we had seen the blow's instant fall! His mind turns to Antonio, and the thrice told

> let him look to his bond.

is a rope of salvation for him; it knots up the speech in a dreadful strength. Then, on a sudden, upon the good young Salarino's reasonable supposition that what a moneylender wants is his money back; who on earth would take flesh instead?—

> What's that good for?

—there flashes out the savagery stripped naked of

> To bait fish withal: if it will feed nothing else, it will feed
> my revenge.

Now we have it; and one salutes such purity of hatred. There
follows the famous speech—no need to quote it—mounting in
passionate logic, from its

> He hath disgraced me . . . and what's his reason?
> I am a Jew.

to the height of

> If a Jew wrong a Christian, what is his humility? Re-
> venge. If a Christian wrong a Jew, what should his suffer-
> ence be by Christian example? Why, revenge. The villainy
> you teach me I will execute, and it shall go hard but I will
> better the instruction.

This is a Shylock born of the old story, but transformed, and
here a theme of high tragedy, of the one seemingly never-ending
tragedy of the world. It is the theme for a greater play than
Shakespeare was yet to write. But if this one cannot be sustained on such a height, he has at least for the moment raised
it there.

Solanio and Salarino are quite oblivious to the great moral
issue opened out to them; though they depart a little sobered—
this Jew seems a dangerous fellow. There follows the remarkable
passage with Tubal; of gruesome comedy, the apocalyptic Shylock shrunk already to the man telling his ill-luck against his
enemy's, weighing each in scales (love for his daughter, a memory of his dead wife thrown in!) as he is used to weigh the coin
which is all these Christians have left him for his pride. It is
technically a notable passage, in that it is without conflict or contrast, things generally necessary to dramatic dialogue; but the
breaking of a rule will be an improvement, now and then, upon
obedience to it. So Shakespeare, for a finish, lowers the scene
from its crisis, from that confronting of Christian and Jew, of
hate with hate, to this raucous assonance of these two of a kind
and mind, standing cheek to cheek in common cause, the excellent Tubal fueling up revenge.

Such a finish, ousting all nobility, both shows us another facet

of Shylock himself (solid figure enough now to be turned any
way his maker will) and is, as we saw, a shadow against which
the high romance of Bassanio's wooing will in a moment shine
the more brightly. Sharp upon the heels of this, he comes again;
but once more apocalyptic, law incarnate now.

> *Shylock.* Gaoler, look to him; tell me not of mercy;
> This is the fool that lent out money gratis:
> Gaoler, look to him.
>
> *Antonio.*   Hear me yet, good Shylock.
>
> *Shylock.* I'll have my bond; speak not against my bond:
> I have sworn an oath that I will have my bond.

Verse and its dignity are needed for this scene; and note the recurring knell of the phrases:

> I'll have my bond; I will not hear thee speak:
> I'll have my bond, and therefore speak no more.
> I'll not be made a soft and dull-eyed fool,
> To shake the head, relent, and sigh, and yield
> To Christian intercessors. Follow not;
> I'll have no speaking: I will have my bond.

Here is a Shylock primed for the play's great scene; and Shakespeare's Shylock wrought ready for a catastrophe, which is a
deeper one by far than that the story yields. For not in the missing of his vengeance on Antonio will be this Shylock's tragedy,
but in the betrayal of the faith on which he builds.

> I've sworn an oath that I will have my bond. . . .

How many times has the synagogue not heard it sworn?

> An oath, an oath. I have an oath in Heaven. . . .

He has made his covenant with an unshakable God:

> What judgment shall I dread, doing no wrong?

—and he is to find himself betrayed.

It is the apocalyptic Shylock that comes slowly into court, solitary and silent, to face and to outface the Duke and all the moral
power of Venice.[13] When he does speak he answers the Duke

as an equal, setting a sterner sanction against easy magnanimity —at other people's expense! One could complain that this first appeal for mercy discounts Portia's. To some extent it does; but the more famous speech escapes comparison by coming when the spell of the young doctor is freshly cast on us, and by its finer content and larger scope. Structurally, the Duke's speech is the more important, for it sets the lists, defines the issue and provokes that

> I have possessed your grace of what I purpose;
> And by our holy Sabbath have I sworn
> To have the due and forfeit of my bond. . . .

So confident is he that he is tempted to shift ground a little and let yet another Shylock peep—the least likable of all. He goes on

> You'll ask me, why I rather choose to have
> A weight of carrion flesh, than to receive
> Three thousand ducats: I'll not answer that,
> But say it is my humour. . . .

Legality gives license to the hard heart. Mark the progression. While the sufferer cried

> The villainy you teach me I will execute, and it shall go hard but I will better the instruction.

with the law on his side it is

> What judgment shall I dread, doing no wrong?

from which he passes, by an easy turn, to the mere moral anarchy of

> The pound of flesh, which I demand of him,
> Is dearly bought; 'tis mine, and I will have it. . . .

and in satanic heroism stands defiant:

> If you deny me, fie upon your law!
> There is no force in the decrees of Venice.
> I stand for judgment. Answer: shall I have it?

There is a dreadful silence. For who, dwelling unquestioningly under covenant of law, shall gainsay him?

It says much for the mental hypnosis which the make-believe of the theater can induce that this scene of the trial holds us so spellbound. Its poetry adds to the enchantment—let anyone try rewriting it in prose—and the exotic atmosphere helps. But how much more is due to the embroidering of character upon story so richly that the quality of the fabric comes to matter little! Shakespeare, at any rate, has us now upon the elemental heights of drama. He cannot keep us there. Portia must perform her conjuring trick; perhaps this is why he gives Shylock full scope before she arrives. But he brings us down with great skill, maneuvering character to the needs of the story, and turning story to character's account.

The coming of the young judge's clerk does not impress Shylock. How should it. Little Nerissa! He has won, what doubt of it? He can indulge then—why not?—the lodged hate and loathing he bears Antonio. The Duke is busy with Bellario's letter and the eyes of the court are off him. From avenger he degenerates to butcher. To be caught, lickerish-lipped, by Bassanio; and Gratiano's rough tongue serves him as but another whetstone for savagery! He turns surly at first sight of the wise young judge—what need of such a fine fellow and more fine talk—and surlier still when it is talk of mercy. He stands there, he tells them yet again, asking no favors, giving none.

> My deeds upon my head! I crave the law,
> The penalty and forfeit of my bond.

Why does Shakespeare now delay the catastrophe by a hundred lines, and let Portia play cat-and-mouse with her victim? From the story's standpoint, of course, to keep up the excitement a while longer. We guess there is a way out. We wonder what it can be; and yet, with that knife shining, Antonio's doom seems to come nearer and nearer. This is dramatic child's play, and excellent of its sort. But into it much finer stuff is woven. We are to have more than a trick brought off; there must be a better victory; this faith in which Shylock abides must be broken. So first she leads him on. Infatuate, finding her all on his side, he finally and formally refuses the

money—walks into the trap. Next she plays upon his fanatical
trust in his bond, sets him searching in mean mockery for a
charitable comma in it—had one escaped his cold eye—even as
the Pharisees searched their code to convict Christ. Fold by
fold, the prophetic dignity falls from him. While Antonio takes
his selfless farewell of his friend, Shylock must stand clutching
his bond and his knife, only contemptible in his triumph. She
leads him on to a last slaveringly exultant cry: then the blow
falls.

Note that the tables are very precisely turned on him.

> if thou tak'st more,
> Or less, than just a pound, be it so much
> As makes it light or heavy in the substance,
> Or the division of the twentieth part
> Of one poor scruple, nay, if the scale do turn
> But in the estimation of a hair . . .

is exact retaliation for Shylock's insistence upon the letter of
his bond. Gratiano is there to mock him with his own words,
and to sound, besides, a harsher note of retribution than Portia
can; for the pendulum of sympathy now swings back a little—
more than a little, we are apt to feel. But the true catastrophe
is clear. Shylock stood for law and the letter of the law; and it
seemed, in its kind, a noble thing to stand for, ennobling him.
It betrays him, and in the man himself there is no virtue left.

> Is *that* the law?

he gasps helplessly. It is his only thought. The pride and power
in which legality had wrapped him, by which he had outfaced
them all, and held Venice herself to ransom, are gone. He stands
stripped, once more the sordid Jew that they may spit upon,
greedy for money, and hurriedly keen to profit by his shame.

> I take this offer then; pay the bond thrice,
> And let the Christian go.

Here is Shakespeare's Shylock's fall, and not in the trick the
law plays him.

He is given just a chance—would the story let him take it!—

to regain tragic dignity. What is passing in his mind that prompts
Portia's

> Why doth the Jew pause? Take thy forfeiture. [14]

No, nothing, it would seem, but the thought that he will be
well out of the mess with his three thousand ducats safe.

Shakespeare has still to bring his theme full circle. He does
it with doubled regard to character and story.

> Why, then the devil give him good of it!
> I'll stay no longer question.

If he were not made to stay, by every canon of theatrical justice
Shylock would be let off too lightly; wherefore we find that
the law has another hold on him. It is but a logical extending
of retribution, which Gratiano is quick to reduce to its brutal
absurdity. Here is Shylock with no more right to a cord with
which to hang himself than had Antonio a bandage for his
wound. These quibbling ironies are for the layman among the
few delights of law. Something of the villainy the Jew taught
them the Christians will now execute; and Shylock, as helpless
as Antonio was, takes on a victim's dignity in turn. He stays
silent while his fate, and the varieties of official and unofficial
mercy to be shown him, are canvassed. [15] He is allowed no comment upon his impoverishing for the benefit of "his son Lorenzo"
or upon his forced apostasy. But could eloquence serve better
than such a silence?

> *Portia.*   Art thou contented, Jew? What dost thou say?
> *Shylock.* I am content.

With the three words of submission the swung pendulum of
the drama comes to rest. And for the last of him we have only

> I pray you give me leave to go from hence;
> I am not well. Send the deed after me,
> And I will sign it.

Here is the unapproachable Shakespeare. "I am not well."
It nears banality and achieves perfection in its simplicity. And
what a completing of the picture of Shylock! His deep offense
has been against human kindness; he had scorned compassion

and prayed God himself in aid of his vengeance. So Shakespeare dismisses him upon an all but ridiculous appeal to our pity, such as an ailing child might make that had been naughty; and we should put the naughtiness aside. He passes out silently, leaving the gibing Gratiano the last word, and the play's action sweeps on without pause. There can be no greater error than to gerrymander Shylock a strenuously "effective exit"—and most Shylocks commit it. From the character's point of view the significant simplicity of that

I am not well.

is spoiled; and from the point of view of the play the technical skill with which Shakespeare abstracts from his comedy this tragic and dominating figure and avoids anticlimax after is nullified.

THE RETURN TO COMEDY

The tragic interest is posted to oblivion cavalierly indeed. Seven lines suffice, and the Duke's processional departure. The business of the rings is then briskly dispatched, and made the brisker by the businesslike matter of the signing of the deed being tacked to it. Thence to Belmont; and while Lorenzo and Jessica paint its moonlit beauty for us, Balthasar and his clerk have time to change costume and tire their heads again for Portia and Nerissa. They have evidently, as we saw, none too much time; for Launcelot is allowed a last—and an incongruously superflous—piece of clowning. But the musicians can play ahead for an extra minute or two if hooks and eyes refuse to fasten, and no one will notice the delay. The last stretch of dialogue is lively; a comic quartet coming after the consort of viols, and it asks for a like virtuosity. The play ends, pleasantly and with formality, as a fairy tale should. One may wonder that the last speech is left (against tradition) to Gratiano; but one practical reason is plain. Portia and Bassanio, Antonio, Lorenzo and Jessica must pace off the stage in their stately Venetian way, while Gratiano's harmless ribaldry is tossed to the audience as an epilogue. Then he and Nerissa, now with less dignity than ever to lose, skip quickly after.

ACT-DIVISION AND STAGING

However well the First Folio's five-act rule may fit other plays, and whatever, in Elizabethan stage practice, division into five acts implied, there is ample evidence that *The Merchant of Venice* was meant to be played without an effective break. The scenes, and the padding in them, that give time for Portia and Nerissa to change clothes, are one sign of it. The first of these is padding unalloyed, and very poor padding at that. For the second, Shakespeare finds better and pleasanter excuse; but in part, at least, we owe that charming duet between Lorenzo and Jessica to this practical need.[16]

A case of a sort can be made out for the division in the Folio. Granted five acts, this fourth and fifth are manifest; the beginnings and finishings of the first three make useful milestones in the story, but others every bit as useful could be set up. It is worth noting that this act-division does nothing to elucidate the complex time-scheme of our anxious editors; but the Folio's expert play-divider would be no more bothered by that problem than Shakespeare had been. Nor was he concerned to end his acts memorably; the second leaves Aragon in our minds and the third ends with Jessica and Lorenzo's and the play's worst scene.[17] There might, however, be good enough reason in the Elizabethan theater for making an act's first scene arresting and for letting its last tail away; for they had, of course, no curtain to lower upon a climax, and after an interval interest would need quick rekindling. No producer today, one hopes, will want to lower a picture-stage curtain at such points. Nor, if he is wise, while his stories are working to their joint crisis will he give us pause to think by what strange leaps in time and space they travel.

But surely there are many signs that—however, for convenience sake, it is to be acted, with or without pause—Shakespeare has conceived and constructed the play indivisibly. There is the alternating between Venice and Belmont, and the spinning-out of the Portia story to fit with the other; neither device gains by or countenances act-division. There is the unhesitating sweep of the action up to the trial-scene, and indeed beyond it. One can parcel it up in various ways—the Folio's and half a dozen others—and on various pleas; but will any one of them make the story clearer; will it not, on the contrary, do something to disclose its confusions? Prose and blank verse, rhymed couplets and a quatrain are used indifferently for tags; so these form no consistent punctuation. There is no scene, not even the trial-scene, that ends with a full close, until the play ends. There is, in fact, no inherent, no dramatic pause in the action at all; nor can any be made which will not be rather hindrance than help to a performance.

Well-paced acting will take the play straight through in the traditional, vague two hours. But if, for the weakness of the flesh, there must be pauses, division into three parts will be a little less awkward than into two. If you do not stop before the trial-scene you cannot, of course, stop at all; the play will be virtually over. You may reasonably pause at the end of the Folio's Act III. This alone, though, will make very unequal division. For an earlier pause, the moment of Bassanio's departure from Venice will serve.[18] This splits the first three acts of the Folio all but exactly in two. Delay the pause another scene and we shall have done with Morocco. The second part would then begin with the tale of how Shylock took his loss and our first news of Antonio's losses, and would develop this interest till the eve of the trial. Incidentally it would hold all the inordinate time-telescoping; a helpful quickening, this, to its pulse. But these divisions and the choice of them have no other validity than convenience; the play must be thought of as an integral whole.

Needless to say that the confusion of scene-divisions in most modern editions (a very riot of it when Jessica is eloping) is not Shakespeare's; nor is the expert of the Folio responsible, nor even Rowe, who contents himself with marking the moves from Venice to Belmont and back. [19] For a century editors disputed as to when *Venice, a street,* shifted to *A room in Shylock's house,* or to *Another street,* or to *Before Shylock's house,* and chopped up the action and checked its impetus, when one glance at Shakespeare's stage, its doors and balcony and traverses, shows with what swift unity the play and its playing flow on. And whatever picturing of Venice and Belmont a producer may design, this swift-flowing unity he must on no account obstruct. Let that be clear.

But there is little difficulty in the play's production, once its form is recognized, its temper felt, the tune of its verse and the rhythm of its prose rightly caught. The text is very free from errors, there are no puzzles in the actual stagecraft. The music may come from Elizabethan stock, and the costuming is obvious. Nothing is needed but perception and good taste, and from the actors, acting.

NOTES

1. If the effect is one and the same, one might think the question unimportant. But Daniel, making out his three months, is generous of "intervals," not only between acts, but between scenes; and even Furness, on his subtler scent, can say, "One is always conscious that between the acts of a play a certain space of time elapses. To convey this impression is one of the purposes for which a drama is divided into acts." Therefore an important and a much-disputed question is involved—and begged. And, in practice, the pernicious hanging-up of performances by these pauses is encouraged, to which scenery and its shifting is already a sufficient temptation.

2. See also Preface to *Antony and Cleopatro*.

3. It is, one may say, a commonplace of stagecraft, Elizabethan or other; but none the less worthy for that.

4. And such interest as there is in Aragon's scene is now lessened, perhaps, by our knowledge that Bassanio is on his way; even more, by the talk in the scene before of Antonio's misfortune. But Shakespeare, as his wont is, plucks some little advantage from the poverty of the business by capping Aragon's vapidity with the excitement of the news of Bassanio's arrival.

5. Though there are commentators who maintain that Nerissa— even Portia, perhaps—gives Bassanio the hint to choose lead, or has it sung to him:

> Tell me, where is fancy *bred*,
> In the heart, or in the *head*?
> How begot, how *nourished*?

And if he'll only listen carefully he will note that they all rhyme
with *lead*.

Shakespeare was surely of a simpler mind than this—his audiences too. And he had some slight sense of the fitness of things.
Would he—how *could* he?—wind up this innocent fairy tale with
such a slim trick? Besides, how was it to be worked; how is an
audience to be let into the secret? Are they likely to tag extra
rhymes to the words of a song as they listen to it? Or is Nerissa
—not Portia, surely!—at some point to tip Bassanio "the wink"
while he smiles knowingly back to assure her that he has "cot-
toned on"? Where, oh, where indeed, are such dramatic fancies
bred? Not in any head that will think out the effect of their
realization.

6. Little to be found in him, upon analysis, to refute the frigid
verdict lately passed upon him by that distinguished and en-
lightened—but in this instance, surely, most mistakenly whimsi-
cal—critic, Sir Arthur Quiller-Couch, of fortune-hunter, hypocrite
and worse. Is anything more certain than that Shakespeare did
not *mean* to present us with such a hero? If Sir Arthur were
producing the play, one pities the actor asked to give effect to
his verdict.

7. Possible extra time was needed for the shifting of the caskets and their furniture and the setting of the chairs of state
for the Duke and the Magnificoes. But in that case these last
must have been very elaborate.

8. For the bearing of this upon the question of act-division,
see p. 66.

9. But Rosencrantz and Guildenstern, as Shakespeare wrote
them, are not the mere puppets that the usual mangling of the
text leaves them.

10. It is worth remarking that the word "sad," as Shakespeare
uses it, may mean rather solemn and serious than definitely
miserable.

11. This is one of the ever-recurring small strokes of stagecraft that are hardly appreciable apart from an Elizabethan
stage. Shylock and Bassanio are to the front of the platform.
Antonio, near the door, is by convention any convenient distance off; by impression, too, with no realistic scenery to destroy

the impression. Shylock is left isolated, so isolated that the long aside has all the importance and the force of a soliloquy.

12. And so strange has this seemed to many a producer of the play and actor of Shylock, that we have been given scenes of pantomime in which Shylock comes back from Bassanio's supper to find Jessica flown. The solitary figure with a lantern, the un-answered rapping at the door, has become all but traditional. Irving did it, Coghlan had already done something of the sort, and—I fancy—Booth. An ingenious variation upon a theme by Shakespeare, that yet merely enfeebles the theme. The length-ier elaboration of a Shylock seen distracted at the discovery of his loss is, of course, even more inadmissible, since Shakespeare has deliberately avoided the situation.

13. Upon the modern stage he usually has Tubal for a com-panion; one has even seen him seconded by a small crowd of sympathetic Jews. How any producer can bring himself so to discount the poignant sight of that drab, heroic figure, lonely amid the magnificence around, passes understanding!

14. See Furness for an elaborate, illuminating and witty com-ment upon the situation.

15. It is hard to see why Antonio's taking the money to pass on to "the gentleman that lately stole his daughter" and provid-ing that, for his half-pardon "he presently become a Christian," should be so reprobated by some critics. If we have less con-fidence today than had Antonio in the efficacy of baptism, have we none left in the rightfulness of reparation? Not much in its efficacy, perhaps. Antonio, one must insist, does not mean to keep any of the money for himself. One hopes he never lapsed into self-righteousness in recalling this. Nothing is said, how-ever, about the original three thousand ducats!

16. The two scenes are, to a line, of the same length. Add to the one the opening of the trial-scene, and to the other, for safety's sake, twenty bars or so of music, and we have the time allotted for the change of costume.

17. Furness sees dramatic point in the second act ending with Bassanio on the doorstep. I suggest that Nerissa's tag is meant to keep Belmont a little in our minds during the strenuous scene between Shylock and Tubal which follows; but that, if anything, it tells against an act-pause falling here, rather than for it.

18. There is, as we have seen, a possible contracting of the action here that gives a summariness to the last few lines and suggests (to the modern ear, truly) a "curtain."

19. Lord Lansdowne's Jew held the stage in Rowe's time; and for this reason, it may just possibly be, he does not trouble to bring the play into closer relation with his own theater.

Caroline F E. Spurgeon

THE IMAGERY OF *ROMEO AND JULIET*

IT HAS NOT, so far as I know, ever yet been noticed that recurrent images play a part in raising, developing, sustaining, and repeating emotion in the tragedies, which is somewhat analogous to the action of a recurrent theme or "motif" in a musical fugue or sonato, or in one of Wagner's operas.

Perhaps, however, a more exact analogy to the function of Shakespeare's images in this respect is the unique work of another great artist, of the peculiar quality of which they constantly remind one, that is, Blake's illustrations to his prophetic books. These are not, for the most part, illustrations in the ordinary sense of the term, the translation by the artist of some incident in the narrative into a visual picture; they are rather a running accompaniment to the words in another medium, sometimes symbolically emphasizing or interpreting certain aspects of the thought, sometimes supplying frankly only decoration or atmosphere, sometimes grotesque and even repellent, vivid, strange, arresting, sometimes drawn with an almost unearthly beauty of form and colour. Thus, as the leaping tongues of flame which illuminate the pages of *The Marriage of Heaven and Hell* show the visual form which Blake's thought evoked in his mind, and symbolize for us the purity, the beauty, and the two-edged quality of life and danger in his words, so the recurrent images in *Macbeth* or *Hamlet* reveal the dominant picture or sensation—and for Shakespeare the two are identical—in terms of which he sees and feels the main problem or theme

From *Leading Motives in the Imagery of Shakespeare's Tragedies*, paragraphs 1-17. The Shakespeare Association Lecture for 1930. Reprinted by permission of the Association.

of the play, thus giving us an unerring clue to the way he looked at it, as well as a direct glimpse into the working of his mind and imagination.

These dominating images are a characteristic of Shakespeare's work throughout, but whereas in the earlier plays they are often rather obvious and of set design, taken over in some cases with the story itself from a hint in the original narrative; in the later plays, and especially in the great tragedies, they are born of the emotions of the theme, and are, as in *Macbeth,* subtle, complex, varied, but intensely vivid and revealing; or as in *Lear,* so constant and all-pervading as to be reiterated, not only in the word-pictures, but also in the single words themselves.

Any reader, of course, must be aware of certain recurrent symbolic imagery in Shakespeare, such as that of a tree and its branches, and of planting, lopping, or rooting up, which runs through the English historical plays; they are conscious of the imaginative effect of the animal imagery in *Lear,* or of the flash of explosives in *Romeo and Juliet,* but it was not until the last few years, when in the course of an intensive study of Shakespeare's imagery I had listed and classified and card-indexed and counted every image in every play thrice over, that the actual facts as to these dominating pictures stared me in the face.

I found that there is a certain range of images, and roughly a certain proportion of these, to be expected in every play, and that certain familiar categories, of nature, animals, and what one may call "everyday" or "domestic," easily come first. But in addition to this normal grouping, I have found, especially in the tragedies, certain groups of images which, as it were, stick out in each particular play and immediately attract attention because they are peculiar either in subject or quantity, or both.

These seem to form the floating image or images in Shakespeare's mind called forth by that particular play, and I propose now, as briefly as possible, just to look at the tragedies from the point of view of these groups of images only.

In *Romeo and Juliet* the beauty and ardour of young love is seen by Shakespeare as the irradiating glory of sunlight and starlight in a dark world. The dominating image is *light,* every form and manifestation of it; the sun, moon, stars, fire, lightning, the flash of gunpowder, and the reflected light of beauty and of love; while by contrast we have night, darkness, clouds, rain, mist, and smoke.

Each of the lovers thinks of the other as light; Romeo's overpowering impression when he first catches sight of Juliet on the fateful evening at the Capulets' ball is seen in his exclamation,

> O, she doth teach the torches to burn bright!

To Juliet, Romeo, is "day in night"; to Romeo, Juliet is the sun rising from the east, and when they soar to love's ecstasy, each alike pictures the other as stars in heaven, shedding such brightness as puts to shame the heavenly bodies themselves.

The intensity of feeling in both lovers purges even the most highly affected and euphuistic conceits of their artificiality, and transforms them into the exquisite and passionate expression of love's rhapsody.

Thus Romeo plays with the old conceit that two of the fairest stars in heaven, having some business on earth, have entreated Juliet's eyes to take their place till they return, and he conjectures,

> What if her eyes were there, they in her head?

If so,

> The brightness of her cheek would shame those stars,
> As day-light doth a lamp:

and then comes the rush of feeling, the overpowering realization and immortal expression of the transforming glory of love,

> her eyes in heaven
> Would through the airy region stream so bright
> That birds would sing and think it were not night.

And Juliet, in her invocation to night, using an even more extravagant conceit such as Cowley or Cleveland at his wildest never exceeded, transmutes it into the perfect and natural expression of a girl whose lover to her not only radiates light but is, indeed, very light itself:

> Give me my Romeo; and, when he shall die,
> Take him and cut him out in little stars,

> And he will make the face of heaven so fine,
> That all the world will be in love with night,
> And pay no worship to the garish sun.

Love is described by Romeo, before he knows what it really is, as

> a smoke raised with the fume of sighs;
> Being purged, a fire sparkling in lovers' eyes;

and the messengers of love are seen by Juliet, when she is chafing under the nurse's delay, as one of the most exquisite effects in nature, especially on the English hills in spring, of the swift, magical, transforming power of light; "love's heralds," she cries, "should be thoughts,

> Which ten times faster glide than the sun's beams,
> Driving back shadows over louring hills."

The irradiating quality of the beauty of love is noticed by both lovers; by Juliet in her first ecstasy, when she declares that lovers' "own beauties" are sufficient light for them to see by, and at the end by Romeo, when, thinking her dead, he gazes on her and cries

> her beauty makes
> This vault a feasting presence full of light.

There can be no question, I think, that Shakespeare saw the story, in its swift and tragic beauty, as an almost blinding flash of light, suddenly ignited and as swiftly quenched. He quite deliberately compresses the action from over nine months to the almost incredibly short period of five days; so that the lovers meet on Sunday, are wedded on Monday, part at dawn on Tuesday, and are reunited in death on the night of Thursday. The sensation of swiftness and brilliance, accompanied by danger and destruction, is accentuated again and again; by Juliet when she avows their bethrothal

> is too rash, too unadvised, too sudden,
> Too like the lightning, which doth cease to be
> Ere one can say 'It lightens';

and by Romeo and the Friar, who instinctively make repeated use of the image of the quick destructive flash of gunpowder (III. iii. 103, 132; v. i. 63). Indeed the Friar, in his well-known answer to Romeo's prayer for instant marriage, succinctly, in the last nine words, sums up the whole movement of the play,

> These violent delights have violent ends,
> And in their triumph die; like fire and powder
> Which as they kiss consume.

Even old Capulet, whom one does not think of as a poetical person, though he uses many images—some of great beauty—carries on the idea of light to represent love and youth and beauty, and of the clouding of the sun for grief and sorrow. He promises Paris that on the evening of the ball he shall see at his house

> Earth-treading stars that make dark heaven light,

and when he encounters Juliet weeping, as he thinks for her cousin Tybalt's death, he clothes his comment in similar nature-imagery of light quenched in darkness,

> When the sun sets, the air doth drizzle dew;
> But for the sunset of my brother's son
> It rains downright.

In addition to this more definite symbolic imagery we find that radiant light, sunshine, starlight, moonbeams, sunrise and sunset, the sparkle of fire, a meteor, candles, torches, quick-coming darkness, clouds, mist, rain, and night, form a pictorial background or running accompaniment to the play, which augments unconsciously in us this same sensation.

We meet it at once in the Prince's description of the attitude of the rival houses

> That quench the fire of your pernicious rage
> With purple fountains issuing from your veins;

and later, in the talk of Benvolio and Montagu about the rising sun, the dew, and clouds (I. i. 117-18, 130-36), followed by Romeo's definition of love (I. i. 189-90), Capulet's words just quoted, Benvolio's riming proverb about fire (I. ii. 46), the talk of Romeo and Mercutio about torches, candles, lights, and lamps

(I. iv. 35-45), the flashing lights and torches of the ball, four
times accentuated (I. v. 28, 45, 88, 126), Romeo's conception of
Juliet as a "bright angel," "as glorious to this night"

> As is a winged messenger of heaven;

the moonlight in the orchard, the sunrise Friar Lawrence watches
from his cell, the sun clearing from heaven Romeo's sighs (II. iii.
73), the exquisite light and shadow swiftly chasing over Juliet's
words in the orchard (II. v. 4-11), the "black fate" of the day on
which Mercutio was killed, the "fire-eyed fury" which leads
Romeo to challenge Tybalt, their fight, to which they go "like
lightning," the sunset which Juliet so ardently desires to be
swift "and bring in cloudy night immediately," the exquisite play
of quivering light from darkness through dawn, till

> jocund day
> Stands tip-toe on the misty mountain tops,

which forms the theme of the lovers' parting song; and at the
last, Romeo's anguished reply to Juliet, pointing the contrast
between the coming day and their own great sorrow,

> More light and light: more dark and dark our woes!

And then at the end we see the darkness of the churchyard, lit
by the glittering torch of Paris, quickly quenched; Romeo's
arrival with his torch, the swift fight and death, the dark vault,
which is not a grave but a lantern irradiated by Juliet's beauty,
Romeo's grim jest on the "lightning before death," followed
immediately by the self-slaughter of the "star-crossed" lovers,
the gathering together of the stricken mourners as the day
breaks, and the "glooming" peace of the overcast morning when

> The sun for sorrow will not show his head.

Shakespeare's extraordinary susceptibility to suggestion and
readiness to borrow is well exemplified in this running imagery.
He took the idea from the last place we should expect, from the
wooden doggerel of Arthur Brooke, and the germ of it is in
the sing-song line in which Brooke describes the attitude of
the lovers,

> For each of them to other is as to the world the sun.

Their mutual feeling and the feud of the families is constantly referred to by Brooke as "fire" or "flame"; in the beginning, he speaks of the feud as a "mighty fire"; the families "bathe in blood of smarting wounds," and the Prince hopes he may "quench the sparks that burned within their breast." These three images are combined and unified by Shakespeare in the two lines already quoted (I. i. 83-4).

Other suggestions also come from Brooke, such as the emphasis on the bright light of the torches at the ball; and Romeo's first sight of Juliet, which is a "sudden kindled fire"; her first impression of him when he

> in her sight did seem to pass the rest as far
> As Phoebus' shining beams do pass the brightness of a star;

and his description in his first talk to her, of the

> quick sparks and glowing furious glead
> . . . from your beauty's pleasant eyne, Love causéd to
> proceed
> Which have so set on fire each feeling part of mine
> That lo, my mind doth melt away, my outward parts do
> pine,

which is transmuted to the delightful image of the stars which have changed places with her eyes (II. ii. 15-22).

But although Shakespeare took the idea from his original it scarcely needs saying that, in taking it, he has transformed a few conventional and obvious similes of little poetic worth into a continuous and consistent running image of exquisite beauty, building up a definite picture and atmosphere of brilliance swiftly quenched, which powerfully affects the imagination of the reader.

Northrop Frye

THE ARGUMENT OF COMEDY

THE GREEKS produced two kinds of comedy, Old Comedy, represented by the eleven extant plays of Aristophanes, and New Comedy, of which the best known exponent is Menander. About two dozen New Comedies survive in the work of Plautus and Terence. Old Comedy, however, was out of date before Aristophanes himself was dead; and today, when we speak of comedy, we normally think of something that derives from the Menandrine tradition.

New Comedy unfolds from what may be described as a comic Oedipus situation. Its main theme is the successful effort of a young man to outwit an opponent and possess the girl of his choice. The opponent is usually the father (*senex*), and the psychological descent of the heroine from the mother is also sometimes hinted at. The father frequently wants the same girl, and is cheated out of her by the son, the mother thus becoming the son's ally. The girl is usually a slave or courtesan, and the plot turns on a *cognitio* or discovery of birth which makes her marriageable. Thus it turns out that she is not under an insuperable taboo after all but is an accessible object of desire, so that the plot follows the regular wish-fulfillment pattern. Often the central Oedipus situation is thinly concealed by surrogates or doubles of the main characters, as when the heroine is discovered to be the hero's sister, and has to be married off to his best friend. In Congreve's *Love for Love,* to take a modern instance well within the Menandrine tradition, there are two Oedipus themes in

From *English Institute Essays,* 1948, 1949, pp. 58-73. Copyright 1949 by Columbia University Press. Reprinted by permission of the publisher.

counterpoint: the hero cheats his father out of the heroine, and his best friend violates the wife of an impotent old man who is the heroine's guardian. Whether this analysis is sound or not, New Comedy is certainly concerned with the maneuvering of a young man toward a young woman, and marriage is the tonic chord on which it ends. The normal comic resolution is the surrender of the *senex* to the hero, never the reverse. Shakespeare tried to reverse the pattern in *All's Well That Ends Well*, where the king of France forces Bertram to marry Helena, and the critics have not yet stopped making faces over it.

New Comedy has the blessing of Aristotle, who greatly preferred it to its predecessor, and it exhibits the general pattern of Aristotelian causation. It has a material cause in the young man's sexual desire, and a formal cause in the social order represented by the *senex*, with which the hero comes to terms when he gratifies his desire. It has an efficient cause in the character who brings about the final situation. In classical times this character is a tricky slave; Renaissance dramatists often use some adaptation of the medieval "vice"; modern writers generally like to pretend that nature or at least the natural course of events, is the efficient cause. The final cause is the audience, which is expected by its applause to take part in the comic resolution. All this takes place on a single order of existence. The action of New Comedy tends to become probable rather than fantastic, and it moves toward realism and away from myth and romance. The one romantic (originally mythical) feature in it, the fact that the hero or heroine turns out to be freeborn or someone's heir, is precisely the feature that trained New Comedy audiences tire of most quickly.

The conventions of New Comedy are the conventions of Jonson and Molière, and a fortiori of the English Restoration and the French rococo. When Ibsen started giving ironic twists to the same formulas, his startled hearers took them for portents of a social revolution. Even the old chestnut about the heroine's being really the hero's sister turns up in *Ghosts* and *Little Eyolf*. The average movie of today is a rigidly conventionalized New Comedy proceeding toward an act which, like death in Greek tragedy, takes place offstage, and is symbolized by the final embrace.

In all good New Comedy there is a social as well as an individual theme which must be sought in the general atmosphere of reconciliation that makes the final marriage possible. As the hero gets closer to the heroine and opposition is overcome, all the right-thinking people come over to his side. Thus a new social unit is formed on the stage, and the moment that this social unit crystallizes is the moment of the comic resolution. In the last scene, when the dramatist usually tries to get all his characters on the stage at once, the audience witnesses the birth of a renewed sense of social integration. In comedy as in life the regular expression of this is a festival, whether a marriage, a dance, or a feast. Old Comedy has, besides a marriage, a *komos,* the processional dance from which comedy derives its name; and the masque, which is a by-form of comedy, also ends in a dance.

This new social integration may be called, first, a kind of moral norm and, second, the pattern of a free society. We can see this more clearly if we look at the sort of characters who impede the progress of the comedy toward the hero's victory. These are always people who are in some kind of mental bondage, who are helplessly driven by ruling passions, neurotic compulsions, social rituals, and selfishness. The miser, the hypochondriac, the hypocrite, the pedant, the snob: these are humors, people who do not fully know what they are doing, who are slaves to a predictable self-imposed pattern of behavior. What we call the moral norm is, then, not morality but deliverance from moral bondage. Comedy is designed not to condemn evil, but to ridicule a lack of self-knowledge. It finds the virtues of Malvolio and Angelo as comic as the vices of Shylock.

The essential comic resolution, therefore, is an individual release which is also a social reconciliation. The normal individual is freed from the bonds of a humorous society, and a normal society is freed from the bonds imposed on it by humorous individuals. The Oedipus pattern we noted in New Comedy belongs to the individual side of this, and the sense of the ridiculousness of the humor to the social side. But all real comedy is based on the principle that these two forms of release are ultimately the same: this principle may be seen at its most concentrated in *The Tempest.* The rule holds whether the resolution is expressed in social terms, as in *The Merchant of Venice,* or in individual terms, as in Ibsen's *An Enemy of the People.*

The freer the society, the greater the variety of individuals it can tolerate, and the natural tendency of comedy is to include as many as possible in its final festival. The motto of comedy is Terence's "Nothing human is alien to me." This may be one reason for the traditional comic importance of the parasite, who has no business to be at the festival but is nevertheless there. The spirit of reconciliation which pervades the comedies of Shakespeare is not to be ascribed to a personal attitude of his own, about which we know nothing whatever, but to his impersonal concentration on the laws of comic form.

Hence the moral quality of the society presented is not the point of the comic resolution. In Jonson's *Volpone* the final assertion of the moral norm takes the form of a social revenge on Volpone, and the play ends with a great bustle of sentences to penal servitude and the galleys. One feels perhaps that the audience's sense of the moral norm does not need so much hard labor. In *The Alchemist,* when Lovewit returns to his house, the virtuous characters have proved so weak and the rascals so ingenious that the action dissolves in laughter. Whichever is morally the better ending, that of *The Alchemist* is more concentrated comedy. *Volpone* is starting to move toward tragedy, toward the vision of a greatness which develops *hybris* and catastrophe.

The same principle is even clearer in Aristophanes. Aristophanes is the most personal of writers: his opinions on every subject are written all over his plays, and we have no doubt of his moral attitude. We know that he wanted peace with Sparta and that he hated Cleon, and when his comedy depicts the attaining of peace and the defeat of Cleon we know that he approved and wanted his audience to approve. But in *Ecclesiazusae* a band of women in disguise railroad a communistic scheme through the Assembly, which is a horrid parody of Plato's *Republic,* and proceed to inaugurate Plato's sexual communism with some astonishing improvements. Presumably Aristophanes did not applaud this, yet the comedy follows the same pattern and the same resolution. In *The Birds* the Peisthetairos who defies Zeus and blocks out Olympus with his Cloud-Cuckoo-

Land is accorded the same triumph that is given to the Trygaeus of the *Peace* who flies to heaven and brings a golden age back to Athens.

Comedy, then, may show virtue her own feature and scorn her own image—for Hamlet's famous definition of drama was originally a definition of comedy. It may emphasize the birth of an ideal society as you like it, or the tawdriness of the sham society which is the way of the world. There is an important parallel here with tragedy. Tragedy, we are told, is expected to raise but not ultimately to accept the emotions of pity and terror. These I take to be the sense of moral good and evil, respectively, which we attach to the tragic hero. He may be as good as Caesar, and so appeal to our pity, or as bad as Macbeth, and so appeal to terror, but the particular thing called tragedy that happens to him does not depend on his moral status. The tragic catharsis passes beyond moral judgment, and while it is quite possible to construct a moral tragedy, what tragedy gains in morality it loses in cathartic power. The same is true of the comic catharsis, which raises sympathy and ridicule on a moral basis, but passes beyond both.

Many things are involved in the tragic catharsis, but one of them is a mental or imaginative form of the sacrificial ritual out of which tragedy arose. This is the ritual of the struggle, death, and rebirth of a God-Man, which is linked to the yearly triumph of spring over winter. The tragic hero is not really killed, and the audience no longer eats his body and drinks his blood, but the corresponding thing in art still takes place. The audience enters into communion with the body of the hero, becoming thereby a single body itself. Comedy grows out of the same ritual, for in the ritual the tragic story has a comic sequel. Divine men do not die: they die and rise again. The ritual pattern behind the catharsis of comedy is the resurrection that follows the death, the epiphany or manifestation of the risen hero. This is clear enough in Aristophanes, where the hero is treated as a risen God-Man, led in triumph with the divine honors of the Olympic victor, rejuvenated, or hailed as a new Zeus. In New Comedy the new human body is, as we have seen, both a hero and a social group. Aristophanes is not only closer to the ritual pattern, but contemporary with Plato; and his comedy, unlike Menander's, is

Platonic and dialectic: it seeks not the entelechy of the soul but the Form of the Good, and finds it in the resurrection of the soul from the world of the cave to the sunlight. The audience gains a vision of that resurrection whether the conclusion is joyful or ironic, just as in tragedy it gains a vision of a heroic death whether the hero is morally innocent or guilty.

Two things follow from this: first, that tragedy is really implicit or uncompleted comedy; second, that comedy contains a potential tragedy within itself. With regard to the latter, Aristophanes is full of traces of the original death of the hero which preceded his resurrection in the ritual. Even in New Comedy the dramatist usually tries to bring his action as close to a tragic overthrow of the hero as he can get it, and reverses this movement as suddenly as possible. In Plautus the tricky slave is often forgiven or even freed after having been threatened with all the brutalities that a very brutal dramatist can think of, including crucifixion. Thus the resolution of New Comedy seems to be a realistic foreshortening of a death-and-resurrection pattern, in which the struggle and rebirth of a divine hero has shrunk into a marriage, the freeing of a slave, and the triumph of a young man over an older one.

As for the conception of tragedy as implicit comedy, we may notice how often tragedy closes on the major chord of comedy: the Aeschylean trilogy, for instance, proceeds to what is really a comic resolution, and so do many tragedies of Euripides. From the point of view of Christianity, too, tragedy is an episode in that larger scheme of redemption and resurrection to which Dante gave the name of *commedia*. This conception of *commedia* enters drama with the miracle-play cycles, where such tragedies as the Fall and the Crucifixion are episodes of a dramatic scheme in which the divine comedy has the last word. The sense of tragedy as a prelude to comedy is hardly separable from anything explicitly Christian. The serenity of the final double chorus in the St. Matthew Passion would hardly be attainable if composer and audience did not know that there was more to the story. Nor would the death of Samson lead to "calm of mind all passion spent" if Samson were not a prototype of the rising Christ.

New Comedy is thus contained, so to speak, within the symbolic structure of Old Comedy, which in its turn is contained within the Christian conception of _commedia_. This sounds like a logically exhaustive classification, but we have still not caught Shakespeare in it.

It is only in Jonson and the Restoration writers that English comedy can be called a form of New Comedy. The earlier tradition established by Peele and developed by Lyly, Greene, and the masque writers, which uses themes from romance and folklore and avoids the comedy of manners, is the one followed by Shakespeare. These themes are largely medieval in origin, and derive, not from the mysteries or the moralities or the interludes, but from a fourth dramatic tradition. This is the drama of folk ritual, of the St. George play and the mummers' play, of the feast of the ass and the Boy Bishop, and of all the dramatic activity that punctuated the Christian calendar with the rituals of an immemorial paganism. We may call this the drama of the green world, and its theme is once again the triumph of life over the waste land, the death and revival of the year impersonated by figures still human, and once divine as well.

When Shakespeare began to study Plautus and Terence, his dramatic instinct, stimulated by his predecessors, divined that there was a profounder pattern in the argument of comedy than appears in either of them. At once—for the process is beginning in _The Comedy of Errors_—he started groping toward that profounder pattern, the ritual of death and revival that also underlies Aristophanes, of which an exact equivalent lay ready to hand in the drama of the green world. This parallelism largely accounts for the resemblances to Greek ritual which Colin Still has pointed out in _The Tempest_.

The Two Gentlemen of Verona is an orthodox New Comedy except for one thing. The hero Valentine becomes captain of a band of outlaws in a forest, and all the other characters are gathered into this forest and become converted. Thus the action of the comedy begins in a world represented as a normal world, moves into the green world, goes into a metamorphosis there in which the comic resolution is achieved, and returns to the normal world. The forest in this play is the embryonic form of the fairy world of _A Midsummer Night's Dream_, the Forest of Arden in _As You Like It_, Windsor Forest in _The Merry Wives of Windsor_, and the pastoral world of the mythical sea-coasted Bohemia in *The Winter's Tale*. In all these comedies there is the same rhythmic movement from normal world to green world and back again. Nor is this second world confined to the forest comedies. In *The Merchant of Venice* the two worlds are a little harder to see, yet Venice is clearly not the same world as that of Portia's mysterious house in Belmont, where there are caskets teaching that gold and silver are corruptible goods, and from whence proceed the wonderful cosmological harmonies of the fifth act. In *The Tempest* the entire action takes place in the second world, and the same may be said of *Twelfth Night*, which, as its title implies, presents a carnival society, not so much a green world as an evergreen one. The second world is absent from the so-called problem comedies, which is one of the things that makes them problem comedies.

The green world charges the comedies with a symbolism in which the comic resolution contains a suggestion of the old ritual pattern of the victory of summer over winter. This is explicit in *Love's Labour's Lost*. In this very masque-like play, the comic contest takes the form of the medieval debate of winter and spring. In *The Merry Wives of Windsor* there is an elaborate ritual of the defeat of winter, known to folklorists as "carrying out Death," of which Falstaff is the victim; and Falstaff must have felt that, after being thrown into the water, dressed up as a witch and beaten out of a house with curses, and finally supplied with a beast's head and singed with candles while he said, "Divide me like a brib'd buck, each a haunch," he had done about all that could reasonably be asked of any fertility spirit.

The association of this symbolism with the death and revival of human beings is more elusive, but still perceptible. The fact that the heroine often brings about the comic resolution by disguising herself as a boy is familiar enough. In the Hero of *Much Ado About Nothing* and the Helena of *All's Well That Ends Well*, this theme of the withdrawal and return of the heroine comes as close to a death and revival as Elizabethan conventions will allow. The Thaisa of *Pericles* and the Fidele of *Cymbeline* are beginning to crack the conventions, and with the disappearance and revival of Hermione in *The Winter's Tale*, who actually returns once as a ghost in a dream, the original nature-myth of

Demeter and Proserpine is openly established. The fact that the dying and reviving character is usually female strengthens the feeling that there is something maternal about the green world, in which the new order of the comic resolution is nourished and brought to birth. However, a similar theme which is very like the rejuvenation of the *senex* so frequent in Aristophanes occurs in the folklore motif of the healing of the impotent king on which *All's Well That Ends Well* is based, and this theme is probably involved in the symbolism of Prospero.

The conception of a second world bursts the boundaries of Menandrine comedy, yet it is clear that the world of Puck is no world of eternal forms or divine revelation. Shakespeare's comedy is not Aristotelian and realistic like Menander's, nor Platonic and dialectic like Aristophanes', nor Thomist and sacramental like Dante's, but a fourth kind. It is an Elizabethan kind, and is not confined either to Shakespeare or to the drama. Spenser's epic is a wonderful contrapuntal intermingling of two orders of existence, one the red and white world of English history, the other the green world of the Faerie Queene. The latter is a world of crusading virtues proceeding from the Faerie Queene's court and designed to return to that court when the destiny of the other world is fulfilled. The fact that the Faerie Queene's knights are sent out during the twelve days of the Christmas festival suggests our next point.

Shakespeare too has his green world of comedy and his red and white world of history. The story of the latter is at one point interrupted by an invasion from the comic world, when Falstaff *senex et parasitus* throws his gigantic shadow over Prince Henry, assuming on one occasion the role of his father. Clearly, if the Prince is ever to conquer France he must reassert the moral norm. The moral norm is duly reasserted, but the rejection of Falstaff is not a comic resolution. In comedy the moral norm is not morality but deliverance, and we certainly do not feel delivered from Falstaff as we feel delivered from Shylock with his absurd and vicious bond. The moral norm does not carry with it the vision of a free society: Falstaff will always keep a bit of that in his tavern.

Falstaff is a mock king, a lord of misrule, and his tavern is a Saturnalia. Yet we are reminded of the original meaning of the

Saturnalia, as a rite intended to recall the golden age of Saturn. Falstaff's world is not a golden world, but as long as we remember it we cannot forget that the world of *Henry V* is an iron one. We are reminded too of another traditional denizen of the green world, Robin Hood, the outlaw who manages to suggest a better kind of society than those who make him an outlaw can produce. The outlaws in *The Two Gentlemen of Verona* compare themselves, in spite of the Italian setting, to Robin Hood, and in *As You Like It* Charles the wrestler says of Duke Senior's followers: "There they live like the old Robin Hood of England: they say many young gentlemen flock to him every day, and fleet the time carelessly, as they did in the golden world."

In the histories, therefore, the comic Saturnalia is a temporary reversal of normal standards, comic "relief" as it is called, which subsides and allows the history to continue. In the comedies, the green world suggests an original golden age which the normal world has usurped and which makes us wonder if it is not the normal world that is the real Saturnalia. In *Cymbeline* the green world finally triumphs over a historical theme, the reason being perhaps that in that play the incarnation of Christ, which is contemporary with Cymbeline, takes place offstage, and accounts for the halcyon peace with which the play concludes. From then on in Shakespeare's plays, the green world has it all its own way, and both in *Cymbeline* and in *Henry VIII* there may be suggestions that Shakespeare, like Spenser, is moving toward a synthesis of the two worlds, a wedding of Prince Arthur and the Faerie Queene.

This world of fairies, dreams, disembodied souls, and pastoral lovers may not be a "real" world, but, if not, there is something equally illusory in the stumbling and blinded follies of the "normal" world, of Theseus' Athens with its idiotic marriage law, of Duke Frederick and his melancholy tyranny, of Leontes and his mad jealousy, of the Court Party with their plots and intrigues. The famous speech of Prospero about the dream nature of reality applies equally to Milan and the enchanted island. We spend our lives partly in a waking world we call normal and partly in a dream world which we create out of our own desires. Shakespeare endows both worlds with equal imaginative power, brings them opposite one another, and makes each world seem

about the "good people," and would even have shared in the
habits of thought and imagination from which those beliefs took
their rise. It is certainly not so with Shakespeare, who, for good
or for evil, is a thorough child of the Renascence, and exhibits
not only the Renascence love of quaint lore plundered from
every quarter, but also the Renascence positive spirit, for which
such lore has little meaning otherwise than as material for deliberate poetic craft. He takes his superstitions from learned and
literary sources, just as he takes his natural history from the
bestiaries, no less freely than from his own observation. Even
when his material is of English origin, it is not always clear
whether he has drawn it from reminiscences of his own Warwick-
shire boyhood or from some popular book, such as Reginald
Scot's *Discovery of Witchcraft* or Harsnet's *Declaration of Popish
Impostures*. It must not be assumed, therefore, that Shakespeare's use of the supernatural for dramatic purposes implies a
belief in its actual and objective existence. Where it is not merely
imposed upon him by his historical sources, it seems to serve one
of two ends. Either it attunes the minds of the audience to a
tragic or ironical issue, as for example in the terrible dreams of
Richard Crookback before Bosworth Field; or it is a symbol,
introduced by the poet as a recognition of a mystery, an unex-
plained element in the course of human affairs upon earth. This
is its really important function in some of the greatest plays. It is
Shakespeare's confession of ignorance, of the fact that in his
observation of life he has come just there upon something which
baffles analysis, something which is, but which cannot be quite
accounted for. Thus in *Macbeth* the witches symbolize the
double mystery of temptation and retribution; in *The Tempest*
the magic arts of Prospero and the spiritual forces which are at
his beck and call symbolize the mystery of an overruling Providence, and perhaps at the same time something of the mystery
of the creative poetic imagination. The agency of the fairies in
A Midsummer Night's Dream is capable of a similar explanation.

Of course the play is primarily a court revel. It was doubtless
written for a wedding, and possibly for a wedding at which
Elizabeth was present. It has the profusion of dance and song,
the picturesque staging and pretty costumes, the sprinkling of
courtly compliment, the piquant contrast of poetry and clown-

ing, which were the delight of the nobles and maids of honour
who assembled at Gloriana's palace of Greenwich. But at the
same time it is a true comedy, a deliberate picture of life as life
reveals itself to the shrewd insight of the comic spirit. The theme
is love—an obvious theme for a wedding play, even if it were not
the one about which Shakespeare's imagination was principally
exercised at the moment. He had written *The Two Gentlemen of
Verona,* and had either written or was on the point of writing
Romeo and Juliet, with its tragic burden of two lives ruined and
at the same time ennobled by love. Even in *Romeo and Juliet*
the comic as well as the tragic view of love is present. It is
incarnate in the critical wit of Mercutio. But in *A Midsummer
Night's Dream* it has undisputed sway. We have no longer to
do with Dante's "lord of terrible aspect," but rather with the
roguish little Cupid of Ovid, the irresponsible child-god, with
his blinded eyes and his erring arrows. "Hast been in love?" says
the young shepherd to the old one in *As You Like It,* then—

> How many actions most ridiculous
> Hast thou been drawn to by thy fantasy?

Love, as interpreted by the comic spirit, is a certain fine lunacy
in the brain of youth; not an integral part of life, but a disturbing
element in it. The lover is a being of strange caprices and strange
infidelities, beyond the control of reason, and swayed with every
gust of passion. He is at odds for the time with all the established
order of things, a rebel against the authority of parents, a rebel
against friendship, a rebel against his own vows. This is love as
it figures in comedy, and in the presentation and analysis of this
lies the point of the play.

Bearing then in mind this central idea of the lawlessness and
the laughableness of love, one may observe how carefully, for
all the apparent whimsicality of structure, it is kept to the front
in the working out of the plot. As is generally the case in Shakespeare's comedies, this is composed of several stories, which are
woven together with remarkable ingenuity. You have the story of
Theseus' wedding, the story of the Athenian lovers, the story of
the quarrel of Oberon and Titania, the story of the handicraftsmen's play, and finally the story or interlude of Pyramus and
Thisbe. It is the first of these which serves as the link that holds

is generally only a passing fever. There is a period of *Sturm und Drang*, and then the man or woman begins to take life seriously, and is ready to submit to its discipline and to accept its reasonable responsibilities. And so by the side of Lysander and Demetrius we have the grave figure of the Athenian duke, Theseus. Theseus has had his wayward youth; he has "played with light loves in the portal," with Perigenia and Aegles and the rest; ay, and in the glimmering night even with Queen Titania herself. Moreover, in his passion for Hippolyta he has approached her through deeds of violence; he has "won her love, doing her injuries." But now, like the Henry the Fifth of whom he is a prototype, he has put away childish things; he stands forth as the serene law-abiding king, no less than the still loving and tender husband. Thus the story of Theseus' wedding not only, as has been said, serves to hold the plot together, but also contributes its share to the illustration of the central idea.

When we turn to the fairies, we find that what enters into human life only as a transitory disturbing element, is in them the normal law of their being. They are irresponsible creatures throughout, eternal children. They belong to the winds and the clouds and the flowers, to all in nature that is beautiful and gracious and fleeting; but of the characteristics by which man differs from these, the sense of law and the instinct of self-control, they show no trace. Puck, the fairy jester, is a buffoon of spirits, whose sport it is to bring perplexity upon hapless mortals. Oberon and Titania will be jealous and be reconciled to each other a dozen times a day, while for culmination of their story you have the absurd spectacle of a fairy in love with an ass. So that in them is represented, as it were *in vacuo*, the very quality of which it is the object of the play to discern the partial and occasional workings in the heart of humanity.

In the story of the handicraftsmen, the central idea does not find any direct illustration. The story is required, partly to introduce the interlude, but still more to provide that comic contrast which was always an essential feature of a mask, or a play written on the lines of a mask. It is ingeniously interwoven into the fairy story by making Bottom the instrument of Oberon's revenge upon Titania. And it is in the person of Bottom that the whole humour of the thing consists. He is, with the possible exception of the Nurse in *Romeo and Juliet,* the first of Shake-speare's supreme comic creations, greater than the Costard of *Love's Labour's Lost* or the Launce of *The Two Gentlemen of Verona,* as the masterpiece is greater than the imperfect sketch. From beginning to end of the play his absolute self-possession never for a moment fails him. He lords it over his fellow-actors, as though he, and not Quince, were poet and stage-manager in one; he accepts the amorous attentions of a queen with calm serenity as no more than might naturally have been expected; nor does he ever, either before or after his transformation, betray the slightest suspicion of the fact that he is after all only an ass. It has often been thought that in the rehearsal scenes Shake-speare was drawing upon the humours of such rustic actors as might have ventured a Whitsun pastoral at Stratford-upon-Avon; yet one fears that the foibles of the green-room are much the same in the humblest and the loftiest walks of the profession, and who shall say that the poet is not poking good-humoured fun at some of his fellows of the Lord Chamberlain's company?

Finally, with the interlude, we come back to the central idea once more. For in the ill-starred loves of Pyramus and Thisbe, their assignation, their elopement, and their terrible end, we have but a burlesque presentment of the same theme which has occupied us throughout. It is all a matter of how the poet chooses to put it. Precisely the same situation that in *Romeo and Juliet* will ask our tears, shall here move unextinguishable laughter. And so the serious interest of the play dissolves in mirth, and while the musicians break into the exquisite poetry of the epithalamium, the playwright stands and watches us with the smile of wise tolerance on his lips.

M. C. Bradbrook

MUCH ADO ABOUT NOTHING

IF *Romeo and Juliet* was a tragedy with its full complement of comedy, and *The Merchant of Venice* a comedy with an infusion of tragic pity and fear, *Much Ado About Nothing* is a comedy of Masks where the deeper issues are overlaid with mirth, and appear only at the climax of the play, the church scene. It is for this reason that so very mechanical a villain as Don John becomes a necessity of the plot. A true villain, like Shylock or Edmund or Richard III, would destroy the comedy: those who protest at the insufficiency of Don John should consider what would happen to the total composition if he were other than he is.[1] The old worn device of a maid dressing up in her mistress's clothes—one of the commonplaces of European fiction for centuries—is also used for a special purpose. It is not perhaps so incredible as modern readers tend to think it: the story of Gratiano and Nerissa should have served as reminder that gentlewomen really might ape their mistresses,[2] and talking with a man out at a window had happened in Shakespeare before without incurring moral disapprobation, even of the strictest; it was only as it happened on her wedding eve to the betrothed Hero that it took on the colouring of perfidy as well as lightness. Nevertheless the convention is used in a frankly conventional way; Margaret does not intervene when Claudio lodges his accusation, and Claudio does not fall upon the interloper and run him through like the hero of *A Blot in the Scutcheon,* both of which are obvious, natural, and probable, but inappropriate things for them to do.

From *Shakespeare and Elizabethan Poetry,* 1951, pp. 179-88. Reprinted by permission of Chatto and Windus Ltd.

In *Much Ado*, as Masefield pointed out,[3] the two plots are
linked by the common theme of credulity and self-deception.
Claudio believes first that Don Pedro, then that Hero plays him
false: Benedick and Beatrice believe the stories of their friends,
thereby building a truth upon a fabulous basis. Dogberry and
Verges need no one to lay them a trap; they are perpetually
deceiving themselves, and invent a wonderful fabrication from
the conversation of Borachio and Conrad. Yet it is they who unmask the villainy, thus robbing it of a good deal of its sinister
value.

Credulity and foolish mistakings are the natural effects of
love: we have already seen Valentine unable to fathom Silvia's
meaning in asking him to write a love-letter, and the courtly
ladies of *Love's Labour's Lost* are unable to distinguish between
jest and earnest—though here perhaps the fault lies rather with
their lovers, who are so unpracticed at expressing their feelings.
Love's power to trip the heels, baffle the wits, and transform
the person is a staple of Shakespearean comedy. Within the
frame of a formal narrative, with its set situations—their staginess
underlined rather than disguised—Shakespeare develops the personal and natural feelings of his lovers, working by implication
and by strong use of contrast.

It does not need a critic to observe that Benedick and Beatrice
are flirting from the beginning. The technique of a "merry war"
is not unknown to clowns, and if Shakespeare had not happened
to have met it in real life, he could have found it plentifully
enough in literature.

Nevertheless discussions as to whether Benedick and Beatrice
are "really" in love will lead precisely nowhere. That in a sense
is the point of their wit-combat; what they think they are, what
their friends think they are, what they really might be, are left
as a series of alluring possibilities. "I confesse nothing nor I
deny nothing" says Beatrice at the climax of the church scene;
it was a situation to which the practice of courtship must have
given precedents enough. The dancing spray of the dialogue
could not, at all events, rise from mutual boredom.

As in *Love's Labour's Lost*, but not in *Two Gentlemen of
Verona* and *Twelfth Night*, the jesting is extremely broad. If
Beatrice is translated into modern English some of her language

would not be heard far west of Leicester Square. Yet she is hit,
as Phoebe and Olivia were to be hit, by a good scolding from
another woman. It seems to have been Shakespeare's grand
strategy for subduing the female sex. Benedick on the other hand
is caught with an appeal to his pity. The means are nicely varied;
so are the responses. His long, natural and entertaining soliloquy,
"Love me? why it must be requited," is based on the soliloquies
of Berowne (*Love's Labour's Lost*, III, i, 184-215: IV, iii, 1-21),
in its use of the debating form, with questions and answers, and
the picture of the reluctant lover haled into love, against his will
but not unwillingly. Benedick like Berowne takes to sonnetting,
though more unsuccessfully: but his physical transformation is
not of the old fashion, to let himself appear distraught and
ungartered; on the contrary, like Orlando, he goes point-devise
and shaves himself, which may be a proof merely that he is
ignorant of the rules. His wooing—and his sparring—is all conducted in russet yeas and honest kersey noes: the language of
the play is in revolt against courtly decorum throughout.

Yet Beatrice's reaction to the news is given in ten rhymed lines
of extreme formality:

> What fire is in mine eares? can this be true?
> Stand I condemned for pride and scorn so much?
> Contempt farewell, and maiden pride adew,
> No glory liues behind the back of such.
> And *Benedick,* loue on, I will requite thee,
> Taming my wild heart to thy louing hand:
> If thou dost loue, my kindenesse shall incite thee
> To binde our loues up in a holy band.
> For others say thou dost deserue, and I
> Believe it better than reportingly.
>
> (III, i, 107-16.)

This cannot be carelessness, remains of an old play, or laziness:
it is a most important moment in the story. Yet here is the verbal
equivalent of the dummy villain. Beatrice is to be shown still
preserving some of her defences until the climax of the church
scene, her next encounter with Benedick, and therefore nothing
personal enters into her confession because her feeling must be
held back for the critical release. He, being given the wooer's

role, can be allowed to speak his mind after the eavesdropping.

Both Benedick and Beatrice are comic without being ridiculous, and they provide the audience with the same kind of mirth that they are supposed to provide their friends. Their transparent attempts at disguising their feelings under the form of a toothache and a cold in the head, their slight peevishness and their extreme gullibility, Benedick's halting sonnet and February face, and Beatrice's extraordinary taciturnity, allow their friends to tease them, and the audience to indulge that particularly pleasing kind of superiority which arises when one's own predicaments are recognizably displayed in larger forms than life. If the two were not so admirable in all their more important actions—if Benedick were not so honest and soldierly, Beatrice so constant and loyal—there would be a good deal less pleasure in this identification. But to see characters in all other respects heroic reduced to such complete helplessness by Nature's ruthless device for ensuring that "the world must be peopled" is exhilarating in the extreme. It was a form of entertainment which was to be exploited much more coarsely by Fletcher with his conquering heroes reduced to absolute imbecility, like Arbaces, and his heroines of a wide-eyed innocence verging on impropriety, like Ordella.[4] To an age brought up on the Platonic politenesses, such a display of Nature must have been doubly engaging. The frank bawdiness and the human inconsistencies of Benedick and Beatrice must be seen against the proprieties of Valentine and Silvia, the stately splendour of Belmont, to win their full value.

To make the human relationship between two lovers display itself through the wit-combat of courtly love, by the simple process of extending the role of "unwilling" lover to the lady as well as the gentleman [5] was a stroke of genius which once achieved, takes on the appearance of the obvious. To quarrel was the stock recipe for comedy. Beatrice may indeed have owed something to the earlier Kate of *The Taming of the Shrew,* for her wit was certainly more forcible as well as more nimble than stage tradition would allow the court. Rosaline of *Love's Labour's Lost* is, like Beatrice, tilting against a professed enemy to her sex and is therefore justified of her tartness; Rosalind of *As You Like It* is speaking in the role of a pert page. Beatrice is called on for a moment of clarity which all the merry wars, the evasions and dissemblings serve to throw into high relief—the moment when she is confronted and in her turn confronts Benedick with a choice. Like the choice of the caskets, it is perilous: Benedick hesitates. For he has "to give and hazard" something which he weighs with the whole world.

> *Beatrice.* I love you with so much of my heart, that none is left to protest.
> *Benedick.* Come, bid me doe anything for thee.
> *Beatrice.* Kill *Claudio.*
> *Benedick.* Ha, not for the wide world.
> *Beatrice.* You kill me to denie it, farewell.
>
> (IV, i, 291ff)

Beatrice's passion is no assertion of principle: it is blind, savage and generous, offering Benedick simply the testimony of character, the testimony of her unshakable faith in her cousin's innocence. This is weighed against the sworn ocular proof of his two closest friends.[6] His acceptance of the challenge is prosaic in manner as well as in form.

> Enough, I am engaged, I will challenge him, I will kiss your hand and so leave you: by this hand Claudio shall render me a deere account: as you heare of me so thinke of me: goe comfort your cousin, I must say she is dead, and so farewell.
>
> (IV, i, 339ff)

These are the sort of old ends that were flouted by Claudio and Don Pedro; they are part of Benedick's soldierly plainness, and it is this quality—his readiness to act on his belief without hesitation and without requiring more conviction than Beatrice's oath and his own intuition—which gives him an easy lead among Shakespeare's heroes of comedy.

Claudio has on the other hand been the object of a good deal of critical venom. He has much larger stretches of flat dialogue to sustain but his part is developed from a courtly to a natural one in the course of his wooing. In contrast to Benedick and Beatrice, Claudio and Hero are silent lovers. Hero chatters to Beatrice and her women or under the protection of a mask (II, i, 90-104): Claudio, "Lord Lack beard," is similarly at ease with

Benedick and the Prince, but he can only introduce Hero's name
in his conversation by asking the Prince a question whose answer
is already known to him (I, i, 304-306). He and Hero have seen
each other in public; but virtually all he knows of her is her
looks. He has fallen in love with a pretty face and a modest
manner. It is quite natural to him to think that the Prince must
want Hero too. Fancy is not bred altogether in his eyes, nor,
though it has an interest, in his liver.

In the betrothal scene both the lovers are prompted by
Beatrice:

> *Leonato.* . . . his grace hath made the match, and all
> grace say, Amen to it.
> *Beatrice.* Speake Count, tis your Qu.
> *Claudio.* Silence is the perfectest Herrault of Ioy, I were
> but little happy if I could say, how much? Lady, as you are
> mine, I am yours, I giue away myself for you and dote upon
> the exchange.
> *Beatrice.* Speake cosin . . .
>
> (II, i, 316ff)

Like Bassanio Claudio is bereft of words; but when Pedro asks
him to name the marriage day, his precipitate "To-morrow, my
lord" is as telling as the fact that he has not exchanged one word
more with Hero nor she with him—except in his ear, to be interpreted by Beatrice to the company.

So the shock of the ocular proof which Don John offers has
little but Hero's appearance to contradict it; and hence the agony
of Claudio's dilemma. Claudio's idealization of Hero is shown
by his first comment, "Is it not a modest young lady?" He is hor-
ribly mocked, as he takes it, by the "seeming" which she maintains under his accusations.

> Behold how like a maid she blushes here! . . .
> Would you not sweare
> All you that see her, that she were a maide,
> By these exterior shewes?
>
> (IV, i, 34-40.)

When he speaks of his own behavior, "like a brother to a sister,"
Hero asks:

> And seem'd I ever otherwise to you?

The word is match to tinder.

> Out on thee seeming, I will write against it,
> You seeme to me as Dian in her orb.

That is, she *still* "seems" so. The speech looks back to Bassanio's
comment on the caskets and the false seeming of gold; it looks
forward to Hamlet's "Seems, madam! nay, it is, I know not
seemes." The lament which follows, lovely in its rhythm—

> O *Hero*! what a *Hero* hadst thou beene
> If halfe thy outward graces had been placed
> About thy thoughts and counsels of thy heart?
> But fair thee well, most foul, most faire, farewell
> Thou pure impiety and impious purity—

has not the agonized force of his question to Leonato:

> Is this face *Hero's*? are our eyes our own?

So Troilus, looking at Cressid, was to exclaim, "This is and is
not Cressid" while Thersites commented, "Wil he swagger himself out on's eyes?"

And Borachio, confessing his villainy to the Prince, says, "I
haue deceiued euen your verie eies." It is the "image of *Hero*"
that then reappears to Claudio "in the rare semblance that I
lou'd it first."

Hero has indeed nothing but her image, her appearance with
which to defend herself. Like Desdemona, Hermione or Imogen
she is too shocked at first even for a verbal denial. She is left
with nothing but a bare protest when the Friar puts his gentle
question to her (but be it noted, the question contains a trap).
The Friar can read faces: he takes as sure testimony what to
Claudio had been hideous "seeming," [7] and what he proposes is
that Claudio should be left with the memory of Hero's image
which will in time work its conviction upon him also.

> The Idea of her life shall sweetly creep
> Into his study of imagination.
> And every lovely Organ of her life,
> Shall come apparel'd in more precious habite,

More mouing delicate and full of life
Into the eye and prospect of his soule
Than when she liv'd indeed.

                              (IV, i, 226-32.)

The relation of the men and women of the play depends upon
such an attraction and such an imperfect knowledge: but they
each know their own sex extremely well. Hero knows the surest
way to catch Beatrice and sometimes explains her meaning to
others.[8] Beatrice champions her cousin sooner than the girl's
own father dares to do. Claudio, the Prince and Benedick are a
sufficiently good set of messmates (princely aloofness a little
slackened in the field) for Benedick's challenge to Claudio to
extend as far as an indirect giving of the lie to Don Pedro as
well:

> My lord, for your manie courtesies I thank you, I must
> discontinue your companie . . . you haue among you
> kill'd a sweet and innocent Ladie.

                              (v, i, 195ff)

Claudio's flippancy about the pitiful insults of Leonato and
Antonio (though he behaved admirably in their presence) and
his readiness to take a second bride in reparation for the first
create difficulties for the modern reader where they are not
likely to have existed for an Elizabethan. Leonato's challenge in
the presence of the Prince was a social outrage which would
have landed the greatest nobleman in prison (Benedick draws
Claudio aside to make his defiance). As for the marriage, it may
rank with other fictions; by this time the audience and everyone
but Claudio can see the happy conclusion, and to treat Claudio
as an independent character at this point, and upbraid him for
his failure to lodge an objection—like Bassanio when he was asked
for the ring—is to abandon all sense of theatrical propriety and
comic decorum for the sake of a psychological consistency which
would defeat its own ends. Claudio cannot now be made into a
tragic character or allowed more than a pretty lyric by way of
remorse. In the church scene he had spoken out, and spoken the
words which his earlier character warranted. There is no further
role for him, or for Hero, save to make a pair in the final dance.

They each sink back into the kind of formality which the plot allowed, and the conclusion belongs to Benedick and Beatrice. The full story was not to be told till Shakespeare wrote *Cymbeline,* and depicted remorse in Posthumus, with constancy in Imogen.

In both *Much Ado* and *The Merchant of Venice* the clowns are ingeniously but loosely attached to the main plot by a few lines of intrigue—Gobbo acts as go-between for Jessica, Dogberry serves to keep Borachio in safe custody till Act V. Their real function is to act as parody or, in musical analogy, as undersong; Lancelot's debate with the fiend about his leaving his master, "who (God blesse the marke) is a kind of deuill," is a very pretty speech for the clown and reflects in a charmingly direct manner upon the brisk decision of Jessica, to leave her Hell. Dogberry and Verges are clearly reincarnations of Gobbo and his father, and their role of comic policeman was one of the oldest and most assured cards in popular comedy. But their parts are confined to scenes immediately preceding and following the church scene, where the relief of their broad comedy is most tellingly juxtaposed with the straightforward drama of the main plot. As interludes between the wit combats of Benedick and Beatrice they would have been unnecessary. The clowns of the later comedies were more closely woven into the main structure of the play, and indeed Feste is the central figure of *Twelfth Night;* but here the low comedy serves rather by contrast to strengthen the range and complexity of "interchangeable variety."

This variety, which, if it did not extend to hornpipes and funerals, extended to wedding festivity and mock-funerals, is marked by a strict control. Nothing could be further than the masterly shaping of Shakespeare's art from the wild incongruities of the Elizabethan hacks or the baroque eclecticism of the Jacobeans. The nearest analogue to the bold contrasts of these middle comedies is probably to be found in Chaucer, where the Canterbury Pilgrims tell their tales and conduct their debates in such a way as to bring out the individuality of each, whilst subordinating it to the whole pattern. Shakespeare, like Chaucer, drew largely from life, though both his heroic and his low characters were also recognized literary types. Shakespeare, like Chaucer, defined his characters largely in terms of their idiom, their own private speech. Both are given to raising moral issues, but not to pronouncing on them, except by implication. Both present a picture of the world which is above all wise and humane.

NOTES

1. It is clear that Don John has been fighting his brother and that this has been the subject of the recent wars: Don John hates Claudio because he won glory in the wars by Don John's overthrow (I, iii, 67-71): Don John is virtually a released prisoner of war. This might have been made plain in the staging. His bastardy, which explains his malignity, is not revealed till Act V, but it should be clear from the way he is treated that he is not really the heir of Arragon.

2. Borachio says that they shall hear him call Margaret Hero and hear Margaret term him Claudio (II, ii, 44-5). It would not help the plot to hear Margaret call him Claudio: but it suggests that she will wear her mistress's clothes and use her name in the kind of court game that is familiar from courtesy books and other plays (e.g. *Cynthia's Revels*), i.e. she will assume a character as a kind of masquerade (that of the bride of to-morrow) in order to be courted with a more highflown set of compliments by her sweetheart. If this is the explanation, Leonato seems to be right in dropping his first view that Margaret was an accomplice (v, i, 309-12) and accepting that she was in fault against her will (v, iv, 4-6). But the whole point is left extremely vague.

3. In his book on Shakespeare in the Home University Library series.

4. Arbaces is the hero of *A King and No King*, Ordella the heroine of *Thierry and Theodoret*.

5. The unwilling lover had been studied already in Berowne.

6. At first "attired in wonder," Benedick is apparently convinced by the Friar, as the first words of his colloquy with Beatrice show, that Hero is innocent: it follows, as Beatrice convinces him, that Claudio must have wronged her.

7. Claudio like Posthumus is to be converted simply by the beauty of Hero as it survives in his memory, and his conversion will depend on the strength of his first impressions conquering

his "knowledge." Compare Othello as he looks at the sleeping Desdemona:

> Be thus when thou art dead, and I will kill thee
> And loue thee after.

8. E.g. i, i, 35-6. It is Hero who convicts Beatrice in the end by producing the poem stolen from her pocket, containing her affection unto Benedick.

Harold Jenkins

AS YOU LIKE IT [1]

A MASTERPIECE is not to be explained, and to attempt to explain it is apt to seem ridiculous. I must say at once that I propose nothing so ambitious. I merely hope, by looking at one play, even in what must necessarily be a very fragmentary way and with my own imperfect sight, to illustrate something of what Shakespeare's method in comedy may be. And I have chosen *As You Like It* because it seems to me to exhibit, most clearly of all the comedies, Shakespeare's characteristic excellences in this kind. This is not to say that *As You Like It* is exactly a representative specimen. Indeed I am going to suggest that it is not. In this play, what I take to be Shakespeare's distinctive virtues as a writer of comedy have their fullest scope; but in order that they may have it, certain of the usual ingredients of Shakespeare's comedy, or indeed of any comedy, have to be—not of course eliminated, but very much circumscribed. In *As You Like It*, I suggest, Shakespeare took his comedy in one direction nearly as far as it could go. And then, as occasionally happens in Shakespeare's career, when he has developed his art far in one direction, in the comedy which succeeds he seems to readjust his course.

If our chronology is right, after *As You Like It* comes, among the comedies, *Twelfth Night*. And while we may accept that *Twelfth Night* is, as Sir Edmund Chambers says, very much akin to *As You Like It* "in style and temper," in some important respects it returns to the method and structure of the previous comedy of *Much Ado About Nothing*. Sandwiched between these

From *Shakespeare Survey*, 8, 1955, pp. 40-51. Reprinted by permission of the editors and the Cambridge University Press.

two, *As You Like It* is conspicuously lacking in comedy's more robust and boisterous elements—the pomps of Dogberry and the romps of Sir Toby. More significantly, it has nothing which corresponds to the splendid theatricalism of the church scene in *Much Ado,* nothing which answers to those crucial bits of trickery by which Benedick and Beatrice in turn are hoodwinked into love. Even if, as may be objected, they are not hoodwinked but merely tricked into removing their hoods, still those stratagems in Leonato's orchard are necessary if the happy ending proper to the comedy is to be brought about. These ambushes, if I may call them so—they are really inverted ambushes—are paralleled, or should one say parodied, in *Twelfth Night* in the scene where Malvolio is persuaded that he too is beloved. And this ambush too is necessary if, as the comedy demands, Malvolio is to have his sanity called in question and his authority undermined. The slandering of Hero in *Much Ado* also is to have its counterpart in *Twelfth Night.* For the slandering of Hero, with its culmination in the church scene, forces one pair of lovers violently apart while bringing another pair together. And in *Twelfth Night* the confusion of identities holds one pair of lovers—Orsino and Viola —temporarily apart, yet forces another pair—Olivia and Sebastian—with some violence together. A satisfactory outcome in *Much Ado* and *Twelfth Night* depends on such embroilments; and the same is even more true in an earlier comedy like *A Midsummer Night's Dream.* In *As You Like It* I can hardly say that such embroilments do not occur, but they are not structural to anything like the same degree. Without the heroine's masculine disguise Phebe would not have married Silvius any more than in *Twelfth Night* Olivia would have married Sebastian; but the confusions of identity in *As You Like It* have no influence whatever upon the ultimate destiny of Rosalind and Orlando, or of the kingdom of Duke Senior, or of the estate of Sir Rowland de Boys. Yet these are the destinies with which the action of the play is concerned. It is in the defectiveness of its action that *As You Like It* differs from the rest of the major comedies—in its dearth not only of big theatrical scenes but of events linked together by the logical intricacies of cause and effect. Of comedy, as of tragedy, action is the first essential; but *As You Like It* suggests that action is not, if I may adapt a phrase of Marston's, "the life of these things." It may be merely the foundation on which they are built. And *As You Like It* further shows that on a very flimsy foundation, if only you are skilful enough, a very elaborate structure may be poised. But the method has its dangers, and though Shakespeare's skill conceals these dangers from us, *Twelfth Night,* as I said, returns to a more orthodox scheme.

The story which provides the action for *As You Like It* belongs to the world of fairy-tale or folk-lore. This is a world which supplied the plots of a number of Shakespeare's plays, including the greatest, notably *King Lear*. And fairy-tales have many advantages for the dramatist, among which is their total disregard of practical probabilities. In fairy-tales, for example, evil is always absolute, clearly recognized, and finally overthrown; all of which may have something to do with the Aristotelian theory that while history records what has happened, poetry shows what should happen. Relaxing the more prosaic demands of verisimilitude, the fairy-tale invites the imagination. It can certainly provide a convenient road into the Forest of Arden. And this is not less true for Shakespeare because the road had already been built for him by Lodge.

A man has died and left three sons. Three is the inevitable number, and though Shakespeare, like Lodge, forgets to do much with the middle one, he is not therefore unimportant. The eldest brother is wicked, the youngest virtuous—and does fabulous feats of strength, notably destroying a giant in the shape of Charles the wrestler, who has torn other hopeful youths to pieces. Orlando therefore wins the princess, herself the victim of a wicked uncle, who has usurped her father's throne. This is the *story* of *As You Like It*. And Shakespeare, making the journey of the imagination far more quickly than Lodge, gets most of it over in the first act. That is what is remarkable. By the time we reach the second act Rosalind has already come safe to the Forest of Arden, by the aid of her man's disguise. From this disguise, as everybody knows, springs the principal comic situation of the play. But such is the inconsequential nature of the action that this comic situation develops only when the practical need for the disguise is past. The course of true love has not run smooth. But most of its obstacles have really disappeared before the main comedy begins. It only remains for the wicked to be converted, as they duly are at the end, all in comedy's good but arbitrary time, when the wicked eldest brother makes a suitable husband for the second princess. Or a most *un*suitable husband, as all the critics have complained. But this, I think, is to misunderstand. Instead of lamenting that Celia should be thrown away on Oliver, he having been much too wicked to deserve her, we should rather see that Oliver's getting this reward is a seal set on his conversion, and a sign of how good he has now become.

The first act of *As You Like It* has to supply the necessary minimum of event. But, Quiller-Couch notwithstanding, this first act is something more than mechanical.[2] It is for one thing a feat of compression, rapid, lucid and, incidentally, theatrical. In fifty lines we know all about the three brothers and the youngest is at the eldest's throat. In three hundred more we know all about the banished Duke and where and how he lives, and the giant has been destroyed before our eyes. But there is more to the first act than this. Before we enter Arden, to "fleet the time carelessly, as they did in the golden world," we must be able to contrast its simple life with the brittle refinement of the court. This surely is the point of some of what "Q" called the "rather pointless choplogic"; and also of the courtier figure of Le Beau, a little sketch for Osric, with his foppery of diction and his expert knowledge of sport. Le Beau's notion of sport provokes Touchstone's pointed comment on the courtier's values: "Thus men may grow wiser every day: it is the first time that ever I heard breaking of ribs was sport for ladies." This *is* the callousness one learns at a court ruled by a tyrannous Duke, whose malevolent rage against Rosalind and Orlando not only drives them both to Arden but completes the picture of the world they leave behind.

This first act, then, shows some instinct for dramatic preparation, though we may grant that Shakespeare's haste to get ahead makes him curiously perfunctory. He is in two minds about when Duke Senior was banished; and about which Duke is to be called Frederick; and whether Rosalind or Celia is the taller. He has not quite decided about the character of Touchstone. I do not think these are signs of revision. They simply show Shakespeare plunging into his play with some of its details still but half-shaped in his mind. The strangest of these details is the mysterious middle brother, called Fernandyne by Lodge but merely "Second Brother" in *As You Like It*, when at length he makes his appearance at the end. Yet in the fifth line of the play he was already christened Jaques. And Shakespeare of course afterwards gave this name to someone else. It seems clear enough that these two men with the same name were originally meant to be one. As things turned out Jaques could claim to have acquired his famous melancholy from travel and experience; but I suspect that it really began in the schoolbooks which were studied with such profit by Jaques de Boys. Though he grew into something very different, Jaques surely had his beginnings in the family of De Boys and in such an academy as that in Navarre where four young men turned their backs on love and life in the belief that they could supply the want of experience by study and contemplation.

Interesting as it might be to develop this idea, the im-portant point of comparison between *As You Like It* and *Love's Labour's Lost* is of another kind. And to this I should like briefly to refer before I come to discuss the main part of *As You Like It*. *Love's Labour's Lost* is the one play before *As You Like It* in which Shakespeare sought to write a comedy with the minimum of action. Four young men make a vow to have nothing to do with a woman; each breaks his oath and ends vowing to serve a woman. That is the story; far slighter than in *As You Like It*. Yet, in contrast with *As You Like It*, the careful and conspicuous organization of *Love's Labour's Lost* distributes its thin action evenly through the play. And the characters always act in concert. In the first act the men, all together, make their vow; in the second the ladies, all together, arrive and the temptation begins. The climax duly comes, where you would expect it, in a big scene in Act IV, when each in turn breaks his vow and all together are found out. *Love's Labour's Lost* is the most formally constructed of all the com-edies. When the ladies and gentlemen temporarily exchange partners, this is done symmetrically and to order. Indeed the movement of the whole play is like a well-ordered dance in which each of the participants repeats the steps of the others. But this is exactly what does *not* happen in *As You Like It*, where the characters do *not* keep in step. When they *seem* to be doing the same thing they are really doing something dif-

ferent, and if they ever echo one another they mean quite
different things by what they say—as could easily be illustrated
from the little quartet of lovers in the fifth act ("And so am I
for Phebe.—And I for Ganymede.—And I for Rosalind.—And I
for no woman"), where the similarity of the tune they sing
conceals their different situations. The pattern of *As You Like It*
comes not from a mere repetition of steps, but from constant
little shifts and changes. The formal parallelisms of *Love's
Labour's Lost* are replaced by a more complex design, one
loose enough to hold all sorts of asymmetries within it.

But of course the effect of variations upon a theme instead
of simple repetitions is not new in *As You Like It*. It is the tendency of Shakespeare's comedy from the start. In *Love's Labour's
Lost* itself the courtly gestures of the four young men are bur-
lesqued by those of a fantastic knight, and while the four young
men are vowing not to see a woman, Costard the clown is
"taken with a wench." Moreover, one of the four, though he
goes through the movements with the others, has some trouble
to keep in step, and is always threatening to break out of the
ring. Even when he makes his vow with the others, he knows
that necessity will make him break it. As he joins in their purposes he knows them to be foolish and he mocks at ideals
which he at the same time pursues. Human activity offers itself to the dramatist in a large variety of forms and the same
individual can play contradictory parts. The drunken tinker in
The Taming of the Shrew does not know whether he may not
really be a noble lord. Although Shakespeare did not invent
this situation, it was just the thing to appeal to him. For he
knew that a man is very easily "translated." In the middle of
his fairy play he put a man with an ass's head. In perhaps
the most remarkable encounter in Shakespeare the daintiest
fairy queen caresses a man turned brute, who, with a fairy
kingdom around him, can think only of scratching his itch.
When the animal appears in a man it may terrify his fellows;
it may also attract to it his finest dreams and fancies, corrupting them, or being uplifted by them to a vision of new wonder.
Shakespeare of course does nothing as crude as *say* this. He
knows as well as the Duke in Arden that sermons may be found
in stones, but much better than the Duke that it is tedious to

preach them, a thing, incidentally, he does not permit the Duke
to do. What Shakespeare characteristically does in his comedy
is to set together the contrasting elements in human nature and
leave them by their juxtaposition or interaction to comment
on one another.

In *As You Like It* the art of comic juxtaposition is at its
subtlest. It is to give it fullest scope that the action can be
pushed up into a corner, and the usual entanglements of plotting,
though not dispensed with altogether, can be loosened. Freedom, of course, is in the hospitable air of Arden, where convenient caves stand ready to receive outlaws, alfresco meals
are abundantly provided, with a concert of birds and running
brooks, and there is no worse hardship than a salubrious winter
wind. This is "the golden world" to which, with the beginning
of his second act, Shakespeare at once transports us, such a
world as has been the dream of poets since at least the time of
Virgil when, wearied with the toilings and wranglings of society, they yearn for the simplicity and innocence of what they
choose to think man's natural state.[3] It is of course a very literary
tradition that Shakespeare is here using, but the long vogue of
the pastoral suggests that it is connected with a universal impulse of the human mind, to which Shakespeare in *As You
Like It* gives permanent expression. But this aspect of the play
is merely the one which confronts us most conspicuously. There
are many others. *As You Like It* has been too often praised for
its idyllic quality alone, as though it were some mere May-
morning frolic prolonged into a lotos-eating afternoon. A contrast with the ideal state was necessitated by the literary tradition itself, since the poet seeking an escape into the simple
life was expected to hint at the ills of the society he was escap-
ing from. That meant especially the courts of princes, where
life—it was axiomatic—was at its most artificial. And the vivid
sketching in of the courtly half of the antithesis is, as I have
shown, an important function of *As You Like It's* maligned first
act. With the first speech of the banished Duke at the opening
of the second act, the complete contrast is before us; for, while
introducing us to Arden, this speech brings into sharp focus
that first act which has just culminated in the usurper's murderous malice. "Are not these woods more free from peril than the

envious court?" Though the contrast is traditional, it comes
upon us here, like so many things in Shakespeare, with the vitality of fresh experience. The Forest of Arden comes to life in
numerous little touches of the country-side, and the heartless
self-seeking of the outer world is concentrated into phrases
which have the force of permanent truth. The line that "Q"
admired—"And unregarded age in corners thrown"—might have
come from one of the sonnets, and when Orlando observes how
"none will sweat but for promotion" we recognize the fashion
of our times as well as his. As the play proceeds, it is easy
enough for Shakespeare to keep us ever aware of the forest,
what with Amiens to sing for us, the procession home after
the killing of the deer, an empty cottage standing ready for
Rosalind and Celia, surrounded by olive-trees beyond a willow
stream, and a good supply of oaks for Orlando or Oliver to
lie under. It cannot have been quite so easy to keep us in touch
with the court life we have now abandoned; but nothing is
neater in the construction of the play than those well-placed
little scenes which, by despatching first Orlando and then Oliver
to the forest, do what is still required by the story and give
the illusion that an action is still going briskly forward, while
at the same time they renew our acquaintance with the wicked
world. After the first scene in the ideal world of Arden and a
sentimental discourse on the deer, there is Frederick again in
one of his rages, sending for Oliver, who, an act later, when
we are well acclimatized to the forest, duly turns up at court.
Then occurs a scene of eighteen lines, in which Shakespeare
gives as vivid a sketch of the unjust tyrant as one could hope
to find. The tyrant prides himself upon his mercy, punishes one
man for his brother's sins, and finds in his victim's excuses further cause of offence. Oliver's plaint that he had never loved
his brother brings the instant retort, "More villain thou. Well,
push him out of doors." As this eruption dies down, there appears in the Forest of Arden the cause of all the trouble
quietly hanging his verses on a tree.

The contrast between court and country is thus presented
and our preference is very plain. Yet as a counterpoise to all
this, there is one man in the country-side who actually prefers
the court. Finding himself in Arden, Touchstone decides: "When

I was at home, I was in a better place." It is no doubt important that he is a fool, whose values may well be topsy-turvy. But in one word he reminds us that there are such things as domestic comforts. And presently we find that the old man whom society throws into the corner is likely in the "uncouth forest" to die of hunger and exposure to the "bleak air." There is clearly something to be said on the other side; the fool may anatomize the wise man's folly. And there is also Jaques to point out that the natural life in Arden, where men usurp the forest from the deer and kill them in their "native dwelling-place," while deer, like men, are in distress abandoned by their friends, is as cruel and unnatural as the other. When Amiens sings under the greenwood tree and turns "his merry note unto the sweet bird's throat," inviting us to shun ambition and be pleased with what we get, Jaques adds a further stanza to the song which suggests that to leave your "wealth and ease" is the act of an ass or a fool. Most of us, I suppose, have moods in which we would certainly agree with him, and it is a mark of Shakespeare's mature comedy that he permits this criticism of his ideal world in the very centre of it. The triumphal procession after the killing of the deer, a symbolic ritual of the forester's prowess, is accompanied by a mocking song, while the slayer of the deer is given its horns to wear as a somewhat ambiguous trophy.

It is Jaques, mostly, with the touch of the medieval buffoon in him, who contributes this grotesque element to the songs and rituals of Arden. Like Touchstone he is not impressed by Arden, but unlike Touchstone he does not prefer the court. Indeed, as we have seen, he is able to show that they are very much alike, infected by the same diseases. No doubt his is a jaundiced view of life, and it is strange that some earlier critics should have thought it might be Shakespeare's. Shakespeare's contemporaries would hardly have had difficulty in recognizing in Jaques a variant of the Elizabethan melancholy man—the epithet is applied to him often enough—though I remain a little sceptical when I am told by O. J. Campbell that from the first moment they heard Jaques described, the Elizabethans would have perceived "the unnatural melancholy produced by the adustion of phlegm." [4] Whatever its physiological kind, the im-

portant thing about his melancholy is that it is not the fatigue
of spirits of the man who has found the world too much for
him, but an active principle manifesting itself in tireless and
exuberant antics. Far from being a morose man, whether he
is weeping with the stag or jeering at the huntsman, he throws
himself into these things with something akin to passion. His
misanthropy is a form of self-indulgence, as is plain enough in
his very first words:

> *Jaques.* More, more, I prithee, more.
> *Amiens.* It will make you melancholy, Monsier Jaques.
> *Jaques.* I thank it. More, I prithee, more. I can
>   suck melancholy out of a song.

His own comparison with a weasel sucking eggs suggests what
a ferocious and life-destroying thing this passion is. Shakespeare's
final dismissal of Jaques is profound. Far from making Celia
a better husband than Oliver, as George Sand apparently
thought, he is the one person in the play who could not be allowed to marry anyone, since he can have nothing to do with
either love or generation. His attempt to forward the nuptials
of Touchstone and Audrey serves only to postpone them. He
is of course the one consistent character in the play in that he
declines to go back with the others to the court that they have
scorned. Yet how *can* he go back when the court has been converted? Jaques's occupation's gone. And he will not easily
thrive away from the social life on which he feeds. It is notable
that the place he really covets, or affects to, is that of the motley fool, licensed to mock at society, indulged by society but
not of it. Yet, seeking for a fool, he has only to look in the
brook to find one; and it is the romantic hero who will tell him so.

Shakespeare, then, builds up his ideal world and lets his
idealists scorn the real one. But into their midst he introduces
people who mock their ideals and others who mock *them*. One
must not say that Shakespeare never judges, but one judgement
is always being modified by another. Opposite views may contradict one another, but of course they do not cancel out. Instead they add up to an all-embracing view far larger and more
satisfying than any one of them in itself.

Now when Orlando tells Jaques that he may see a fool by

looking in the brook, this is not the first time that Jaques and
Orlando meet; and the relations between the two of them are
worth a moment's glance. Their first encounter occurs in public
when the Duke and his retinue are met for one of their forest
repasts. Jaques has just been eloquent about the vices of man-
kind and is justifying the satirist who scourges them, when he
is confronted with the romantic hero in his most heroic attitude, rushing into the middle of the scene with drawn sword,[5]
crying, "Forbear, and eat no more." But Jaques is not the man
to be discomposed, even when a sudden interruption throws
him off his hobby-horse. When he has inquired, "Of what kind
should this cock come off?", the heroic attitude begins to look
extravagant. The hero stands his ground: "Forbear, I say: He
dies that touches any of this fruit"; at which Jaques nonchalantly
helps himself to a grape, saying, "An you will not be answered
with reason (raisin), I must die." Heroism now appears
thoroughly deflated, or would do if Jaques were attended to by
the company at large. The hero is in fact saved by the Duke's
"civility"; and their talk of "gentleness" and "nurture" even
throws back into perspective Jaques's recent attack upon society. The situation as a whole retains its equilibrium. And yet
as a result of this little incident we are bound to feel that the
romantic hero is very vulnerable to the ridicule of the satirist,
until their duel of wit in the following act readjusts our view
by allowing Orlando his retort.

There is a formal point to notice here, easy to miss but full
of meaning. The wit-combat between Jaques and the hero is
matched an act or so later—there is no strict regularity about
these things—by a similar wit-combat between Jaques and the
heroine. On each occasion Jaques is worsted and departs, leaving Rosalind and Orlando to come together. In fact the dis-
comfiture of Monsieur Melancholy by one or other of the lovers
is the prelude to each of the two big love-scenes of the play.
And this arrangement makes a point more prettily than any
action-plot involving Jaques could do. The mocking words of
Jaques's farewell are in each case illuminating: "Farewell, good
Signior Love"; and "Nay, then, God be wi' you, an you talk in
blank verse." The gibe at blank verse is not an incidental or
decorative jest. It makes it clear that, however we judge of

them, the melancholy spirit of Jaques and the romantic emotion
of Rosalind and Orlando cannot mingle. Shakespeare dismisses
the melancholy man before he gives the lovers their scope. And
in this I follow his example.

So far I have dealt only with the immigrants to Arden. There
is of course a native population. The natural world of the poet's
dreams has always been inhabited by shepherds, who from the
time of Theocritus have piped their songs of love. And Rosalind and Celia have been in the forest for only twenty lines
when two shepherds appear pat before them. In an earlier
comedy perhaps these might have been a similar pair singing
comparable love-ditties. But in *As You Like It*—Shakespeare
making the most of what is offered him by Lodge—they are a
contrasting pair. One is young and one is old, one is in love
and one is not. The lover is the standard type. But the notion
of love has undergone a change since classical times and the
shepherds of Renaissance pastorals have all been bred in the
schools of courtly love. So young Silvius is the faithful abject
lover who finds disdain in his fair shepherdess's eye and sighs
"upon a midnight pillow"—Shakespeare always fixes on a detail
in which a whole situation is epitomized. There are of course
many other lovers in the play, but the story of Silvius and Phebe
is of the pure pastoral world, the familiar literary norm against
which all the others may be measured. First against Silvius and
Phebe are set Rosalind and Orlando, and the immediate result
of this is that Rosalind and Orlando, though they clearly belong to the pastoral world, seem much closer to the ordinary
one. Indeed, since Silvius and Phebe relieve them of the necessity of displaying the lovers' more extravagant postures, Rosalind
and Orlando are freer to act like human beings. Rosalind need
only play at taunting her adorer while allowing her real woman's
heart to be in love with him in earnest. In an earlier comedy
like *The Two Gentlemen of Verona* the heroes themselves had
to undergo those "bitter fasts, with penitential groans, With
nightly tears and daily heart-sore sighs," and these are what, as
H. B. Charlton says, may make Valentine look a fool. But with
Silvius to take this burden from him, Orlando can really be
a hero, performing the traditional hero's fabulous feats, and
upon occasion may even be a common man like ourselves. He

has, for example, the very human trait of unpunctuality; he is twice late for an appointment. And although on one occasion he has the perfect excuse of a bloody accident, on the other he has nothing to say, beyond "My fair Rosalind, I come within an hour of my promise." Such engaging casualness is of course outside Silvius's range. And although Orlando has his due share of lovers' sighs and is indeed the "unfortunate he" who hangs the verses on the trees, in so human a creature these love-gestures appear not as his *raison d'être* but as an aberration. A delightful aberration, no doubt—"I would not be cured, youth," he says—but still an aberration that can be the legitimate subject of our mockery. Lying contemplating his love under an oak, ne seems to Celia "like a dropped acorn," and both the ladies smile at his youthful lack of beard. But Orlando is robust enough to stand their mockery and ours, and Shakespeare's superb dramatic tact arranges that Orlando shall draw our laughter towards him so that he may protect the fragile Silvius from the ridicule which would destroy *him*. Rosalind alone is privileged to make fun of Silvius; and that because searching his wounds, she finds her own. The encounters which do not occur have their significance as well as those which do: Touchstone is only once, and Jaques never, allowed a sight of Silvius before the final scene of the play. Silvius has not to be destroyed or the play will lack something near its centre.

If in a pastoral play the ideal shepherd is satirized it must be indirectly. But that he is, through his complete unreality, a likely target for satire has been commonly recognized by the poets, who have therefore had a habit of providing him with a burlesque counterpart to redress the balance and show that they did know what rustics were like in real life. As Gay was to put it in his proem to *The Shepherd's Week*, the shepherd "sleepeth not under myrtle shades, but under a hedge"; and so when Gay's shepherd makes love it is in a sly kiss behind a haycock to the accompaniment of the lady's yells of laughter. This may have been the method of Shakespeare's William, for, far from inditing verses to his mistress, William is singularly tongue-tied; though he is "five and twenty" and thinks he has "a pretty wit," the biggest of his eleven speeches is only seven

words long. And his partner is just as much a contrast to the
shepherdess of pastoral legend. She thanks the gods she is not
beautiful, does not even know the meaning of "poetical," and
her sheep, alas, are goats.

Shakespeare, then, presents the conventional pastoral, and
duly burlesques it. But with a surer knowledge of life than
many poets have had, he seems to suspect that the burlesque
as well as the convention may also miss the truth. Do shepherds
really sleep under hedges? In order to be unsophisticated, must
they be stupid too? So among his varied array of shepherds,
Silvius and Ganymede and William, Shakespeare introduces
yet another shepherd, the only one who knows anything of
sheep, whose hands even get greasy with handling them. It
does not matter that Shakespeare got the hint for Corin from
Corydon in Lodge. For Lodge found Corydon in literature and
for Corin Shakespeare went to life. Lodge's Corydon, though
he may make the king smile with his clownish salutation, has
evidently been bred at court himself. Would he ever else ac-
cost a lady in distress in strains like these

> If I should not, fair damosel, occasion offence, or renew
> your griets by rubbing the scar, I would fain crave so
> much favour as to know the cause of your misfortunes.

Shakespeare s Corin speaks at once of grazing and shearing
and an unkind master; and when he talks about the shepherd's
life he shows that he knows the value of money and that fat
sheep need good pasture. His greatest pride is to see his ewes
graze and his lambs suck. This is the note of his philosophy,
and it it has its limitations, it is far from despicable and is
splendidly anchored to fact. His attitude to love is that of the
fully sane man undisturbed by illusions. Being a man, he has
been in love and can still guess what it is like; but it is so
long ago he has forgotten all the details. How little he belongs
to Arcadia may be discovered from Sidney, whose shepherd-
boy went on piping "as though he should never be old." In
As You Like It perpetual youth is the happiness of Silvius, and
his fate. *That* much of the difference between Silvius and Corin
is apparent from the short dialogue of twenty lines which first
introduces them together to us.

In Corin Shakespeare provides us with a touchstone with which to test the pastoral. Corin's dialogue with the Touchstone of the court, dropped into the middle of the play, adds to the conventional antithesis between courtier and countryman a glimpse of the real thing. Our picture of the court as a place of tyranny, ambition and corruption is no doubt true enough. But its colours are modified somewhat when Touchstone gives us the court's plain routine. For him, as he lets us know on another occasion, the court is the place where he has trod a measure, flattered a lady, been smooth with his enemy and undone three tailors. Though Touchstone seeks to entangle Corin in the fantastications of his wit, his arguments to show that the court is better than the sheepfarm have a way of recoiling on himself. What emerges from the encounter of these two realists is that ewe and ram, like man and woman, are put together and that though the courtier perfumes his body it sweats like any other creature's. In city or country, *all* ways of life are at bottom the same, and we recognize a conclusion that Jaques, by a different route, has helped us to reach before.

The melancholy moralizings of Jaques and the Robin Hood raptures of the Duke, though in contrast, are equally the product of man's spirit. There has to be someone in Arden to remind us of the indispensable flesh. It was a shrewd irony of Shakespeare's to give this office to the jester. Whether he is wiser or more foolish than other men it is never possible to decide, but Touchstone is, as well as the most artificial wit, the most natural man of them all; and the most conscious of his corporal needs. After the journey to the forest Rosalind complains of a weariness of spirits, to which Touchstone retorts "I care not for my spirits, if my legs were not weary." And when he displays his wit at the expense of Orlando's bad verses, saying "I'll rhyme you so eight years together," he remembers to add "dinners and suppers and sleeping-hours excepted." A "material fool," as Jaques notes. This preoccupation with the physical makes Touchstone the obvious choice for the sensual lover who will burlesque the romantic dream. So Touchstone not only deprives the yokel William of his mistress, but steals his part in the play, making it in the process of infinitely greater significance. However, Shakespeare from the beginning cast

Touchstone for this burlesque role, though he may not have
seen at first what form the burlesque would take. When Silvius
first exhibits his love to us, and reminds Rosalind of hers, Touchstone completes the trio on his discordant note:

> I remember, when I was in love I broke my sword upon
> a stone and bid him take that for coming a-night to Jane
> Smile; and I remember the kissing of . . . the cow's dugs
> that her pretty chopt hands had milked.

This sort of extravagance—in the burlesque-chivalrous vein—is
not, I think, developed; but an indecent jest about a peascod
does point forward to the animal lust which propels him towards
Audrey, and his amour with her forms the perfect contrast to
the three idealized courtships of the play. If we need a formal
juxtaposition of the two kinds of love to point the matter further, I note that it is just when Rosalind has met Orlando in the
forest and Orlando has promised to woo her "by the faith of
[his] love" and "with all [his] heart" that we see Touchstone
courting the goat-girl regretting that fair women should be
honest and talking of sexual desire.

The fool is not only a material touchstone; he is also the
time-keeper of the play. At least, in the forest, where "there's no
clock," he carries a time-piece with him; and it provokes the
reflection: "It is ten o'clock . . . 'Tis but an hour ago since it
was nine, And after one hour more 'twill be eleven." The people
of Arcadia will do well to take note of this, but if all you can
do with your hours is to count them, this undeniable truth may
seem a trifle futile. Touchstone, to do him justice, goes on:
"And so, from hour to hour, we ripe and ripe, And then, from
hour to hour, we rot and rot." He dares to speak in Arcadia,
where one can never grow old, of Time's inevitable processes of
maturity and decay. By this the ideal life of the banished Duke
is mocked, and since Touchstone's words are repeated by
Jaques with delighted and uproarious laughter, the mockery is
double. Yet, in accordance with the play's principle of counter-
ing one view with another, there are two things that may be
noted: first, that in a later scene Touchstone, who sums up life
as riping and rotting, is compared by Rosalind to a medlar,
which is rotten before it is ripe; and second, that it is at this

very point, when the ideal life is doubly mocked, that the Duke administers to the mocker Jaques a direct and fierce rebuke, charging the mocker of the world's vices with having lived a vicious life himself.

The satirist, of course, is far from silenced; it is now that he ridicules the romantic hero, and presently he delivers his famous speech on the seven ages of man, brilliantly summing up the course of human life, but omitting to notice anything in it that is noble or even pleasant. However, as has often been observed, though the seven ages speech ends with a description of man's final decrepitude— "sans teeth, sans eyes, sans taste, sans everything"—it has not yet left the speaker's tongue when an aged man appears who is at once addressed as "venerable." There is always this readjustment of the point of view. Senility and venerableness—are they different things or different ways of looking at the same? Certainly the entry of the venerable Adam does not disproves what Jaques says; Shakespeare seeks no cheap antithesis. "Sans teeth"—Adam himself has admitted to being toothless, Orlando has called him "a rotten tree," and his helplessness is only too visible when he is *carried* on to the stage. Yet he *is* carried, tenderly, by the master whom he has followed "to the last gasp, with truth and loyalty." Here is the glimpse of human virtue that the seven ages speech omitted. And then it is upon this moving spectacle of mutual affection and devotion that Amiens sings his song, "Blow, blow, thou winter wind, Thou art not so unkind As man's ingratitude." Placed here, this lovely lyric, blend of joy and pathos, has a special poignancy.

The arrangement of the play depends upon many such piquant but seemingly casual juxtapositions. *As You Like It* contemplates life within and without Arden, with numerous shifts of angle, alternating valuations, and variations of mood. As for action, incident—life in the Forest of Arden does not easily lend itself to those. I have suggested that Shakespeare does something to supply this want by a glance or two back at what is happening at court. And departures from the court are matched by arrivals in the forest. For events, of course, even in Arden do sometimes occur. Orlando arrives dramatically, even melodramatically. Presently Rosalind learns that he is about. A little later on they meet. Later still Oliver arrives and is rescued

from a lioness. Shakespeare still keeps up a sense of things going on. But the manner of the play, when once it settles down in
the forest, is to let two people drift together, talk a little, and
part, to be followed by two more. Sometimes a pair will be
watched by others, who will sometimes comment on what they
see. Sometimes of course there is a larger group, once or twice
even a crowded stage; but most often two at a time. When they
part they may arrange to meet again, or they may not. Through
the three middle acts of the play, though there are two instances of love at first sight (one of them only reported), it is
rare that anything happens in any particular encounter between
these people of the sort that changes the course of their lives,
anything, that is to say, that goes to make what is usually called
a plot. Yet the meetings may properly be called "encounters,"
because of the impact the contrasting characters make on one
another and the sparkle of wit they kindle in one another. What
is important in each meeting is our impression of those who
meet and of their different attitudes to one another or to one
another's views of life, an impression which is deepened or
modified each time they reappear with the same or different
partners. As I describe it, this may all sound rather static, but
such is the ease and rapidity with which pairs and groups
break up, re-form, and succeed one another on the stage that
there is a sense of fluid movement. All is done with the utmost
lightness and gaiety, but as the lovers move through the forest,
part and meet again, or mingle with the other characters in
their constantly changing pairs and groups, every view of life
that is presented seems, sooner or later, to find its opposite.
Life is "but a flower in spring time, the only pretty ring time,"
but for the unromantic Touchstone there is "no great matter in
the ditty" and he counts it but time lost—his eye no doubt still
on his timepiece—"to hear such a foolish song." A quartet of
lovers avowing their love is broken up when one of them says

> Pray you, no more of this; 'tis like the howling of Irish
>   wolves against the moon.

And the one who says this is she who cannot tell "how many
fathom deep" she is in love. Dominating the centre of the play,
playing both the man's and woman's parts, counsellor in love

and yet its victim, Rosalind gathers up into herself many of its roles and many of its meanings. Around her in the forest, where the banished Duke presides, is the perfect happiness of the simple life, an illusion, much mocked at, but still cherished. She herself, beloved of the hero, has all the sanity to recognize that "love is merely a madness" and that lovers should be whipped as madmen are, but admits that "the whippers are in love too." Heroine of numerous masquerades, she is none the less always constant and never more true than when insisting that she is counterfeiting. For she is an expert in those dark riddles which mean exactly what they say. Though things are rarely what they seem, they may sometimes be so in a deeper sense. What is wisdom and what is folly is of course never decided—you may have it "as you like it." Or, as Touchstone rejoined to Rosalind, after her gibe about the medlar, "You have said; but whether wisely or no, let the forest judge."

It may be possible to suggest that the forest gives its verdict. For if *As You Like It* proclaims no final truth, its ultimate effect is not negative. Longing to escape to our enchanted world, we are constantly brought up against reality; sanity, practical wisdom sees through our illusions. Yet in *As You Like It* ideals, though always on the point of dissolving, are for ever recreating themselves. They do not delude the eye of reason, yet faith in them is not extinguished in spite of all that reason can do. "I would not be cured, youth."

NOTES

1. A lecture delivered to the Shakespeare Conference at Stratford-upon-Avon, 18 August 1953.
2. Quiller-Couch, *Shakespeare's Workmanship* (1918), p. 130. In spite of some radical disagreement, I have got a number of hints from "Q"'s essay.
3. This is not to imply that Shakespeare's "golden world" is at all the same as the primitive life of the mythical golden age, in which, by contrast with the Forest of Arden, there was no winter wind, sheep went unshorn, and man, at peace with all creatures, neither killed the deer nor was threatened by the snake and lion. Virgil associated the simplicity of pastoral life

with the golden age, and the two ideals were frequently combined, not to say confused, by later pastoralists (cf. Roy Walker, *The Golden Feast*, 1952, p. 133).

4. *Huntington Library Bulletin*, VIII (1935), 85.

5. *"Enter Orlando"* says the Folio simply, but the dialogue justifies Theobald's *"with Sword drawn."*

Joseph H. Summers

THE MASKS OF *TWELFTH NIGHT*

LOVE and its fulfillment are primary in Shakespeare's comedies.
Its conflicts are often presented in terms of the battle of the
generations. At the beginning of the plays the bliss of the
young lovers is usually barred by an older generation of parents
and rulers, a group which has supposedly experienced its own
fulfillment in the past and which is now concerned with preserving old forms or fulfilling new ambitions. The comedies usually
end with the triumph of young love, a triumph in which the
lovers make peace with their elders and themselves assume
adulthood and often power. The revolutionary force of love becomes an added element of vitality in a re-established society.

Twelfth Night does not follow the customary pattern. In this
play the responsible older generation has been abolished, and
there are no parents at all. In the first act we are rapidly introduced into a world in which the ruler is a love-sick Duke—in
which young ladies, fatherless and motherless, embark on disguised actions, or rule, after a fashion, their own households, and
in which the only individuals possibly over thirty are drunkards,
jokesters, and gulls, totally without authority. All the external
barriers to fulfillment have been eliminated in what becomes
almost a parody of the state desired by the ordinary young
lovers, the Hermias and Lysanders—or even the Rosalinds and
Orlandos. According to the strictly romantic formula, the happy
ending should be already achieved at the beginning of the
play: we should abandon the theater for the rites of love. But
the slightly stunned inhabitants of Illyria discover that they are

From *The University of Kansas City Review*, Vol. 22, Autumn
1955, pp. 25-32. Copyright 1955 by the University of Kansas City.
Reprinted by permission of the editor and the author.

anything but free. Their own actions provide the barriers, for most of them know neither themselves, nor others, nor their social world.

For his festival entertainment, Shakespeare freshly organized all the usual material of the romances—the twins, the exile, the impersonations—to provide significant movement for a dance of maskers. Every character has his mask, for the assumption of the play is that no one is without a mask in the serio-comic business of the pursuit of happiness. The character without disguises who is not ridiculous is outside the realm of comedy. Within comedy, the character who thinks it is possible to live without assuming a mask is merely too naive to recognize the mask he has already assumed. He is the chief object of laughter. As a general rule, we laugh with the characters who know the role they are playing and we laugh at those who do not; we can crudely divide the cast of *Twelfth Night* into those two categories.

But matters are more complicated than this, and roles have a way of shifting. All the butts except perhaps Sir Andrew Ague-cheek have moments in which they are the masters of our laughter; yet all the masters have moments in which they appear as fools. In our proper confusion, we must remember the alternative title of the play, "What You Will." It may indicate that everyone is free to invent his own title for the proceedings. It also tells the author's intention to fulfill our desires: we wish to share in the triumphs of love and we wish to laugh; we wish our fools occasionally to be wise, and we are insistent that our wisest dramatic figures experience our common fallibility. Most significantly, the title may hint that what "we" collectively "will" creates all the comic masks—that society determines the forms of comedy more directly than it determines those of any other literary genre.

At the opening of the play Orsino and Olivia accept the aristocratic (and literary) ideas of the romantic lover and the grief-stricken lady as realities rather than as ideas. They are comic characters exactly because of that confusion. Orsino glories in the proper moodiness and fickleness of the literary lover; only our own romanticism can blind us to the absurdities in his opening speech. Orsino first wishes the music to continue so that the appetite of love may "surfeit"; immediately, however, he demands that the musicians stop the music they are playing to repeat an isolated phrase—an awkward procedure and a comic bit of stage business which is rarely utilized in productions. Four lines later the music must stop entirely because the repeated "strain" no longer *is* sweet, and the appetite is truly about to "surfeit." He then exclaims that the spirit of love is so "quick and fresh" that like the sea (hardly a model of freshness)

> naught enters there,
> Of what validity and pitch soe'er,
> But falls into abatement and low price,
> Even in a minute!

Orsino is a victim of a type of madness to which the most admirable characters are sometimes subject. Its usual causes are boredom, lack of physical love, and excessive imagination, and the victim is unaware that he is in love with love rather than with a person.

In the same scene, before we ever see the lady, Olivia's state is as nicely defined. Valentine, Orsino's messenger, has acquired something of his master's extraordinary language, and his report on his love mission manages both to please the Duke and to convey his own incredulity at the excess of Olivia's vow for her brother. In his speech the fresh and the salt are again confused. It is impossible to keep fresh something so ephemeral as grief; Olivia can make it last and "season" it, however, by the process of pickling—the natural effect of "eye-offending brine." Orsino feels unbounded admiration for the depth of soul indicated by Olivia's vow and at the same time he assumes that the vow can easily be broken by a lover. He departs for "sweet *beds* ot flow'rs" which are somehow to provide a *canopy* for "love-thoughts."

Both Orsino and Olivia have adopted currently fashionable literary postures; yet neither of them is a fool. We are glad to be reassured by the Captain that Orsino is "A noble duke, in nature as in name," and that his present infatuation is only a month old. Sir Toby's later remark "What a plague means my niece, to take the death of her brother thus?" indicates that

Olivia too had seemed an unlikely candidate for affectation. She is also an unconvincing practitioner. Although at our first glimpse of her she is properly the grief-stricken lady ("Take the fool away"), her propriety collapses under Feste's famous catechism. We discover that Olivia is already bored and that she really desires to love. Outraged nature has its full and comic revenge when Olivia falls passionately in love with a male exterior and acts with an aggressiveness which makes Orsino seem almost feminine. Still properly an actor in comedy, Olivia quickly changes from the character who has confused herself with a socially attractive mask to one who fails to perceive the mask which society has imposed on another.

Viola's situation allows time for neither love- nor grief-in-idleness. A virgin, shipwrecked in a strange land, possessing only wit and intelligence and the Captain's friendship, she must act immediately if she is to preserve herself. She, like Olivia, has "lost" a brother, but the luxury of conventional mourning is quickly exchanged for a *willed* hope that, as she was saved, "so perchance may he be." With Viola's wish for time to know what her "estate is," before she is "delivered to the world," we are reminded that society often requires a mask, neither for the relief of boredom nor the enjoyment of acting, but merely for self-preservation. While Antonio, "friend to Sebastian," almost loses his life because of his failure to assume a disguise, Viola suffers from no failure of discretion or imagination. She must assume a disguise as a boy and she must have help in preparing it.

Although she knows the ways of the world, Viola takes the necessary chance and wills to trust the Captain:

> There is a fair behavior in thee, Captain.
> And though that Nature with a beauteous wall
> Doth oft close in pollution, yet of thee
> I will believe thou hast a mind that suits
> With this thy fair and outward character.

We have in this second scene not only the beginning of one strand of the complicated intrigue, but also the creation of the one character active in the intrigue who provides a measure for the comic excesses of all the others. (Feste's role as observer is analogous to Viola's role as "actor.") Although Viola chooses to impersonate Cesario from necessity, she later plays her part with undisguised enjoyment. She misses none of the opportunities for parody, for confession, and for *double entendre* which the mask affords, and she never forgets or lets us forget the biological distance between Viola and Cesario. Except in the fencing match with Sir Andrew Aguecheek, she anticipates and directs our perception of the ludicrous in her own role as well as in the roles of Orsino and Olivia.

Sebastian is the reality of which Cesario is the artful imitation. Viola's twin assumes no disguises; Viola and the inhabitants of Illyria have assumed it for him. He is, to the eye, identical with Viola, and his early scenes with Antonio serve to remind us firmly of his existence as well as to introduce an initial exhilarating confusion at the entrance of either of the twins. When he truly enters the action of the play in Act IV he is certainly the object of our laughter, not because he has confused himself with an ideal or improper mask, but because he so righteously and ineffectually insists on his own identity in the face of unanimous public opposition. Our attitude quickly changes, however, to a mixture of amused patronization and identification: we do, after all, *know* so much more than does Sebastian; yet, within the context of the play, we can hardly keep from identifying with the gentleman who, practically if not idealistically, decides not to reject the reality of a passionate Olivia just because he has never seen her before:

> Or I am mad, or else this is a dream.
> Let fancy still my sense in Lethe steep.
> If it be thus to dream, still let me sleep!

The other characters in the play do not truly belong to an aristocracy of taste and leisure. For some of them, that is the chief problem. Malvolio and Sir Andrew Aguecheek are ruled by their mistaken notions of the proper role of an upper-class gentleman, and they fail to perceive the comic gaps between themselves and their ideal roles, and between those ideals and the social reality. Sick with self-love as he is, Malvolio is also sick with his desire to rise in society: "an affectioned ass, that cons state without book and utters it by great swaths: the best persuaded of himself, so crammed, as he thinks, with excellencies, that it is his grounds of faith that all that look on him love him." Although he knows it without, he has learned his "state" by book —but such a pupil inevitably distorts the text. He dreams of ruling a thrifty and solemn household while he plays with "some rich jewel," a dream characteristically attractive to the *arriviste* and absolutely impossible to the *arrive*. We, like Maria, "can hardly forbear hurling things at him." His is as absurd as the reverse image which possesses Sir Andrew, a carpet-knight rightly described by Sir Toby as "an ass-head and a coxcomb and a knave, a thin-faced knave, a gull!" In the gallery of false images Sir Andrew's roaring boy hangs opposite Malvolio's burgher. Although in a low moment Sir Andrew may think that he has "no more wit than a Christian or an ordinary man has," he never has such grave self-doubt for long. Like a true gull, he tries to assume the particular role which, of all others, he is most poorly equipped to play: drinker, fighter, wencher.

Sir Andrew, however, would hardly exist without Sir Toby Belch: the gull must have his guller. Sir Toby may fulfill Sir Andrew's idea of what a gentleman should be, but Sir Toby himself has no such odd idea of gentility. (Sir Andrew may be "a dear manikin to you, Sir Toby," but Sir Toby has a superlatively good reason for allowing him to be: "I have been dear to him, lad, some two thousand strong, or so.") Even at his most drunken, we are delightfully unsure whether we laugh at or with Sir Toby, whether he is or is not fully conscious of the effects as well as the causes of his "mistakes," his verbal confusions, and even his belches. Like another drunken knight, and like Viola, Toby possesses a range of dramatic talents and he enjoys using them. He is equally effective as the fearless man of action, as the practitioner of noble "gentleness" with the "mad" Malvolio, and as the experienced alcoholic guide to Sir Andrew. His joy is in the jest as well as in the bottle, and he can bring himself to abandon the latter long enough to marry Maria simply in admiration for her ability as an intriguer. But like other knowing players, Sir Toby is vulnerable to deception. He is object rather than master of our laughter from the time when he mistakes Sebastian for Cesario and attempts to assert his masculine ability as a swordsman.

In the business of masking, Feste is the one professional among a crowd of amateurs; he does it for a living. He never makes the amateur's mistake of confusing his personality with his mask—he wears not motley in his brain. Viola recognizes his wisdom and some kinship in the fact that each "must observe their mood on whom he jests." But though Feste may have deliberately chosen his role, society determines its conditions. Now that he is growing old, the conditions become difficult: "Go to, you're a dry fool, I'll no more of you. Besides, you grow dishonest." While all the other characters are concerned with gaining something they do not have, Feste's struggle is to retain his mask and to make it again ingratiating. He is able to penetrate all the masks of the others, and he succeeds in retaining his own.

However fanciful its dreams of desire, the play moves within a context of an almost real world, from one disguise and half-understood intrigue to another, until all its elements are whirled into a complexly related and moving figure. With the constant contrasts and parallels and reversals in character, situation, and intrigue, we find ourselves at last, along with Malvolio and Olivia and Viola and the rest, in a state of real delirium. Until the concluding scene, however, we can largely agree with Sebastian: if we dream, we do not wish to wake; if this is madness, it is still comic madness, and we do not envy the sane. The attempts at false and inflexible authority are being defeated, the pretentious are being deflated, and the very sentimentality of the likable sentimentalists has led them close to biological reality. We are particularly delighted with Viola. Young, intelligent, zestful, she is a realist. She cuts through the subterfuges and disguises of the others with absolute clarity, and she provides us with a center for the movement, a standard of normality which is never dull. In her rejection of the artificial myths of love, moreover, Viola never becomes the advocate of a far more terrifying myth, the myth of absolute rationality. In a completely rational world, Shakespeare never tires of pointing out, what we know as love could not exist. We have never desired such a world.

From the time of her first aside to the audience after she has seen Orsino ("Yet a barful strife!/Whoe'er I woo, myself would be his wife"), Viola directly admits her irrational love. She differs, then, from Orsino and Olivia not in any invulnerability to

blindness and passion, but in the clarity and simplicity with
which she recognizes and accepts her state. Reason is not abandoned: she rationally admits her irrationality and her inability
to cope with the situation:

> O Time, thou must untangle this, not I!
> It is too hard a knot for me to untie!

Viola needs a miracle. Although she may imagine herself as
"Patience on a monument, smiling at grief," she remains as close
as possible to her loved one and waits for the miracle to happen.
Since we have seen Sebastian, we know that the miracle will
occur; yet through our identification with Viola we come to know
the comic burden, the masker's increasing weariness of the mask
which implies that love is still pursued rather than possessed.

The burden becomes comically unbearable only in the final
scene, when it is cast off. Here Shakespeare underscores all those
possibilities of violence and death which are usually submerged
in comedy. Antonio is arrested and in danger of his life. Orsino,
finally recognizing the hopelessness of his suit to Olivia, shows
the vicious side of sentimentality. After considering the possibility
of killing Olivia "like to the Egyptian thief," he determines to do
violence to "Cesario":

> Come, boy, with me. My thoughts are ripe in mischief.
> I'll sacrifice the lamb that I do love,
> To spite a raven's heart within a dove.

Olivia is hysterical at what seems to be the baseness of Cesario.
Sir Toby has a broken pate to show for his one major failure to
penetrate a mask. The dance must stop. The miracle must occur.

The entrance of Sebastian is "what we will." It is the most
dramatic moment of the play. The confrontation of Sebastian and
Cesario-Viola, those identical images, concludes the formal plot
and provides the means for the discarding of all the lovers' masks.
The moment must be savored and fully realized. As Viola and
Sebastian chant their traditional formulas of proof, both the audience and the other characters on the stage undistractedly view
the physical image of the duality which has made the confusion
and the play. The masks and the play are to be abandoned for a
vision of delight beyond delight, in which lovers have neither to

wear nor to penetrate disguises since they are at last invulnerable to error and laughter.

Yet the play does not resolve into a magic blessing of the world's fertility as does *A Midsummer Night's Dream*. We have been promised a happy ending, and we receive it. We are grateful that the proper Jacks and Jills have found each other, but the miracle is a limited miracle, available only to the young and the lucky. Not every Jack has his Jill even in Illyria, and after the general unmasking, those without love may seem even lonelier. Malvolio, of course, is justly punished. He has earned his mad scene, and with the aid of Feste he has made it comic. As a result of his humiliation he has also earned some sort of redress. Yet he is ridiculous in his arrogance to the end, and his threatened revenge, now that he is powerless to effect it, sustains the comedy and the characterization and prevents the obtrusion of destructive pathos.

It is Feste rather than Malvolio who finally reminds us of the limitations and the costs of the romantic vision of happiness with which we have been seduced. However burdensome, masking is his career, and romantic love provides no end for it. Alone on the stage at the end of the play, he sings a song of unfulfilled love which shows the other side of the coin. For Feste, as for his audience, the mask can never be finally discarded: the rain it raineth every day. His song has those overtones, I believe, but they are only overtones. The music, here and elsewhere in the play, provides an element in which oppositions may be resolved. And the song itself, like the movement which must accompany it, is crude and witty as well as graceful and nostalgic. However far it may have missed the conventionally happy ending, Feste's saga of misfortunes in love is comic, even from his own point of view. The exaggeration so often operative in the refrains of Elizabethan lyrics emphasizes that the watery as well as the sunny vision can become funny: it doesn't rain every day by a long shot.

The song, which begins as the wittiest observer's comment on the denouement of the play, ends as a dissolution of the dramatic fiction:

> A great while ago the world begun,
>   With hey, ho, the wind and the rain,

But that's all one, our play is done,
And we'll strive to please you every day.

The audience has been a participant in the festivity. As the fictional lovers have unmasked to reveal or realize their "true" identities, it is only proper that the clown, the only character who might move freely in the environs of Bankside, as well as in the realm of Illyria, should unmask the whole proceeding for the imitation of a desired world which it has been. The audience must be returned from "What You Will" to its own less patterned world where the sea rarely disgorges siblings given up for lost, where mistaken marriages rarely turn out well, where Violas rarely catch Dukes, and where Malvolios too often rule households with disturbing propriety. The lovers have met, and Feste announces that present laughter has come to an end. But the actors, those true and untiring maskers, will continue to "strive to please" us. They will find few occasions in the future in which their efforts will be more sure of success.

Twelfth Night is the climax of Shakespeare's early achievement in comedy. The effects and values of the earlier comedies are here subtly embodied in the most complex structure which Shakespeare had yet created. But the play also looks forward: the pressure to dissolve the comedy, to realize and finally abandon the burden of laughter, is an intrinsic part of its "perfection." Viola's clear-eyed and affirmative vision of her own and the world's irrationality is a triumph and we desire it; yet we realize its vulnerability, and we come to realize that virtue in disguise is only totally triumphant when evil is not in disguise—is not truly present at all. Having solved magnificently the problems of this particular form of comedy, Shakespeare was evidently not tempted to repeat his triumph. After *Twelfth Night* the so-called comedies require for their happy resolutions more radical characters and devices—omniscient and omnipresent Dukes, magic, and resurrection. More obvious miracles are needed for comedy to exist in a world in which evil also exists, not merely incipiently but with power.

E. M. W. Tillyard

RICHARD II

Richard II is imperfectly executed, and yet, that imperfection granted, perfectly planned as part of a great structure. It is sharply contrasted, in its extreme formality of shape and style, with the subtler and more fluid nature of *Henry IV;* but it is a necessary and deliberate contrast; resembling a stiff recitative composed to introduce a varied and flexible *aria.* Coming after *King John* the play would appear the strangest relapse into the official self which Shakespeare had been shedding; taken with *Henry IV* it shows that Shakespeare, while retaining and using this official self, could develop with brilliant success the new qualities of character and style manifested in the Bastard. *Richard II* therefore betokens no relapse but is an organic part of one of Shakespeare's major achievements.

But the imperfections are undoubted and must be faced. As a separate play *Richard II* lacks the sustained vitality of *Richard III,* being less interesting and less exacting in structure and containing a good deal of verse which by the best Shakespearean standards can only be called indifferent. Not that there is anything wrong with the structure, which is that of *2 Henry VI,* the rise of one great man at the expense of another; but it is simple, as befits an exordium and does not serve through the excitement of its complications to make the utmost demand on the powers of the author. For illustrating the indifferent verse I need not go beyond the frequent stretches of couplet-writing and the occasional quatrains that make such a contrast to the verse of

From *Shakespeare's History Plays, 1946,* pp. 244-63. Copyright 1946, by The Macmillan Co. Reprinted by permission of The Macmillan Company and Chatto and Windus Ltd.

Henry IV. It is not that these have not got their function, which
will be dealt with later, but that as poetry they are indifferent
stuff. They are as necessary as the stiff lines in *3 Henry VI* spoken
by the Father who has killed his Son, and the Son who has killed
his Father; but they are little better poetically. For present
purposes it does not matter in the least whether they are relics
of an old play, by Shakespeare or by someone else, or whether
Shakespeare wrote them with the rest. They occur throughout
the play and with the exception of perhaps two couplets are not
conspicuously worse in the fifth act than anywhere else. There
is no need for a theory that in this act, to save time, Shakespeare
hurriedly began copying chunks from an old play. Until there is
decisive proof of this, it is simplest to think that Shakespeare
wrote his couplets along with the rest, intending a deliberate
contrast. He had done the same thing with the Talbots' death in
1 Henry VI, while, to account for the indifferent quality, one may
remember that he was never very good at the couplet. The best
couplets in *A Midsummer Night's Dream* are weak compared
with the best blank verse in that play, while few of the final
couplets of the sonnets are more than a competent close to far
higher verse.

I turn now to a larger quality of the play, of which the couplets
are one of several indications.

Of all Shakespeare's plays *Richard II* is the most formal and
ceremonial. It is not only that Richard himself is a true king in
appearance, in his command of the trappings of royalty, while
being deficient in the solid virtues of the ruler; that is a commonplace: the ceremonial character of the play extends much wider
than Richard's own nature or the exquisite patterns of his poetic
speech.

First, the very actions tend to be symbolic rather than real.
There is all the pomp of a tournament without the physical meeting of the two armed knights. There is a great army of Welshmen
assembled to support Richard, but they never fight. Bolingbroke
before Flint Castle speaks of the terrible clash there should be
when he and Richard meet:

Methinks King Richard and myself should meet
With no less terror than the elements

Of fire and water, when their thundering shock
At meeting tears the cloudy cheeks of heaven.

But instead of a clash there is a highly ceremonious encounter
leading to the effortless submission of Richard. There are violent
challenges before Henry in Westminster Hall, but the issue is
postponed. The climax of the play is the ceremony of Richard's
deposition. And finally Richard, imprisoned at Pomfret, erects
his own lonely state and his own griefs into a gigantic ceremony.
He arranges his own thoughts into classes corresponding with
men's estates in real life; king and beggar, divine, soldier, and
middle man. His own sighs keep a ceremonial order like a clock:

> Now, sir, the sound that tells what hour it is
> Are clamorous groans, which strike upon my heart,
> Which is the bell: so sighs and tears and groans
> Show minutes, times, and hours.

Second, in places where emotion rises, where there is strong
mental action, Shakespeare evades direct or naturalistic presentation and resorts to convention and conceit. He had done the same
when Arthur pleaded with Hubert for his eyes in *King John,* but
that was exceptional to a play which contained the agonies of
Constance and the Bastard's perplexities over Arthur's body.
Emotionally Richard's parting from his queen could have been
a great thing in the play: actually it is an exchange of frigidly
ingenious couplets.

Rich.
> Go, count thy way with sighs; I mine with groans.

Qu.
> So longest way shall have the longest moans.

Rich.
> Twice for one step I'll groan, the way being short,
> And piece the way out with a heavy heart.

This is indeed the language of ceremony not of passion. Exactly
the same happens when the Duchess of York pleads with Henry
against her husband for her son Aumerle's life. Before the climax,
when York gives the news of his son's treachery, there had been
a show of feeling; but with the entry of the Duchess, when emo-

tion should culminate, all is changed to prettiness and formal antiphony. This is how the Duchess compares her own quality of pleading with her husband's:

> Pleads he in earnest? look upon his face;
> His eyes do drop no tears, his prayers are jest;
> His words come from his mouth, ours from our breast:
> He prays but faintly and would be denied;
> We pray with heart and soul and all beside:
> His weary joints would gladly rise, I know;
> Our knees shall kneel till to the ground they grow:
> His prayers are full of false hypocrisy;
> Ours of true zeal and deep integrity.

And to "frame" the scene, to make it unmistakably a piece of deliberate ceremonial, Bolingbroke falls into the normal language of drama when having forgiven Aumerle he vows to punish the other conspirators:

> But for our trusty brother-in-law and the abbot,
> And all the rest of that consorted crew,
> Destruction straight shall dog them at the heels.

The case of Gaunt is different but more complicated. When he has the state of England in mind and reproves Richard, though he can be rhetorical and play on words, he speaks the language of passion:

> Now He that made me knows I see thee ill.
> Thy death-bed is no lesser than thy land
> Wherein thou liest in reputation sick.
> And thou, too careless patient as thou art,
> Commit'st thy anointed body to the cure
> Of those physicians that first wounded thee.
> A thousand flatterers sit within thy crown,
> Whose compass is no bigger than thy head.

But in the scene of private feeling, when he parts from his banished son, both speakers, ceasing to be specifically themselves, exchange the most exquisitely formal commonplaces traditionally deemed appropriate to such a situation.

Go, say I sent thee for to purchase honour
And not the king exil'd thee; or suppose
Devouring pestilence hangs in our air
And thou art flying to a fresher clime.
Look, what thy soul holds dear, imagine it
To lie that way thou go'st, not whence thou com'st.
Suppose the singing birds musicians,
The grass whereon thou tread'st the presence strew'd,
The flowers fair ladies, and thy steps no more
Than a delightful measure or a dance;
For gnarling sorrow hath less power to bite
The man that mocks at it and sets it light.

Superficially this may be maturer verse than the couplets quoted,
but it is just as formal, just as mindful of propriety and as un-
mindful of nature as Richard and his queen taking leave.
Richard's sudden start into action when attacked by his murderers is exceptional, serving to set off by contrast the lack of
action that has prevailed and to link the play with the next of
the series. His groom, who appears in the same scene, is a realistic
character alien to the rest of the play and serves the same function as Richard in action.

Thirdly, there is an elaboration and a formality in the cosmic
references, scarcely to be matched in Shakespeare. These are
usually brief and incidental, showing indeed how intimate a
part they were of the things accepted and familiar in Shakespeare's mind. But in *Richard II* they are positively paraded. The
great speech of Richard in Pomfret Castle is a tissue of them:
first the peopling of his prison room with his thoughts, making
its microcosm correspond with the orders of the body politic;
then the doctrine of the universe as a musical harmony; then the
fantasy of his own griefs arranged in a pattern like the working
of a clock, symbol of regularity opposed to discord; and finally
madness as the counterpart in man's mental kingdom of discord
or chaos. Throughout the play the great commonplace of the
king on earth duplicating the sun in heaven is exploited with a
persistence unmatched anywhere else in Shakespeare. Finally
(for I omit minor references to cosmic lore) there is the scene
(III.4) of the gardeners, with the elaborate comparison of the

state to the botanical microcosm of the garden. But this is a
scene so typical of the whole trend of the play that I will speak
of it generally and not merely as another illustration of the traditional correspondences.

The scene begins with a few exquisitely musical lines of
dialogue between the queen and two ladies. She refines her grief
in a vein of high ceremony and sophistication. She begins by
asking what sport they can devise in this garden to drive away
care. But to every sport proposed there is a witty objection.

> *Lady.*
>> Madam, we'll tell tales.
>
> *Queen.*
>> Of sorrow or of joy?
>
> *Lady.*
>>> Of either, madam.
>
> *Queen.*
>> Of neither, girl:
>> For if of joy, being altogether wanting,
>> It doth remember me the more of sorrow;
>> Or if of grief, being altogether had,
>> It adds more sorrow to my want of joy.
>> For what I have I need not to repeat,
>> And what I want it boots not to complain.

Shakespeare uses language here like a very accomplished musi-
cian doing exercises over the whole compass of the violin. Then
there enter a gardener and two servants: clearly to balance the
queen and her ladies and through that balance to suggest that
the gardener within the walls of his little plot of land is a king.
Nothing could illustrate better the different expectations of a
modern and of an Elizabethan audience than the way they would
take the gardener's opening words:

> Go, bind thou up yon dangling apricocks,
> Which, like unruly children, make their sire
> Stoop with oppression of their prodigal weight.

The first thought of a modern audience is: what a ridiculous
way for a gardener to talk. The first thought of an Elizabethan
would have been: what is the symbolic meaning of those words,

spoken by this king of the garden, and how does it bear on the play? And it would very quickly conclude that the apricots had grown inflated and overweening in the sun of the royal favour; that oppression was used with a political as well as a physical meaning; and that the apricots threatened, unless restrained, to upset the proper relation between parent and offspring, to offend against the great principle of order. And the rest of the gardener's speech would bear out this interpretation.

> Go thou, and like an executioner
> Cut off the heads of too fast growing sprays,
> That look too lofty in our commonwealth.
> All must be even in our government.
> You thus employ'd, I will go root away
> The noisome weeds, which without profit suck
> The soil's fertility from wholesome flowers.

In fact the scene turns out to be an elaborate political allegory with the Earl of Wiltshire, Bushy, and Green standing for the noxious weeds which Richard, the bad gardener, allowed to flourish and which Henry, the new gardener, has rooted up. It ends with the queen coming forward and joining in the talk. She confirms the gardener's regal and moral function by calling him "old Adam's likeness," but curses him for his ill news about Richard and Bolingbroke. The intensively symbolic character of the scene is confirmed when the gardener at the end proposes to plant a bank with rue where the queen let fall her tears, as a memorial:

> Rue, even for ruth, here shortly shall be seen
> In the remembrance of a weeping queen.

In passing, for it is not my immediate concern, let me add that the gardener gives both the pattern and the moral of the play. The pattern is the weighing of the fortunes of Richard and Bolingbroke:

> Their fortunes both are weigh'd.
> In your lord's scale is nothing but himself
> And some few vanities that make him light;

> But in the balance of great Bolingbroke
> Besides himself are all the English peers,
> And with that odds he weighs King Richard down.

For the moral, though he deplores Richard's inefficiency, the gardener calls the news of his fall "black tidings" and he sympathises with the queen's sorrow. And he is himself, in his microcosmic garden, what neither Richard nor Bolingbroke separately is, the authentic gardener-king, no usurper, and the just represser of vices, the man who makes "all even in our government."

The one close Shakespearean analogy with this gardener is Iden, the unambitious squire in his Kentish garden, who stands for "degree" in 2 *Henry VI*. But he comes in as an obvious foil to the realistic disorder just exhibited in Cade's rebellion. Why was it that in *Richard II*, when he was so much more mature, when his brilliant realism in *King John* showed him capable of making his gardeners as human and as amusing as the grave-diggers in *Hamlet*, Shakespeare chose to present them with a degree of formality unequalled in any play he wrote? It is, in a different form, the same question as that which was implied by my discussion of the other formal or ceremonial features of the play: namely, why did Shakespeare in *Richard II* make the ceremonial or ritual form of writing, found in differing quantities in the *Henry VI* plays and in *Richard III*, not merely one of the principal means of expression but the very essence of the play?

These are the first questions we must answer if we are to understand the true nature of *Richard II*. And here let me repeat that though Richard himself is a very important part of the play's ceremonial content, that content is larger and more important than Richard. With that caution, I will try to explain how the ritual or ceremonial element in *Richard II* differs from that in the earlier History Plays, and through such an explanation to conjecture a new interpretation of the play. There is no finer instance or ceremonial writing than the scene or the ghosts at the end of *Richard III*. But it is subservient to a piece of action, to the Battle of Bosworth with the overthrow of a tyrant and the triumph of a righteous prince. Its duty is to make that action a matter of high, mysterious, religious import. We are not invited to dwell on the ritual happenings as on a resting-place, to deduce from them the ideas into which the mind settles when the action of the play is over. But in *Richard II*, with all the emphasis and the point taken out of the action, we are invited, again and again, to dwell on the sheer ceremony of the various situations. The main point of the tournament between Bolingbroke and Mowbray is the way it is conducted; tne point of Gaunt's parting with Bolingbroke is the sheer propriety of the sentiments they utter; the portents, put so fittingly into the mouth of a Welshman, are more exciting because they are appropriate than because they precipitate an event; Richard is ever more concerned with how he behaves, with the fitness of his conduct to the occasion, than with what he actually does; the gardener may foretell the deposition of Richard yet he is far more interesting as representing a static principle of order; when Richard is deposed, it is the precise manner that comes before all—

> With mine own tears I wash away my balm,
> With mine own hands I give away my crown,
> With mine own tongue deny my sacred state,
> With mine own breath release all duty's rites.

We are in fact in a world where means matter more than ends, where it is more important to keep strictly the rules of an elaborate game than either to win or to lose it.

Now though compared with ourselves the Elizabethans put a high value on means as against ends they did not go to the extreme. It was in the Middle Ages that means were so elaborated, that the rules of the game of life were so lavishly and so minutely set forth. *Richard II* is Shakespeare's picture of that life.

Of course it would be absurd to suggest that Shakespeare pictured the age of Richard II after tne fashion of a modern historian. But there are signs elsewhere in Shakespeare of at least a feeling after historical verity; and there are special reasons why the age of Richard II should have struck the imaginations of the Elizabethans.

I noted above that at the end of *2 Henry VI* Clifford and York, though enemies, do utter some of the chivalric sentiments proper to medieval warfare. Such sentiments do not recur in *3 Henry VI*, where we have instead the full barbarities of Wakefield and Towton. Shakespeare is probably recording the historical fact

that the decencies of the knightly code went down under the
stress of civil carnage. But the really convincing analogy with
Richard II is the play of *Julius Caesar*. There, however slender
Shakespeare's equipment as historian and however much of his
own time he slips in, he does succeed in giving his picture of
antique Rome, of the dignity of its government and of the stoic
creed of its great men. T. S. Eliot has rightly noted how much
essential history Shakespeare extracted from Plutarch. And if
from Plutarch, why not from Froissart likewise?

Till recently Shakespeare's debt to Berner's translation of
Froissart's Chronicle has been almost passed over, but now it is
rightly agreed that it was considerable. To recognise the debt
helps one to understand the play. For instance, one of the minor
puzzles of the play is plain if we grant Shakespeare's acquaintance with Froissart. When York, horrified at Richard's confiscat-
ing Gaunt's property the moment he died, goes on to enumerate
all Richard's crimes, he mentions "the prevention of poor Bolingbroke about his marriage." There is nothing more about this in
the play, but there is a great deal about it in Froissart—Richard
had brought charges against the exile Bolingbroke which induced
the French king to break off Bolingbroke's engagement with the
daughter of the Duke of Berry, the king's cousin. If Shakespeare
had been full of Froissart when writing *Richard II* he could
easily have slipped in this isolated reference. But quite apart
from any tangible signs of imitation it is scarcely conceivable
that Shakespeare should not have read so famous a book as
Berners's Froissart, or that having read it he should not have
been impressed by the bright pictures of chivalric life in those
pages. Now among Shakespeare's History Plays *Richard II* is the
only one that falls within the period of time covered by Froissart.
All the more reason why on this unique occasion he should heed
this great original. Now though Froissart is greatly interested in
motives, he also writes with an eye unmatched among chroniclers
for its eager observation of external things and with a mind
similarly unmatched for the high value it placed on the proper
disposition of those things. In fact he showed a lively belief in
ceremony and in the proprieties of heraldry akin to Elizabethan
belief yet altogether more firmly attached to the general scheme
of ideas that prevailed at the time. Shakespeare's brilliant wit

must have grasped this; and *Richard II* may be his intuitive rendering of Froissart's medievalism.

But there were other reasons why the reign of Richard II should be notable. A. B. Steel, his most recent historian, begins his study by noting that Richard was the last king of the old medieval order:

> the last king ruling by hereditary right, direct and undisputed, from the Conqueror. The kings of the next hundred and ten years . . . were essentially kings *de facto* not *de jure*, successful usurpers recognised after the event, upon conditions, by their fellow-magnates or by parliament.

Shakespeare, deeply interested in titles as he had showed himself to be in his early History Plays, must have known this very well; and Gaunt's famous speech on England cannot be fully understood without this knowledge. He calls England

> This nurse, this teeming womb of royal kings,
> Fear'd by their breed and famous by their birth,
> Renowned for their deeds as far from home,
> For Christian service and true chivalry,
> As is the sepulchre in stubborn Jewry
> Of the world's ransom, blessed Mary's son.

Richard was no crusader, but he was authentic heir of the crusading Plantagenets. Henry was different, a usurper; and it is with reference to this passage that we must read the lines in *Richard II* and *Henry IV* which recount his desire and his failure to go to Palestine. That honour was reserved for the authentic Plantagenet kings. Richard then had the full sanctity of medieval kingship and the strong pathos of being the last king to possess it. Shakespeare probably realised that however powerful the Tudors were and however undisputed their hold over their country's church, they had not the same sanctity as the medieval kings. He was therefore ready to draw from certain French treatises, anti-Lancastrian in tone, that made Richard a martyr and compared him to Christ and his accusers to so many Pilates giving him over to the wishes of the London mob. Shakespeare's Richard says at his deposition:

> Though some of you with Pilate wash your hands,
> Showing an outward pity; yet you Pilates
> Have here deliver'd me to my sour cross,
> And water cannot wash away your sin.

Holy and virtuous as the Earl of Richmond is in *Richard III*, he does not pretend to the same kingly sanctity as Richard II. Such sanctity belongs to a more antique, more exotically ritual world; and Shakespeare composed his play accordingly.

Not only did Richard in himself hold a position unique among English kings, he maintained a court of excessive splendour. Froissart writes as follows in the last pages of his chronicle:

> This King Richard reigned king of England twenty-two year in great prosperity, holding great estate and signory. There was never before any king of England that spent so much in his house as he did by a hundred thousand florins every year. For I, Sir John Froissart, canon and treasurer of Chinay, knew it well, for I was in his court more than a quarter of a year together and he made me good cheer. . . . And when I departed from him it was at Windsor; and at my departing the king sent me by a knight of his, Sir John Golofer, a goblet of silver and gilt weighing two mark of silver and within it a hundred nobles, by the which I am as yet the better and shall be as long as I live; wherefore I am bound to pray to God for his soul and with much sorrow I write of his death.

But Shakespeare need not have gone to Froissart for such information. In an age that was both passionately admiring of royal magnificence and far more retentive of tradition than our own the glories of Richard's court must have persisted as a legend. Anyhow that Shakespeare was aware of them is plain from Richard's address to his own likeness in the mirror:

> Was this face the face
> That every day under his household roof
> Did keep ten thousand men?

The legend must have persisted of this court's continental elegance, of the curiosities of its dress, of such a thing as Anne of Bohemia introducing the custom of riding side-saddle, of Richard's invention of the handkerchief for nasal use. Then there were the poets. Shakespeare must have associated the beginnings of English poetry with Chaucer and Gower; and they wrote mainly in Richard's reign. There must have been much medieval art, far more than now survives, visible in the great houses of Elizabeth's day, illuminated books and tapestry; and it would be generally associated with the most brilliant reign of the Middle Ages. Finally in Richard's reign there was the glamour of a still intact nobility: a very powerful glamour in an age still devoted to heraldry and yet possessing an aristocracy who, compared with the great men of Richard's day, were upstarts.

All these facts would have a strong, if unconscious, effect on Shakespeare's mind and induce him to present the age of Richard in a brilliant yet remote and unrealistic manner. He was already master of a certain antique lore and of a certain kind of ceremonial writing: it was natural that he should use them, but with a different turn, to do this particular work. Thus he makes more solemn and elaborates the inherited notions of cosmic correspondences and chivalric procedure and he makes his ritual style a central and not peripheral concern. Hence the portentous solemnity of the moralising gardeners, the powerful emphasis on the isolated symbol of the rue-tree, the elaborate circumstances of the tournament between Bolingbroke and Mowbray, and the unique artifice of Richard's great speeches: speeches which are the true centre of the play but central with a far wider reference than to the mere character of Richard.

In speaking of medieval illuminated books and tapestry I do not wish to imply anything too literal: that Shakespeare had actual examples of such things in mind when he wrote *Richard II*. But it is true that many passages in this play call them up and that unconscious memory of them *might* have given Shakespeare help. Take a passage from one of Richard's best known speeches.

> For God's sake, let us sit upon the ground
> And tell sad stories of the death of kings:
> How some have been depos'd, some slain in war,
> Some haunted by the ghosts they have depos'd,
> Some poison'd by their wives, some sleeping kill'd;

All murder'd: for within the hollow crown
That rounds the mortal temples of a king
Keeps Death his court, and there the antic sits,
Scoffing his state and grinning at his pomp,
Allowing him a breath, a little scene,
To monarchise, be fear'd, and kill with looks,
Infusing him with self and vain conceit,
As if this flesh which walls about our life
Were brass impregnable, and, humour'd thus,
Comes at the last and with a little pin
Bores through his castle wall, and farewell king!

Critics have seen a reference here to the *Mirror for Magistrates,*
but Chaucer's Monk's Tale would suit much better. Death, keeping his court, is a pure medieval motive. Still, these motives were
inherited and need imply nothing unusual. But Death the skele-
ton watching and mocking the king in his trappings is a clear
and concrete image that reminds one of the visual arts: and
above all the exquisiteness, the very remoteness from what could
have happened in an actual physical attempt, of someone boring
through the castle wall with a little pin precisely recaptures the
technique of medieval illumination. Before the tournament
Bolingbroke prays God:

> And with thy blessings steel my lance's point
> That it may enter Mowbray's waxen coat.

That again is just like medieval illumination. When a wound is
given in medieval art there is no fusion of thing striking with
thing stricken; the blow simply rests in a pre-existing hole, while
any blood that spouts out had pre-existed just as surely. This is
the kind of picture called up by Mowbray's "waxen coat." Or
take this comparison. If anywhere in *Henry IV* we might expect
medievalism it is in the description of the Prince performing the
most spectacular of chivalric actions: vaulting onto his horse in
full armour.

> I saw young Harry, with his beaver on,
> His cuisses on his thighs, gallantly arm'd,
> Rise from the ground like feather'd Mercury,
> And vaulted with such ease into his seat,

> As if an angel dropp'd down from the clouds,
> To turn and wind a fiery Pegasus
> And witch the world with noble horsemanship.

There is nothing medieval here. It is a description recalling the art of the high Renaissance with fused colours and subtle transitions. Set beside it Gaunt's advice to Bolingbroke about to go into exile:

> Suppose the singing birds musicians,
> The grass whereon thou tread'st the presence strew d,
> The flowers fair ladies, and thy steps no more
> Than a delightful measure or a dance.

Here each item is distinct, and the lines evoke the mincing figures of a medieval tapestry in a setting of birds and flowers.

The case for the essential medievalism of *Richard II* is even stronger when it is seen that the conspirators, working as such, do not share the ceremonial style used to represent Richard and his court. Once again the usual explanation of such a contrast is too narrow. It has been the habit to contrast the "poetry" of Richard with the practical common sense of Bolingbroke. But the "poetry" of Richard is all part of a world of gorgeous tournaments, conventionally mournful queens, and impossibly sententious gardeners, while Bolingbroke's common sense extends to his backers, in particular to that most important character, Northumberland. We have in fact the contrast not only of two characters but of two ways of life.

One example of the two different ways of life has occurred already: in the contrast noted between the mannered pleading of the Duchess of York for Aumerle's life and Henry's vigorous resolve immediately after to punish the conspirators. The Duchess and her family belong to the old order where the means, the style, the embroidery matter more than what they further or express. Henry belongs to a new order, where action is quick and leads somewhere. But other examples are needed to back up what to many readers will doubtless seem a dangerous and forced theory of the play's significance. First, a new kind of vigour, the vigour of strong and swift action, enters the verse of the play at II. 1. 224, when, after Richard has seized Gaunt's

property and announced his coming journey to Ireland, Northumberland, Ross, and Willoughby remain behind and hatch their
conspiracy. Northumberland's last speech especially has a different vigour from any vigorous writing that has gone before:
from the vigour of the jousters' mutual defiance or York's moral
indignation at the king's excesses. After enumerating Bolingbroke's supporters in Brittany, he goes on:

> All these well furnish'd by the Duke of Brittain
> With eight tall ships, three thousand men of war,
> Are making hither with all due expedience
> And shortly mean to touch our northern shore:
> Perhaps they had ere this, but that they stay
> The first departing of the king for Ireland.
> If then we shall shake off our slavish yoke,
> Imp out our drooping country's broken wing,
> Redeem from broken pawn the blemish'd crown,
> Wipe off the dust that hides our sceptre's gift
> And make high majesty look like itself,
> Away with me in post to Ravenspurgh.

The four lines describing by different metaphors how the land is
to be restored are not in a ritual manner but in Shakespeare's
normal idiom of Elizabethan exuberance. It is not for nothing
that the next scene shows the Queen exchanging elegant conceits about her sorrow for Richard's absence with Bushy and
Green. But the largest contrast comes at the beginning of the
third act. It begins with a very fine speech of Bolingbroke recounting to Bushy and Green all their crimes, before they are
executed. It has the full accent of the world of action, where
people want to get things and are roused to passion in their
attempts:

> Bring forth these men.
> Bushy and Green, I will not vex your souls
> (Since presently your souls must part your bodies)
> With too much urging your pernicious lives,
> For 'twere no charity.

That is the beginning, and the speech goes on to things themselves not to the way they are done or are embroidered. And when

at the end Bolingbroke recounts his own injuries it is with plain
and understandable passion:

> Myself a prince by fortune of my birth,
> Near to the king in blood, and near in love
> Till you did make him misinterpret me,
> Have stoop'd my neck under your injuries
> And sigh'd my English breath in foreign clouds,
> Eating the bitter bread of banishment.

The scene is followed by Richard's landing in Wales, his pitiful
inability to act, and his wonderful self-dramatisation. As a display of externals, as an exaltation of means over ends (here carried to a frivolous excess), it is wonderful; yet it contains no
lines that for the weight of unaffected passion come near Bolingbroke's single line,

> Eating the bitter bread of banishment.

The world for which Bolingbroke stands, though it is a usurping
world, displays a greater sincerity of personal emotion.

Thus *Richard II*, although reputed so simple and homogeneous
a play, is built on a contrast. The world of medieval refinement
is indeed the main object of presentation but it is threatened and
in the end superseded by the more familiar world of the present.

In carrying out his object Shakespeare shows the greatest skill
in keeping the emphasis sufficiently on Richard, while hinting
that in Bolingbroke's world there is the probability of development. In other words he makes the world of Bolingbroke not so
much defective as embryonic. It is not allowed to compete with
Richard's but it is ready to grow to its proper fulness in the next
plays. This is especially true of the conspirators' characters.
Hotspur, for instance, is faintly drawn yet in one place he
speaks with a hearty abruptness that shows his creator had conceived the whole character already. It is when Hotspur first
meets Bolingbroke, near Berkeley Castle. Northumberland asks
him if he has forgotten the Duke of Hereford, and Hotspur
replies:

> No, my good lord, for that is not forgot
> Which ne'er I did remember: to my knowledge
> I never in my life did look on him.

At the beginning of the same scene Northumberland's elaborate compliments to Bolingbroke show his politic nature: it is the same man who at the beginning of *2 Henry IV* lies "crafty-sick." Bolingbroke too is consistent with his later self, though we are shown only certain elements in his character. What marks out the later Bolingbroke and makes him a rather pathetic figure is his bewilderment. For all his political acumen he does not know himself completely or his way about the world. And the reason is that he has relied in large part on fortune. Dover Wilson remarked truly of him in *Richard II* that though he acts forcibly he appears to be borne upward by a power beyond his volition. He is made the first mover of trouble in the matter of the tournament and he wants to do something about Woodstock's murder. But he has no steady policy and having once set events in motion is the servant of fortune. As such, he is not in control of events, though by his adroitness he may deal with the unpredictable as it occurs. Now a man who, lacking a steady policy, begins a course of action will be led into those "by-paths and indirect crook'd ways" of which Henry speaks to his son in *2 Henry IV*. Shakespeare says nothing of them in *Richard II*, but they are yet the inevitable result of Henry's character as shown in that play. It is worth anticipating and saying that Prince Hal differs from his father in having perfect knowledge both of himself and of the world around him. Of all types of men he is the least subject to the sway of fortune.

Another quality shown only in embryo is humour. It is nearly absent but there is just a touch: sufficient to assure us that Shakespeare has it there all the time in readiness. It occurs in the scene where Aumerle describes to Richard his parting from Bolingbroke.

Rich.

> And say, what store of parting tears were shed?

Aum.

> Faith, none for me: except the north-east wind
> Which then blew bitterly against our faces,
> Awak'd the sleeping rheum, and so by chance
> Did grace our hollow parting with a tear.

Richard II thus at once possesses a dominant theme and contains within itself the elements of those different things that are to be the theme of its successors.

It must not be thought, because Shakespeare treated history, as described above, in a way new to him that he has lost interest in his old themes. On the contrary he is interested as much as ever in the theme of civil war, in the kingly type, and in the general fortunes of England. And I will say a little on each of these before trying to sum up the play's meaning in the tetralogy to which it belongs.

Richard II does its work in proclaiming the great theme of the whole cycle of Shakespeare's History Plays: the beginning in prosperity, the distortion of prosperity by a crime, civil war, and ultimate renewal of prosperity. The last stage falls outside the play's scope, but the second scene with the Duchess of Gloucester's enumeration of Edward III's seven sons, her account of Gloucester's death, and her call for vengeance is a worthy exordium of the whole cycle. The speeches of the Bishop of Carlisle and of Richard to Northumberland, parts of which were quoted near the beginning of this chapter, are worthy statements of the disorder that follows the deposition of the rightful king. In doctrine the play is entirely orthodox. Shakespeare knows that Richard's crimes never amounted to tyranny and hence that outright rebellion against him was a crime. He leaves uncertain the question of who murdered Woodstock and never says that Richard was personally responsible. The king's uncles hold perfectly correct opinions. Gaunt refuses the Duchess of Gloucester's request for vengeance, the matter being for God's decision alone. Even on his deathbed, when lamenting the state of the realm and calling Richard the landlord and not the king of England, he never preaches rebellion. And he mentions deposition only in the sense that Richard by his own conduct is deposing himself. York utters the most correct sentiments. Like the Bastard he is for supporting the existing government. And though he changes allegiance he is never for rebellion. As stated above, the gardener was against the deposition of Richard.

As well as being a study of medievalism, Richard takes his place among Shakespeare's many studies of the kingly nature. He is a king by unquestioned title and by his external graces

alone. But others have written so well on Richard's character that
I need say no more.

Lastly, for political motives, there is the old Morality theme of
Respublica. One of Shakespeare's debts in *Richard II* is to *Woodstock;* and this play is constructed very plainly on the Morality
pattern, with the king's three uncles led by Woodstock inducing
him to virtue, and Tressilian, Bushy and Green to vice. There
are traces of this motive in Shakespeare's play, but with Woodstock dead before the action begins and Gaunt dying early in it
the balance of good and evil influences is destroyed. Bushy,
Green and Bagot, however, remain very plainly Morality figures
and were probably marked in some way by their dress as abstract
vices. If Shakespeare really confused Bagot with the Earl of Wiltshire (according to a conjecture of Dover Wilson) he need not
be following an old play heedlessly: he would in any case look
on them all as a gang of bad characters, far more important as a
gang than as individuals, hence not worth being careful over
separately. Once again, as in the earlier tetralogy, England herself, and not the protagonist, is the main concern. Gaunt speaks
her praises, the gardener in describing his own symbolic garden
has her in mind. As part of the great cycle of English history covered by Hall's chronicle the events of the reign of Richard II
take their proper place. But here something fresh has happened.
The early tetralogy had as its concern the fortunes of England in
that exciting and instructive stretch of her history. *Richard II*
has this concern too, but it also deals with England herself, the
nature and not merely the fortunes of England. In *Richard II* it
is the old brilliant medieval England of the last Plantagenet in
the authentic succession; in *Henry IV* it will be the England not
of the Middle Ages but of Shakespeare himself. We can now see
how the epic comes in and how *Richard II* contributes to an
epic effect. Those works which we honour by the epic title
always, among other things, express the feelings or the habits of
a large group of men, often of a nation. However centrally
human, however powerful, a work may be, we shall not give it
the epic title for these qualities alone. It is not the parting of
Hector and Andromache or the ransoming of Hector's body that
make the *Iliad* an epic; it is that the *Iliad* expresses a whole way
of life. Shakespeare, it seems, as well as exploiting the most

central human affairs, as he was to do in his tragedies, was also impelled to fulfil through the drama that peculiarly epic function which is usually fulfilled through the narrative. Inspired partly perhaps by the example of Daniel and certainly by his own genius, he combined with the grim didactic exposition of the fortunes of England during her terrible ordeal of civil war his epic version of what England was.

This new turn given to the History Play is a great stroke of Shakespeare's genius. Through it he goes beyond anything in Hall or Daniel or even Spenser. Hall and Daniel see English history in a solemn and moral light and they are impressive writers. Spenser is a great philosophical poet and epitomises the ethos of the Elizabethan age. But none of these can truly picture England. Of the epic writers Sidney in *Arcadia* comes nearest to doing this. It is indeed only in patches that authentic England appears through mythical Arcadia, but that it can this description of Kalander's house in the second chapter of the book is sufficient proof:

> The house itself was built of fair and strong stone, not affecting so much any extraordinary kind of fineness as an honourable representing of a firm stateliness: the lights doors and stairs rather directed to the use of the guest than to the eye of the artificer, and yet, as the one chiefly heeded, so the other not neglected; each place handsome without curiosity and homely without loathsomeness; not so dainty as not to be trod on nor yet slubbered up with good fellowship; all more lasting than beautiful but that the consideration of the exceeding lastingness made the eye believe it was exceedingly beautiful.

This expresses the authentic genius of English domestic architecture.

Of this great new epic attempt *Richard II* is only the prelude. What of England it pictures is not only antique but partial: the confined world of a medieval courtly class. In his next plays Shakespeare was to picture (with much else) the whole land, as he knew it, in his own day, with its multifarious layers of society and manners of living.

Leonard F. Dean

RICHARD II: THE STATE AND
THE IMAGE OF THE THEATER

ONE WAY to describe the passage from *Richard II* to *Henry V*
is to say that the first play is a picture of a sick state in which
appearance and reality are at odds and that the last play is a
picture of a healthy state in which political appearance and
reality are unified in terms of the Elizabethan ideal of mon-
archy. This essay suggests that one sign of the political sickness
in *Richard II* is the presence, explicit or implied, of the Renaissance comparison between the state and the theater.[1] As the
suggestion is developed, the reader will be asked to grant that
political problems are also philosophical problems, and that plot
and character may be controlled expressions of a general moral
theme as well as dramatic accounts of typical personalities or
recurrent historical situations.[2] Examples of the state-theater
comparison from More and Machiavelli will be reviewed, not
to prove direct indebtedness by Shakespeare, but to show how
the comparison was available in two pertinent contexts, Christian humanism and Renaissance Realpolitic.

In More's *The Four Last Things* the image of "the lorel who
playeth the lord in a stage play"[3] serves the theme of *contemptus mundi*. The proud lord is told not to be so naïve as to
confuse a temporary role with lasting reality. Only a simple-
minded person will be "earnestly proud" of the "gay golden
gown" which has been assigned to him for the performance.
Death, like the end of the play, will show him who he really is.

From *Publications of the Modern Language Association*, Vol. 67,
1952, pp. 211-18. Reprinted by permission of the editor, *PMLA*,
and the author.

The make-believe lord will soon "walk a knave in his old coat," and the king likewise will "be borne out of his princely palace, laid in the ground and left there alone, where every lewd lad will be bold to tread on his head." We recall that Richard asks, as he nears the deposition, "What must the King do now?" and that he answers that he must lose name, jewels, gay apparel, "And my large kingdom for a little grave; . . . Or I'll be buried in the King's highway, . . . where subjects' feet / May hourly trample on their sovereign's head" (III.iii.143ff.). More turns directly from "the example of plays and players, which be too merry for this matter," to an image of the world as a prison—"all the while we live in this world we be but prisoners, and be within a sure prison, out of which there can be no escape." Richard also studies "how I may compare / This prison where I live unto the world"; and Shakespeare combines the images as Richard mentally populates his prison: "Thus play I in one person many people" (v.v).

In his *History of Richard III* (which Shakespeare had read in Holinshed), More uses the image of the stage play with greater complexity and applies it directly to politics. It is part of his comment on Richard's attempt to engineer a coronation.[4] The puzzled "on-lookers" try to adjust themselves to the mock coronation by recalling the difference between a stage play and real life. Their instinctive honesty, they reason, must be suppressed just as is the naïve inclination to recognize their friend the "souter" under the robes of the "Sultan." The comparison of the state to a theater, along with the sardonic pun on "scaffolds" and the dramatic scene of the spectators' humble puzzlement, enables More to imply that the lesson from proper behavior at a stage play can be applied to a state ceremony only when it in turn is a truly expressive fiction rather than a hypocritical disguise. If the central ritual of society, the coronation, is false, an instrument of self-interest rather than of renewed civic vitality and order, then the argument from dramatic aesthetics to social action is rendered fallacious. The "on-lookers" are stultified, not reborn with the new king; things are "done in good order" but only "for the manner sake." It should be noticed that the "commoners" are all the people who watch the histrionic actions of the "noble" performers. They are primarily a

part of a metaphor rather than a representation of a particular
political group. They are in effect all "poor men" who are
forced into "not be a-knowen what they know." It should also
be noticed that the pressure to act a part is two-way: the "on-
lookers" can not call things by their right names, but neither
can the king. The most efficient ruler (a Bolingbroke, for example) is still obliged to be a part of the play; he must try to
satisfy the "on-lookers" even though he scorns them. Fear of
political revolt is not emphasized as the cause of his play-acting; he is simply not allowed any being or existence outside
of the theater. The emphasis is not on personality or politics in
the modern sense, but on the general moral predicament. Christian humanism denies the possibility of release from play-acting
through secular policy, no matter how shrewd or skilful. The
release can come only in absolute or other-worldly terms. This
may be illustrated from More's *Utopia*.

The main framework of the first book of the *Utopia* is a dialogue between speakers named More and Hythloday about
the possibility of putting ideal values into practice. The book
ends with More's admonition that the idealist must remember
that life is a comedy: "What parte soever yowe have taken
upon yowe, playe that as well as yowe canne, & make the beste
of yt; and doo not therefore dysturbe & brynge owt of ordre
the hole matter, beycause that an othere, whyche is meryere &
bettere, cummethe to yowre remembraunce. So the case stondeth
in a common wealthe; & so yt ys in the consultatyons of Kynges
& prynces." [5] The first book criticizes Hythloday's unbending
idealism; he would disrupt the play, and the play is all there is. In
the second book Hythloday is freed from the actual world and
from the image of the theater which represents it, and is allowed to present a speculative account of a static and rationally
ideal society.

Although Machiavelli scorned the idealism of the utopists,
his realism was not a denial of the necessity for political play-
acting, but a change in point ot view toward it. Machiavelli's
prince, like More's Richard III, is obliged to pretend to be
virtuous in order to satisfy and manipulate the "on-lookers."
But whereas More implies that the best ruler in this world is
the one who consciously and reluctantly exercises as little du-

plicity as possible, Machiavelli implies that it is the one whose duplicity is complete. The "commoners" make the play-acting, the fox-like duplicity, necessary; they also make its success almost impossible, and thus call for the lion. The ideal Machiavellian state may be thought of as a theater in which the spectators are hypnotized by a perfect royal performance.

In turning now to *Richard II*, the first important point for the present discussion, and one that has not been emphasized,[6] is that Shakespeare's practical decision to follow Halle in beginning *Richard II* and the Henriad with the ordeal by combat between Bolingbroke and Mowbray not only provided him with a spectacular opening scene but also immediately involved him in the theatricalism of politics, and this presumably opened the way for the use of such an established motif as the state-stage comparison. The ordeal by combat was a social institution, like the courtroom process which developed from it, that was deliberately designed to impose a stereotyped or unnatural character upon the participants. The real feelings of Richard, Bolingbroke, Mowbray, and even Gaunt are necessarily masked to a large extent by the calculated neutrality of the ceremony. We sense at once that the king and the nobles are reading lines, that their social behavior is play-acting. Our subsequent judgment that the ceremony is a hypocritical disguise, that it will not cure the disorder which it is momentarily suppressing, is the product both of the glib ritualistic style and of those few lines in which contrary emotions come to the surface and announce themselves through a complication of the normally neutral and ceremonial tone. Most readers have heard the sarcasm in Richard's comment on Bolingbroke's charges against Mowbray: "How high a pitch his resolution soars." They have heard the private irony and the general mockery of noble sentiments in the king's assertion: "impartial are our eyes and ears. / Were he my brother, nay, my kingdom's heir . . ."

The last scene of the first act makes all of this explicit. The historical or social purpose of the ordeal by combat was well enough understood, and it had been stated by the king in his farewell to Bolingbroke: "Farewell, my blood; which if to-day thou shed, / Lament we may, but not revenge thee dead." By sublimating the issue and the participants, by purifying their motives, the ceremony was meant through its deliberate impersonality to end the call of blood for blood. But when the king and his followers are finally alone, they remove their masks, and we see that the ritual has left the actuality untouched. Their cynical scorn is emphasized by the manner in which they mock the elaborately formal language of the ceremony: "How far brought you high Herford on his way? / I brought high Herford, if you call him so, / But to the next highway, and there I left him. / And say, what store of parting tears were shed . . ." Aumerle exclaims that he was so revolted by the part he was expected to play that he saved himself by a kind of double hypocrisy, pretending that he was too choked with emotion to say farewell. And on the other side, Bolingbroke is also described as busy play-acting, paying "courtship to the common people; . . . wooing poor craftsmen with the craft of smiles." Richard accepts such behavior as a matter of course; it is simply a fact that must be faced and answered with force or guile.

In this theatrical state of England, well-meaning "on-lookers" like Gaunt and York are stultified. It is useless or dangerous for them to call things by their right names. Gaunt is obliged to mock his name, the thing he stands for, and to accept from Richard the insinuation that his very dying words are merely unbecoming play-acting. Gaunt's comparison of Eden and England emphasizes the distance this society has fallen from the state in which man and his function or role are indivisible and naturally good. Even the "charters and customary rights" of Time (in York's words), the laws which are man's best instrument in building a contractual state that will at least help to repair his fall, are here perverted imitations of themselves, "inky blots and rotten parchment bonds." York attempts to withdraw ("I'll not be by the while"), but Richard assigns him a surrogate role, "lord governor of England." He does not "Know how or which way to order these affairs / Thus thrust disorderly into my hands," but "somewhat we must do."

In this dilemma York is confronted by Bolingbroke, who is presented in a series of tableaux which define him as a man of policy adjusting his appearance to changing audiences. To the opportunistic elder nobles his "discourse hath been as sugar";

to the honorable young Percy he offers a gentleman's "covenant" sealing "heart" and "hand"; to the lawful York he presents a humble knee and challenges law for his proper "rights
and royalties"; to unnamed "on-lookers" he recites reasons for
the execution of Bushy and Green, to wash their "blood / From
off my hands here in the view of men . . ." Faced with this
situation, in which illegalities are compounded and the distance
from the ideal doubled, York is as stultified by the behavior
of Bolingbroke as Gaunt was by that of Richard. His only recourse is to "remain as neuter."

At this point Shakespeare returns to Richard, and in the interest of theme gives him a character that has scarcely been
prepared for in the first act. He now becomes the eloquent
spokesman for the ideal. In traditional imagery (garden, sun,
time, Christ, etc.), he identifies himself with perfect majesty
and that absolute value which has contempt for the world and
its ceremonies. But since Richard has been discredited from
the start as a Christian king and since he has now failed as a
politician, we read this in terms of personality as sentimentalizing and in terms of theme as another way of emphasizing the
emptiness of the name without the thing. It is this Richard of
course who has been called histrionic, but there is no reason to
think of him as being any more so than the politic Bolingbroke.
Neither is allowed to exist outside of the theater of the state.
Changes and developments which seem to be in the interest
of characterization are more basically another view of the general moral sickness, in which "Each substance of a grief," to
borrow Bushy's words, "hath twenty shadows . . ." The Bolingbroke "who never clogs his impulse to action with play-
acting" must still do everything for "the manner sake." Richard
would welcome a forthright and quicker end: "they well deserve to have," he urges, "That know the strong'st and surest
way to get . . . For do we must what force will have us do."
But before he can obtain the release of unconsciousness, he
must mount the "scaffold" and play out the scene which Bolingbroke is equally obliged to help enact. "What must the King
do now?" asks Richard approaching the "stage," and he wishes
now for roles from *contemptus mundi* that he has not earned.
Then with a self-consciousness that Bolingbroke cannot afford

to show and that must be stultified in himself, Richard concludes: "Well, well, I see / I talk but idly, and you laugh at me." But presumably Bolingbroke does not and can not laugh. He is in fact out of earshot, on the edge of the "stage." He confers sharply about tactics with the stage manager Northumberland: "What says his Majesty?" The answer is crudely psychological and practical: "Sorrow and grief of heart / Makes him speak fondly, like a frantic man; / Yet he is come." Then Richard enters and Bolingbroke advances, kneels, and begins to speak his lines in the mummery: "Stand all apart, / And show fair duty to his Majesty."

The garden scene (III.iv), which follows, and which is set off by its allegorical mode from the rest of the play, re-asserts the ideal of the state as Eden and the possibility of its approximation by an Adam-like king through keeping "law and form and due proportion" in the "sea-walled garden"—a possibility perverted by both Richard and Bolingbroke. The next scene (IV.i), the appellants before Bolingbroke, parallels the opening action of the play and shows that the political mode has not been really altered despite the change in rulers. This is attested by Bolingbroke's command: "Fetch hither Richard, that in common view / He may surrender; so we shall proceed / Without suspicion." Once more the care for the "common view" may be read as an extension of the theatrical trope rather than as simply fear of popular uprising. Much of the deposition scene, as many have observed, is an exchange of "stage directions": "Here, cousin, seize the crown—Now mark me—Read o'er this paper—Urge it no more—Mark, silent king—Say that again." Richard must go through the mockery of legal confession, but Bolingbroke too must suit his pace and words to Richard's, or "The commons will not then be satisfi'd." When Bolingbroke is "silent" it is not for lack of histrionic ability, as has often been suggested, but because his politic role will not let him speak his true thoughts. When Richard sees in the mirror that the "silence in the tortured soul" is the final "substance," we may understand, as the blindly patronizing Bolingbroke and Northumberland cannot, that the discovery applies not exclusively to the personality of Richard but also to the moral situation, that extinction of consciousness is the only successful end to this play. Again the mode has not been changed, but merely the principals, as York observes: "As in a theatre, the eyes of men, / After a well-grac'd actor leaves the stage, / Are idly bent on him that enters next . . ." The Abbot of Westminster likewise describes the scene as a "woeful pageant"; his solution, however, serves only to continue the theatrical events: "a plot / to rid the realm of this pernicious blot . . . shall show us all a merry day." That day is another scene stage-managed by Bolingbroke as he adjusts his policy to circumstances. He is, first, "smooth as oil" (to borrow his words from *I Henry IV*) with the deluded Duchess and her son: "Our scene is alter'd from a serious thing, / And now chang'd to 'The Beggar and the King'"; then he is "Mighty and to be fear'd" as he orders "for our trusty brother-in-law and the abbot . . . Destruction straight . . ." The politic actor is exposed by the Duchess' unwitting irony: "A god on earth thou art," and by the murderous Exton's closing quotation from this "god": "Have I no friend will rid me of this living fear?" And the exposure is completed at the end of the play when Bolingbroke is faced with Exton and his own doubleness: "The guilt of conscience take thou for thy labour, / But neither my good word nor princely favour."

Richard's famous prison speech in the next to the last scene is often read as the climax of his ineffectual attitudinizing; it is also (as has been suggested in connection with More's *The Four Last Things*) a dramatic analysis of the moral dilemma in the theater-like state. Richard's thoughts are "like the people of this world. For no thought is contented." His acting "in one person many persons" leads to the same judgment: "And none contented." The source of the discontent is the dualism at the basis of the stage play. "Things divine" (urged by More) are hard; "Thoughts tending to ambition . . . do plot unlikely wonders"; and as a result all "Thoughts tending to content flatter themselves." Time therefore cannot be redeemed, concludes Richard, and "any man that but man is / With nothing shall be pleased, till he be eas'd / With being nothing." But of course one who will succeed in "Redeeming time when men think least [he] will" has already been introduced. Bolingbroke's "unthrifty son" will miraculously resolve the dualism of the theatrical state. It is not surprising that the dying father is made to describe the coming change in terms of the state-stage comparison:

> God knows, my son,
> By what by-paths and indirect crook'd ways
> I met this crown; and I myself know well
> How troublesome it sat upon my head . . .
> For all my reign hath been but as a scene
> Acting that argument; and now my death
> Changes the mode. . . .
>
> (*II Henry IV* IV.v.184-200)

NOTES

1. The state-theater comparison is not noticed by Richard D. Altick in his "Symphonic Imagery in *Richard II*," *PMLA*, LXII (1947), 339-365. Altick does, however, follow Mark Van Doren, *Shakespeare* (New York, 1939), pp. 85-87, in remarking the insistent use of *tongue, mouth, speech, word,* and this leads him to the conclusion: "That words are mere conventional sounds moulded by the tongue, and reality is something else again, is constantly on the minds of all the characters" (p. 350). He also suggests that "the tragic sense of unsubstantiality in this play—the confusion of appearance and reality" is supported by the repeated use of *hollow* and *face* (pp. 350-351, 363).

2. The interpretation which emphasizes the contrasting personalities of Richard and Bolingbroke is widely known. According to it, the theatrical and narcissistic Richard, a poet manqué, goes down before the efficient Bolingbroke, who, in Oscar J. Campbell's words, "never clogs his impulse to action with play-acting or sentimentalizing" (*The Living Shakespeare*, New York, 1949, p. 181). The possible implications of the play as a mirror of a recurrent historical pattern have been stressed by Lily B. Campbell in *Shakespeare's "Histories"* (San Marino, 1947), pp. 168-212: "Shakespeare thus offered the follies of Richard II only as a background for the presentation of the problem that was so often discussed during Elizabeth's reign, the problem of the deposition of a king . . . He used Richard II as the accepted pattern of a deposed king, but he used his

pattern to set forth the political ethics of the Tudors in regard to the rights and duties of a king. It might equally well have served as a warning to Elizabeth and to any who desired to usurp her throne" (pp. 211-212).

3. *The English Works,* ed. W. E. Campbell and A. W. Reed (London and New York, 1931), I, 479; see pp. 462 and 482-483 for the stage image in conjunction with the unweeded garden, sickness, deposition and execution.

4. *English Works,* I, 447-8.

5. *The Utopia,* ed. J. H. Lupton (Oxford, 1895), pp. 98-9.

6. It is not discussed in the best and latest account of the play's sources: Matthew W. Black, "The Sources of Shakespeare's *Richard II," Joseph Quincy Adams Memorial Studies* (Washington, 1948), pp. 199-216. The first act offers little or no evidence for the interpretation which stresses the contrast between the personalities of Richard and Bolingbroke. Miss Campbell is mainly interested at this point in the possible resemblance between Bolingbroke and "the Earl of Essex, famous for his courtesy and in love with the power which popularity brought" (p. 198). E. M. W. Tillyard in *Shakespeare's History Plays* (New York, 1946) does deal at length with Act I, but he interprets the two tones or styles here and elsewhere in the play as representative of two eras, medieval and modern, that are at a moment of transition: "the 'poetry' of Richard is all of a world of gorgeous tournaments, conventionally mournful queens, and impossibly sententious gardeners, while Bolingbroke's common sense extends to his backers, in particular to that most important character, Northumberland. We have in fact the contrast not only of two characters but of two ways of life" (p. 258).

C. L. Barber

SATURNALIA IN THE HENRIAD

MY GENERAL CONCERN is with the relation of comedy to analogous forms of symbolic action in folk rituals: not only the
likenesses of comedy to ritual, but the differences, the features
of comic form which make it comedy and not ritual. I want to
point out what seem to me striking analogies between the
comedy in the two parts of *Henry IV* and the customary misrule of traditional saturnalian holidays.[1] These analogies, I
think, prove to be useful critical tools: they lead us to see
structure in the play. And they also raise fascinating historical
and theoretical questions about the relation of drama to other
products of culture. One way in which our time has been
seeing the universal in literature has been to find in complex
literary works patterns which are analogous to myths and rituals
and which can be regarded as archetypes, in some sense primitive or fundamental. I find this approach very exciting indeed.
But at the same time, such analysis can be misleading if it
leads to equating the literary form with primitive analogues.
When we deal with so developed an art as Shakespeare's, in so
complex an epoch as the Renaissance, primitive patterns may
be seen in literature mainly because literary imagination, exploiting the heritage of literary form, disengages them from the
suggestions of a complex culture. And the primitive levels are
articulated in the course of reunderstanding their nature—in-

From *English Stage Comedy: English Institute Essays,* 1954, pp.
22-51. Copyright 1955 by Columbia University Press. Reprinted by
permission of the publisher and the author. The original title was
"From Ritual to Comedy: An Examination of *Henry IV.*" It has been
retitled by the author.

deed, the primitive can be fully expressed only on condition that the artist can deal with it in a most civilized way. Shakespeare presents patterns analogous to magic and ritual in the process of redefining magic as imagination, ritual as social action.

Shakespeare was neither primitive nor primitivistic, for in his culture what we search out and call primitive was in the blood and bone as a matter of course. The problem was to deal with it, to master it. The Renaissance was a moment when educated men were modifying a ceremonial conception of human life to create a historical conception. The ceremonial view, which assumed that names and meanings are fixed and final, expressed experience as pageant and ritual—pageant where the right names could march in proper order, or ritual where names could be changed in the right, the proper way. The historical view expresses life as drama. People in drama are not identical with their names, for they gain and lose their names, their status, and meaning—and not by settled ritual: the gaining and losing of names, of meaning, is beyond the control of any set ritual sequence. Shakespeare's plays are full of pageantry and of action patterned in a ritualistic way. But the pageants are regularly interrupted; the rituals are abortive or perverted; or if they succeed, they succeed against odds or in an unexpected fashion. The people in the plays try to organize their lives by pageant and ritual, but the plays are dramatic precisely because the effort fails. This failure drama presents as history and personality; in the largest perspective, as destiny. At the heart of the plays there is, I think, a fascination with the individualistic use or abuse of ritual—with magic.

There is an intoxication with the possibility of an omnipotence of mind by which words might become things, by which a man might "gain a deity," might achieve, by making his own ritual, an unlimited power to incarnate meaning. This fascination is expressed in the poetry by which Shakespeare's people envisage their ideal selves. But his drama also expresses an equal and complementary awareness that magic is delusory, that words can become things or lead to deeds only within a social group, by virtue of a historical and psychological situation beyond the mind and discourse of any one man. This awareness of limitations is expressed by the ironies, whether comic or tragic, which Shakespeare embodies in the dramatic situations of his speakers, the ironies which bring down the selves or meanings which fly high in winged words.

We can explore one instance of this dramatic tension by looking in *Henry IV* at the relation of Shakespeare's festive comedy to ritual prototypes. As I see it, the gay comedy in Shakespeare is fundamentally saturnalian rather than satiric. A saturnalian pattern for organizing experience came to Shakespeare from many sources, in both social and artistic tradition. In the theatrical institution of clowning, the clown or Vice, when Shakespeare started to write, was a recognized anarchist who made aberration obvious by carrying release to absurd extremes. The cult of fools and folly, half social and half literary, embodied a similar polarization of experience. In social life, folly was customarily cultivated on traditional holidays such as Shrove Tuesday, Hocktide, May Day, Whitsuntide, Midsummer Eve, Harvest Home, and the twelve days of Christmas ending with Twelfth Night. The festival occasion provides a paradigm for the organization of impulse and awareness not only in those comedies where Shakespeare drew largely and directly on holiday motifs, like *Love's Labour's Lost*, *A Midsummer Night's Dream*, and *Twelfth Night*, but also in plays where there is relatively little direct use of holiday, notably *As You Like It* and *Henry IV*. The language that described festive occasions, or was used in them, provides a vocabulary for making explicit the "form of mirth" in the plays about pleasure. The attitudes adopted on holiday were archetypes in English Renaissance culture for the attitudes adopted about pleasure whenever people set out to have a good time. So Shakespeare's gay comedy dramatizes pleasure as release from normal limitations, and the judgments implicit in its humor primarily concern the relation between man and the nature celebrated by holiday, not relations between social classes or types. The plays give form to feeling and knowledge by a movement which can be summarized in the formula: *through release to clarification.*

I cannot even survey Shakespeare's development in relation to this holiday tradition here. My view, briefly, is that, although he began writing comedy with literary models (Plautus,

Italian comedy, and narrative romances), he found a satisfactory form for the whole play only when, in *Love's Labour's Lost* and *A Midsummer Night's Dream,* he shaped the whole action so as to express the release of a revel and so provide occasion for comic clarification of the relation between man's vital energies and the rest of his experience.

My thesis is that, in creating the Falstaff comedy, Shakespeare fused two main saturnalian traditions: the clowning customary on the stage, and the folly customary on holiday. Northrop Frye has effectively summarized the holiday aspect of Falstaff in saying that he is "a mock king, a lord of misrule, and his tavern is a saturnalia." [2] To see Falstaff in this role is not to suppose that Shakespeare arbitrarily imitates festivities at the Inns of Court or elsewhere, though such experience obviously is used. Rather, it seems to me Shakespeare arrives at such a figure by developing the saturnalian implications of the clown's role in the directions suggested by the saturnalian customs and sensibility of his time and in response to the need for such a role within the imaginative economy of the whole complex historical drama which he was working out.

The tradition of clowning had been from long before Shakespeare integrally related to the use of double plots. William Empson has made some fine observations here, to which I am indebted.[3] It was of course a practice, going back at least as far as the *Second Shepherd's Play,* for the clowns to present a burlesque version of actions performed seriously by their betters. Wagner's conjuring in *Dr. Faustus* is an obvious example. In the drama just before Shakespeare began writing, there are a great many parallels of this sort between the low comedy and the main action. One suspects that they often resulted from the initiative of the clown performer—he was, as Sidney said, thrust in "by head and shoulders to play a part in majestical matters"—and the handiest part to play was a low take-off of what the high people were doing. Though Sidney objected that the procedure was "without decency or decorum," such burlesque, when properly controlled, had an artistic logic which Shakespeare was quick to develop.

At the simplest level the clowns were foils, as one of the aristocrats remarks in *Love's Labour's Lost:*

'Tis some policy
To have one show worse than the king's and his company.

But burlesque could also have a positive effect, as a vehicle
for expressing aberrant impulse and thought. When the aberration was made relevant to the main action, clowning could
provide both release for impulses which run counter to decorum and the clarification about limits which comes from
going beyond the limit. Shakespeare used this movement from
release to clarification with masterful control in clown episodes
as early as *Henry VI, Part II.* The scenes of the Jack Cade rebellion in that history are an astonishingly consistent expression
of anarchy by clowning: the popular rising is presented throughout as a saturnalia, ignorantly undertaken in earnest; Cade's
motto is "then are we in order when we are most out of order."

The implications of a saturnalian attitude are more drastically
and complexly expressed in *Henry IV* than anywhere else, because here saturnalia is presented along with other kinds of
experience, in an environment, so that Shakespeare dramatizes
not only holiday but also the need for holiday and the need to
limit holiday. Misrule is more drastic and meaningful here than
in, say, *Twelfth Night*, because misrule is presented along
with rule and along with the tensions that challenge rule. In
the idyllic plays there is a humor of perspective which recognizes the limitations of the reigning festive moment by looking
outward, from it, to the work-a-day world beyond. But in the
two parts of *Henry IV*, holiday is balanced against everyday
and doomsday within the play. The comedy expresses impulses
and awareness excluded by the urgency and decorum of political
life, so that the comic and serious strains are contrapuntal, each
conveying ironies limiting the other.

The issue, so far as it concerns Prince Hal, can be summarized quite adequately in our key terms. As the nonhistorical
material came to Shakespeare in *The Famous Victories of
Henry the Fifth*, the prince was cast in the traditional role of
the prodigal son while his disreputable companions functioned
as tempters in the same general fashion as the Vice of the
morality plays. At one level Shakespeare keeps this pattern, but
he shifts the emphasis away from simple moral terms. The issue,

in his hands, is not whether Hal will be good or bad but whether he will be noble or degenerate, whether his holiday will become his everyday. The interregnum of a Lord of Misrule, delightful in its moment, might develop into the anarchic reign of a favorite dominating a dissolute king. Hal's secret, which he confides early to the audience, is that for him Falstaff is merely a pastime, to be dismissed in due course:

> If all the year were playing holidays,
> To sport would be as tedious as to work.

The prince's sports, accordingly, express not dissoluteness but a fine excess of vitality—"as full of spirit as the month of May"—together with a capacity for occasionally looking at the world as though it were upside down. His energy is controlled by an inclusive awareness of the rhythm in which he is living: despite appearances, he will not make the mistake which undid Richard II, who played at saturnalia until it caught up with him in earnest. During the battle of Shrewsbury (when, in Hotspur's phrase, "Doomsday is near"), Hal dismisses Falstaff with "What! is't a time to jest and dally now?" This sense of timing, of the relation of holiday to everyday, contributes to establishing the prince as an inclusive, sovereign nature. At the close of battle, in the moment of stillness when Hal stands poised above the prostrate bodies of Hotspur and Falstaff, his position on the stage and his lines about the two heroes express a nature which includes within a larger order the now subordinated parts of life which are represented in those two: in Hotspur, honor, the social obligation to courage and self-sacrifice, a value which has been isolated in this magnificently anarchical feudal lord to become almost the whole of life; and in Falstaff, the complementary *joie de vivre* which rejects all social obligations because "I like not such grinning honour as Sir Walter hath." At this point, Shakespeare was in a wonderful position to end *Henry IV;* he could have left Falstaff really dead, since he is effectually dead for the Prince. Instead the dramatist brought him back to life, jumping up like Bottom after Pyramus in a triumph which reminds one of the comic resurrections in the St. George plays.

When Falstaff jumps up, his apology for counterfeiting cuts deeply indeed, because it does not apply merely to himself; we can relate it, as Empson has shown, to the counterfeiting of the king. Bolingbroke knows when it is time to counterfeit, both in this battle, where he survives because he has many marching in his coats, and throughout the political career where, as he acknowledges to Hal, he manipulates the symbols of majesty with a calculating concern for ulterior results. L. C. Knights, noticing this relation and the burlesque, elsewhere in Falstaff's part, of the attitudes of chivalry, concluded with nineteenth-century critics like Ulrici and Victor Hugo that the comedy should be taken as a devastating satire on war and government.[4] But this is obviously an impossible, anachronistic view, based on the assumption of the age of individualism that politics and war are unnatural activities that can be done without. Knights would have it that the audience should feel a jeering response when Henry sonorously declares, after Shrewsbury: "Thus ever did rebellion find rebuke." This interpretation makes a shambles of the heroic moments of the play—makes them clearly impossible to act. My own view, as my introductory remarks will have made clear, is that the dynamic relation of comedy and serious action is saturnalian rather than satiric, that the misrule works, through the whole dramatic rhythm, to consolidate rule. But it is also true, as Empson remarks, that "the double plot is carrying a fearful strain here."[5] Shakespeare is putting an enormous pressure on the comedy to resolve the challenge posed by the ironic perceptions presented in his serious action.

This can be made clearer, I hope, by reference now to the scapegoat aspect of saturnalian ritual. We do not need to assume that Shakespeare had any such ritual patterns consciously in mind; whatever his conscious intention, it seems to me that these analogues illuminate patterns which his poetic drama presents concretely and dramatically. After such figures as the Mardi Gras or Carnival have presided over a revel, they are frequently turned on by their followers, tried in some sort of court, convicted of sins notorious in the village during the last year, and burned or buried in effigy to signify a new start. In other ceremonies described in *The Golden Bough*, mockery kings appear as recognizable substitutes for real kings, stand trial in their stead, and carry away the evils of their realms into exile or death. One such scapegoat figure, as remote as could be from Shakespeare, is the Tibetan King of the Years, who enjoyed, until very recently at least, ten days' misrule during the annual holiday of Buddhist monks at Lhasa. At the climax of his ceremony, after doing what he liked while collecting bad luck by shaking a black yak's tail over the people, he mounted the temple steps and ridiculed the representative of the Grand Lama, proclaiming heresies like "What we perceive through the five senses is no illusion. All you teach is untrue." A few minutes later, discredited by a cast of loaded dice, he was chased off to exile and possible death in the mountains.[6] One cannot help thinking of Falstaff's catechism on honor, spoken just before another valuation of honor is expressed in the elevated blank verse of a hero confronting death: "Can honour . . . take away the grief of a wound? No. . . . What is honour? a word. What is that word, honour? Air." And Hal's final expulsion of Falstaff appears in the light of these analogies to carry out an impersonal pattern, not merely political but ritual in character. After the guilty reign of Bolingbroke, the prince is making a fresh start as the new king. At a level beneath the moral notions of a personal reform, we can see a nonlogical process of purification by sacrifice —the sacrifice of Falstaff. The career of the old king, a successful usurper whose conduct of affairs has been skeptical and opportunistic, has cast doubt on the validity of the whole conception of a divinely ordained and chivalrous kingship to which Shakespeare and his society were committed. And before Bolingbroke, Richard II had given occasion for doubts about the rituals of kingship in an opposite way, by trying to use them magically. Shakespeare had shown Richard assuming that the symbols of majesty should be absolutes, that the names of legitimate power should be transcendently effective regardless of social forces. Now both these attitudes have been projected also in Falstaff; he carries to comically delightful and degraded extremes both a magical use of moral sanctions and the complementary opportunistic manipulation and skepticism. So the ritual analogy suggests that by turning on Falstaff as a scapegoat, as the villagers turned on their Mardi Gras, the prince can free himself from the sins, the "bad luck," of Richard's reign and of his father s reign, to become a king in whom chivalry and a sense of divine ordination are restored.

Now this process of carrying off bad luck, if it is to be made *dramatically* cogent, as a symbolic action accomplished in and by dramatic form, cannot take place magically in Shakespeare's play: the magical analogy can be only a useful way of organizing our awareness of a complex symbolic action. The expulsion of evil works as dramatic form only in so far as it is realized in a movement from participation to rejection which happens, moment by moment, in our response to Falstaff's clowning misrule. We watch Falstaff adopt one posture after another, in the effort to give himself meaning at no cost; and moment by moment we see that the meaning is specious. So our participation is repeatedly diverted to laughter. The laughter signalizes our mastery by understanding of the tendency which has been misapplied or carried to an extreme; this mastery leaves us free to laugh off energy originally mobilized to respond to a valid meaning.

Consider, for example, the use of magical notions of royal power in the most famous of all Falstaff's burlesques:

> By the Lord, I knew ye as well as he that made ye . . . .
> was it for me to kill the heir-apparent? Should I turn upon
> the true prince? Why, thou knowest I am as valiant as
> Hercules; but beware instinct; the lion will not touch the
> true prince. Instinct is a great matter, I was a coward on
> instinct. I shall think the better of myself and thee during
> my life; I for a valiant lion, and thou for a true prince. But,
> by the Lord, lads, I am glad you have the money. Hostess,
> clap to the doors: watch to-night, pray to-morrow.

Here Falstaff has recourse to the brave conception that legitimate kingship has a magical potency. This is the sort of absolutist appeal to sanctions which Richard II keeps falling back on in his desperate "conjuration" by hyperbole:

> So when this thief, this traitor, Bolingbroke
>
> .   .   .   .   .
>
> Shall see us rising in our throne, the east,
> His treasons will sit blushing in his face,
> Not able to endure the sight of day. . . .

The breath of worldly men cannot depose
The deputy elected by the Lord.
For every man that Bolingbroke hath press'd
To lift shrewd steel against our golden crown,
God for his Richard hath in heavenly pay
A glorious angel.

In Richard's case, a tragic irony enforces the fact that heavenly angels are of no avail if one's coffers are empty and the Welsh army have dispersed. In Falstaff's case, the irony is comically obvious, the "lies are like the father that begets them; gross as a mountain, open, palpable." Hal stands for the judgment side of our response, while Falstaff embodies the enthusiastic, irrepressible conviction of fantasy's omnipotence. The Prince keeps returning to Falstaff's bogus "instinct": "Now, sirs . . . you are lions too, you ran away upon instinct, you will not touch the true prince; no, fie!" After enjoying the experience of seeing through such notions of magical majesty, he is never apt to make the mistake of assuming that, just because he is king, lions like Northumberland will not touch him. King Richard's bad luck came precisely from such an assumption—unexamined, of course, as fatal assumptions always are. Freud's account of bad luck, in *The Psychopathology of Everyday Life,* sees it as the expression of unconscious motives which resist the conscious goals of the personality. This view helps to explain how the acting out of disruptive motives in saturnalia or in comedy can serve to master potential aberration by revaluing it in relation to the whole of experience. So Falstaff, in acting out this absolutist aberration, is taking away what might have been Hal's bad luck, taking it away in a real, though not magical way: the comedy is a civilized equivalent of the primitive rite. I hope it will be clear by analogy that a similar mastery of potential aberration is promoted by the experience of seeing through Falstaff's burlesque of the sort of headlong chivalry presented seriously in Hotspur.

In order to put the symbolic action of the comedy in larger perspective, it will be worth while to consider further, for a moment, the relation of language to stage action and dramatic situation in *Richard II.* That play is a pioneering exploration of the semantics of royalty, shot through with talk about the potency and impotence of language. In the first part, we see a Richard who is possessor of an apparently magical omnipotence: for example, when he commutes Bolingbroke's banishment from ten to six years, Bolingbroke exclaims:

> How long a time lies in one little word!
> Four lagging winters and four wanton springs
> End in a word: such is the breath of kings.

Richard assumes he has such magic breath inevitably, regardless of the breath of worldly men. When he shouts things like "Is not the king's name twenty thousand names? Arm, arm, my name!" he carries the absolutist assumption to the giddiest verge of absurdity. When we analyze the magical substitution of words for things in such lines, looking at them from outside the rhythm of feeling in which they occur, it seems scarcely plausible that a drama should be built around the impulse to adopt such an assumption. It seems especially implausible in our own age, when we are so conscious, on an abstract level, of the dependence of verbal efficacy on the social group. The analytical situation involves a misleading perspective, however; for, whatever your assumptions about semantics, when you have to act, to be somebody or become somebody, there is a moment when you have to have faith that the unknown world beyond will respond to the names you commit yourself to as right names.[7] The Elizabethan mind, moreover, generally assumed that one played one's part in a divinely ordained pageant where each man *was* his name and the role his name implied. The expression of this faith, and of the outrage of it, is particularly drastic in the Elizabethan drama, which can be regarded, from this vantage, as an art form developed to express the shock and exhilaration of the discovery that life is not pageantry. As Professor Tillyard has pointed out, *Richard II* is the most ceremonial of all Shakespeare's plays, and the ceremony all comes to nothing.[8] In Richard's deposition scene, one way in which anguish at his fall is expressed is by a focus on his loss of names: he responds to Northumberland's "My Lord—" by flinging out

> No Lord of thine, thou haught insulting man,
> Nor no man's lord; I have no name, no title,

> No, not that name was given me at the font,
> But 'tis usurp'd: alack the heavy day!
> That I have worn so many winters out,
> And know not now what name to call myself.
> O! that I were a mockery king of snow,
> Standing before the sun of Bolingbroke,
> To melt myself away in water-drops.

His next move is to call for the looking glass in which he stares at his face to look for the meaning the face has lost. To lose one's meaning, one's social role, is to be reduced to mere body.

Here again the tragedy can be used to illuminate the comedy. Since the Elizabethan drama was a double medium of words and of physical gestures, it frequently expressed the pathos of the loss of meaning by emphasizing moments when word and gesture, name and body, no longer go together, just as it presented the excitement of a gain of meaning by showing a body seizing on names when a hero creates his identity. In the deposition scene, Richard says "mark me how I will undo myself." Then he gives away by physical gestures the symbolic meanings which have constituted that self. When at last he has no name, the anguish is that the face, the body, remain when the meaning is gone. Of course there is also a narcissism in Richard's lines which, beneath the surface of his self-pity, relishes such reduction to his body, a self-love which looks towards fulfillment in that final reduction of all to the body which is death. This narcissistic need for the physical is the other side of the attitude that the magic of the crown should altogether transcend the physical—and the human:

> Cover your heads, and mock not flesh and blood
> With solemn reverence: throw away respect,
> Tradition, form, and ceremonious duty,
> For you have but mistook me all this while:
> I live with bread like you, feel want,
> Taste grief, need friends: subjected thus,
> How can you say to me I am a king?

In expressing the disappointment of Richard's magical expectations, as well as their sweeping magnificence, the lines make manifest the aberration which is mastered in the play by tragic form.

The same sort of impulse is expressed and mastered by comic form in the *Henry IV* comedy. When Richard wishes he were a mockery king of snow, to melt before the sun of Bolingbroke, the image expresses on one side the wish to escape from the body with which he is left when his meaning has gone—to weep himself away in water drops. But the lines also look wistfully towards games of mock royalty where, since the whole thing is based on snow, the collapse of meaning need not hurt. Falstaff is such a mockery king. To be sure, he is flesh and blood, of a kind: he is tallow, anyway. He "sweats to death And lards the lean earth as he walks along." (The image is strikingly reminiscent of Richard's melting snowman.) Of course he is not just a mockery, not just his role, not just bombast. Shakespeare, as always, makes the symbolic role the product of a life which includes contradictions of it, such as the morning-after regrets when Falstaff thinks of the inside of a church and notices that his skin hangs about him like an old lady's loose gown. Falstaff is human enough so that "Were't not for laughing, . . . [we] should pity him." But we do laugh, because when Falstaff's meanings collapse, almost nothing but make-believe has been lost

> *Prince:* Do thou stand for my father, and examine me upon the particulars of my life.
> *Falstaff:* Shall I? content: this chair shall be my state, this dagger my sceptre, and this cushion my crown.
> *Prince:* Thy state is taken for a joint-stool, thy golden sceptre for a leaden dagger, and thy precious rich crown for a pitiful bald crown!

Falstaff's effort to make his body and furnishings mean sovereignty is doomed from the start; he must work with a leaden dagger, the equivalent of a Vice's dagger of lath. But Falstaff does have golden words, and an inexhaustible vitality in using them. He can name himself nobly, reordering the world verbally so as to do himself credit:

> No, good my lord; banish Peto, banish Bardolph, banish Poins; but for sweet Jack Falstaff, kind Jack Falstaff, true

> Jack Falstaff, valiant Jack Falstaff, and therefore more
> valiant being, as he is, old Jack Falstaff, banish not him thy
> Harry's company: banish not him thy Harry's company:
> Banish plump Jack, and banish all the world.

I quote such familiar lines to recall their effect of incantation:
they embody an effort at a kind of magical naming. Each repetition of "sweet Jack Falstaff, kind Jack Falstaff" aggrandizes an
identity which the serial clauses caress and cherish. At the very
end, in "plump Jack," the disreputable belly is glorified.

In valid heroic and majestic action, the bodies of the personages are constantly being elevated by becoming the vehicles of
social meanings; in the comedy, such elevation becomes burlesque, and by the repeated failures to achieve a fusion of body
and symbol, abstract meanings keep falling back into the physical. "A plague of sighing and grief! it blows a man up like a
bladder." The repetition of such joking about Falstaff's belly
makes it meaningful in a very special way, as a symbol of the
process of inflation and reduction. So it represents the power of
the individual life to continue despite the collapse of social roles.
This continuing on beyond definitions is after all what we call
"the body" in one main meaning of the term: Falstaff's belly is
thus the essence of body—an essence which can be defined only
dynamically, by failures of meaning. The effect of indestructible
vitality is reinforced by the association of Falstaff's figure with
the gay eating and drinking of Shrove Tuesday and Carnival.
Whereas, in the tragedy, the reduction is to a body which can
only die, here reduction is to a body which typifies our power
to eat and drink our way through a shambles of intellectual and
moral contradictions.

So we cannot resist sharing Falstaff's genial self-love when he
commends his vision of plump Jack to the Prince, just as we share
the ingenuous self-love of a little child. But the dramatist is ever
on the alert to enforce the ironies that dog the tendency of
fantasy to equate the self with "all the world." So a most monstrous watch comes beating at the doors which have been clapped
to against care; everyday breaks in on holiday.

Part I can be summarized, in terms of our analogy, as the
reign of Carnival; *Part II* as his trial. To put Carnival on trial, run

him out of town, and burn or bury him is in folk custom a way
of limiting, by ritual, the attitudes and impulses set loose by
ritual. Such a trial, though conducted no doubt with gay hoots
and jeers, serves to swing the mind round to a new vantage,
where it sees misrule no longer as a benign release for the individual, but as a source of destructive consequences for society.
This sort of reckoning is what *Part II* brings to Falstaff.

But Falstaff proves extremely difficult to bring to book—more
difficult than an ordinary mummery king—because his burlesque
and mockery are developed to a point where the mood of a
moment crystallizes as a settled attitude of skepticism. In a static,
monolithic society, a Lord of Misrule can be put back in his place
after the revel with relative ease. The festive burlesque of solemn
sanctities does not seriously threaten social values in a monolithic
culture, because the license depends utterly upon what it mocks:
liberty is unable to envisage any alternative to the accepted order
except the standing of it on its head. But Shakespeare's culture
was not monolithic: though its moralists assumed a single order,
skepticism was beginning to have ground to stand on and look
about—especially in and around London. So a Lord of Misrule
figure, brought up, so to speak, from the country to the city, or
from the traditional past into the changing present, could become
on the Bankside the mouthpiece not merely for the dependent
holiday skepticism which is endemic in a traditional society, but
also for a dangerously self-sufficient everyday skepticism. When
such a figure is set in an environment of sober-blooded great men
behaving as opportunistically as he, the effect is to raise radical
questions about social sanctities. At the end of *Part II*, the expulsion of Falstaff is presented by the dramatist as getting rid of
this threat; he has recourse to a primitive procedure to meet a
modern challenge. We shall find reason to question whether this
use of ritual succeeds.

But the main body of *Part II*, what I am seeing as the trial as
against the execution, is of course wonderfully effective drama.
The first step in trying Carnival, the first step in ceasing to be
his subjects, would be to stop calling him "My Lord" and call him
instead by his right name, Misrule. Now this is just the step
which Falstaff himself takes for us at the outset of *Part II;* when
we first see him, he is setting himself up as an institution, con-

gratulating himself on his powers *as* buffoon and wit. He glories
in his role with what Dover Wilson has aptly called "comic
hubris." [9] In the saturnalian scenes of *Part I,* where we first see
him, it is impossible to say just who he is, for he is constantly
renaming himself:

> . . . let not us that are squires of the night's body be
> called thieves of the day's beauty: let us be Diana's foresters,
> gentlemen of the shade, minions of the moon; and let men
> say, we be men of good government. . . .

Here Misrule is asking to be called Good Government, as it is his
nature to do—though of course he does so with a wink which
sets real good government at naught. But in *Part II,* Falstaff sets
himself up at the outset as Falstaff:

> I am not only witty in myself, but the cause that wit is in
> other men.

> .   .   .   .   .

> A pox of this gout! or, a gout of this pox! for the one or the
> other plays the rogue with my great toe. 'Tis no matter if I
> do halt; I have the wars for my colour, and my pension shall
> seem the more reasonable. A good wit will make use of any-
> thing; I will turn diseases to commodity.

In the early portion of *Part I* he never spoke in asides, but now
he constantly confides his schemes and his sense of himself to the
audience. We do not have to see through him, but watch instead
from inside his façades as he imposes them on others. Instead of
warm amplifications centered on himself, his talk now consists
chiefly of bland impudence or dry, denigrating comments on the
way of the world. Much of the comedy is an almost Jonsonian
spectacle where we relish a witty knave gulling fools.

It is this self-conscious Falstaff, confident of setting up his
holiday license on an everyday basis, who at once encounters,
of all awkward people, the Lord Chief Justice. From there on,
during the first two acts, he is constantly put in the position of
answering his way of life; in effect he is repeatedly called to trial
and keeps eluding it only by a "more than impudent sauciness"
and the privilege of his official employment in the wars. Mistress

Quickly's attempt to arrest him is wonderfully ineffectual; but he notably fails to thrust the Lord Chief Justice from a level consideration. Hal and Poins then disguise themselves, not this time for the sake of the incomprehensible lies that Falstaff will tell, but in order to try him, to see him "bestow himself . . . in his true colours." So during the first two acts we are repeatedly put in the position of judging him, although we continue to laugh with him. A vantage is thus established from which we watch him in action in Gloucestershire, where the Justice he has to deal with is so shallow that Falstaff's progress is a triumph. The comedy is still delightful; Falstaff is still the greatest of wits; but we are constantly shown that fun involves fraud. Falstaff himself tells us so, with proud relish. Towards the end of the play, Hal's reconciliation with his father and then with the Lord Chief Justice reemphasizes the detached vantage of judgment. So no leading remarks are necessary to assure our noting and marking when we hear Falstaff shouting, "Let us take any man's horses; the laws of England are at my commandment. Happy are they which have been my friends, and woe unto my lord chief justice!" The next moment we watch Doll and the Hostess being hauled off by beadles because "the man is dead that you and Pistol beat among you."

Many of the basic structures in this action no doubt were shaped by morality-play encounters between Virtues and Vices, encounters which from our vantage today can be seen as part of the festive and scapegoat pattern. The trial of Falstaff is so effective *as drama* because no one conducts it—it happens. Falstaff, being a dramatic character, not a mummery, does not know when he has had his day. And he does not even recognize the authority who will finally sentence him: he mistakes Hal for a bastard son of the king's. The result of the trial is to make us see perfectly the necessity for the rejection of Falstaff as a man, as a favorite for a king, as the leader of an interest at court.

But, in justifying the rejection of Falstaff as a mode of awareness, I do not think that the dramatist is equally successful. The problem is not in justifying rejection morally but in making the process cogent *dramatically*, as in *Part I* we reject magical majesty or intransigent chivalry. The bad luck which in *Part II* Falstaff goes about collecting, by shaking the black yak's tail of his wit over people's heads, is the impulse to assume that nothing is sacred. In a play concerned with ruthless political maneuver, much of it conducted by impersonal state functionaries, Falstaff turns up as a functionary too, with his own version of maneuver and impersonality: "If the young dace be a bait for the old pike, I see no reason in the law of nature but I may snap at him." Now this attitude is a most appropriate response to the behavior of the high factions beneath whose struggles Falstaff plies his retail trade. In the Gaultree parleys, Lord John rebukes the Archbishop for his use of the counterfeited zeal of God—and then himself uses a counterfeited zeal of gentlemanly friendship to trick the rebels into disbanding their forces. The difference between his behavior and Falstaff's is of course that Lancaster has the sanction of the state on his side, a sanction supported, if not by legitimacy, at least by the desperate need for social order. This is a real difference, but a bare and harsh one. After all, Falstaff's little commonwealth of man has its pragmatic needs too: as he explains blandly to the Justice, he needs great infamy, because "he that buckles him in my belt cannot live in less."

The trouble with trying to get rid of this attitude merely by getting rid of Falstaff is that the attitude is too pervasive in the whole society of the play, whether public or private. It is too obviously *not* just a saturnalian mood, an extravagant aberration; it is presented instead as in grain, as the way of the world. Shakespeare might have let the play end with this attitude dominant, a harsh recognition that life is a nasty business where the big fishes eat the little fishes, with the single redeeming consideration that political order is better than anarchy, so that there is a pragmatic virtue in loyalty to the power of the state. But instead the dramatist undertakes, in the last part of the play, to expel this view of the world and to dramatize the creation of legitimacy and sanctified social power. Although the final scenes are fascinating, with all sorts of illuminations, it seems to me that at this level they partly fail.

We have seen that Shakespeare typically uses ritual patterns of behavior and thought precisely in the course of making clear, by tragic or comic irony, that rituals have no *magical* efficacy. The reason for his failure at the close of *Part II* is that at this point he uses ritual, not ironically transformed into drama, but magically. To do this involves a restriction instead of an extension of awareness. An extension of control and awareness is consummated in the epiphany of Hal's majesty while he is standing over Hotspur and Falstaff at the end of *Part I*. But *Part II* ends with a drastic restriction of awareness which goes with the embracing of magical modes of thought, not humorously but sentimentally.

It is true that the latter half of *Part II* very effectively builds up to this finale by recurrent expression of a laboring need to be rid of a growth or humor. King Henry talks of the body of his kingdom as foul with rank diseases, and recalls Richard's prophecy that "foul sin gathering head Shall break into corruption." There are a number of other images of expulsion, of which I can notice here only the very striking case where the rebels speak of the need to "purge the obstructions which begin to stop Our very veins of life." Henry himself, of course, is sick in the last half of the play, and there are repeated suggestions that his sickness is the consequence both of his sinful usurpation and of the struggle to defend it. Since his usurpation was almost a public duty, and his defense of order clearly for England's sake as well as his own advantage, he becomes in these last scenes almost a sacrificial figure, a king who sins for the sake of society, suffers for society in suffering for his sin, and carries his sin off into death. Hal speaks of the crown having "fed upon the body of my father." Henry, in his last long speech, summarizes this pattern in saying:

> God knows, my son,
> By what by-paths and indirect crook'd ways
> I met this crown; and I myself know well
> How troublesome it sat upon my head:
> To thee it shall descend with better quiet,
> Better opinion, better confirmation;
> For all the soil of the achievement goes
> With me into the earth.

The same image of burying sin occurs in some curious lines with which Hal reassures his brothers:

> My father is gone wild into his grave,
> For in his tomb lie my affections.

This conceit not only suggests an expulsion of evil, but hints at the patricidal motive which is referred to explicitly elsewhere in these final scenes and is the complement of the father-son atonement.

Now this sacrificial imagery, where used by and about the old king, is effectively dramatic, because it does not ask the audience to abandon any part of the awareness of the human, social situation which the play as a whole has expressed. But the case is altered when Hal turns on "that father ruffian" Falstaff. The new king's whip-lash lines stress Falstaff's age and glance at his death:

> I know thee not, old man: fall to thy prayers;
> How ill white hairs become a fool and jester!
> I have long dream'd of such a kind of man,
> So surfeit-swell'd, so old, and so profane;
> But being awak'd, I do despise my dream.
> Make less thy body hence, and more thy grace;
> Leave gormandising; know the grave doth gape
> For thee thrice wider than for other men.

The priggish tone, to which so many readers, including Bradley, have objected, can be explained at one level as appropriate to the solemn occasion of a coronation. But it goes with a drastic narrowing of awareness. There are of course occasions in life when people close off parts of their minds—a coronation is a case in point: Shakespeare, it can be argued, is simply putting such an occasion into his play. But even his genius could not get around the fact that to block off awareness of irony is contradictory to the very nature of drama, which has as one of its functions the extension of such awareness. Hal's lines, redefining his holiday with Falstaff as a dream, and then despising the dream, seek to invalidate that holiday pole of life, instead of including it, as his lines on his old acquaintance did at the end of *Part I*. Elsewhere in Shakespeare, to dismiss dreams categorically is foolhardy. And those lines about the thrice-wide grave: are they a threat or a joke? We cannot tell, because the sort of awareness that would confirm a joke is being damped out: "Reply not to me with a fool-born jest." If ironies about Hal were expressed by the context, we could take the scene as the representation of his

becoming a prig. But there is simply a blur in the tone, a blur
which results, I think, from a retreat into magic by the *dramatist,*
as distinct from his characters. Magically, the line about burying
the belly is exactly the appropriate threat. It goes with the other
images of burying sin and wildness and conveys the idea that
the grave can swallow what Falstaff's belly stands for. To assume
that one can cope with a pervasive attitude of mind by dealing
physically with its most prominent symbol—what is this but
magic-mongering? It is the same sort of juggling which we get
in Henry IV's sentimental lines taking literally the name of the
Jerusalem chamber in the palace:

> Laud be to God! Even there my life must end.
> It hath been prophesied to me many years
> I should not die but in Jerusalem.

One can imagine making a mockery of Henry's pious ejaculation
by catcalling a version of his final lines at the close of *Richard II:*

> Is this that voyage to the Holy Land
> To wash the blood from off your guilty hand?

An inhibition of irony goes here with Henry's making the symbol
do for the thing, just as it does with Hal's expulsion of Falstaff.
A return to an official view of the sanctity of state is achieved by
sentimental use of magical relations.

Henry IV is only one instance, but we can now at least suggest a few tentative conclusions of a general sort about the relation of comedy to ritual. It appears from this example that
comedy uses ritual in the process of redefining ritual as the expression of particular personalities in particular circumstances.
The heritage of ritual gives universality and depth. The persons
of the drama make the customary gestures developed in ritual
observance, and, in doing so, they project in a wholehearted way
attitudes which are not normally articulated at large. At the same
time, the dramatization of such gestures involves being aware of
their relation to the whole of experience in a way which is not
necessary for the celebrants of a ritual proper. In the actual
observance of customary misrule, the control of the disruptive
motives which the festivity expresses is achieved by the group's
recognition of the place of the whole business within the larger

rhythm of their continuing social life. No one need decide, therefore, whether the identifications involved in the ceremony are magically valid or merely expressive. But in the drama, perspective and control depend on presenting, along with the ritual gestures, an expression of a social situation out of which they grow. So the drama controls magic by reunderstanding it as imagination: dramatic irony constantly dogs the wish that the mock king be real, that the self be all the world or set all the world at naught. When, through a failure of irony, the dramatist presents ritual as magically valid, the result is sentimental, since drama lacks the kind of control which comes when the auditors are participants. Sentimental "drama," that which succeeds in being neither comedy nor tragedy, can be regarded from this vantage as theater used as a substitute for ritual, without the commitment to participation proper to ritual nor the commitment to the fullest understanding proper to comedy or tragedy.

Historically, Shakespeare's drama can be seen as part of the process by which our culture has moved from absolutist modes of thought towards a historical and psychological view of man by which all the world is a stage. But though the Renaissance moment made the tension between a magical and an empirical view of man particularly acute, this pull is of course always present: it is the tension between the heart and the world. By incarnating ritual as plot and character, the dramatist finds an embodiment for the heart's drastic gestures while recognizing how the world keeps comically and tragically giving them the lie.

NOTES

1. This paper is a development of an interpretation of *Henry IV* originally sketched in a more general article, "The Saturnalian Pattern in Shakespeare's Comedy," *Sewanee Review*, LIX (Autumn, 1951), 593-611. A number of sentences from the earlier account are included here in the course of setting up the problem of distinguishing comedy from ritual.

2. "The Argument of Comedy," *English Institute Essays, 1948*, ed. by D. A. Robertson, Jr. (New York, 1949), p. 71. Mr. Frye's essay brilliantly summarizes Shakespeare's relation to the whole tradition of literary comedy. His account of the way comic form

expresses reconciliation is a more generalized description than mine here; it outlines an "argument" which fits the saturnalian pole of comic release as well as the idyllic and millennial.

3. Mr. Empson's discussion of the effects achieved by such double plots is in *English Pastoral Poetry* (New York, 1938), chap. II.

4. "A Note on Comedy," *Determinations*, ed. by F. R. Leavis (London, 1934).

5. *Op. cit.* p. 46.

6. See James G. Frazer, *The Scapegoat* (London, 1914), pp. 218-23.

7. I am indebted to my colleagues Professor Theodore Baird and Professor G. Armour Craig for this general conception of the relations of names to developing situations.

8. See *Shakespeare's History Plays* (New York, 1946), pp. 245ff.

9. *The Fortunes of Falstaff* (New York, 1944), chap. v, "Falstaff High on Fortune's Wheel."

D. A. Traversi

HENRY V

THE POLITICAL SUCCESS aimed at by Henry IV is finally achieved, in the last play of the series, by his son. The general theme of *Henry V*, already approached in its predecessors, is the establishment in England of an order based on consecrated authority and crowned successfully by action against France. The conditions of this order are, again in accordance with the main conception, moral as well as political. The crime of regicide which had stood between Bolingbroke and the attainment of peace no longer hangs over Henry V—unless as a disturbing memory—and the crusading purpose which had run as an unfulfilled aspiration through the father's life is replaced by the reality, at once brilliant and ruthless, of the son's victorious campaign.

This, as critics have not always realized, is less a conclusion than a point of departure for the understanding of *Henry V*. It was the conditions of kingship, rather than its results, that really interested Shakespeare in these plays; and those conditions are viewed, by the time the last of them came to be conceived, in a light definitely akin to the tragic. The problem of political unity and that of personal order have been brought in the course of these historical studies into the closest relationship. Just as the state, already in *Henry IV*—Part II, is regarded in its divisions as a diseased body ravaged by a consuming fever, so is the individual seen increasingly as torn between the violence of his passions and the direction of reason; and just as the political remedy lies in unquestioned allegiance to an authority divinely constituted, so does personal coherence depend upon the submission

From *An Approach to Shakespeare,* 2nd revised edition, 1956, pp. 35-49. Reprinted by permission of Sands and Company Ltd.

of our uncontrolled desires to reason. The link between the two
states, political and personal, is provided in these plays by concentration upon the figure of the king. The problem of the state
becomes, in a very real sense, that of the individual at its head.
The king, who rightly demands unquestioning allegiance from
his subjects, is first called upon to show, through the perfection
of his self-control, a complete and selfless devotion to his office.
The personal implications of that devotion are considered in
Henry V.

It demands, in the first place, an absolute measure of self-
domination. Called upon to exercise justice and shape policies
for the common good, the king can allow no trace of selfishness
or frailty to affect his decisions. He must continually examine his
motives, subdue them in the light of reason; and this means that
he is engaged in a continual struggle against his share of human
weakness. As the play proceeds, we become increasingly aware
that there is in Henry an uneasy balance between violent passion,
in certain of its forms, and cold self-control. The control is, indeed, an essential part of his political capacity, but it has behind
it an unmistakable sense of constraint which makes itself felt
in his greeting to the French ambassador:

> We are no tyrant, but a Christian king;
> Unto whose grace our passion is as subject
> As are our wretches fettered in our prisons. (I, ii)

The harshness of the comparison is, to say the least, remarkable.
Such self-control is necessarily precarious. The passions, "fettered," treated with a disdain similar to that which, as Prince Hal,
he had already displayed to normal human feelings when his success as monarch depended upon the renunciation of his past, may
be expected to break out in forms not altogether creditable. Almost at once they do so. The French ambassadors, in fulfilling
their mission by presenting him with the Dauphin's tennis balls,
touch upon Henry's most noticeable weakness; they expose him
to ridicule and, worse still, they refer—by the observation that
"You cannot revel into dukedoms here"—to the abjured but not
forgotten past. Henry's reaction, in spite of an opening affirmation of self-control, takes the form of one of those outbursts which
are habitual with him whenever his will is crossed:

> . . . *I* will rise there with so full a glory
> That *I* will dazzle all the eyes of France,
> Yea, strike the Dauphin blind to look on us.
> And tell the pleasant prince this mock of his
> Hath turned his balls to gun-stones; and his soul
> Shall stand sore charged for the wasteful vengeance
> That shall fly with them: for many a thousand widows
> Shall this his mock mock out of their dear husbands;
> Mock mothers from their sons, mock castles down;
> And some are yet ungotten and unborn
> That shall have cause to curse the Dauphin's scorn.
>
> (i, ii)

"*I* will rise there"; "*I* will dazzle all the eyes of France." The Dauphin's gibe has set free Henry's "fettered" passions and they express themselves frankly in a cumulative vision of destruction. The tone of the utterance—the impact of "strike," the harsh reference to the balls which have been turned to gun-*stones,* the sense of irresistible, ruinous force behind "mock castles down"— reflects the new feeling and already recalls the later, more masterly picture of Coriolanus in action.[1] The sense of power, inhuman and destructive, has at last been unleashed in the king. The responsibility for coming events, already assumed in the same scene by the Archbishop, has now been further fastened upon the Dauphin, and Henry is in a position to announce his coming descent upon France with a phrase that incorporates into his new vehemence the convenient certainty of righteousness:

> But all this lies within the will of God.
> To whom I do appeal.

No doubt the conviction is, as far as it goes, sincere, for the will of God and the will of Henry, now fused in the egoistic passion released by the Dauphin's jest, have become identical.

It is not until the opening of the French campaign that Henry's utterances and preparations are openly translated into action. The poetry of war in this play deserves careful attention, for much of it is unmistakably associated with the element of constraint already noted in his character. The rhetoric with which he incites

his men to battle before the walls of Harfleur has about it a
strong flavour of artificiality and strain:

> . . . then imitate the action of the tiger;
> Stiffen the sinews, summon up the blood,
> Disguise fair nature with hard-favour'd rage;
> Then lend the eye a terrible aspect;
> Let it pry through the portage of the head
> Like the brass cannon; let the brow o'erwhelm it
> As fearfully as doth a galled rock
> O'erhang and jutty his confounded base,
> Swill'd with the wild and wasteful ocean.
> Now set the teeth and stretch the nostril wide,
> Hold hard the breath and bend up every spirit
> To his full height.
>
>   (III, i)

There is about this incitation something forced, incongruous, even
slightly absurd. The action of the warrior is an imitation, and an
imitation of a wild beast at that, carried out by a deliberate exclusion of "fair nature." The blood is to be summoned up, the
sinews stiffened to the necessary degree of artificial bestiality,
while the involved rhetorical comparisons which follow the
references to the "brass cannon" and the "galled rock" strengthen
the impression of unreality. In stressing this note of inhumanity
Shakespeare does not intend to deny the poetry of war which
he expresses most fully in certain passages from the various prologues of this play; [2] but, as later in *Coriolanus,* he balances the
conception of the warrior in his triumphant energy as "a grey-
hound straining at the leash" against that, not less forcible, of a
ruthless and inhuman engine of destruction. Both ruthlessness
and splendour are inseparable aspects of the complete picture.

Henry's treatment of the governor and citizens of Harfleur,
which immediately follows (III, iii), relates this conception of
the warrior to tensions already apparent in the king's own character. Not for the first time, Shakespeare places the two scenes
together to enforce a contrast.[3] The words in which Henry
presents his ultimatum are full of that sense of conflict between
control and passion which is so repeatedly stressed in his earlier
utterances. The grotesque inhumanity of his words, however, is

balanced by a suggestion of tragic destiny. Beneath his callousness there is a sense that the horrors of war, once unloosed, once freed from the sternest self-control, are irresistible. His soldiers, he warns the governor, are still held uneasily in check. "The cool and temperate wind of grace," whose control over passion has already been indicated as the mark of a Christian soldier, still exercises its authority; but "licentious wickedness" and "the filthy and contagious clouds" of "*heady* murder" threaten to break out at any moment. In his catalogue of the horrors of unbridled war stress is laid continually upon rape and the crimes of "blood." The "fresh-fair virgins" of Harfleur will become the victims of the soldiery, whose destructive atrocities are significantly referred to in terms of "liberty":

> What rein can hold licentious wickedness
> When down the hill he holds his fierce career?

The processes of evil, once unleashed, move along courses fatally determined; but Henry, as usual, having described them in words which emphasize their horror, disclaims all responsibility for them, just as he had once disclaimed all responsibility for the outbreak of the war. The whole matter, thus taken out of his hands becomes indifferent to him:

> What is't to me, *when you yourselves are cause,*
> If your pure maidens fall into the hand
> Of hot and forcing violation?

> (III, iii)

Yet this very assertion of indifference implies, at bottom, a sense of the tragedy of the royal position. Only this denial of responsibility, Shakespeare would seem to say, only the exclusion of humanity and the acceptance of a complete dualism between controlling "grace" and the promptings of irresponsible passion, make possible that success in war which is, for the purposes of this play, the crown of kingship.

For it would be wrong to suppose that Shakespeare, in portraying Henry, intends to stress a note of hypocrisy. His purpose is rather to bring out certain contradictions, human and moral, which seem to be inherent in the notion of a successful king. As the play proceeds, Henry seems increasingly to be, at

least in the moral sense, the victim of his position. The cunning
calculations of the Archbishop, with which the play opens, have
already given some hint of the world in which he moves and
which, as king, he has to mould to his own purposes; and the
treasonable activities of Cambridge, Grey, and Scroop are further indications of the duplicity with which monarchs are fated
by their position to deal. Somewhere at the heart of this court
there is a fundamental fault which must constantly be allowed
for by a successful ruler. It appears to Henry, in his dealings
with the conspirators, as something deep-rooted enough to be
associated with the original fall of man:

> Seem they religious?
> Why, so did'st thou: or are they spare in diet,
> Free from gross passion or of mirth or anger,
> Constant in spirit, not swerving with the blood,
> Garnish'd and decked in modest complement,
> Not working with the eye without the ear,
> And but in purged judgement trusting neither?
> Such and so finely bolted did'st thou seem:
> And thus thy fall hath left a kind of blot,
> To mark the full-fraught man and best indued
> With some suspicion. I will weep for thee;
> For this revolt of thine, methinks, is like
> Another fall of man.
>
> (II, ii)

It is remarkable that Henry, in meditating on this betrayal,
should return once more to that theme of control, of freedom
from passion, which is so prominent in his own nature. By con-
centrating on the functioning of the body, and on the sense of
mutual divergence between eye, ear, and judgement in the infinitely difficult balance of the personality, Shakespeare sets
spiritual control in contrast with a sense of anarchy which proceeds, most typically, from his contemplation of physical processes. "Gross passion"—the adjective is significant—is associated
with the irrational "swerving of the blood," and the judgement
which controls it needs to be "purged" by fasting ("spare in
diet") before it can attain a scarcely human freedom from "mirth
or anger." By emphasizing the difficult and even unnatural nature

of such control, Shakespeare casts doubt, at least by implication, upon that of Henry himself; but it is also seen to be necessary, inseparable from his office. The administration of justice, upon which depends order within the kingdom and success in its foreign wars, demands from the monarch an impersonality which borders on the inhuman. The state must be purged of "treason lurking in its way" before it can be led, with that single-mindedness of purpose which is both Henry's strength and his limitation, to the victorious enterprise in France.

It is clear, indeed, that *Henry V* represents, however tentatively, a step in the realization of themes fully developed only in the tragedies. Inheriting from his sources a conception of Henry as the victorious king, perfectly aware of his responsibilities and religiously devoted to the idea of duty, Shakespeare emphasizes the difficulties of the conception, the obstacles, both personal and political, which lie between it and fulfilment. When he discusses, during his debate with Williams and Bates on the eve of Agincourt (IV, i), the implications of his power, he approaches closely the spirit in which the great tragedies were to be conceived: "The king is but a man as I am; the violet smells to him as it doth to me; . . . all his senses have but human conditions: his ceremonies laid by, in his nakedness he appears but a man; and though his affections are higher mounted than ours, yet when they stoop they stoop with the like wing." The universality of the argument, in the true tragic fashion, transcends the royal situation. Men, differentiated by vain "ceremony," are united in their common weakness, and the most notable feature of human behaviour seems to the speaker to be its domination by impulse, its helplessness before the stooping of the affections. In this respect, at least, the king is one with his men; and just because he is so like them, because his senses too "have but human conditions," are constantly liable to break through the guard of rigid self-control imposed upon him by his vocation, there is something precarious and disproportionate in his absolute claim upon the allegiance of his followers.

The royal isolation is further underlined by Williams when he points out the spiritual consequences of a conflict for which the king, as unquestioned head of his army, is alone responsible: "For how can they [his soldiers] charitably dispose of anything

when blood is their argument? Now, if these men do not die
well, it will be a black matter for the king that led them to it."
These words repeat once more, but with a greater urgency, a
preoccupation with the horrors of war which Henry has already
expressed, even if he succeeded in shaking off responsibility for
them, to the French ambassadors and to the governor of Harfleur.
They imply, beyond the religious sense of responsibility which
derives from the traditional conception of Henry's character, a
contrast—already familiar—between the Christian law of "charity"
and the "blood"-spurred impulse to destruction that threatens it
in the acts of war with the consequences of unleashed brutality.
The connection between this conflict of flesh and spirit and the
tendency of human societies, states and families alike, to dissolve
by the questioning of "degree" into individual anarchy is not
established in this play as it is in the tragedies which followed.
But Hamlet himself might have reflected like Henry on the precarious basis of human pretensions, and Angelo defined in similar
terms the catastrophic realization of it brought about by his fatal
encounter with Isabella. Had Henry once followed his line of
speculation far enough to doubt the validity of his motives for
action, or—on the other hand—had he given free play to the
sinister impulses dimly recognized in himself, the resemblance
would have been complete; as it is, there is only a premonition, a
first indication of possibilities brought more fully to light in later
plays.

For the moment, Henry counters the implications of Williams's
argument by pointing out that soldiers "purpose not their death,
when they purpose their services." His sombre view of human
nature, however, impresses itself upon the king, attaches itself
to his own meditations, and is profoundly echoed in his own
words. Connecting war with sin, and in particular with overriding
passion, he repeats the tone of earlier statements: "Besides, there
is no king, be his cause never so spotless, if it come to the arbitra-
ment of swords, can try it out with all unspotted soldiers: some
peradventure have on them the guilt of premeditated and contrived murder; some, of beguiling virgins with the broken seals of
perjury." The result is, in part, a fresh emphasis upon meticulous
self-examination as a means of conserving spiritual health—"therefore should every soldier in the wars do as every sick man in his

bed, wash every mote out of his conscience"—and in the soliloquy
which brings the scene to an end, one of those outbursts of nostalgic craving for release which have appeared already in the
Second Part of *Henry IV* and which will be repeated more
urgently, with a more directly *physical* apprehension of existence,
in Hamlet's meditations and in the Duke's incitations to Claudio
in *Measure for Measure:*

> What infinite heart's ease
> Must kings neglect, that private men enjoy!
>
> (IV, i)

The craving for "heart's ease" in this long speech is still, generally
speaking, that of *Henry IV:* a desire to be freed from the burden
of an office in which human purposes seem fatally divorced from
human achievement. The development of the verse is still pains-
taking, leisurely in the expansion of its long periods, and a little
rhetorical; but there are moments which anticipate the association in *Hamlet* of this familiar nostalgia with a desire to be freed
from the incumbrances, the "fardels," the "things rank and gross
in nature," by which the flesh persistently seems to obstruct the
unimpeded workings of the spirit. Greatness is a "fiery fever"
which consumes its royal victim like a bodily disease, and the
contrasted peace of the humble subject is described with a curious ambiguity of tone:

> Not all these, laid in bed majestical,
> Can sleep so soundly as the wretched slave,
> Who with a body fill'd and vacant mind
> Gets him to rest, cramm'd with distressful bread.
>
> (IV, i)

In the association of peace with bodily fulness and vacancy of
mind, in the impression, harshly and directly physical, behind
"fill'd" and "cramm'd," there is a distinct suggestion of certain
descriptions of satiated, idle contentment in plays as far apart as
Troilus and Cressida and *Coriolanus.* Here already such imagery
represents a kind of residue, intractable and irreducible, in direct
contrast to the king's unceasing emphasis on the need for spiritual
discipline. It is no more than a suggestion, unabsorbed as yet into
the main imaginative design of the play; but, tentative as it is, it

does stand in a certain relationship to the clash of flesh and spirit, "passion" and "grace" which exacts continual vigilance from Henry, and which is slowly moving through these developments of imagery to more open dramatic realization.

A similar potential cleavage can be traced in the treatment of the two sides drawn up in battle at Agincourt. Shakespeare differentiates between the French and English forces in a way which dimly foreshadows the balance held in *Troilus and Cressida* between Greeks and Trojans, though here it is true that the unfavourable estimate of the English, which is scarcely compatible with the spirit of the play, is expressed only in the words of their enemies. The English are still morally worthy of their victory, but the French account of them at least anticipates the possibility of criticism. The French, combining a touch of the unsubstantial chivalry of Troilus with a more than Trojan emptiness, are, like the Trojans, defeated; the English, represented by them as gross and dull-witted, are as undeniably successful as the Greeks. Shakespeare's handling of the battle itself carries on this conception. The French, trusting in a thin and rhetorical belief in their own aristocratic superiority, rush hastily and incompetently to their deaths; the English, deriving their spirit from their king, win the day by their perseverance and self-control. Self-control, however, which is—as in Henry himself—not without some suggestion of harshness and inhumanity. Henry's righteousness does not prevent him from inflicting merciless reprisals on his prisoners, and there is something sardonic about Gower's comment that "the king, most worthily, hath caused every soldier to cut his prisoner's throat. O 'tis a gallant king" (IV, vii). By such excellence, Shakespeare would seem to say, must wars be won.

There is, indeed, a good deal of throat-cutting in this play. The king's ruthlessness, a logical consequence of his efficiency, needs to be seen against the human background which Shakespeare provided for it, most noticeably in the comic scenes which turn on the behaviour of the common soldiery. There is little room in *Henry V* for the distinctive note of comedy. Shakespeare's delineation of character is as clear-cut as ever, and his dialogue abundantly if discreetly flavoured with the sense of humanity; but there is about the humour of these scenes a cer-

tain dessicated flatness that contrasts sharply with the exuberance
of earlier plays. Bardolph, Pistol, and the others, no longer en-
livened by contact with Falstaff, quarrel like curs, and their jokes
turn largely upon the bawdyhouses which will inevitably swallow
them up when they return to England, and upon the cutting of
throats. "Men may sleep and they may have their throats about
them at that time; and some say knives have edges" (ii, ii).
Nym's remark, itself dark and enigmatic, is prefaced by a sombre,
fatalistic "things must be as they may," which modifies the comic
sententiousness of the speaker and implies a certain resigned
acceptance of the ordering of things. The humorous conception
of the character is toned down to fit in with a spirit no longer
essentially humorous; and this applies not only to Nym but to
his companions in arms. Fluellen and Gower, Williams and Bates
are distinguished, not by comic vitality or by the penetration of
their comments on men and events, but by their qualities of
common sense, by a tough sense of loyalty and dedication to
the work in hand; and it is by their devotion to the strictly practical virtues and by their definition of their various national
idiosyncracies that they live. This is no longer the world of
Henry IV—Part I. Falstaff himself, out of place in such company,
is remembered only in his death,[4] serving as a kind of measure
by contrast with which Shakespeare emphasizes his changing
vision of humanity. This death—it is worth noting—is ascribed
directly to the king, who "has killed his heart"; and Nym, repeating that phrase of resignation which conveys so much more than
he realizes of the spirit of this new world, relates Henry's treatment of him to an obscure, inherent fatality: "The king is a good
king; but it must be as it may; he passes some humours and
careers" (ii, i). His companions who remain must now accommodate themselves to the times. They do so by abandoning
domestic crime to follow their king to France. War and its
prospects of plunder are for them no more and no less than a
means of livelihood and an alternative to preying upon one
another. As Bardolph puts it: "We must to France together;
why the devil should we keep knives to cut one another's
throats?" (ii, i).

It is indeed significant, in making a final estimate of this play,
that the account in it of the death of Falstaff is, by common

consent, the most human and deeply felt thing in the entire action. In an action where the touchstone of conduct is success, and in which humanity has to accommodate itself to the claims of expediency, there is no place for Falstaff. Shakespeare had already recognized this, and prepared us for the necessary changes, in the "rejection" scene and in the events leading up to it; and now his end affects us tragically as the last glimpse of another and less sombre world. No doubt there is a patriotic purpose, not irrelevant to the play, and no doubt Shakespeare drew the character of his successful monarch with that purpose in mind. One aim does not, in Shakespeare, exclude another; and the fact remains that as we consider the uncompromising study of achieved success which rounds off this trilogy, a certain coldness takes possession of us, as it took possession of the limbs of the dying Falstaff, so that we find ourselves in a mood that already anticipates the great tragedies.[5]

NOTES

1. *Coriolanus* ii, ii.
2. See especially the Prologues to Acts iii and iv.
3. We have discussed a similar use of dramatic contrast in relation to *Henry IV*.
4. It might be added that his posthumous appearance, so to call it, in *The Merry Wives of Windsor* does not affect our main argument. The Falstaff of this comedy, as has been often observed, is no more than the halfhearted revival of a character originally conceived in a very different spirit.
5. The interpretation of *Henry V* here suggested receives some corroboration from H. Granville-Barker's *From Henry V to Hamlet* (British Academy Lecture, 1925).

Brents Stirling

"OR ELSE WERE THIS A SAVAGE SPECTACLE"

MODERN READERS are prone to find the tragedy of Brutus in his rigid devotion to justice and fair play. Many members of the Globe audience, however, believed that his virtues were complicated by self-deception and doubtful principle. In sixteenth-century views of history the conspiracy against Caesar often represented a flouting of unitary sovereignty, that prime point of Tudor policy, and exemplified the anarchy thought to accompany "democratic" or constitutional checks upon authority. Certain judgments of Elizabethan political writers who refer to Brutus are quite clear upon this point.[1] Although naturally aware of his disinterested honor and liberality, contemporary audiences could thus perceive in him a conflict between questionable goals and honorable action, a contradiction lying in his attempt to redeem morally confused ends by morally clarified means. The Elizabethan tragedy of Brutus, like that of Othello, is marked by an integrity of conduct which leads the protagonist into evil and reassures him in his error.

The distinction between modern and Elizabethan views of *Julius Caesar* is not the point of our inquiry, but it is a necessary beginning, for the older view of Brutus determines both the symbolic quality and the structure of the play. I hope to show that a sixteenth-century idea of Brutus is as thoroughly related to Shakespeare's art as it is to his meaning.

When a dramatist wishes to present an idea, his traditional method, of course, is to settle upon an episode in which the idea

From *Unity in Shakespearian Tragedy: the Interplay of Theme and Character*, 1956, pp. 40-54. Copyright 1956 by Columbia University Press. Reprinted by permission of the author and the publisher.

arises naturally but vividly from action and situation. Such an episode in *Julius Caesar* is the one in which Brutus resolves to exalt not only the mission but the tactics of conspiracy: having accepted republicanism as an honorable end, he sets out to dignify assassination, the means, by lifting it to a level of rite and ceremony.[2] In ii.i, as Cassius urges the killing of Antony as a necessary accompaniment to the death of Caesar, Brutus declares that "such a course will seem too bloody . . . ,/ To cut the head off and then hack the limbs." With this thought a sense of purpose comes over him: "Let's be sacrificers, but not butchers, Caius." Here his conflict seems to be resolved, and for the first time he is more than a reluctant presence among the conspirators as he expands the theme which ends his hesitation and frees his moral imagination:

> We all stand up against the spirit of Caesar,
> And in the spirit of men there is no blood;
> Oh, that we then could come by Caesar's spirit,
> And not dismember Caesar! But, alas,
> Caesar must bleed for it! And, gentle friends,
> Let's kill him boldly, but not wrathfully;
> Let's carve him as a dish fit for the gods,
> Not hew him as a carcass fit for hounds.

This proposed conversion of bloodshed to ritual is the manner in which an abstract Brutus will be presented in terms of concrete art. From the suggestion of Plutarch that Brutus' first error lay in sparing Antony, Shakespeare moves to the image of Antony as a limb of Caesar, a limb not to be hacked because hacking is no part of ceremonial sacrifice. From Plutarch's description of Brutus as high-minded, gentle and disinterested, Shakespeare proceeds to the Brutus of symbolic action. Gentleness and disinterestedness become embodied in the act of "unwrathful" blood sacrifice. High-mindedness becomes objectified in ceremonial observance.

A skeptical reader may ask why the episode just described is any more significant than a number of others such as Brutus' scene with Portia or his quarrel with Cassius. If more significant, it is so only because of its relation to a thematic design. I agree, moreover, that Shakespeare gains his effects by variety; as a recognition, in fact, of his complexity I hope to show that the structure of *Julius Caesar* is marked by reference both varied and apt to Brutus' sacrificial rite, and that this process includes expository preparation in earlier scenes, emphasis upon "mock-ceremony" in both earlier and later scenes, and repeated comment by Antony upon butchery under the guise of sacrifice—ironical comment which takes final form in the parley before Philippi.

Derived in large measure from Plutarch, but never mechanically or unselectively, the theme of incantation and ritual is thus prominent throughout *Julius Caesar,* and this is no less true at the beginning than during the crucial episodes of Acts II and III. In the opening scene of the play we are confronted with a Roman populace rebuked by Marullus for ceremonial idolatry of Caesar:

> And do you now put on your best attire?
> And do you now cull out a holiday?
> And do you now strew flowers in his way
> That comes in triumph over Pompey's blood?

For this transgression Marullus prescribes a counter-observance by the citizens in immediate expiation of their folly:

> Run to your houses, fall upon your knees,
> Pray to the gods to intermit this plague
> That needs must light on this ingratitude.

To which Flavius adds:

> Go, go, good countrymen, and for this fault,
> Assemble all the poor men of your sort;
> Draw them to Tiber banks, and weep your tears
> Into the channel, till the lowest stream
> Do kiss the most exalted shores of all.

And after committing the populace to these rites of atonement for their festal celebration of Caesar, the two tribunes themselves leave to remove the devotional symbols set up for his welcoming. "Go you . . . towards the Capitol;/ This way will I. Disrobe the images/ If you do find them decked with ceremonies./ . . . let

no images/ Be hung wtih Caesar's trophies." It is the hope of
Flavius that these disenchantments will make Caesar "fly an
ordinary pitch,/ Who else would soar above the view of men."

Act I, scene ii is equally unusual in carrying the theme of
ritual. It is apparent that Shakespeare had a wide choice of
means for staging the entry of Caesar and his retinue; yet he
selects an entry based upon Plutarch's description of the "feast
Lupercalia" in which the rite of touching or striking barren
women by runners of the course is made prominent. Caesar,
moreover, after ordering Calpurnia to be so touched by Antony,
commands: "Set on; and leave no ceremony out." It can be said,
in fact, that the whole of this scene is written with ceremonial
observance as a background. Its beginning, already described,
is followed by a touch of solemnity in the soothsayer's words;
next comes its main expository function, the sounding of Brutus
by Cassius, and throughout this interchange come at intervals
the shouts and flourishes of a symbolic spectacle. When the
scene is again varied by a formal reentry and exit of Caesar's
train, Casca remains behind to make a mockery of the rite which
has loomed so large from off-stage. Significantly, in Casca's
travesty of the ceremonial crown-offering and of the token offering by Caesar of his throat for cutting, Shakespeare has added a
satirical note which does not appear in Plutarch.

The process, then, in each of the two opening episodes has
been the bringing of serious ritual into great prominence, and
of subjecting it to satirical treatment. In the first scene the
tribunes denounce the punctilio planned for Caesar's entry, send
the idolatrous crowd to rites of purification, and set off themselves to desecrate the devotional images. In the second scene a
multiple emphasis of ceremony is capped by Casca's satire which
twists the crown ritual into imbecile mummery. At this point,
and in conformity with the mood set by Casca, occurs Cassius'
mockery in soliloquy of Brutus:

> Well, Brutus, thou art noble; yet I see
> Thy honorable mettle may be wrought
> From that it is dispos'd; therefore it is meet
> That noble minds keep ever with their likes;
> For who is so firm that cannot be seduc'd?

The next scene (I.iii) is packed with omens and supernatural portents, a note which is carried directly into II.i where Brutus, on receiving the mysterious papers which have been left to prompt his action, remarks,

> The exhalations whizzing in the air
> Give so much light that I may read by them.

Appropriately, the letters read under this weird glow evoke his first real commitment to the "cause":

> O Rome, I make thee promise
> If the redress will follow, thou receivest
> Thy full petition at the hand of Brutus!

Now appear his lines on the interim "between the acting of a dreadful thing / And the first motion" in which "the state of man / Like to a little kingdom, suffers then / The nature of a insurrection." This conventional symbolizing of political convulsion by inward insurrection is followed by the soliloquy on conspiracy:

> O, then by day
> Where wilt thou find a cavern dark enough
> To mask thy monstrous visage? Seek none, Conspiracy!
> Hide it in smiles and affability.

The conflict within Brutus thus becomes clear in this scene. First, the participant in revolution suffers revolution within himself; then the hater of conspiracy and lover of plain dealing must call upon Conspiracy to hide in smiling courtesy.

We have now reached the critical point (II.i.154ff.) to which attention was first called, an outward presentation of Brutus' crisis through his acceptance of an assassin's role upon condition that the assassins become sacrificers. Already a theme well established in preceding scenes, the idea of ritual is again made prominent. As the soliloquy on conspiracy closes, the plotters gather, and the issue becomes the taking of an oath. Brutus rejects this as an idle ceremony unsuited to men joined in the honesty of a cause and turns now to the prospect of Caesar's death. This time, however, honorable men do need ceremony,

ceremony which will purify the violent act of all taint of butchery
and raise it to the level of sacrifice. But although Brutus has
steadied himself with a formula his conflict is still unresolved,
for as he sets his course he "unconsciously" reveals the evasion
which Antony later will amplify: to transmute political killing
into ritual is to cloak it with appearances. We began with Brutus' passage on carving Caesar as a dish for the gods; these are
the lines which complete it:

> And let our hearts, as subtle masters do,
> Stir up their servants to an act of rage,
> And after seem to chide 'em. This shall make
> Our purpose necessary and not envious;
> Which so appearing to the common eyes,
> We shall be called purgers, not murderers.

The contradiction is interesting. In an anticlimax, Brutus has
ended his great invocation to ritual with a note on practical
politics: our hearts shall stir us and afterward seem to chide us;
we shall thus "appear" to the citizenry as purgers, not murderers.

Shakespeare never presents Brutus as a demagogue, but there
are ironical traces of the politician in him which suggest Covell's adverse picture of Roman liberators.[3] It is curious, in
fact, that although Brutus is commonly thought to be uncon-
cerned over public favor, he expresses clear concern for it in
the passage just quoted and in III.i.244-51, where he sanctions
Antony's funeral speech only if Antony agrees to tell the crowd
that he speaks by generous permission, and only if he agrees to
utter no evil of the conspiracy. Nor is Brutus' speech in the
Forum wholly the nonpolitical performance it is supposed to be;
certainly Shakespeare's Roman citizens are the best judges of it,
and they react tempestuously. Although compressed, it scarcely
discloses aloofness or an avoidance of popular emotive themes.

Act II, scene ii now shifts to the house of Caesar, but the
emphasis on ritual continues as before. With dramatic irony, in
view of Brutus' recent lines on sacrificial murder, Caesar commands, "Go bid the priests do present sacrifice." Calpurnia
who has "never stood on ceremonies" (omens) is now terrified
by them. News comes that the augurers, plucking the entrails
of an offering, have failed to find a heart. Calpurnia has dreamed

that smiling Romans have laved their hands in blood running from Caesar's statue, and Decius Brutus gives this its favorable interpretation which sends Caesar to his death.

The vivid assassination scene carries out Brutus' ritual prescription in dramatic detail, for the killing is staged with a formalized approach, ending in kneeling, by one conspirator after another until the victim is surrounded. This is met by a series of retorts from Caesar ending in "Hence! Wilt thou lift up Olympus," and the "sacrifice" is climaxed with his "Et tu Brute!" The conspirators ceremonially bathe their hands in Caesar's blood, and Brutus pronounces upon "this our lofty scene" with the prophecy that it "shall be acted over / In states unborn and accents yet unknown!"

The mockery in counterritual now begins as a servant of Antony enters (III.i.121) and confronts Brutus:

> Thus, Brutus, did my master bid me kneel,
> Thus did Mark Antony bid me fall down;
> And being prostrate, thus he bade me say:
> Brutus is noble, wise, valiant, and honest.

Here a threefold repetition, "kneel," "fall down," and "being prostrate," brings the ceremonial irony close to satire. Following this worship of the new idol by his messenger, Antony appears in person and with dramatic timing offers himself as a victim. In one speech he evokes both the holy scene which the conspirators so desired and the savagery which underlay it:

> Now, whilst your purpled hands do reek and smoke,
> Fulfill your pleasure. Live a thousand years,
> I shall not find myself so apt to die;
> No place will please me so, no mean of death,
> As here by Caesar, and by you cut off.

The murder scene is thus hallowed by Antony in a manner which quite reverses its sanctification by the conspirators. Brutus, forbearing, attempts to mollify Antony with his cherished theme of purgation:

> Our hearts you see not. They are pitiful,
> And pity to the general wrong of Rome—

As fire drives out fire, so pity pity—
Hath done this deed on Caesar.

Antony's response is again one of counterceremony, the shaking
of hands in formal sequence which serves to make each conspirator stand alone and unprotected by the rite of blood which
had united him with the others. The assassins had agreed as a
token of solidarity that each of them should stab Caesar. Antony
seems to allude to this:

Let each man render me his bloody hand.
First, Marcus Brutus, will I shake with you;
Now, Caius Cassius, do I take your hand;
Now, Decius Brutus, yours; now yours, Mettellus;
Yours, Cinna; and, my valiant Casca, yours;
Though last, not least in love, yours, good Trebonius.
Gentlemen all,—alas what shall I say?

It is then that Antony, addressing the body of Caesar, suddenly
delivers his first profanation of the ritual sacrifice:

Here wast thou bay'd brave hart;
Here didst thou fall; and here thy hunters stand,
Sign'd in thy spoil, and crimson'd in thy lethe.

And lest the allusion escape, Shakespeare continues Antony's
inversion of Brutus' ceremonial formula: the dish carved for
the gods is doubly transformed into the carcass hewn for hounds
with further hunting metaphors of Caesar as a hart in the forest and as "a deer strucken by many princes." Brutus agrees to
give reasons why Caesar was dangerous, "or else were this a
savage spectacle," and the stage is set for what may be called
the play's chief counterritual. Only Brutus, who planned the
rite of sacrifice, could with such apt irony arrange the "true
rites" and "ceremonies" which are to doom the conspiracy.

I will myself into the pulpit first
And show the reason of our Caesar's death.
What Antony shall speak, I will protest
He speaks by leave and by permission,
And that we are contented Caesar shall
Have all true rites and lawful ceremonies.

But exactly after the manner of his speech announcing the ritual sacrifice (ii.i) Brutus concludes again on a note of policy: "It shall advantage more than do us wrong."

Next follows Antony *solus* rendering his prophecy of "domestic fury and fierce civil strife" symbolized in Caesar's ghost which will

> Cry "Havoc," and let slip the dogs of war,
> That this foul deed shall smell above the earth.

The passage is similar in utterance, function, and dramatic placement to Carlisle's prophecy on the deposition of Richard II, and for that reason it is to be taken seriously as a choric interpretation of Caesar's death. Significantly, the beginning lines again deride Brutus' erstwhile phrase, "sacrificers but not butchers":

> O, pardon me, thou bleeding piece of earth,
> That I am meek and gentle with these butchers!

It is unnecessary to elaborate upon the Forum scene; Antony's oration follows the speech of Brutus with consequences familiar to all readers. But there is an element in Antony's turning of the tables which is just as remarkable as the well-known irony of his references to "honorable men." If we remember that Shakespeare has emphasized ritual at various planes of seriousness and of derision, the conclusion of Antony's speech to the populace will link itself with the previous theme. For here Antony reenacts the death of Caesar in a ritual of his own, one intended to show that the original "lofty scene" presented a base carnage. Holding Caesar's bloody mantle as a talisman, he reproduces *seriatim* the sacrificial strokes, but he does so in terms of the "rent" Casca made and the "cursed steel" that Brutus plucked away with the blood of Caesar following it. Again, each conspirator had struck individually at Caesar and had symbolically involved himself with the others; for the second time Antony reminds us of this ritual bond by recounting each stroke, and his recreation of the rite becomes a mockery of it. Brutus' transformation of blood into the heady wine of sacrifice is reversed both in substance and in ceremony.

For the "realists" among the conspirators what has occurred can be summed up in the bare action of the play: the killing of Caesar has been accomplished, but the fruits of it have been spoiled by Brutus' insistence that Antony live and that he speak at Caesar's funeral. "The which," as North's Plutarch has it, "marred all." With reference to Brutus, however, something much more significant has been enacted; the "insurrection," the contradiction, within him has taken outward form in his attempt to purify assassination through ceremony. This act, not to be found in Plutarch,[4] symbolizes the "Elizabethan" Brutus compelled by honor to join with conspirators but required by conscience to reject Conspiracy.

We have followed the ritual theme in *Julius Caesar* from early scenes to the point of Antony's oration, at which it is completely defined. There remains, however, a terminal appearance of the theme in the first scene of Act V. The ultimate clash between the idealism of Brutus and Antony's contempt for it comes during the parley on the eve of Philippi, at which Antony again drives home the old issue of ceremonial imposture. Brutus has observed that his enemy wisely threats before he stings; the reply is Antony's last disposition of the sacrificial rite:

> Villains, you did not so when your vile daggers
> Hack'd one another in the sides of Caesar,
> You show'd your teeth like apes, and fawn'd like
> hounds,
> And bow'd like bondmen, kissing Caesar's feet;
> Whilst damned Casca, like a cur, behind
> Struck Caesar on the neck.

Antony invokes the "hacking" which Brutus earlier foreswore, and he again inverts the cherished formula of sacrifice: once more the dish carved for gods becomes the carcass hewn for hounds. Over the body of Caesar he had previously employed the hunting-hound figure ("Here wast thou bay'd, brave hart."); the apes, the hounds, and the cur of these lines complete his vengeful irony of metaphor.

What, finally, is to be inferred from Antony's concluding passage on "the noblest Roman of them all"? Commonly found there is a broad vindication of Brutus which would deny an ironical interpretation. When Antony's elegiac speech is read plainly, however, its meaning is quite limited: it declares simply that Brutus was the only conspirator untouched by envy, and that, in intention, he acted "in a general honest thought / And common good to all." The Elizabethan view of Brutus as tragically misguided is thus consistent with Antony's pronouncement that he was the only disinterested member of the conspiracy. But Brutus is not to be summed up in an epitaph; as the impersonal member of a conspiracy motivated largely by personal ends, he sought in a complex way to resolve his contradiction by depersonalizing, ritualizing, the means.

Shakespeare's achievement, however, is not confined to the characterization of a major figure, for we have seen that the ceremonial motive extends beyond the personality of Brutus into the structure of the play. Exposition stressing the idea of ritual observance leads to the episode in which Brutus formulates the "sacrifice," and clear resolution of the idea follows in event and commentary. Structural craftsmanship thus supplements characterization and the two combine, as in *Richard II*, to state the political philosophy implicit in the play.

NOTES

1. See the discussion in J. E. Phillips's *The State in Shakespeare's Greek and Roman Plays* (New York, 1940), pp. 172ff. Mr. Phillips quotes at length from such typical spokesmen as Sir Thomas Elyot and Thomas Craig. His analysis of *Julius Caesar* on this basis is also illuminating. See also the present author's *The Populace in Shakespeare* (New York, 1949), p. 147, for a condemnation by William Covell of Romans who aroused civil dissension by covering their purposes "with the fine terms of a common good, of the freedom of the people, of justice. . . .". The parallel with Brutus is a very close one, and Covell, moreover, explicitly avows a topical relation of such Roman history to the civil tensions of Elizabethan England.

2. My article on the ritual theme in *Julius Caesar* (*PMLA*, LXVI, pp. 765ff.) appeared in 1951 as an early draft of this chapter. Some of my principal observations have been repeated by Ernest

Schanzer in a recent essay ("The Tragedy of Shakespeare's Brutus," *ELH* (March, 1955), pp. 1ff.; see pp. 6-8).

3. See the reference and quotation in note 1.

4. A reference at this point to Plutarch will serve both to clarify my meaning and to allay some natural doubts concerning the dramatist's intention. While it is true that the ritual murder of Caesar is Shakespeare's own contribution, the expository preparation for it in Act I comes from an episode in Plutarch in which Antony concludes the Lupercalian rites by offering a laurel crown twice to Caesar, and in which the tribunes are described as desecrating ritual offerings (*Shakespeare's Plutarch*, I, 92-3; see also II, 19-20). Hence we have basic ritual materials for Shakespeare's first two scenes present in one convenient block of his source which also offered a convenient beginning for the play. Does this prevent us from attaching significance to the unusual presence of ritual elements in the exposition scenes? I believe it does not, for two reasons. First, the choice of source material by a dramatist is itself significant; Shakespeare could have started the play with other episodes in Plutarch or with scenes of his own invention. Secondly, it is immaterial whether he began *Julius Caesar* with this episode in his source and, because of its wealth of ritual detail, was led to the theme of ritualized assassination, or whether he began with the theme and chose source materials for exposition which agreed with it. In either case the same remarkable unity between earlier and later parts of the play would have been achieved, and it is this unity which is important. Guesses about its origin in the playwright's composition are profitless. We do know that Shakespeare's Brutus plans the killing of Caesar as ritual, while Plutarch presents it as the very opposite of this. Plutarch's description of the assassination emphasizes, in fact, its resemblance to the hunting down of an animal, the very effect Brutus seeks explicitly to avoid in the "carcass-hounds" figure, and the one which Antony magnifies in his counteremphasis of imagery drawn from hunting. North notes it thus: "Caesar turned him nowhere but he was stricken at by some . . . and was hacked and mangled among them, as a wild beast taken of hunters." (*Shakespeare's Plutarch*, I, 101-2.)

Roy Walker

HAMLET: THE OPENING SCENE

Hamlet opens with a brief dialogue between two honest soldiers, the sentinels Francisco and Bernardo. Francisco, leaving
the stage almost at once, is seen no more. Marcellus, the third
honest soldier, enters with the scholar Horatio. In the second
scene Bernardo attests the appearance of the Ghost and then,
like Francisco, disappears from the play. Marcellus is in the
Ghost scenes at the end of Act One but is not seen afterwards.
Who are these soldiers? What is their deeper purpose in the
tragedy? Why does the Ghost first appear to them? And why
does it on this, the third night of its manifestation, come *twice*
before them?

The scenes in which the soldiers appear are at night and
out-of-doors. At the end of the first and fifth scenes the darkness
is giving place to dawn and the Ghost is compelled by approaching day to hasten his departure. Is this no more than traditional
ghost lore? The only other outdoor scenes take place by day.
After the night of the ghostly revelation Hamlet does not walk
out in the air again until near the end of the Fourth Act, when
again he finds himself among soldiers—this time the army of
young Fortinbras—and again he is stirred to action, or to the
resolve to act. These are soldiers that go to their graves like
beds, and in the last outdoor scene, in Act Five, Hamlet is in
the graveyard, where he struggles with Laertes over Ophelia's
dead body.

Neither Second Quarto nor Folio defines the situation of
scene one and the later Ghost scenes of the First Act. It is vari-

From *The Time Is Out of Joint,* 1948, pp. 4-9. Reprinted by permission of Andrew Dakers Ltd. Retitled by the editor.

ously indicated by later editors as the battlements or "a platform
before the castle."[1] Except for the Fortinbras and Graveyard
scenes all the action passes within the walls of the fortress. (I
suppose Polonius and his family to be domiciled within the
castle. The point need not be considered too curiously; it is
sufficient that no dramatic indication of separation between the
dwellings of the King and Polonius is given by the poet.)
Ophelia wanders from the castle only to meet muddy death
in the glassy stream. Hamlet himself is dispatched from it to
death which he escapes by luck and cunning and returns to
the fortress and to death. The walls of Elsinore are the confines
of the prison which is Denmark, the limits of the natural world
in which the tragedy takes place. To pass beyond the walls of
the castle is to pass from life towards death,[2] or, as the Ghost
does, to come from the world of the dead to the realm of the
living, revealing what lives among the dead and what dies in
the midst of life.

On the walls of this fortress we find Francisco, an armed
sentinel pledged to the defence of Denmark, standing guard in
the cold at midnight, peering outwards through the gloom for
the first sign of approaching danger. What it may be he knows
no better than Marcellus. For this is no routine watch, it is
strict and most observant, the counterpart of intense preparation
by day and night against a threatened attack, by whom, from
whence, the soldiers do not know.

From behind the sentinel a second figure emerges, hesitates,
and cries, "Who's there?" This should be the challenge of the
sentinel, but it is he who is challenged. He asserts his duty in
startled tones, "Nay, answer me; stand and unfold yourself."
The other replies in evident relief, "Long live the king." The
watchword and the familiar voice identify the speaker—"Bernardo?" "He."

It is a watchword indeed. These are the soldiers of the king,
but of which king? Long live the king who died and now re-
visits the glimpses of the moon? Or Long live the king who
killed the king, and who by the king's command shall die at
the hand of him who should be king and who dies himself in
the moment of becoming king? Long live the king! The phrase
echoes ironically in the memory. This is a loyalty true and valid

within its narrow limits, but there is not magic enough in the formula of allegiance to reigning power to unriddle the whole duty of man in such a world as this. The soldiers wield the power of death, but all their numbers cannot try the cause. They are powerless before the catastrophe which is

> the imposthume of much wealth and peace,
> That inward breaks, and shows no cause without
> Why the man dies.
>
> (IV. iv. 27-9)

Why did Bernardo challenge the sentinel? Because on the two preceding nights he and his comrade Marcellus have seen the dreaded sight, the apparition of the king to whom they gave their allegiance but two months past. Loyal vigilance has done the sentinel's job at Elsinore, and done it well. They have been the first to apprehend the approach of danger. On this third night, glimpsing the motionless figure of Francisco in the darkness, Bernardo is for a panic-stricken moment uncertain if this is the sentry to whose relief he has come or the silent martial figure of the king that's dead, and in sudden fear he cried out his challenge, "Who's there?"

Francisco has not seen the Ghost, nor have the others talked of it, but some premonition of evil troubles him, he is "sick at heart." Bernardo's quick enquiry, "Have you had quiet guard?" is answered by "Not a mouse stirring" and, fearing that the apparition may come upon him before his friends arrive, he urges the departing sentry to hurry Horatio and Marcellus to him, and at that moment they appear. Aware of the limitation of their understanding, the honest soldiers have entreated the scholar Horatio to share their watch, to speak to the Ghost. As he listens with tolerant scepticism to their story the spirit silently enters

> that fair and warlike form
> In which the majesty of buried Denmark
> Did sometimes march
>
> (I. i. 47-9)

departing when Horatio at last finds words and roughly charges it to speak.

Soon the three fall to talking of the significance of this visitation. Is it not somehow connected with their strict and most observant watch, with the day and night labour to produce the implements of war? Horatio attributes these preparations to apprehension of an impending Norwegian attack led by young Fortinbras, a prince of Norway whose kingly father was slain by King Hamlet, and whose sickly uncle (as we learn in the next scene) has ascended the throne of Norway. Bernardo seizes on the explanation:

> I think it be no other but e'en so:
> Well may it sort that this portentous figure
> Comes armed through our watch, so like the king
> That was and is the question of these wars.
>
> (I. i. 108-11)

Aggression from Norway to wrest back by force territories won by force from Norway! The danger is the familiar outward threat of war, the Ghost nothing more incomprehensible than a portent of war.

But Horatio, musing on forewarnings of "some strange eruption to our State," speaks of the fall of Julius Caesar and of the signs and portents that preceded it, speaks wiser than he knows, for Caesar fell not to a foreign conqueror but at the hands of his own people. Those signs and portents in old Rome heralded disaster, declares Horatio:

> And even the like precurse of fierce events,
> As harbingers preceding still the fates
> And prologue to the omen coming on,
> Have heaven and earth together demonstrated
> Unto our climatures and countrymen.
>
> (I. i. 121-5)

At these prophetic words the Ghost returns. For a moment it seems about to speak in response to Horatio's earnest conjuration, but a cock crows and as the spirit moves away, Horatio cries out, "Stop it, Marcellus."

Marcellus: Shall I strike at it with my partisan?
Horatio: Do, if it will not stand.
Bernardo: 'Tis here!

Horatio: 'Tis here!

                          Exit Ghost

Marcellus: 'Tis gone!
          We do it wrong, being so majestical,
          To offer it the show of violence;
          For it is, as the air, invulnerable,
          And our vain blows malicious mockery.

                                    (I. i. 140-46)

The soldiers' simple theory that the danger is an external attack against which their weapons guard the State of Denmark
will be shattered, when Fortinbras marches into Elsinore without striking a blow and mounts the Danish throne.

Shakespeare has shown us in this first scene of the play that
great evils threaten the little world of Elsinore, that they come
from within, that the castle walls no more protect the Court
of Denmark than might the walls of Jericho, that the soldier's
weapon is grotesquely inadequate to hinder the impending
doom or to command it to utterance in the everyday language
of humanity. The Ghost is prologue, prologue to the omen coming on, and that omen is Hamlet, prince of Denmark, who,
standing in a unique relationship to the Ghost, to the throne,
and therefore to the State, is capable of receiving the Ghost's
revelation and becoming the human instrument of the Ghost's
dread purpose, as the Ghost itself is the instrument of the unseen
Fates or forces by which it is doomed for a certain term to
walk the night. Soon enough the night will come down on Denmark again, the long night of the ending of the old order and
the birth of the new. But it touches not the soldiers who soon
now sink out of sight, or the scholar who is not of Elsinore but
Wittenberg, something of an onlooker at the tragedy although
a true and faithful friend to its hero-victim. Now, for the only
time in the play we share in a morning's holy office.[3] Night,
like Hamlet in his suits of solemn black, passes from the stage
and dawn, as fair as sweet Ophelia, touches us with beauty, as
Horatio says:

          But look, the Morn, in russet mantle clad,
          Walks o'er the dew of yon high eastern hill.

                                    (I. i. 166-7)

NOTES

1. From the allusions I. ii. 213 and 251-2.

2. Rosencrantz and Guildenstern also go from the castle to death; lesser figures drawn into the orbit of Hamlet's destiny. Cornelius and Voltimand go and return, and so does Laertes. These ambassadors, like Reynaldo, are not within the central focus of the drama. Laertes, at first a minor figure, is drawn into the King's orbit on his return to Elsinore, and thus involved in the final catastrophe. The characters of the play compose a hierarchy in which the subsidiary and less symbolic persons serve to heighten our awareness of the destiny that shapes the ends of the principal characters.

3. Cf. *Cymbeline*. III. iii. 4.

W. H. Clemen

THE IMAGERY OF *HAMLET*

THE surprisingly new possibilities of language which make this play appear a turning-point in the development of Shakespeare's style [1] seem to have their origin in the personality of Hamlet. The new language comes from him, in him it attains to perfection. The language of the King and the Queen, of Laertes and Polonius, although subtly adapted to their character, still treads the well-worn paths; it is less novel, because the people by whom it is spoken are not in need of a new form of expression—on the contrary, they may be more aptly characterized by a conventional mode of speech. But Hamlet's nature can only find expression in a wholly new language. This also applies to the imagery in the play. It is Hamlet who creates the most significant images, images marking the atmosphere and theme of the play, which are paler and less pregnant in the speech of the other characters. Hamlet's way of employing images is unique in Shakespeare's drama. When he begins to speak, the images fairly stream to him without the slightest effort—not as similes or conscious paraphrases, but as immediate and spontaneous visions.[2] Hamlet's imagery shows us that whenever he thinks and speaks, he is at the same time a visionary, a seer, for whom the living things of the world about him embody and symbolize thought. His first monologue may show this; the short space of time which lies between his father's death and his mother's remarriage is to him a series of pictures taken from real life:

From *The Development of Shakespeare's Imagery*, 1951, pp. 106-18. Copyright 1951 by Harvard University Press. Reprinted by permission of Harvard University Press and Methuen and Co., Ltd. The title has been changed from *Hamlet* by the editor.

> A little month, or ere those shoes were old
> With which she follow'd my poor father's body
> Like Niobe, all tears:
>
> > (I. ii. 147)

> Ere yet the salt of most unrighteous tears
> Had left the flushing in her galled eyes,
>
> > (I. ii. 154)

or a little later, addressed to Horatio:

> > the funeral baked meats
> > Did coldly furnish forth the marriage tables.
> >
> > > (I. ii. 180)

These are no poetic similes, but keen observations of reality. Hamlet does not translate the general thought into an image paraphrasing it; on the contrary, he uses the opposite method: he refers the generalization to the events and objects of the reality underlying the thought. This sense of reality finds expression in all the images Hamlet employs. Peculiar to them all is that closeness to reality which is often carried to the point of an unsparing poignancy.[3] They are mostly very concrete and precise, simple and, as to their subject matter, easy to understand; common and ordinary things, things familiar to the man in the street dominate, rather than lofty, strange or rare objects.[4] Illuminating in this connection is the absence of hyperbole,[5] of great dimensions in his imagery. In contrast to Othello or Lear, for example, who awaken heaven and the elements in their imagery [6] and who lend expression to their mighty passions in images of soaring magnificence, Hamlet prefers to keep his language within the scope of reality, indeed, within the everyday world. It is not spacious scenery and nature which dominate in Hamlet's imagery, but rather trades and callings, objects of daily use, popular games and technical terms; his images are not beautiful, poetic, magnificent, but they always hit their mark, the matter in question, with surprisingly unerring sureness. They do not waft the things of reality into a dreamworld of the imagination; on the contrary, they make them truly *real*, they reveal their inmost, naked being. All this, the wealth of realistic observation, of real objects, of associations taken from everyday life, is enough to prove that Hamlet is no abstract thinker and dreamer. As his imagery betrays to us, he is rather a man gifted with greater powers of observation than the others. He is capable of scanning reality with a keener eye and of pene- trating the veil of semblance even to the very core of things. "I know not seems."

At the same time, Hamlet's imagery reveals the hero's wide educational background, his many-sidedness and the extra- ordinary range of his experience.[7] That metaphors taken from natural sciences are specially frequent in Hamlet's language again emphasizes his power of observation, his critical objec- tive way of looking at things.[8] But Hamlet is also at home in classical antiquity or Greek mythology,[9] in the terminology of law,[10] he is not only familiar with the theatre and with acting —as everyone knows—but also with the fine arts,[11] with falconry and hunting,[12] with the soldier's trade and strategy,[13] with the courtier's way of life. All these spheres disclosing Hamlet's per- sonality as that of a "courtier, soldier and scholar" (in Ophelia's words, III. i. 159) are evoked by the imagery which, however, turns them to living account by a fit application to situations, persons and moods. Hamlet commands so many levels of ex- pression that he can attune his diction as well as his imagery to the situation and to the person to whom he is speaking. This adaptability and versatility is another feature in Hamlet's use of language which can also be traced in his imagery.

At the same time, this wide range of imagery can, in certain passages, serve to give relief to his conflicting moods, to his being torn between extremes and to the abruptness of his changes of mood. This characteristic which has been particularly emphasized and partly attributed to "melancholy" by L. L. Schücking and John Dover Wilson,[14] also expresses itself in the sudden change of language and in the juxtaposition of pas- sages which are sharply contrasted in their diction. With no other character in Shakespeare do we find this sharp contrast between images marked by a pensive mood and those which unsparingly use vulgar words and display a frivolous and sar- castic disgust for the world.[15]

Let us consider further how Hamlet's use of imagery reflects his ability to penetrate to the real nature of men and things

and his relentless breaking down of the barriers raised by hypocrisy. Many of his images seem in fact designed to unmask men;
they are meant to strip them of their fine appearances and to
show them up in their true nature. Thus, by means of the
simile of fortune's pipe, Hamlet shows Rosencrantz and Guildenstern that he has seen through their intent, and thus he un-
masks Rosencrantz when he calls him a "sponge," "that soaks
up the king's countenance" (IV. ii. 16). He splits his mother's
heart "in twain," because he tells her the truth from which she
shrinks and which she conceals from herself. And again it is
by means of images that he seeks to lead her to a recognition of
the truth. He renews the memory of his father in her by means
of that forceful description of his outward appearance which
could be compared with Hyperion, Mars and Mercury. On the
other hand, another series of comparisons seeks to bring home
to his mother the real nature of Claudius:

> a mildew'd ear,
> Blasting his wholesome brother.
>
> > (III. iv. 64)
>
> a vice of kings;
> A cutpurse of the empire and the rule,
> That from a shelf the precious diadem stole,
> And put it in his pocket!
>
> . . . . . .
>
> A king of shreds and patches,
>
> > (III. iv. 98)

So Hamlet sees through men and things. He perceives what is
false, visualizing his recognition through imagery.

Hamlet's imagery, which thus calls things by their right
names, acquires a peculiar freedom from his feigned madness.
Hamlet needs images for his "antic disposition." He would betray himself if he used open direct language. Hence he must
speak ambiguously and cloak his real meaning under quibbles
and puns,[16] images and parables. The other characters do not
understand him and continue to think he is mad, but the audience can gain an insight into the true situation. Under the protection of that mask of "antic disposition," Hamlet says more

shrewd things than all the rest of the courtiers together.[17] So we find the images here in an entirely new role, unique in Shakespeare's drama. Only the images of the fool in *King Lear* have a similar function.

Hamlet suffers an injustice when he is accused of merely theoretical and abstract speculation which would lead him away from reality. His thoughts carry further than those of others, because he sees more and deeper than they, not because he would leave reality unheeded. It is true that his is a nature more prone to thought than to action; but that signifies by no means, as the Hamlet critics would often have us believe, that he is a philosopher and dreamer and no man of the world. When, in the graveyard scene, he holds Yorick's skull in his hand, he sees *more* in it than the others, for whom the skull is merely a lifeless object. And precisely because he is more deeply moved by the reality and significance of these earthly remains, his fantasy is able to follow the "noble dust of Alexander" through all its metamorphoses. The comparisons which spring from this faculty of thinking a thing to the end, as it were, derive in fact from a more intense experience of reality.

It is a fundamental tenet of Hamlet criticism that Hamlet's over-developed intellect makes it impossible for him to act. In this connection the following famous passage is generally quoted:

> And thus the native hue of resolution
> Is sicklied o'er with the pale cast of thought,
> And enterprises of great pith and moment
> With this regard their currents turn awry,
> And lose the name of action.—
>
> (III. i. 85)

The customary interpretation of this passage, "reflection hinders action," does it an injustice. For Hamlet does not say "reflection hinders action," he simply utters this image. The fact that he does not utter that general maxim, but this image, makes all the difference. For this image is the unique and specific form of expression of the thought underlying it, it cannot be separated from it. If we say "reflection hinders action," we make a false generalization; we replace a specific formulation by an apothegm. And thereby we eradicate in this passage that quality which is peculiarly Shakespeare's or, what is more, peculiarly Hamlet's. Here the image does not serve the purpose of merely casting a decorative cloak about the thought; it is much rather an intrinsic part of the thought.

"Reflection hinders action"—this phrase carries in it something absolute, something damning. We sense a moralizing undertone. Action and reflection are thus conceived of as two mutually inimical abstract principles. But not so in Shakespeare's metaphorical language. "Native hue of resolution" suggests that Shakespeare viewed resolution as an innate human quality, not as a moral virtue to be consciously striven after. But the Hamlet-criticism of the nineteenth century saw the problem in this light of a moral virtue. We see, then, that a careful consideration of Shakespeare's imagery may sometimes correct false interpretations.[18]

"Reflection hinders action." Polonius, the sententious lover of maxims, could have said this, for a general saying carries no sense of personal obligation; it places a distance between the speaker and what he would say. But just as it is characteristic of Polonius to utter banalities and sententious effusions,[19] so, too, it is characteristic of Hamlet, to express even those things which would have permitted of a generalizing formulation, in a language which bears the stamp of a unique and personal experience.

Hamlet sees this problem under the aspect of a process of the human organism.[20] The original bright colouring of the skin is concealed by an ailment. Thus the relation between thought and action appears not as an opposition between two abstract principles between which a free choice is possible, but as an unavoidable condition of human nature. The image of the leprous ailment emphasizes the malignant, disabling, slowly disintegrating nature of the process. It is by no mere chance that Hamlet employs just this image. Perusing the description which the ghost of Hamlet's father gives of his poisoning by Claudius (I. v. 63) one cannot help being struck by the vividness with which the process of poisoning, the malicious spreading of the disease, is portrayed:

> And in the porches of mine ears did pour
> The leperous distilment; whose effect

Holds such an enmity with blood of man
That swift as quicksilver it courses through
The natural gates and alleys of the body,
And with a sudden vigour it doth posset
And curd, like eager droppings into milk,
The thin and wholesome blood: so did it mine;
And a most instant tetter bark'd about,
Most lazar-like, with vile and loathsome crust,
All my smooth body.

(I. v. 63)

A real event described at the beginning of the drama has exercised a profound influence upon the whole imagery of the play. What is later metaphor, is here still reality. The picture of the leprous skin disease, which is here—in the first act—described by Hamlet's father, has buried itself deep in Hamlet's imagination and continues to lead its subterranean existence, as it were, until it reappears in metaphorical form.

As Miss Spurgeon has shown, the idea of an ulcer dominates the imagery, infecting and fatally eating away the whole body; on every occasion repulsive images of sickness make their appearance.[21] It is certain that this imagery is derived from that one real event. Hamlet's father describes in that passage how the poison invades the body during sleep and how the healthy organism is destroyed from within, not having a chance to defend itself against attack. But this now becomes the *leitmotif* of the imagery: the individual occurrence is expanded into a symbol for the central problem of the play. The corruption of land and people throughout Denmark is understood as an imperceptible and irresistible process of poisoning. And, furthermore, this poisoning reappears as a *leitmotif* in the action as well—as a poisoning in the "dumb-show," and finally, as the poisoning of all the major characters in the last act. Thus imagery and action continually play into each other's hands and we see how the term "dramatic imagery" gains a new significance.

The imagery appears to be influenced by yet another event in the action underlying the play: Hamlet feels himself to be sullied by his mother's incest which, according to the conception of the time, she committed in marrying Claudius. For him this is a

poisoning idea which finds expression in his language. Professor
Dover Wilson has defended the reading of the Second Quarto
with convincing arguments: [22]

> O, that this too too sullied flesh would melt,
> Thaw and resolve itself into a dew!
>
> (I. ii. 129)

It is therefore probable that this idea is present in Hamlet's mind
at many moments when images of decay and rot appear in his
language.

The *leitmotif* occasionally appears in a disguised form at a
point where it seems to have no real connection with the main
issue of the play, for instance, in the following passage:

> So, oft it chances in particular men,
> That for some vicious mole of nature in them,
> As, in their birth—wherein they are not guilty
> Since nature cannot choose his origin—
> By the o'er growth of some complexion,
> Oft breaking down the pales and forts of reason,
> Or by some habit, that too much o'er-leavens
> The form of plausive manners, that these men,
> Carrying, I say, the stamp of one defect,
> Being nature's livery, or fortune's star,
> Their virtues else—be they as pure as grace,
> As infinite as man may undergo—
> Shall in the general censure take corruption
> From that particular fault: the dram of eale
> Doth all the noble substance of a doubt
> To his own scandal.
>
> (I. iv. 23)

Hamlet has spoken of the excessive revels and drinking-bouts
among his people and has said that this was disparaging to the
Danes in the eyes of the other peoples. Then follows this general
reflection. The question arises: why does Hamlet speak in such
detail of these matters here? For at this point in the play he has
as yet heard nothing of his uncle's murderous deed. And still he
touches in this speech upon that *leitmòtif* of the whole play; he

describes how human nature may be brought to decay through a tiny birth-mark, just as from one "dram of evil" [23] a destructive effect may spread over the whole organism. "O'er-leavens" already points to "sicklied o'er," and, as in the passage discussed, the notion of the human body is in the background. As in later passages, the balance of the powers in man is the theme here, and "corruption," a basic motif in the whole play, already makes its appearance. This general reflection on gradual and irresistible infection is made in passing, as it were. Thus Shakespeare makes use of every opportunity to suggest the fundamental theme of the play. When the King says to Laertes in the fourth act:

> There lives within the very flame of love
> A kind of wick or snuff that will abate it;

the same motif occurs again: corruption through a "dram of evil."

The following passage, too, from Laertes' words of warning to his sister, has never been examined for its value as "dramatic presaging."

> The canker galls the infants of the spring,
> Too oft before their buttons be disclosed,
> And in the morn and liquid dew of youth
> Contagious blastments are most imminent.
>
> (i. iii. 39)

It is no mere chance that this sententious little image,[24] which is so neatly woven in and so conventional, touches upon a motif later to be worked out more clearly. The worm in the bud, like ulcer and eruption, is also an irresistible force destroying the organism from within. Light is cast upon this early passage when, in the last act, it is said of Claudius: "this canker of our nature" (v. ii. 69). But here we still know nothing of the coming developments. The image is a faint warning, preparing the way, together with other hints, for the future.

The Pyrrhus episode [25] which the first Player recites before Hamlet contains features which are also of importance for the theme of the play. For here it is related of Pyrrhus with vigorous emphasis how "Aroused vengeance sets him new a-work" (ii. ii. 510). For Hamlet it must be a gentle warning that vengeance calls forth so bloody a deed in another without delay. On the other hand, the previous lines described Pyrrhus as being in suspense, unable to act, "neutral to his will" as Hamlet still is:

> So, as a painted tyrant, Pyrrhus stood,
> And like a neutral to his will and matter,
> Did nothing.
>
> (II. ii. 502)

The mention of "strumpet Fortune" and the picture of her broken wheel rolled "down the hill of heaven" at the end of this passage, is likewise a hint; in the third act this image of the wheel plunging down from the height, reappears in the conversation between Rosencrantz and the King:

> The cease of majesty
> Dies not alone; but, like a gulf, doth draw
> What's near it with it: it is a massy wheel,
> Fix'd on the summit of the highest mount,
> To whose huge spokes ten thousand lesser things
> Are mortised and adjoin'd; which, when it falls,
> Each small annexment, petty consequence,
> Attends the boisterous ruin.
>
> (III. iii. 15)

Through these images, which are also spun out from a more general reflection, the coming catastrophe is already significantly foreshadowed.

The imagery in Shakespeare's tragedies often shows how a number of other images are grouped around the central symbol which expresses the same idea, but in quite other terms. Several degrees, as it were, of the metaphorical expression of a fundamental idea may be distinguished. Besides images which express a motif with the greatest clarity and emphasis, we find others which utter the thought in a veiled and indirect manner. An examination of the way in which the images are spread over the play, can reveal how subtly Shakespeare modifies and varies according to character and situation.

The most striking images of sickness, which Miss Spurgeon has already listed, make their first appearance, significantly enough, in the second half of the play, and most notably in the scene in which Hamlet seeks to bring his mother to a change of heart. Here the plainness and clarity of the images is meant to awaken the conscience of the Queen; they can scarcely be forceful enough; "let me wring your heart," Hamlet has said at the beginning of the meeting. In the first part of the play the atmosphere of corruption and decay is spread in a more indirect and general way. Hamlet declares in the first and second acts how the world appears to him:

> . . . Ah fie! 'tis an unweeded garden,
> That grows to seed; things rank and gross in nature
> Possess it merely.

(I. ii. 135)

. . . and indeed it goes so heavily with my disposition that this goodly frame, the earth, seems to me a sterile promontory, this most excellent canopy, the air, look you, this brave o'erhanging firmament, this majestical roof fretted with golden fire, why, it appears no other thing to me than a foul and pestilent congregation of vapours.

(II. ii. 309)

The image of weeds, touched upon in the word "unweeded," is related to the imagery of sickness in Shakespeare's work. It appears three times in *Hamlet*. The ghost says to Hamlet:

> And duller shouldst thou be than the fat weed
> That roots itself in ease on Lethe wharf,

(I. v. 32)

In the dialogue with his mother, this image immediately follows upon the image of the ulcer:

> And do not spread the compost on the weeds,
> To make them ranker,

(III. iv. 151)

Images of rot, decay and corruption are especially numerous in the long second scene of the second act. There are, for example, Hamlet's remarks on the maggots which the sun breeds in a dead dog (II. ii. 181), on the deep dungeons in the prison Denmark (II. ii. 249), on the strumpet Fortune (II. ii. 240), who reappears in the speech of the first Player (II. ii. 515), his comparison of himself with a whore, a drab and a scullion (II. ii. 614).

Seen individually, such images do not seem to be very important. But in their totality they contribute considerably to the tone of the play.

NOTES

1. On the style in *Hamlet* see L. L. Schücking, *The Meaning of Hamlet*, London, 1937, I. i. and I. iv.

2. The spontaneous and unpremeditated character of Hamlet's imagery will become obvious through a comparison with Claudius' language. Claudius' speeches are studied and give the impression of having been previously prepared. His images often are consciously inserted. Dr. Schmetz notes that while Claudius often uses comparisons, linking object and image by "as" or "like," Hamlet's imagination fuses both into a metaphor (cf. IV. i. 40-44, IV. v. 94-6 with III. 83-4, III. 407-8). Further examples for Claudius' comparisons: III. iii. 41; IV. vii. 15; IV. xx. 88. This is, of course, only one aspect of the manifold differences between Claudius' and Hamlet's language. The whole problem has been exhaustively dealt with in Dr. Schmetz's study. For the difference between the imagery of Claudius' public and that of his private language, and for further distinguishing features in Claudius' imagery see Una Ellis-Fermor, *The Frontiers of Drama*, London, 1945, p. 88.

3. This, as Dr. Schmetz notes, gives to Hamlet's language sometimes a brutal violence that expresses itself in the use of forceful metaphors: "For I mine eyes will rivet to his face" (III. ii. 90), "Let me wring your heart" (III. iv. 35).

4. After completion of the manuscript, the author became acquainted with Professor Mikhail M. Morozow's article, "The Individualization of Shakespeare's Characters through Imagery" (*Shakespeare Survey, II*, Cambridge, 1949, pp. 83-106). Professor Morozow's more systematic and comprehensive examination of the content of all of Hamlet's images can throw new light on the statements made above and adds a number of acute observations, which have a bearing on the theory put forward in this chapter. Morozow also emphasizes the realistic, common and

popular nature of Hamlet's imagery, his faculty to "see right through people" and his closeness to the common people which does not exclude his scholarship and humanist education.

5. If he makes use of hyperbole in v. i. 304 (at Ophelia's grave) it is to parody Laertes' hyperbolic diction.

6. Hamlet, too, invokes God and the heavenly powers, but these invocations never take the form of grandiose images, they are mostly brief and often restricted to mere references (cf. I. ii. 132, 150, 195; I. v. 92; I. iv. 85; v. ii. 343, 355).

7. For the following cf. Dr. Schmetz's study and Professor Morozow's article.

8. Cf. III. i. 119; I. v. 22, 27, 29; III. iv. 147. For the disease-imagery see below.

9. E.g. I. ii. 140, 149, 153; III. ii. 89, 294; III. iii. 56-8; v. i. 306, 315.

10. v. i. 107 sqq.

11. E.g. his images taken from musical instruments, III. ii. 75.

12. II. ii. 397; III. ii. 361; II. ii. 458.

13. Hamlet speaks of the "pales and forts of reason" (I. iv. 28), wonders whether his mother's heart is "proof and bulwark against sense" (III. iv. 37; cf. III. iv. 208).

14. Cf. L. L. Schücking, *The Meaning of Hamlet*, London, 1937. Hamlet edition (English-German), Leipzig, 1941. J. D. Wilson, *What Happens in Hamlet*, Cambridge, 1935.

15. There are many instances for these contrasts in Hamlet's language. Cf. the transition from the famous monologue in III. i. 56 to his conversation with Ophelia in the same scene (a parallel change in III. ii) or cf. IV. iii. 22; v. i. 230 sqq. Dr. Schmetz notes the following instances of Hamlet's use of vulgar words: "truepenny" (I. v. 150); "old mole" (I. v. 161); "drab" (II. ii. 623); "carrion" (II. ii. 184); "Jowls it to the ground" (v. i. 82); "Knocked about the mazard" (v. i. 95). For further instances of Hamlet's use of coarse and common images see Morozow's article, *loc. cit.*, p. 95.

16. Through John Dover Wilson's edition of *Hamlet* (Cambridge, 1934) many of these puns and quibbles which so far had remained unintelligible (or were falsely understood) have been cleared up. On the importance of quibbles in *Hamlet* see John Dover Wilson's Introduction, p. xxxiii, sqq.

17. Edward Dowden noted this: "Madness possesses exquisite immunities and privileges. From the safe vantage of unintelligibility he can delight himself by uttering his whole mind and sending forth his words among the words of others, with their meaning disguised, as he himself must be, clothed in an antic garb of parable, dark sayings which speak the truth in a mystery" (*Shakespeare, His Mind and Art,* 1877, p. 145). Cf., too, John Dover Wilson's Introduction to *Hamlet,* p. xl.

18. Cf. Spurgeon, *Shakespeare's Imagery,* pp. 318-19.

19. Cf. Edward Dowden: "his wisdom is not the outflow of a rich or deep nature, but the little, accumulated hoard of a long and superficial experience. This is what the sententious manner signifies" (*Shakespeare, His Mind and Art,* p. 142). Professor John W. Draper, reviewing the divergent interpretations of Polonius' character, gives him a far more favourable treatment and considers him "not far removed from the Elizabethan ideal of what a courtier, what a father, what a 'Worthie Priuie Counceller' should be" (*The Hamlet of Shakespeare's Audience,* Durham, 1938, p. 53).

20. For the contemporary scientific background of the disease-imagery in *Hamlet* see John W. Draper, *The Humors and Shakespeare's Characters,* Durham, N. C., 1945.

21. Spurgeon, *Shakespeare's Imagery,* p. 316 sqq.

22. Cf. the note on this passage on p. 151 of John Dover Wilson's edition of *Hamlet* (Cambridge, 1934): " 'Sullied flesh' is the key to the soliloquy and tells us that Hamlet is thinking of the 'kindless' incestuous marriage as a personal defilement. Further, 'sullied' fits the immediate context as 'solid' does not. There is something absurd in associating 'solid flesh' with 'melt' and 'thaw'; whereas Shakespeare always uses 'sully' or 'sullied' elsewhere (cf. *Henry IV,* II. iv. 84; *Winter's Tale,* I. ii. 326) with the image, implicit or explicit, of dirt upon a surface of pure white; and the surface Hamlet obviously has in mind here is snow, symbolical of the nature he shares with his mother, once pure but now befouled."

23. The emendation *evil* has been accepted by several editors, e.g. by John Dover Wilson in the *New Shakespeare* edition.

24. Dr. Schmetz points out that this use of sententious diction betrays a certain immaturity in Laertes, just as his apostrophes

at the sight of the mad Ophelia in IV. v. 155 reveal a hollow pathos, or as his hyperboles at Ophelia's grave impress us as theatrical bombast (v. i. 274).

25. A new and important interpretation of the "Player's Speech" is given by Harry Levin, "An Explication of the Player's Speech," *The Kenyon Review*, XII, 2, 1950.

Maynard Mack

THE WORLD OF *HAMLET*

MY SUBJECT is the world of *Hamlet*. I do not of course mean
Denmark, except as Denmark is given a body by the play; and I
do not mean Elizabethan England, though this is necessarily close
behind the scenes. I mean simply the imaginative environment
that the play asks us to enter when we read it or go to see it.

Great plays, as we know, do present us with something that
can be called a world, a microcosm—a world like our own in
being made of people, actions, situations, thoughts, feelings and
much more, but unlike our own in being perfectly, or almost perfectly, significant and coherent. In a play's world, each part
implies the other parts, and each lives, each means, with the life
and meaning of the rest.

This is the reason, as we also know, that the worlds of great
plays greatly differ. Othello in Hamlet's position, we sometimes
say, would have no problem; but what we are really saying is that
Othello in Hamlet's position would not exist. The conception we
have of Othello is a function of the characters who help define
him, Desdemona, honest Iago, Cassio, and the rest; of his history
of travel and war; of a great storm that divides his ship from
Cassio's, and a handkerchief; of a quiet night in Venice broken by
cries about an old black ram; of a quiet night in Cyprus broken
by sword-play; of a quiet bedroom where a woman goes to bed in
her wedding sheets and a man comes in with a light to put out
the light; and above all, of a language, a language with many
voices in it, gentle, rasping, querulous, or foul, but all counter-
pointing the one great voice:

From *The Yale Review*, Vol. 41, 1952, pp. 502-23. Copyright
1952 by the Yale University Press. Reprinted by permission of the
author and the publisher.

Put up your bright swords, for the dew will rust them.

> O thou weed
> Who art so lovely fair and smell'st so sweet
> That the sense aches at thee. . . .

> Yet I'll not shed her blood
> Nor scar that whiter skin of hers than snow,
> And smooth as monumental alabaster.

> I pray you in your letters,
> When you shall these unlucky deeds relate,
> Speak of me as I am; nothing extenuate,
> Nor set down aught in malice; then must you speak
> Of one that loved not wisely but too well;
> Of one not easily jealous, but being wrought,
> Perplex'd in th' extreme; of one whose hand,
> Like the base Indian, threw a pearl away
> Richer than all his tribe. . . .

Without his particular world of voices, persons, events, the world that both expresses and contains him, Othello is unimaginable. And so, I think, are Antony, King Lear, Macbeth—and Hamlet. We come back then to Hamlet's world, of all the tragic worlds that Shakespeare made, easily the most various and brilliant, the most elusive. It is with no thought of doing justice to it that I have singled out three of its attributes for comment. I know too well, if I may echo a sentiment of Mr. E. M. W. Tillyard's, that no one is likely to accept another man's reading of *Hamlet*, that anyone who tries to throw light on one part of the play usually throws the rest into deeper shadow, and that what I have to say leaves out many problems—to mention only one, the knotty problem of the text. All I would say in defense of the materials I have chosen is that they seem to me interesting, close to the root of the matter even if we continue to differ about what the root of the matter is, and explanatory, in a modest way, of this play's peculiar hold on everyone's imagination, its almost mythic status, one might say, as a paradigm of the life of man.

The first attribute that impresses us, I think, is mysteriousness.

We often hear it said, perhaps with truth, that every great work of art has a mystery at the heart; but the mystery of *Hamlet* is something else. We feel its presence in the numberless explanations that have been brought forward for Hamlet's delay, his madness, his ghost, his treatment of Polonius, or Ophelia, or his mother; and in the controversies that still go on about whether the play is "undoubtedly a failure" (Eliot's phrase) or one of the greatest artistic triumphs; whether, if it is a triumph, it belongs to the highest order of tragedy; whether, if it is such a tragedy, its hero is to be taken as a man of exquisite moral sensibility (Bradley's view) or an egomaniac (Madariaga's view).

Doubtless there have been more of these controversies and explanations than the play requires; for in Hamlet, to paraphrase a remark of Falstaff's, we have a character who is not only mad in himself but a cause that madness is in the rest of us. Still, the very existence of so many theories and counter-theories, many of them formulated by sober heads, gives food for thought. *Hamlet* seems to lie closer to the illogical logic of life than Shakespeare's other tragedies. And while the causes of this situation may be sought by saying that Shakespeare revised the play so often that eventually the motivations were smudged over, or that the original old play has been here or there imperfectly digested, or that the problems of Hamlet lay so close to Shakespeare's heart that he could not quite distance them in the formal terms of art, we have still as critics to deal with effects, not causes. If I may quote again from Mr. Tillyard, the play's very lack of a rigorous type of causal logic seems to be a part of its point.

Moreover, the matter goes deeper than this. Hamlet's world is preëminently in the interrogative mood. It reverberates with questions, anguished, meditative, alarmed. There are questions that in this play, to an extent I think unparalleled in any other, mark the phases and even the nuances of the action, helping to establish its peculiar baffled tone. There are other questions whose interrogations, innocent at first glance, are subsequently seen to have reached beyond their contexts and to point towards some pervasive inscrutability in Hamlet's world as a whole. Such is that tense series of challenges with which the tragedy begins: Bernardo's of Francisco, "Who's there?" Francisco's of Horatio and Marcellus, "Who is there?" Horatio's of the ghost, "What art thou . . . ?" And then there are the famous questions. In them the interrogations seem to point not only beyond the context but beyond the play, out of Hamlet's predicaments into everyone's: "What a piece of work is a man! . . . And yet to me what is this quintessence of dust?" "To be, or not to be, that is the question." "Get thee to a nunnery. Why wouldst thou be a breeder of sinners?" "I am very proud, revengeful, ambitious, with more offences at my beck than I have thoughts to put them in, imagination to give them shape, or time to act them in. What should such fellows as I do crawling between earth and heaven?" "Dost thou think Alexander look'd o' this fashion i' th' earth? . . . And smelt so?"

Further, Hamlet's world is a world of riddles. The hero's own language is often riddling, as the critics have pointed out. When he puns, his puns have receding depths in them, like the one which constitutes his first speech: "A little more than kin, and less than kind." His utterances in madness, even if wild and whirling, are simultaneously, as Polonius discovers, pregnant: "Do you know me, my lord?" "Excellent well. You are a fishmonger." Even the madness itself is riddling: How much is real? How much is feigned? What does it mean? Sane or mad, Hamlet's mind plays restlessly about his world, turning up one riddle upon another. The riddle of character, for example, and how it is that in a man whose virtues else are "pure as grace," some vicious mole of nature, some "dram of eale," can "all the noble substance oft adulter." Or the riddle of the player's art, and how a man can so project himself into a fiction, a dream of passion, that he can weep for Hecuba. Or the riddle of action: how we may think too little—"What to ourselves in passion we propose," says the player-king, "The passion ending, doth the purpose lose"; and again, how we may think too much: "Thus conscience does make cowards of us all, And thus the native hue of resolution Is sicklied o'er with the pale cast of thought."

There are also more immediate riddles. His mother—how could she "on this fair mountain leave to feed, And batten on this moor?" The ghost—which may be a devil, for "the de'il hath power T' assume a pleasing shape." Ophelia—what does her behavior to him mean? Surprising her in her closet, he falls to such perusal of her face as he would draw it. Even the king at his prayers is a riddle. Will a revenge that takes him in the purging of his soul be vengeance, or hire and salary? As for himself, Hamlet realizes, he is the greatest riddle of all—a mystery, he warns Rosencrantz and Guildenstern, from which he will not have the heart plucked out. He cannot tell why he has of late lost all his mirth, forgone all custom of exercises. Still less can he tell why he delays: "I do not know Why yet I live to say, 'This thing's to do,' Sith I have cause and will and strength and means To do't."

Thus the mysteriousness of Hamlet's world is of a piece. It is not simply a matter of missing motivations, to be expunged if only we could find the perfect clue. It is built in. It is evidently an important part of what the play wishes to say to us. And it is certainly an element that the play thrusts upon us from the opening word. Everyone, I think, recalls the mysteriousness of that first scene. The cold middle of the night on the castle platform, the muffled sentries, the uneasy atmosphere of apprehension, the challenges leaping out of the dark, the questions that follow the challenges, feeling out the darkness, searching for identities, for relations, for assurance. "Bernardo?" "Have you had quiet guard?" "Who hath reliev'd you?" "What, is Horatio there?" "What, has this thing appear'd again tonight?" "Looks 'a not like the king?" "How now, Horatio! . . . Is not this something more than fantasy? What think you on 't?" "Is it not like the king?" "Why this same strict and most observant watch . . . ?" "Shall I strike at it with my partisan?" "Do you consent we shall acquaint [young Hamlet] with it?"

We need not be surprised that critics and playgoers alike have been tempted to see in this an evocation not simply of Hamlet's world but of their own. Man in his aspect of bafflement, moving in darkness on a rampart between two worlds, unable to reject, or quite accept, the one that, when he faces it, "to-shakes" his disposition with thoughts beyond the reaches of his soul—comforting himself with hints and guesses. We hear these hints and guesses whispering through the darkness as the several watchers speak. "At least, the whisper goes so," says one. "I think it be no other but e'en so," says another. "I have heard" that on the crowing of the cock "Th' extravagant and erring spirit hies To his confine," says a third. "Some say" at Christmas time "this bird of dawning" sings all night, "And then, they say, no spirit dare stir abroad." "So have I heard," says the first, "and do in part believe it." However we choose to take the scene, it is clear that it creates a world where uncertainties are of the essence.

Meantime, such is Shakespeare's economy, a second attribute of Hamlet's world has been put before us. This is the problematic nature of reality and the relation of reality to appearance. The play begins with an appearance, an "apparition," to use Marcellus's term—the ghost. And the ghost is somehow real, indeed the vehicle of realities. Through its revelation, the glittering surface of Claudius's court is pierced, and Hamlet comes to know, and we do, that the king is not only hateful to him but the murderer of his father, that his mother is guilty of adultery as well as incest. Yet there is a dilemma in the revelation. For possibly the apparition *is* an apparition, a devil who has assumed his father's shape.

This dilemma, once established, recurs on every hand. From the court's point of view, there is Hamlet's madness. Polonius investigates and gets some strange advice about his daughter: "Conception is a blessing, but as your daughter may conceive, friend, look to 't." Rosencrantz and Guildenstern investigate and get the strange confidence that "Man delights not me; no, nor woman neither." Ophelia is "loosed" to Hamlet (Polonius's vulgar word), while Polonius and the king hide behind the arras; and what they hear is a strange indictment of human nature, and a riddling threat: "Those that are married already, all but one, shall live."

On the other hand, from Hamlet's point of view, there is Ophelia. Kneeling here at her prayers, she seems the image of innocence and devotion. Yet she is of the sex for whom he has already found the name Frailty, and she is also, as he seems either madly or sanely to divine, a decoy in a trick. The famous cry— "Get thee to a nunnery"—shows the anguish of his uncertainty. If Ophelia is what she seems, this dirty-minded world of murder, incest, lust, adultery, is no place for her. Were she "as chaste as ice, as pure as snow," she could not escape its calumny. And if she is not what she seems, then a nunnery in its other sense of brothel is relevant to her. In the scene that follows he treats her as if she were indeed an inmate of a brothel.

Likewise, from Hamlet's point of view, there is the enigma of

the king. If the ghost is *only* an appearance, then possibly the
king's appearance is reality. He must try it further. By means of
a second and different kind of "apparition," the play within the
play, he does so. But then, immediately after, he stumbles on
the king at prayer. This appearance has a relish of salvation in
it. If the king dies now, his soul may yet be saved. Yet actually,
as we know, the king's efforts to come to terms with heaven
have been unavailing; his words fly up, his thoughts remain below. If Hamlet means the conventional revenger's reasons that he
gives for sparing Claudius, it was the perfect moment not to
spare him—when the sinner was acknowledging his guilt, yet unrepentant. The perfect moment, but it was hidden, like so much
else in the play, behind an arras.

There are two arrases in his mother's room. Hamlet thrusts his
sword through one of them. Now at last he has got to the heart of
the evil, or so he thinks. But now it is the wrong man; now he
himself is a murderer. The other arras he stabs through with his
words—like daggers, says the queen. He makes her shrink under
the contrast he points between her present husband and his
father. But as the play now stands (matters are somewhat clearer
in the bad Quarto), it is hard to be sure how far the queen grasps
the fact that her second husband is the murderer of her first. And
it is hard to say what may be signified by her inability to see
the ghost, who now for the last time appears. In one sense at
least, the ghost is the supreme reality, representative of the hidden ultimate power, in Bradley's terms—witnessing from beyond
the grave against this hollow world. Yet the man who is capable
of seeing through to this reality, the queen thinks is mad. "To
whom do you speak this?" she cries to her son. "Do you see
nothing there?" he asks, incredulous. And she replies: "Nothing at
all; yet all that is I see." Here certainly we have the imperturb-
able self-confidence of the worldly world, its layers on layers of
habituation, so that when the reality is before its very eyes it
cannot detect its presence.

Like mystery, this problem of reality is central to the play and
written deep into its idiom. Shakespeare's favorite terms in
Hamlet are words of ordinary usage that pose the question of
appearances in a fundamental form. "Apparition" I have already
mentioned. Another term is "seems." When we say, as Ophelia

says of Hamlet leaving her closet, "He seem'd to find his way without his eyes," we mean one thing. When we say, as Hamlet says to his mother in the first court-scene, "Seems, Madam! . . . I know not 'seems,'" we mean another. And when we say, as Hamlet says to Horatio before the play within the play, "And after, we will both our judgments join In censure of his seeming," we mean both at once. The ambiguities of "seem" coil and un-coil throughout this play, and over against them is set the idea of "seeing." So Hamlet challenges the king in his triumphant letter announcing his return to Denmark: "Tomorrow shall I beg leave to see your kingly eyes." Yet "seeing" itself can be am-biguous, as we recognize from Hamlet's uncertainty about the ghost; or from that statement of his mother's already quoted: "Nothing at all; yet all that is I see."

Another term of like importance is "assume." What we assume may be what we are not: "The de'il hath power T' assume a pleasing shape." But it may be what we are: "If it assume my noble father's person, I'll speak to it." And it may be what we are not yet, but would become; thus Hamlet advises his mother, "Assume a virtue, if you have it not." The perplexity in the word points to a real perplexity in Hamlet's and our own experience. We assume our habits—and habits are like costumes, as the word implies: "My father in his habit as he liv'd!" Yet these habits become ourselves in time: "That monster, custom, who all sense doth eat Of habits evil, is angel yet in this, That to the use of actions fair and good He likewise gives a frock or livery That aptly is put on."

Two other terms I wish to instance are "put on" and "shape." The shape of something is the form under which we are accus-tomed to apprehend it: "Do you see yonder cloud that's almost in shape of a camel?" But a shape may also be a disguise—even, in Shakespeare's time, an actor's costume or an actor's role. This is the meaning when the king says to Laertes as they lay the plot against Hamlet's life: "Weigh what convenience both of time and means May fit us to our shape." "Put on" supplies an analogous ambiguity. Shakespeare's mind seems to worry this phrase in the play much as Hamlet's mind worries the problem of acting in a world of surfaces, or the king's mind worries the meaning of Hamlet's transformation. Hamlet has put an antic disposition on, that the king knows. But what does "put on" mean? A mask, or a frock or livery—our "habit"? The king is left guessing, and so are we.

What is found in the play's key terms is also found in its imagery. Miss Spurgeon has called attention to a pattern of disease images in *Hamlet,* to which I shall return. But the play has other patterns equally striking. One of these, as my earlier quotations hint, is based on clothes. In the world of surfaces to which Shakespeare exposes us in Hamlet, clothes are naturally a factor of importance. "The apparel oft proclaims the man," Polonius assures Laertes, cataloguing maxims in the young man's ear as he is about to leave for Paris. Oft, but not always. And so he sends his man Reynaldo to look into Laertes' life there—even, if need be, to put a false dress of accusation upon his son ("What forgeries you please"), the better by indirections to find directions out. On the same grounds, he takes Hamlet's vows to Ophelia as false apparel. They are bawds, he tells her—or if we do not like Theobald's emendation, they are bonds—in masquerade, "Not of that dye which their investments show, But mere implorators of unholy suits."

This breach between the outer and the inner stirs no special emotion in Polonius, because he is always either behind an arras or prying into one, but it shakes Hamlet to the core. Here so recently was his mother in her widow's weeds, the tears still flushing in her galled eyes; yet now within a month, a little month, before even her funeral shoes are old, she has married with his uncle. Her mourning was all clothes. Not so his own, he bitterly replies, when she asks him to cast his "nighted color off." "'Tis not alone my inky cloak, good mother"—and not alone, he adds, the sighs, the tears, the dejected havior of the visage —"that can denote me truly."

> These indeed seem,
> For they are actions that a man might play;
> But I have that within which passes show;
> These but the trappings and the suits of woe.

What we must not overlook here is Hamlet's visible attire, giving the verbal imagery a theatrical extension. Hamlet's apparel now is his inky cloak, mark of his grief for his father, mark also of his character as a man of melancholy, mark possibly too of his being one in whom appearance and reality are attuned. Later, in his madness, with his mind disordered, he will wear his costume in a corresponding disarray, the disarray that Ophelia describes so vividly to Polonius and that producers of the play rarely give sufficient heed to: "Lord Hamlet with his doublet all unbrac'd, No hat upon his head; his stockings foul'd, Ungarter'd, and down-gyved to his ankle." Here the only question will be, as with the madness itself, how much is studied, how much is real. Still later, by a third costume, the simple traveler's garb in which we find him new come from shipboard, Shakespeare will show us that we have a third aspect of the man.

A second pattern of imagery springs from terms of painting: the paints, the colorings, the varnishes that may either conceal, or, as in the painter's art, reveal. Art in Claudius conceals. "The harlot's cheek," he tells us in his one aside, "beautied with plastering art, Is not more ugly to the thing that helps it Than is my deed to my most painted word." Art in Ophelia, loosed to Hamlet in the episode already noticed to which this speech of the king's is prelude, is more complex. She looks so beautiful—"the celestial, and my soul's idol, the most beautified Ophelia," Hamlet has called her in his love letter. But now, what does beautified mean? Perfected with all the innocent beauties of a lovely woman? Or "beautied" like the harlot's cheek? "I have heard of your paintings too, well enough. God hath given you one face, and you make yourselves another."

Yet art, differently used, may serve the truth. By using an "image" (his own word) of a murder done in Vienna, Hamlet cuts through to the king's guilt; holds "as 'twere, the mirror up to nature," shows "virtue her own feature, scorn her own image, and the very age and body of the time"—which is out of joint—"his form and pressure." Something similar he does again in his mother's bedroom, painting for her in words "the rank sweat of an enseamed bed," making her recoil in horror from his "counterfeit presentment of two brothers," and holding, if we may trust a stage tradition, his father's picture beside his uncle's. Here again the verbal imagery is realized visually on the stage.

The most pervasive of Shakespeare's image patterns in this

play, however, is the pattern evolved around the three words, show, act, play. "Show" seems to be Shakespeare's unifying image in *Hamlet*. Through it he pulls together and exhibits in a single focus much of the diverse material in his play. The ideas of seeming, assuming, and putting on; the images of clothing, painting, mirroring; the episode of the dumb show and the play within the play; the characters of Polonius, Laertes, Ophelia, Claudius, Gertrude, Rosencrantz and Guildenstern, Hamlet himself—all these at one time or another, and usually more than once, are drawn into the range of implications flung round the play by "show."

"Act," on the other hand, I take to be the play's radical metaphor. It distills the various perplexities about the character of reality into a residual perplexity about the character of an act. What, this play asks again and again, is an act? What is its relation to the inner act, the intent? "If I drown myself wittingly," says the clown in the graveyard, "it argues an act, and an act hath three branches; it is to act, to do, to perform." Or again, the play asks, how does action relate to passion, that "laps'd in time and passion" I can let "go by Th' important acting of your dread command"; and to thought, which can so sickly o'er the native hue of resolution that "enterprises of great pitch and moment With this regard their currents turn awry, And lose the name of action"; and to words, which are not acts, and so we dare not be content to unpack our hearts with them, and yet are acts of a sort, for we may speak daggers though we use none. Or still again, how does an act (a deed) relate to an act (a pretense)? For an action may be nothing but pretense. So Polonius readying Ophelia for the interview with Hamlet, with "pious action," as he phrases it, "sugar [s] o'er The devil himself." Or it may not be a pretense, yet not what it appears. So Hamlet spares the king, finding him in an act that has some "relish of salvation in 't." Or it may be a pretense that is also the first foothold of a new reality, as when we assume a virtue though we have it not. Or it may be a pretense that is actually a mirroring of reality, like the play within the play, or the tragedy of *Hamlet*.

To this network of implications, the third term, play, adds an additional dimension. "Play" is a more precise word, in Elizabethan parlance at least, for all the elements in *Hamlet* that pertain to the art of the theatre; and it extends their field of reference till we see that every major personage in the tragedy is a player in some sense, and every major episode a play. The court plays, Hamlet plays, the players play, Rosencrantz and Guildenstern try to play on Hamlet, though they cannot play on his recorders—here we have an extension to a musical sense. And the final duel, by a further extension, becomes itself a play, in which everyone but Claudius and Laertes plays his role in ignorance: "The queen desires you to show some gentle entertainment to Laertes before you fall to play." "I . . . will this brother's wager frankly play." "Give him the cup."—"I'll play this bout first."

The full extension of this theme is best evidenced in the play within the play itself. Here, in the bodily presence of these traveling players, bringing with them the latest playhouse gossip out of London, we have suddenly a situation that tends to dissolve the normal barriers between the fictive and the real. For here on the stage before us is a play of false appearances in which an actor called the player-king is playing. But there is also on the stage, Claudius, another player-king, who is a spectator of this player. And there is on the stage, besides, a prince who is a spectator of both these player-kings and who plays with great intensity a player's role himself. And around these kings and that prince is a group of courtly spectators—Gertrude, Rosencrantz, Guildenstern, Polonius, and the rest—and they, as we have come to know, are players too. And lastly there are ourselves, an audience watching all these audiences who are also players. Where, it may suddenly occur to us to ask, does the playing end? Which *are* the guilty creatures sitting at a play? When is an act not an "act"?

The mysteriousness of Hamlet's world, while it pervades the tragedy, finds its point of greatest dramatic concentration in the first act, and its symbol in the first scene. The problems of appearance and reality also pervade the play as a whole, but come to a climax in Acts II and III, and possibly their best symbol is the play within the play. Our third attribute, though again it is one that crops out everywhere, reaches its full development in Acts IV and V. It is not easy to find an appropriate name for this attribute, but perhaps "mortality" will serve, if we remember to mean by mortality the heartache and the thousand natural shocks that flesh is heir to, not simply death.

The powerful sense of mortality in *Hamlet* is conveyed to us, I think, in three ways. First, there is the play's emphasis on human weakness, the instability of human purpose, the subjection of humanity to fortune—all that we might call the aspect of failure in man. Hamlet opens this theme in Act I, when he describes how from that single blemish, perhaps not even the victim's fault, a man's whole character may take corruption. Claudius dwells on it again, to an extent that goes far beyond the needs of the occasion, while engaged in seducing Laertes to step behind the arras of a seemer's world and dispose of Hamlet by a trick. Time qualifies everything, Claudius says, including love, including purpose. As for love—it has a "plurisy" in it and dies of its own too much. As for purpose—"That we would do, We should do when we would, for this 'would' changes, And hath abatements and delays as many As there are tongues, are hands, are accidents; And then this 'should' is like a spendthrift's sigh, That hurts by easing." The player-king, in his long speeches to his queen in the play within the play, sets the matter in a still darker light. She means these protestations of undying love, he knows, but our purposes depend on our memory, and our memory fades fast. Or else, he suggests, we propose something to ourselves in a condition of strong feeling, but then the feeling goes, and with it the resolve. Or else our fortunes change, he adds, and with these our loves: "The great man down, you mark his favorite flies." The subjection of human aims to fortune is a reiterated theme in *Hamlet*, as subsequently in *Lear*. Fortune is the harlot goddess in whose secret parts men like Rosencrantz and Guildenstern live and thrive; the strumpet who threw down Troy and Hecuba and Priam; the outrageous foe whose slings and arrows a man of principle must suffer or seek release in suicide. Horatio suffers them with composure: he is one of the blessed few "Whose blood and judgment are so well co-mingled That they are not a pipe for fortune's finger To sound what stop she please." For Hamlet the task is of a greater difficulty.

Next, and intimately related to this matter of infirmity, is the emphasis on infection—the ulcer, the hidden abscess, "th' imposthume of much wealth and peace That inward breaks and shows no cause without Why the man dies." Miss Spurgeon, who was the first to call attention to this aspect of the play, has well remarked that so far as Shakespeare's pictorial imagination is concerned, the problem in *Hamlet* is not a problem of the will and reason, "of a mind too philosophical or a nature temperamentally unfitted to act quickly," nor even a problem of an individual at all. Rather, it is a condition—"a condition for which the individual himself is apparently not responsible, any more than the sick man is to blame for the infection which strikes and devours him, but which, nevertheless, in its course and development, impartially and relentlessly, annihilates him and others, innocent and guilty alike." "That," she adds, "is the tragedy of *Hamlet,* as it is perhaps the chief tragic mystery of life." This is a perceptive comment, for it reminds us that Hamlet's situation is mainly not of his own manufacture, as are the situations of Shakespeare's other tragic heroes. He has inherited it; he is "born to set it right."

We must not, however, neglect to add to this what another student of Shakespeare's imagery has noticed—that the infection in Denmark is presented alternatively as poison. Here, of course, responsibility is implied, for the poisoner of the play is Claudius. The juice he pours into the ear of the elder Hamlet is a combined poison and disease, a "leperous distilment" that curds "the thin and wholesome blood." From this fatal center, unwholesomeness spreads out till there is something rotten in all Denmark. Hamlet tells us that his "wit's diseased," the queen speaks of her "sick soul," the king is troubled by "the hectic" in his blood, Laertes meditates revenge to warm "the sickness in my heart," the people of the kingdom grow "muddied, Thick and unwholesome in their thoughts"; and even Ophelia's madness is said to be "the poison of deep grief." In the end, all save Ophelia die of that poison in a literal as well as figurative sense.

But the chief form in which the theme of mortality reaches us, it seems to me, is as a profound consciousness of loss. Hamlet's father expresses something of the kind when he tells Hamlet how his "[most] seeming-virtuous queen," betraying a love which "was of that dignity That it went hand in hand even with the vow I made to her in marriage," had chosen to "decline Upon a wretch whose natural gifts were poor To those of mine." "O Hamlet, what a falling off was there!" Ophelia expresses it again, on hearing Hamlet's denunciation of love and woman in the nunnery scene, which she takes to be the product of a disordered brain:

> O what a noble mind is here o'erthrown!
> The courtier's, soldier's, scholar's, eye, tongue, sword;
> Th' expectancy and rose of the fair state,
> The glass of fashion and the mould of form,
> Th' observ'd of all observers, quite, quite down!

The passage invites us to remember that we have never actually seen such a Hamlet—that his mother's marriage has brought a falling off in him before we meet him. And then there is that further falling off, if I may call it so, when Ophelia too goes mad—"Divided from herself and her fair judgment, Without the which we are pictures, or mere beasts."

Time was, the play keeps reminding us, when Denmark was a different place. That was before Hamlet's mother took off "the rose From the fair forehead of an innocent love" and set a blister there. Hamlet then was still "Th' expectancy and rose of the fair state"; Ophelia, the "rose of May." For Denmark was a garden then, when his father ruled. There had been something heroic about his father—a king who met the threats to Denmark in open battle, fought with Norway, smote the sledded Polacks on the ice, slew the elder Fortinbras in an honorable trial of strength. There had been something godlike about his father too: "Hyperion's curls, the front of Jove himself, An eye like Mars . . . , A station like the herald Mercury." But, the ghost reveals, a serpent was in the garden, and "the serpent that did sting thy father's life Now wears his crown." The martial virtues are put by now. The threats to Denmark are attended to by policy, by agents working deviously for and through an uncle. The moral virtues are put by too. Hyperion's throne is occupied by "a vice of kings," "a king of shreds and patches"; Hyperion's bed, by a satyr, a paddock, a bat, a gib, a bloat king with reechy kisses. The garden is unweeded now, and "grows to seed; things rank and gross in nature Possess it merely." Even in himself he feels the taint, the taint of being his mother's son; and that other taint, from an earlier garden, of which he admonishes

Ophelia: "Our virtue cannot so inoculate our old stock but we shall relish of it." "Why wouldst thou be a breeder of sinners?" "What should such fellows as I do crawling between earth and heaven?"

"Hamlet is painfully aware," says Professor Tillyard, "of the baffling human predicament between the angels and the beasts, between the glory of having been made in God's image and the incrimination of being descended from fallen Adam." To this we may add, I think, that Hamlet is more than aware of it; he exemplifies it; and it is for this reason that his problem appeals to us so powerfully as an image of our own.

Hamlet's problem, in its crudest form, is simply the problem of the avenger: he must carry out the injunction of the ghost and kill the king. But this problem, as I ventured to suggest at the outset, is presented in terms of a certain kind of world. The ghost's injunction to act becomes so inextricably bound up for Hamlet with the character of the world in which the action must be taken—its mysteriousness, its baffling appearances, its deep consciousness of infection, frailty, and loss— that he cannot come to terms with either without coming to terms with both.

When we first see him in the play, he is clearly a very young man, sensitive and idealistic, suffering the first shock of growing up. He has taken the garden at face value, we might say, supposing mankind to be only a little lower than the angels. Now in his mother's hasty and incestuous marriage, he discovers evidence of something else, something bestial—though even a beast, he thinks, would have mourned longer. Then comes the revelation of the ghost, bringing a second shock. Not so much because he now knows that his serpent-uncle killed his father; his prophetic soul had almost suspected this. Not entirely, even, because he knows now how far below the angels humanity has fallen in his mother, and how lust—these were the ghost's words— "though to a radiant angel link'd Will sate itself in a celestial bed, And prey on garbage." Rather, because he now sees everywhere, but especially in his own nature, the general taint, taking from life its meaning, from woman her integrity, from the will its strength, turning reason into madness. "Why wouldst thou be a breeder of sinners?" "What should such fellows as I do crawling between earth and heaven?" Hamlet is not the first young man to have felt the heavy and the weary weight of all this unintelligible world; and, like the others, he must come to terms with it.

The ghost's injunction to revenge unfolds a different facet of his problem. The young man growing up is not to be allowed simply to endure a rotten world, he must also act in it. Yet how to begin, among so many enigmatic surfaces? Even Claudius, whom he now knows to be the core of the ulcer, has a plausible exterior. And around Claudius, swathing the evil out of sight, he encounters all those other exteriors, as we have seen. Some of them already deeply infected beneath, like his mother. Some noble, but marked for infection, like Laertes. Some not particularly corrupt but infinitely corruptible, like Rosencrantz and Guildenstern; some mostly weak and foolish like Polonius and Osric. Some, like Ophelia, innocent, yet in their innocence still serving to "skin and film the ulcerous place."

And this is not all. The act required of him, though retributive justice, is one that necessarily involves the doer in the general guilt. Not only because it involves a killing; but because to get at the world of seeming one sometimes has to use its weapons. He himself, before he finishes, has become a player, has put an antic disposition on, has killed a man—the wrong man—has helped drive Ophelia mad, and has sent two friends of his youth to death, mining below their mines, and hoisting the engineer with his own petard. He had never meant to dirty himself with these things, but from the moment of the ghost's challenge to act, this dirtying was inevitable. It is the condition of living at all in such a world. To quote Polonius, who knew that world so well, men become "a little soil'd i' th' working." Here is another matter with which Hamlet has to come to terms.

Human infirmity—all that I have discussed with reference to instability, infection, loss—supplies the problem with its third phase. Hamlet has not only to accept the mystery of man's condition between the angels and the brutes, and not only to act in a perplexing and soiling world. He has also to act within the human limits—"with shabby equipment always deteriorating," if I may adapt some phrases from Eliot's *East Coker*, "In the general mess of imprecision of feeling, Undisciplined squads of emotion." Hamlet is aware of that fine poise of body and mind,

feeling and thought, that suits the action to the word, the word
to the action; that acquires and begets a temperance in the very
torrent, tempest, and whirlwind of passion; but he cannot at
first achieve it in himself. He vacillates between undisciplined
squads of emotion and thinking too precisely on the event. He
learns to his cost how easily action can be lost in "acting," and
loses it there for a time himself. But these again are only the
terms of every man's life. As Anatole France reminds us in a
now famous apostrophe to Hamlet: "What one of us thinks
without contradiction and acts without incoherence? What one
of us is not mad? What one of us does not say with a mixture
of pity, comradeship, admiration, and horror, Goodnight, sweet
Prince!"

In the last act of the play (or so it seems to me, for I know
there can be differences on this point), Hamlet accepts his world
and we discover a different man. Shakespeare does not outline
for us the process of acceptance any more than he had done
with Romeo or was to do with Othello. But he leads us strongly
to expect an altered Hamlet, and then, in my opinion, provides
him. We must recall that at this point Hamlet has been absent
from the stage during several scenes, and that such absences in
Shakespearean tragedy usually warn us to be on the watch for
a new phase in the development of the character. It is so when
we leave King Lear in Gloucester's farmhouse and find him again
in Dover fields. It is so when we leave Macbeth at the witches'
cave and rejoin him at Dunsinane, hearing of the armies that
beset it. Furthermore, and this is an important matter in the
theatre—especially important in a play in which the symbolism
of clothing has figured largely—Hamlet now looks different. He
is wearing a different dress—probably, as Granville-Barker thinks,
his "seagown scarf'd" about him, but in any case no longer the
disordered costume of his antic disposition. The effect is not entirely dissimilar to that in *Lear*, when the old king wakes out
of his madness to find fresh garments on him.

Still more important, Hamlet displays a considerable change
of mood. This is not a matter of the way we take the passage
about defying augury, as Mr. Tillyard among others seems to
think. It is a matter of Hamlet's whole deportment, in which I
feel we may legitimately see the deportment of a man who has

been "illuminated" in the tragic sense. Bradley's term for it is
fatalism, but if this is what we wish to call it, we must at least
acknowledge that it is fatalism of a very distinctive kind—a kind
that Shakespeare has been willing to touch with the associations
of the saying in St. Matthew about the fall of a sparrow, and
with Hamlet's recognition that a divinity shapes our ends. The
point is not that Hamlet has suddenly become religious; he has
been religious all through the play. The point is that he has
now learned, and accepted, the boundaries in which human
action, human judgment, are enclosed.

Till his return from the voyage he had been trying to act beyond these, had been encroaching on the role of providence, if
I may exaggerate to make a vital point. He had been too quick
to take the burden of the whole world and its condition upon
his limited and finite self. Faced with a task of sufficient difficulty in its own right, he had dilated it into a cosmic problem—
as indeed every task is, but if we think about this too precisely
we cannot act at all. The whole time is out of joint, he feels, and
in his young man's egocentricity, he will set it right. Hence he
misjudges Ophelia, seeing in her only a breeder of sinners.
Hence he misjudges himself, seeing himself a vermin crawling
between earth and heaven. Hence he takes it upon himself to
be his mother's conscience, though the ghost has warned that
this is no fit task for him, and returns to repeat the warning:
"Leave her to heaven, And to those thorns that in her bosom
lodge." Even with the king, Hamlet has sought to play at God.
He it must be who decides the issue of Claudius's salvation,
saving him for a more damnable occasion. Now, he has learned
that there are limits to the before and after that human reason
can comprehend. Rashness, even, is sometimes good. Through
rashness he has saved his life from the commission for his death,
"and prais'd be rashness for it." This happy circumstance and
the unexpected arrival of the pirate ship make it plain that the
roles of life are not entirely self-assigned. "There is a divinity
that shapes our ends, Roughhew them how we will." Hamlet is
ready now for what may happen, seeking neither to foreknow
it nor avoid it. "If it be now, 'tis not to come; if it be not to
come, it will be now; if it be not now, yet it will come: the
readiness is all."

The crucial evidence of Hamlet's new frame of mind, as I understand it, is the graveyard scene. Here, in its ultimate symbol, he confronts, recognizes, and accepts the condition of being man. It is not simply that he now accepts death, though Shakespeare shows him accepting it in ever more poignant forms: first, in the imagined persons of the politician, the courtier, and the lawyer, who laid their little schemes "to circumvent God," as Hamlet puts it, but now lie here; then in Yorick, whom he knew and played with as a child; and then in Ophelia. This last death tears from him a final cry of passion, but the striking contrast between his behavior and Laertes's reveals how deeply he has changed.

Still, it is not the fact of death that invests this scene with its peculiar power. It is instead the haunting mystery of life itself that Hamlet's speeches point to, holding in its inscrutable folds those other mysteries that he has wrestled with so long. These he now knows for what they are, and lays them by. The mystery of evil is present here—for this is after all the universal graveyard, where, as the clown says humorously, he holds up Adam's profession; where the scheming politician, the hollow courtier, the tricky lawyer, the emperor and the clown and the beautiful young maiden, all come together in an emblem of the world; where even, Hamlet murmurs, one might expect to stumble on "Cain's jawbone, that did the first murther." The mystery of reality is here too—for death puts the question, "What is real?" in its irreducible form, and in the end uncovers all appearances: "Is this the fine of his fines and the recovery of his recoveries, to have his fine pate full of fine dirt?" "Now get you to my lady's chamber, and tell her, let her paint an inch thick, to this favor she must come." Or if we need more evidence of this mystery, there is the anger of Laertes at the lack of ceremonial trappings, and the ambiguous character of Ophelia's own death. "Is she to be buried in Christian burial when she wilfully seeks her own salvation?" asks the gravedigger. And last of all, but most pervasive of all, there is the mystery of human limitation. The grotesque nature of man's little joys, his big ambitions. The fact that the man who used to bear us on his back is now a skull that smells; that the noble dust of Alexander somewhere plugs a bunghole; that "Imperious Caesar, dead and turn'd to clay,

Might stop a hole to keep the wind away." Above all, the fact that a pit of clay is "meet" for such a guest as man, as the grave-digger tells us in his song, and yet that, despite all frailties and limitations, "That skull had a tongue in it and could sing once."

After the graveyard and what it indicates has come to pass in him, we know that Hamlet is ready for the final contest of mighty opposites. He accepts the world as it is, the world as a duel, in which, whether we know it or not, evil holds the poisoned rapier and the poisoned chalice waits; and in which, if we win at all, it costs not less than everything. I think we understand by the close of Shakespeare's *Hamlet* why it is that unlike the other tragic heroes he is given a soldier's rites upon the stage. For as William Butler Yeats once said, "Why should we honor those who die on the field of battle? A man may show as reckless a courage in entering into the abyss of himself."

S. L. Bethell

TROILUS AND CRESSIDA

Troilus and Cressida is a consciously philosophical play. Normally Shakespeare's philosophical notions are incarnated in character and action; and his poetic thought, always concrete and image-filled, relates to character and action directly, and only indirectly to whatever general truths may be implied. The "To-morrow, and to-morrow" speech (*Macb.* v. v. 19) expresses directly Macbeth's reaction to his wife's death, and merely implies the atheism ("dusty death," "Signifying nothing") which has resulted from his gradual hardening in crime. In *Troilus and Cressida,* on the other hand, the thought, only partially embodied in character and action, flows over into the dialogue, which, though usually concrete enough and full of imagery, is frequently developed almost independently of the situation to which it refers. Ulysses' great speech on "degree" (*T.a.C.* i. iii. 75) begins and ends with Troy, but is much more concerned with generalities of political philosophy than with the Trojan war: in *Troilus and Cressida* the story is an excuse for thought rather than the embodiment of thought. The metaphysical problems of the tragedies must, from the first, have presented themselves to Shakespeare in terms of concrete experience; but in *Troilus and Cressida* he pursues philosophical abstractions with the impassioned eagerness of Donne. Problems of time and value and their mutual relations are thrust forward for the audience's attention:

From *Shakespeare and the Popular Dramatic Tradition,* 1944, pp. 98-105. Reprinted by permission of the executors and Staples Press Limited.

> Time hath, my lord, a wallet at his back,
> Wherein he puts alms for oblivion
>
> (*T.a.C.* III. iii. 145)

As in Donne, philosophy is usually apprehended in terms of sense-experience, but occasionally even the bare bones of abstract thinking appear, e.g. in Troilus' crucial but awkward query: "What is aught, but as 'tis valued?" (II. ii. 52).

In such a play it is no wonder to find characters with something of a "morality" flavour. As Thersites recalls the old Vice, so Ulysses conveys some suggestion of an abstract Worldly Wisdom. Most of the characters in *Troilus and Cressida* express themselves philosophically, but Ulysses has an especially large share of such speeches, including the famous "degree" speech and the speech on Time. With him even more than the others, what he says is infinitely more important than why he says it, and at times even his behaviour is hard to interpret on naturalistic grounds. When Cressida arrives in the Grecian camp, Agamemnon receives her with a kiss:

> Our general doth salute you with a kiss,
>
> (IV. v. 19)

says Nestor. Ulysses comments with a pun:

> Yet is the kindness but particular;
> 'Twere better she were kiss'd in general.
>
> (IV. v. 20)

The others act upon this advice, and Cressida is kissed in turn by all the Greek leaders. When his own turn comes, however, there is a short wit-battle in which Ulysses insultingly rejects the kiss that Cressida is presumably willing to give:

Ulyss.: May I, sweet lady, beg a kiss of you?
Cres.: You may.
Ulyss.:   I do desire it.
Cres.:   Why, beg, then.
Ulyss.: Why then for Venus' sake, give me a kiss
           When Helen is a maid again, and his [*sc.* Menelaus']
Cres.: I am your debtor, claim it when 'tis due.
Ulyss.: Never's my day, and then a kiss of you.

> (IV. v. 47)

When Diomedes leads Cressida away, Ulysses bursts into denunciation:

> Fie, fie upon her!
> There's language in her eye, her cheek, her lip,
> Nay, her foot speaks; her wanton spirits look out
> At every joint and motive of her body.
> O, these encounterers, so glib of tongue,
> That give accosting welcome ere it comes,
> And wide unclasp the tables of their thoughts
> To every ticklish reader! set them down
> For sluttish spoils of opportunity
> And daughters of the game.
>
> (IV. v. 54)

Speaking naturalistically, we should admire this moral rectitude
more heartily, if Ulysses had not himself initiated the general
kissing. Taken conventionally, however, the incident is central
to the Troilus-Cressida theme. The handing over of Cressida to
the Greeks is the handing over of Troilus' ideal love to the sully-
ing of the world: we are to be prepared for his betrayal, and
our knowledge of Cressida's character must be so established
that no psychological doubt remain to befog the philosophical
issue. Ulysses, at least during this incident (episodic intensifica-
tion again!), represents an impersonal Wisdom, whose judgment
we must accept. He devises a test for Cressida which sufficiently
reveals her character and the character of those she has come
among; and his own refusal to kiss her sets him apart from the
others, in judicial aloofness, so that we are prepared to accept
the verdict which he pronounces after Cressida is led away. The
whole passage is in rhyme and full of word-play: this not only
emphasizes the tone of badinage and flirtation, but also serves
to distance or frame the whole incident, which thus appears in
a sort of vocal italics to draw attention to its symbolic function.
To condemn Ulysses' conduct as ungentlemanly would be to
attribute to the character a representational quality which the
passage seems to disallow. There is a suggestion of deity about
Ulysses: we must accept his moral judgments, but we must not
search the morality of his own conduct, which is, as it were, an
Olympian setting of the stage for human conflict. As the embodi-

ment of wisdom, he is to be praised or blamed solely in reference
to that one quality. It is only at times that this hint of allegory
appears in the action and dialogue of Ulysses: Shakespeare's
reversion to an older technique is probably unconscious; but it
is none the less interesting on that account.

Troilus and Cressida, as probably the most intellectual of
Shakespeare's plays, reveals an unusually high degree of con-
ventionalism in the presentation of character; examples can be
found of most of the conventions discussed in this chapter and
the last. Thersites, whose relation to the Vice has already been
mentioned, might perhaps best be classed as a "humour," his
predominant characteristic being a cynical and prurient wit.
Lechery is his favourite theme:

> Nothing but lechery! all incontinent varlets!
>
> (v. i. 105)

He does duty also as a scurrilous chorus upon the futility of
war—a role comparable to that of Falstaff in the battle scenes
of *Henry IV, Part I*. His remark above occurs significantly at
the end of a scene, and the next scene closes with a similar but
even more emphatic outburst:

> Lechery, lechery; still, wars and lechery; nothing else
> holds fashion: a burning devil take them!
>
> (v. ii. 195)

To close two successive scenes of the fifth act in this way is
surely to commend the opinion of Thersites to our very serious
attention. Ajax and Achilles are practically humours: senseless
vanity and strength in Ajax; selfish pride and strength in Achilles.
Helen is also a humour: in the one scene in which she appears,
her only characteristic is a weak and silly sex-obsession:

> Let thy song be love: this love will undo us all. O Cupid,
> Cupid, Cupid!
>
> (iii. i. 119)

Professor Wilson Knight is surely mistaken in considering her to
be a worthy object of Trojan idealism.[1] This scene, which is
almost central in position, is certainly central at any rate to
one theme of the play: the theme of "fair without and foul

within," which I shall later treat more fully. The Helen whose
face had launched a thousand Marlovian ships is subjected to a
remorseless Shakespearean "debunking"; in a few lines the real
Helen is revealed, the inadequate object of so much misplaced
idealism. Other characters in the play are more complex, though
none is seen very clearly in the round.

An interesting example of depersonalisation occurs in Diomedes, the careless and sensual Greek, to whom Cressida so
quickly transfers herself. It is he who rises above the spite and
misrepresentation of war, in pity for both sides, and condemns,
with remarkable moral fervour, the unworthy cause of the whole
dispute:

> For every false drop in her bawdy veins
> A Grecian's life hath sunk; for every scruple
> Of her contaminated carrion weight,
> A Trojan hath been slain: since she could speak,
> She has not given so many good words breath
> As for her Greeks and Trojans suffer'd death.
>
> (IV. i. 69)

This is an unusually clear-sighted view of the matter, but it is
also extremely discourteous, as it is addressed to the culprit,
Paris, and Diomedes has come under a flag of truce. But Paris
takes it very quietly, and replies:

> Fair Diomed, you do as chapmen do,
> Dispraise the thing that you desire to buy.
>
> (IV. i. 75)

The reference to chapmen—hawkers of cheap goods—confirms,
despite the speaker, the attitude to Helen which Diomedes has
already expressed. Clearly Diomedes here steps out of character, and Paris also speaks truer than he knows.

Action as well as character may be symbolic, even action
which is not represented on the stage. Paris' request that Helen
should "help unarm our Hector" (III. i. 163) clinches the Helen
scene and assures its central position. The outward show of
chivalry is there; but we know Hector to be the worthiest of the
Trojans, and Helen a worthless strumpet. That Hector should
yield to fight in such a cause is the undoing of himself and of

Troy: that Helen should play the role of his "fair lady"—a
Helen who can be so much at home with Pandarus—is the
height of Shakespearean irony. In the play's last act, action and
character mingle in what is unique in Shakespeare—a direct
allegorical presentation of his dramatic theme. Hector, despite
the entreaties of Andromache, and the prophetic warnings of
Cassandra, joins the battle, as his honour bids him. The usual
battle confusion is presented in what modern editors unnecessarily divide into a series of short scenes. Near the end of Scene
VI there is a stage direction which reads, in our modern editions,
Enter one in sumptuous armour. In the Quarto and Folios, it
is simply *Enter one in armour,*[2] but Malone's addition of "sumptuous"[3] merely underlines Shakespeare's obvious intention, for
Hector cries out to this anonymous figure:

> Stand, stand, thou Greek; thou art a goodly mark:
> No? Wilt thou not? I like thy armour well;
> I'll frush it and unlock the rivets all,
> But I'll be master of it: wilt thou not, beast, abide?
> Why, then fly on, I'll hunt thee for the hide.
>
> (v. vi. 27)

At the beginning of Scene VIII, we find Hector presumably
standing over the mysterious person whom he has now slain,
and saying:

> Most putrefied core, so fair without,
> Thy goodly armour thus hath cost thy life.
> Now is my day's work done; I'll take good breath:
> Rest, sword; thou hast thy fill of blood and death.
>
> (v. viii. 1)

At this point *"Enter Achilles and Myrmidons,"* and Hector meets
his death unarmed at the hands of the cowardly hero and his
pack. We hear from Troilus, two scenes later, that

> He's dead; and at the murderer's horse's tail,
> In beastly sort, dragg'd through the shameful field.
>
> (v. x. 4)

Shakespeare took the incident of the "one in sumptuous armour"
from Lydgate's *Troye Boke,*[4] but seems to have given it a wider

significance. The crucial question here is, "Why 'putrefied core'?" [5]
There is nothing in Lydgate to explain this remarkable apostrophe. What did Shakespeare intend by it? The "one in sumptuous armour" was surely not dead when he first entered, and
he had had no time to putrefy after being killed. Or does it
mean that he was old, or diseased, or infirm? In any event,
Hector had won the armour which he coveted, so why this apparently embittered comment? I do not see any naturalistic explanation. What I suggest is that Shakespeare saw in the
incident in Lydgate an allegory similar to the "whited sepulchre" of Holy Scripture: "sumptuous armour" stands for the
"outward show" which covers an inner corruption. Perhaps with
the scriptural passage in mind, Shakespeare rendered his symbol complete by adding the "putrefied core," although the reference is incapable of natural explanation, and must be taken by
the audience on an entirely different plane from the rest of the
play. The "sumptuous armour" with its "putrefied core" thus
becomes a symbol of all the play presents to us, an allegorical
enactment of the theme of "fair without, and foul within," which
is applicable almost everywhere in the Troy and Troilus stories
as Shakespeare re-writes them. It applies to the war, with its
false chivalry and inadequate aim; to Helen, to Cressida, and
a good many more of the personages involved; and it applies,
lastly, to the death of Hector, with which it is so closely linked in
presentation. Hector was the best of the Trojans, and better
than the best of the Greeks: he saw, most clearly of them all,
the essential evil of the war, waged to keep Helen from her
lawful husband:

> . . . 'tis mad idolatry
> To make the service greater than the god,
>
> (II. ii. 56)

he said. And yet he concluded for the continuation of the war:

> For 'tis a cause that hath no mean dependance
> Upon our joint and several dignities.
>
> (II. ii. 192)

Later, he ignored Andromache and Cassandra, in order to fulfil the supposed duties of a false conception of honour. Unworthy aims are bound to tarnish the most chivalrous nature:

and so Hector himself, a few moments before he is brutally murdered, so far loses his chivalric courtesy as to call out "beast" after the "one in sumptuous armour," and then: "I'll hunt thee for thy hide"—the least worthy of motives. His death and the shameful treatment of his corpse are perhaps punishment in excess of his swerving, but they point sharply to the previous degradation he had suffered. Even in the *Troye Boke*, there is at least a suggestion that Hector's death was in some sense a consequence of his greed. Shakespeare elaborates the incident, places it at the climax of his play, and removes all possibility of natural explanation, so that he surely meant it to bear the extended significance which I have suggested. Otherwise there seems no point in his choice of this particular incident when so many important happenings in the Troy story are necessarily omitted, and absolutely no point in the further complication of the "putrefied core."

Troilus and Cressida is thus a play which especially calls for the exercise of multi-consciousness. In addition to the usual dual consciousness of play-world and real world, and of past and present time, there is the dual consciousness of story and philosophy, since the two are not wholly merged; there is the dual consciousness of character as representative and as allegorical; and, further, there must be a dual consciousness of certain incidents in their naturalistic and their allegorical significances.

NOTES

1. So at least he implies, in speaking of this scene: "the strains of music," he says, "herald the entry of Helen, queen of romance" (*The Wheel of Fire*, p. 67).

2. and 3. v. *Troilus and Cressida*, in *The Cambridge Shakespeare*, ed. William Aldis Wright (Macmillan, 1894), p. 159, note to l. 27.

4. v. a note of Steevens, in Malone's edition of Shakespeare (pub. 1821), vol. VIII, p. 437:

"This circumstance is taken from Lydgate's poem, p. 196:

'—Guido in his historic doth shew
By worthy Hector's fall, who coveting

To have the sumptuous armour of the king, etc.
So greedy was thereof, that when he had
The body up, and on his horse it bare,
To have the spoil thereof such haste he made
That he did hang his shield without all care
Behind him at his back, the easier
To pull the armour off at his desire,
And by that means his breast clean open lay,' etc.

This furnished Shakespeare with the hint for the following line:

'I am unarm'd; forego this vantage, Greek.' "
Malone obviously borrowed the epithet "sumptuous" from Steevens' quotation or its original.

5. The word is "core," not "corse," and implies a metaphor from rotten fruit.

Harold S. Wilson

ACTION AND SYMBOL IN
MEASURE FOR MEASURE AND *THE TEMPEST*

IF WE COMPARE the dramatic methods of *Measure for Measure*
and *The Tempest* with reference to the directing roles that their
two dukes play—Vincentio of Vienna and Prospero of Milan and
the Magic Island—we may observe a notable difference in their
procedures. Both of them seem to supervise and control the action of their respective plays. But whereas Prospero takes us
immediately into his confidence and explains his purpose as he
goes along, Duke Vincentio never explicitly states his purpose
in *Measure for Measure* and we are left to deduce it from the
course and outcome of the action. The result has been that
Prospero's aims and methods have puzzled no one; [1] but the
reticence of Duke Vincentio has given rise to widespread complaint, if not misunderstanding as well, and *Measure for Measure*
accordingly has often been thought to present a "problem" by
reason of its doubtful morality, its discordant techniques, or
both. The purpose of this paper is to argue that the technique
of *Measure for Measure* is logical and consistent, and to support
this opinion by comparing *Measure for Measure* with *The Tempest*. The two plays have much in common, and the one may be
used to shed light upon the other.

Critical opinions concerning *Measure for Measure* may be
classified, roughly, in four categories. The hostile view of the
play, characteristic of romantic criticism in the nineteenth century, is typified in Coleridge's comment: "The pardon and marriage of Angelo not merely baffles the strong indignant claim of

From *Shakespeare Quarterly*, Vol. 4, 1953, pp. 375-384. Reprinted
by permission of the author and periodical.

justice (for cruelty, with lust and damnable baseness, cannot be forgiven, because we cannot conceive them as being *morally* repented of) but it is likewise degrading to the character of women"; [2] and this view has been associated, in more recent times, with the theory that *Measure for Measure,* like the other "dark" comedies and *Timon of Athens,* reflects Shakespeare's disillusionment and gloomy despair of human virtue during the time he was writing his great tragedies, while he was "in the depths." [3] At the opposite pole is the view of G. Wilson Knight and others that *Measure for Measure* deals with the forgiveness of sin in the spirit of the Sermon on the Mount. [4]

Distinguishable from these two opposing schools of interpretation are two groups of commentators who have been mainly concerned to criticize the dramatic technique of the play. It has been said that the play contains an unassimilated mixture of "realism" and implausible convention, [5] or that it reflects an uncoördinated change in the author's purpose and point of view. [6] The technique of the play has likewise found defenders; [7] but the issue remains open to further argument.

The main difficulty about *Measure for Measure* seems to arise in the following way. In the first act we learn that the Duke is troubled about the corrupt state of Vienna (which his lenient rule has hitherto condoned against his will, and which is illustrated for us in I.ii, in the persons of Lucio, Mistress Overdone, and Claudio), and that he has hit upon the expedient of entrusting reform to Lord Angelo, whose inflexible virtue, he hopes, may correct the abuses without reflecting an inconsistent harshness in his own policy. Some doubts about Angelo's reliability, however, have prompted the Duke to remain in the disguise of a friar as a secret witness of Angelo's rule. From this point (I.iii) we know that the disguised Duke is above all the man to watch, but we may well suppose that his concern is simply for moral reform in Vienna through a stronger exertion of just authority.

In Act II, our attention is concentrated upon the villainy of Angelo, as he tries to seduce Isabella in exchange for her brother's pardon. The disguised Duke learns of Angelo's hypocrisy as he visits her brother Claudio in prison, and we begin to long for him to intervene. Instead, however, he arranges the substitution of Mariana for Isabella in the assignation with Angelo and at the same time deceives Claudio concerning Angelo's motives by pretending to know from the confessional that Angelo's proposal to Isabel is but to test her; thus he prepares Claudio to expect death in a spirit of humble submission (III.i).

We observe the effect of the Duke's designs upon Claudio, but at the same time we cannot help observing the Duke's duplicity; and no hint is given of what his ultimate purpose may be. If we have any doubts about the Duke's behavior, these are strengthened in the following encounter with Lucio, whose impudent aspersions upon the Duke's character leave the bogus friar comically at a loss to answer him; and the Duke's moralizing soliloquy at the end of Act III but restores a balance of ambiguity with the moral earnestness of its rhymed sententiousness. Still, the only motive implied for the Duke's actions is justice:

> Craft against vice I must apply.
> With Angelo tonight shall lie
> His old betrothed but despised;
> So disguise shall, by th' disguised,
> Pay with falseness false exacting,
> And perform an old contracting. (III.ii.291-6) [8]

This is a version of "measure for measure," but it tells us nothing of the retribution we naturally expect to overtake Angelo at the Duke's hands. If justice is his end, it is surely high time he intervened more decisively than this. Under Angelo's regime, the petty offenders are punished with a stern hand—Claudio, Pompey, Mistress Overdone—while licentiousness and evil, in the persons of Lucio and Angelo, have free sway.

Act IV skillfully sets the stage for the climax. The Duke presides at the meeting of Isabella and Mariana; Isabella's embarrassing interview with Angelo, in which she gives her feigned submission, is tactfully reported in a few words, and the arrangements between Isabella and Mariana take place off stage. The contrasting comedy of the following prison scenes, where Pompey becomes Abhorson's apprentice and Barnardine proves indifferent to the sentence of death, is in Shakespeare's best macabre vein. This passage shows us the ordinary workings of

human justice, an ironical light upon the hypocritical pretensions of an Angelo; and the linking of these scenes with the
story of Isabella and Angelo and Claudio has somewhat the same
effect as the grave-diggers' scene linking the death of Ophelia
with the return of Hamlet to Denmark. There is the same contrast of the comic with the deeply serious, and the same jesting
with the theme of mortality.[9]

As the climax approaches, we expect Angelo's villainy to be
unmasked, but we do not know how it is to be managed, any
more than do Isabella and the others who act under the friar's
instructions. He has deceived Isabella, cruelly, as it seems, about
Claudio's fate, tempting her, too, with the prospect of revenge
upon Angelo. Angelo himself has some misgivings:

> Alack, when once our grace we have forgot,
> Nothing goes right; we would, and we would not!
>
> (IV.iv.35-6)

But he is far from penitent, and he is prepared to maintain his
hypocrisy with his customary firmness. His colleague Escalus is
merely bewildered at the Duke's suddenly announced return. All
of this heightens the mood of expectancy with which we await
the outcome of the Duke's elaborate preparations, and the suspense we feel centers upon the Duke's relation to Angelo.

What immediately follows is a false climax. The Duke feigns to
be completely persuaded of Angelo's good faith, and retires,
leaving the helpless Isabella and Mariana to be arranged before
Angelo, and the absent friar to be traduced by Lucio. Even
though we know the outcome of the play well, at a performance
we cannot but be thrilled by the suspense of this moment. Then
follow swiftly the return and accusation of the friar, his unmasking by Lucio and the consequent unmasking of Angelo, the
vindication of Isabella and Mariana, and the confusion of Lucio.
Still the final turning point is not reached. The Duke presses the
charge of justice against the newly married Angelo:

> The very mercy of the law cries out
> Most audible, even from his proper tongue,
> "An Angelo for Claudio! death for death!"

> Haste still pays haste, and leisure answers leisure;
> Like doth quit like, and Measure still for Measure.
> (v.i.412-16)

Isabella provides the solution. We have seen the youthful stern-
ness of her character in her scornful rejection of her brother's
appeal to her to sacrifice herself for him. Now, as Mariana pleads
with her to intercede for Angelo, we are able to appreciate the
struggle it costs her to forgive an enemy; for, owing to the Duke's
deception, she thinks her brother Claudio has been put to death
on Angelo's order. The flimsiness of her excuse for Angelo is
apparent:

> My brother had but justice
> In that he did the thing for which he died.
> For Angelo,
> His act did not o'ertake his bad intent,
> And must be buried but as an intent
> That perish'd by the way. Thoughts are no subjects,
> Intents but merely thoughts.
> (v.i.453-9)

Dr. Johnson wrote of this appeal, "Women think ill of nothing
that raises the credit of their beauty, and are ready, however virtuous, to pardon any act they think incited by their charms." [10]
Such an irony is not beyond Shakespeare's capacity, but it is not
in keeping with the seriousness of this moving scene. It shows
us a vital change in Isabella. Her newly awakened charity can find
an excuse for Angelo where in fact there is none.

At this point, the suspense is relieved by the appearance of the
living Claudio, as the last element of the Duke's design falls into
place. The pattern of the whole action now stands revealed for
the first time, in the general forgiveness of the ending, and we
may at length see a firm consistency of purpose in all the Duke's
proceedings. Claudio did wrong and was brought to repentance
through expecting justice; instead, he received mercy. Angelo
was brought to repent of his wrong-doing in the same way and
with the same consequence. The unrepentant Barnardine and
even the graceless Lucio share in the mercy, that they may yet
find time to remember their sins. Isabella, once intent upon justice,

is offered the choice between justice and mercy, and chooses mercy. Finally, the ambiguous implication preserved in the title of the play stands fully revealed: the measure of justice that Angelo meted to Claudio is in turn meted to Angelo; but the grace that saved Claudio also saves Angelo.

This significant pattern is revealed cumulatively and held in some suspense until the very end, when everything falls into place as an effect of the culminating action; hence there can be no real explanatory comment from the Duke by way of preparation—according to the way the play is designed—and no one else is in a position to supply it. The Duke's purpose must remain something of an enigma till his final action of forgiveness makes it as explicit as it can be made. If Shakespeare had chosen to avoid the ambiguity of the Duke's role, he might have represented him as speaking, near the beginning of the play (and in suitable poetry, rather than this clumsy prose) somewhat to this effect: "I have long been troubled about the corrupt state of Vienna, and I know that my friend Angelo, for all his professed virtue, has shared in it to the extent, at least, of repudiating his betrothal. But I have never cared much simply about punishing offenders. This never does very much good. Any real improvement can come only through a change of heart. I have thought of an ingenious way of testing Angelo, and perhaps bringing about a change of heart in him and others. Watch how I set about it, and, no matter how dubious my conduct may seem, remember that my purpose throughout is to temper justice with mercy and to bring the proud and erring to repentance." But if the Duke had thus explained himself, the whole ensuing action would have been prejudged. Our sense of conflict would have been lessened. The Duke, to be sure, does not really control anyone's actions; on the contrary, he constantly prepares choices for others; but our reliance upon his revealed purposes would lessen the suspense and there would be virtually no surprise in the outcome. Thus all the author's skill goes to maintaining the suspense of the action through the Duke's reticence and the implied ambiguity of his motives and conduct, through the very ambiguity of the play's title, and the significance of the action is revealed through the recurrence of a single theme which builds a symbolic design. The method of *Measure for Measure* might thus be called "symbolic action"; that is, the theme of the play emerges out of the pattern of the action, as a conception and effect embodied in the action without the help of any anticipatory hint or clue.[11]

The symbolic design of the play is likewise implicit in the contrasting interrelations of the main characters as seen through the developing action. Angelo, until the climax is reached, stands for justice as the world knows it; the Duke for justice tempered by mercy, the precedent for which is not human but divine; and he lightly hints at his true role, if we can read his riddle: "There is scarce truth enough alive to make societies secure, but security enough to make fellowships accurst. Much upon this riddle runs the wisdom of the world. This news is old enough, yet it is every day's news" (III.ii.240-44). The Duke, likewise, is "one that, above all other strifes, contended especially to know himself" (III.ii.246-7); but Angelo has never known himself until he is forced to look upon his hypocrisy and acknowledge his errors through the Duke's accusation, and to understand the true status of the sinner through experiencing the forgiveness of Mariana, Isabella, and the Duke acting "like pow'r divine" (v.i.374).

The Angelo whose eyes are sealed to his own shortcomings, the Angelo of the opening of the play, is not altogether unlike Isabella in her narrow holiness and self-righteousness.[12] She preaches eloquently to Angelo, in her first interview with him (II.ii.27ff.), about hating the sin but not the sinner, about forgiveness and mercy; but when it is a case of forgiving her brother Claudio for proposing to sacrifice her virtue to save his life (and Claudio is immediately penitent for the proposal), she storms at him like a virago:

> O you beast!
> O faithless coward! O dishonest wretch!
> Wilt thou be made a man out of my vice?
> Is't not a kind of incest to take life
> From thine own sister's shame? What should I think?
> Heaven shield my mother play'd my father fair!
> For such a warped slip of wilderness
> Ne'er issu'd from his blood. Take my defiance!
> Die, perish! Might but my bending down
> Reprieve thee from thy fate, it should proceed.

I'll pray a thousand prayers for thy death,
No word to save thee.

(III.i.136-47)

And she disdains Claudio's further pleading to be forgiven his moment of weakness, with virginal righteousness. But when the Duke proposes that Mariana should yield herself to Angelo and thus preserve Isabella's chastity, Isabella shows no scruples about submitting Mariana to the offence for which Claudio had suffered the rigor of the law, nor any regret at the memory of her harshness to her brother. It is a wonderful irony, too, that the virginal and self-righteous Isabella should first tempt the virginal and self-righteous Angelo to sin, and that by means of this provocation they should both be brought to participate in the experience of penitence, mercy, and forgiveness. In the end, Isabella is a wiser and finer woman, though scarcely the "thing enskied and sainted" of Lucio's famous tribute; but then, Lucio was hardly a qualified judge in these matters. The Duke, who estimates Isabella more sensibly, evidently proposes to marry her. And so skillful has he been in leading her to forgo self-righteousness and revenge and to prefer forgiveness, that we may hope well of their marriage; for the Duke has shown himself a wise and Christian ruler, and Isabella has learned the Christian virtue of charity.

The Duke has prompted the action from the beginning, and none of the other characters has realized the full scope and significance of his operations. He has deceived them all for their own good, this "duke of dark corners," and, in the end, as Wilson Knight has suggested,[13] the Duke seems almost like the author himself telling us a story, speaking for the puppets and pulling the strings before our eyes, to show us how the mercy of the Sermon on the Mount transcends the limitations of human justice and fills human life with the radiance of love. And yet, while the action is going forward, Angelo and Isabella and Claudio, Lucio and Pompey and Barnardine and the rest, all seem real enough; and everyone, under the Duke's direction, makes some kind of choice, even Barnardine, who chooses not to be bothered. The play is not a parable or an allegory, unless we regard it in only one aspect, its symbolic aspect; it is an action, a drama of men and women lusting and hating, loving and suffering, as well. But it has great dramatic suspense and a most happy ending, and the Duke's conduct, until the end, seems very mysterious and arbitrary; and all this makes the play seem something like a fairy tale too. It is this mingling of effects of successful realism with the more obvious artifice of the Duke's role that apparently sits so ill with some critics; though the same mingling of "art" and "artifice"—to use Professor Stoll's distinction—is to be found in *The Tempest*.

In *The Tempest*, Shakespeare uses essentially the same design but he alters his narrative method. Prospero explains his purposes, during the course of the action, as overtly as the Duke of *Measure for Measure* conceals his. The dramatic situation, too, is handled differently. *Measure for Measure* shows an action *ab ovo*, from its inception through the appointment of Angelo as the Duke's deputy to the general pardon at the end; whereas *The Tempest* shows only the end of an action, the turning point of which has been achieved before the play opens. The wrong suffered by Prospero occurred when Miranda was a child of three. During the years while Miranda has been growing up, Prospero has been maturing his magic arts and biding the moment appointed that shall deliver his enemies into his hands. He has had ample time to digest his resentment and examine his conscience; and his magic has become so powerful that it must serve as an instrument of great evil or great good.

The real conflict of the play's design is the moral conflict of Prospero, but the play itself shows us only the benevolent results of its resolution. The terms of its resolution are marked for us just before the climax, in Prospero's words to Ariel:

> Though with their high wrongs I am struck to th' quick,
> Yet with my nobler reason 'gainst my fury
> Do I take part. The rarer action is
> In virtue than in vengeance. They being penitent,
> The sole drift of my purpose doth extend
> Not a frown further. . . .
>
> (v.i.25-30)

But his choice has been made before the play opens, as the earlier acts imply. The spectacular storm scene with which the play begins is immediately explained as part of Prospero's design:

> Tell your piteous heart
> There's no harm done,

he says to Miranda. We listen, with her, to the account of its causes, and learn from the following dialogue with Ariel (I.ii. 189ff.) what to expect in the ensuing scenes.

This is the epitome of the method used throughout. We witness a succession of spectacles and pseudo-conflicts, preceded or accompanied by the explanatory comment of Prospero. In place of the real conflict of Prospero's choice, we have the balanced pseudo-conflicts of Antonio's design to make Sebastian King of Naples, and the drunken efforts of Caliban and the clowns to become lords of the isle. But we are in no suspense about the outcome of either, for we see (and Prospero himself repeatedly informs us; III.iii.90; IV.i.263-4) that there is no resisting his magic; it paralyzes his opponents, deprives them of reason and boils their brains within their skulls; Caliban and his companions are wracked with cramps and dance up to their chins in the filthy-mantled pool beyond Prospero's cell. In the awakening love of Ferdinand and Miranda, Prospero similarly instructs us concerning his purpose and tactics, though here his magic consists simply in the psychology of opposition and the choice remains the lovers' own.

When we reflect upon it, we cannot help noticing how close the parallel is with *Measure for Measure*. In each play, the action is set going and guided throughout by its duke; yet neither Duke Vincentio nor Prospero controls anyone else's choice; rather, they prepare the conditions in which others choose while taking precautions that no one shall give effect to a choice injurious to others. As Vincentio guides Claudio and Angelo to choose penitence and Isabella to prefer mercy to revenge or justice, so Prospero guides Alonso to choose penitence, Ferdinand to choose the love of Mirando, while he himself forgoes revenge or even justice in favor of mercy; and even Caliban shows signs of amendment at the end. As Barnardine and Lucio in *Measure for Measure* are given the chance to repent, though they remain unmoved, so with Antonio and Sebastian; but though all four are pardoned, they are also curbed of their evil propensities.

The parallelism is not precise—nor should we expect it to be;

Shakespeare does not repeat himself—but it is fundamental, arising as it does out of the identical ruling conception of the two
plays: the virtue of forgiveness and the tempering of justice with
mercy; and the parallel may be carried further. In the two dukes,
there is the suggestion of an earlier unworldliness and a consequent failure to anticipate evil or cope with it—Prospero in failing
to anticipate his brother's plot against him, Vincentio in failing to
curb the evil conditions of Vienna. When each duke begins to
act effectively, his conduct seems to invoke a certain supernatural
aid and sanction. Duke Vincentio's arrangements are compared
with the operation of Divine Grace (*Measure for Measure*,
v.i.374), while Prospero's "white magic" is explained as divinely
sanctioned: Ariel and his fellows are "ministers of fate" (iii.iii.
60ff.), and their powers cannot be used to serve an evil purpose,
as Sycorax discovered. Thus each duke is seen as the human
agent who gives effect to the moral order of things as divinely
authorized. And appropriately, after the wrongs have been
righted and the reconciliations effected, Duke Vincentio lays
aside his friar's robe and returns to his appointed role as ruler of
Vienna; Prospero breaks his staff, drowns his book, and resumes
his natural function as Duke of Milan. Prospero's method
throughout *The Tempest* has been to deceive men for their own
good; so with Duke Vincentio; and *The Tempest* shows us the
same design of "measure for measure": the suffering visited upon
Prospero is in turn meted to his enemies; but the grace that preserved Prospero also preserves them.

When each duke puts off his disguise and stands revealed in
his true temporal status, the Duke of Vienna and the Duke of
Milan, each is seen as a *temporal* authority, the good governor
who knows how to mingle mercy with justice. Mr. Wilson
Knight has associated *Measure for Measure* with the text: "Judge
not, that ye be not judged," and has further written: "The central idea of *Measure for Measure* is this: 'And forgive us our debts
as we forgive our debtors.' Thus 'justice' is a mockery: man, himself a sinner, cannot presume to judge. That is the lesson driven
home in *Measure for Measure*." [14] But this way of putting it over-
looks an important point. Duke Vincentio and Duke Prospero
are both temporal rulers; that is, to a sixteenth-century way of
thought, they are divinely constituted authorities whose duty it is

to rule and judge other men, according to the precept and
example of Scripture, with justice and mercy. This is precisely the
problem with which *Measure for Measure* deals, how to do this;
and it is likewise the difficulty that confronts Prospero. Each of
them solves the problem, though by different means. Duke Vincentio relies upon a conveniently impenetrable disguise and a certain ubiquitousness that makes it possible for him to influence
people's purposes strongly for good; and Prospero has his magic;
but each of them stands revealed at the end in his proper role
as an earthly ruler who judges his subjects with authority. Each
is a type and model of the Christian governor.

Finally, each play contains a subtle implication of the transi-
toriness, the illusion, even, of the life it depicts. In *Measure for
Measure,* this is faintly yet definitely implied through the sustained theatricality of the Duke's role and in his homily to the
penitent Claudio, *de contemptu mundi,* in Act III.[15] In *The
Tempest,* the theme becomes beautifully explicit in Prospero's
famous lines at the end of the Masque of Ceres (iv.i.146-58),
and in the epilogue. Here, the breaking of the dramatic illusion
is deliberate. Before our very eyes, the great Duke of Milan and
the mighty magician vanishes; Prospero stands before us as a
poor player, who entreats our applause. The play itself has been
"such stuff as dreams are made on."

These affiliations between the two plays can hardly be inad-
vertent on Shakespeare's part. *Measure for Measure* is an important *'source"* for *The Tempest*. The later play is a reworking of
the theme of the former, employing a different dramatic method
and calculated for a different dramatic effect. *Measure for Measure* is all action; *The Tempest* is largely spectacle invested with
some of the finest poetry Shakespeare ever wrote. The significance of the one emerges from the pattern of the action, without commentary; of the other, from a succession of magic spells
accompanied by the magician's interpretive comment. The
method of *The Tempest* is less dramatic, less deeply moving,
perhaps; it is pictorially static, "spatial," as Mr. Wilson Knight
calls it; and this effect is in remarkable contrast with the temporal, dynamic movement of *Measure for Measure*. But the
method of *The Tempest* affords very much greater scope for the
decorating of the theme, with the panoply of the court masque,

its gorgeous properties of costume and music and setting, graceful dances and tableaux, and the richer texture of poetic image and symbol. None of these compete with the action or the developing thought of *The Tempest*, made crystal clear in Prospero's explanations. In *Measure for Measure*, the method is indirect and more economical of decoration; and by the same token it is the more deeply stirring; the action contains the thought, the symbolic effect, which is achieved wholly by implication.

NOTES

1. The play, of course, has afforded plenty of complexity to the commentators who have explored the analogies it has suggested to their ingenious fancies—analogies with Shakespeare's own career, with political events of the reign of James, even with the initiation rites of primitive cultures. With these and kindred speculations we shall not here be concerned.

2. *Coleridge's Shakespeare Criticism,* ed. T. M. Raysor (London, 1930), I, 113-14.

3. The origins and development of this view have been set forth at length in the two British Academy Shakespeare Lectures of C. J. Sisson ("The Mythical Sorrows of Shakespeare," 1934) and R. W. Chambers ("The Jacobean Shakespeare and *Measure for Measure,*" 1937).

4. G. Wilson Knight, "*Measure for Measure* and the Gospels," in *The Wheel of Fire* (London, 1930), pp. 80-106; R. W. Chambers, as cited in the preceding note; R. W. Battenhouse, "*Measure for Measure* and Christian Doctrine of the Atonement," *PMLA,* LXI (1946), 1029-59; Elizabeth M. Pope, "The Renaissance Background of *Measure for Measure,*" *Shakespeare Survey,* 2 (Cambridge, 1949), pp. 66-82.

5. W. W. Lawrence, *Shakespeare's Problem Comedies* (New York, 1931), pp. 78-121; Virgil K. Whitaker, "Philosophy and Romance in Shakespeare's 'Problem' Comedies," *The Seventeenth Century* (Stanford, Cal., 1951), pp. 339-54.

6. O. J. Campbell, *Shakespeare's Satire* (London, 1943); see also his *Comicall Satyre and Shakespeare's Troilus and Cressida* (San Marino, Cal., 1938); E. M. W. Tillyard, *Shakespeare's Problem Comedies* (Toronto, 1949); Murray Kreiger, "*Measure for Meas-*

ure and Elizabethan Comedy," *PMLA*, LVI (1951), 775-84. The inference from these adverse criticisms of the play's technique is really in support of the view of the first group of commentators here distinguished, for the ethical unsatisfactoriness of the play may be related to its supposed technical shortcomings.

7. This is the implication of M. C. Bradbrook, "Authority, Truth, and Justice in *Measure for Measure*," *Review of English Studies*, XVII (1941), 385-99, who sees the play as a sustained allegory in dramatic form. See, more particularly, Francis Fergusson, "Philosophy and Theatre in *Measure for Measure*," *The Kenyon Review*, XIV (1952), 103-20, where it is argued that the play is to be understood "both as philosophy and as poetry-of-the-theatre, but that the two are not separate, or merely mechanically combined, but two cognate modes of presenting a single underlying vision of man in society" (p. 104).

8. All references to the text of Shakespeare are taken from the *Complete Works*, ed. G. L. Kittredge (1936).

9. That Barnardine's execution should be deferred and his offences finally pardoned is no sentimental concession to the happy ending but a serious part of the doctrine of the play. How terrible a thing it seemed to Shakespeare's time that a man should die unrepentant is witnessed as late as Shirley's *The Wedding*, where the plot turns upon the idea that it is incredible that a man not utterly abandoned to evil should die with a lie upon his lips. An Iago or a Macbeth may defy heaven; but Barnardine is insensible in his villainy and hence the responsibility for sending him to eternal judgment rests with his earthly judges.

10. *Johnson on Shakespeare*, ed. W. Raleigh (London, 1908), p. 80.

11. In certain ways, the method much resembles that later adapted by Beaumont and Fletcher to more superficial ends in *Philaster;* see a paper by the present writer, "*Philaster* and *Cymbeline*," *English Institute Essays, 1951* (New York, 1952), pp. 146-67. The technique of surprise is, of course, familiar enough throughout the history of drama, or of narrative, for that matter; but the skill and subtlety of its use vary a great deal. In *Measure for Measure*, as is here suggested, Shakespeare provides a masterly example of this dramatic method.

12. It is Lucio, the libertine, we must remember, who sees her,

at the beginning of the play, as "a thing enskied and sainted" (I.iv.34). The same Lucio sees the Duke as "a very superficial, ignorant, unweighing fellow . . ."; who "would have dark deeds darkly answered; he would never bring them to light. . . . The Duke . . . would eat mutton on Fridays. He's not past it yet; . . . he would mouth with a beggar, though she smelt of brown bread and garlic" (III.ii.147,187-195).

13. *The Wheel of Fire*, p. 79; cf. Francis Fergusson in the *Kenyon Review*, XIV (1952), 103ff.

14. *The Wheel of Fire*, pp. 73, 76; cf. also M. C. Bradbrook, as cited in note 7, above.

15. III.i.6-34. See also Francis Fergusson in the *Kenyon Review*, XIV (1952), 117-18, for this and other examples of this theme in *Measure for Measure*.

Elmer Edgar Stoll

SOURCE AND MOTIVE IN
MACBETH AND OTHELLO

The best tragedy—highest tragedy in short—is that of the worthy encompassed by the inevitable.

THOMAS HARDY

SHAKESPEARE, of course, has, like the Greeks—unlike the Bourbon French—no règles, neither rule nor formula. But for all that, why in *Othello* and *Macbeth,* two of the great tragedies that are not histories and that apparently are not in any measure *rifacimenti* of previous plays, does he, in the matter of motivation, deviate so widely and so similarly from his source?

What in *Macbeth* he has omitted and what substituted Sir Arthur Quiller-Couch has made admirably clear, but has not considered the reasons for this or the similarity of procedure in *Othello*. In Holinshed's Chronicle there is the suggestion that, cut off by the nomination of Malcolm as successor to the throne from his own expectations, Macbeth had for his usurpation "a juste quarell so to do (as he tooke the matter)." The crown was then not strictly hereditary, and "by the old lawes of the realme, if he that should succeed were not of able age to take the charge upon himselfe, he that was next of blood should be admitted." [1] "Did Shakespeare use that one hint, enlarge that loophole?" asks Sir Arthur. "He did not."

From *From Shakespeare to Joyce,* 1944, pp. 295-306. Copyright 1944 by Elmer Edgar Stoll. Reprinted by permission of the author and Doubleday & Company, Inc.

Instead of using a paltry chance to condone Macbeth's guilt, he seized on it and plunged it threefold deeper . . .

He made this man, a sworn soldier, murder Duncan, his liege-lord.

He made this man, a host, murder Duncan, a guest within his gates.

He made this man, strong and hale, murder Duncan, old, weak, asleep and defenceless.

He made this man commit murder for nothing but his own advancement.

He made this man murder Duncan, who had steadily advanced him hitherto, who had never been aught but trustful, and who (that no detail of reproach might be wanting) had that very night, as he retired, sent, in most kindly thought, the gift of a diamond to his hostess.

To sum up: instead of extenuating Macbeth's criminality, Shakespeare doubles and redoubles it. [*Shakespeare's Workmanship* (Holt, N. Y., 1930), pp. 19-20.]

And yet Macbeth is the protagonist, the hero, with whom as such, for the right tragic effect, there must, naturally, be some large measure of sympathy. So, having thus put him much farther beyond the reach of our sympathy than in the original, what does the dramatist then do but (indirectly) bring him back within it—in general, by the power of poetry, in particular, by the exhibition of the hero's bravery and virtue at the beginning, by emphasizing the influence of the supernatural presented, and of his wife's inordinate ambition distinctly mentioned, in the source.

There are additional devices which Sir Arthur dwells upon, such as the flattening of the other characters—that the hero and heroine may stand out in high relief, to absorb our interest and (presumably on the principle considered in the preceding chapter) our sympathy also; and such as the keeping of the murders, as the ancients do, in the background, off the stage. "There is some deep law in imaginative illusion," says Watts-Dunton,[2] "whereby the identification of the spectator's personality is with the active character in most dramatic actions rather than the passive." We share the emotions, the perturbations, of Macbeth and his Lady, as even of Clytemnestra and Phaedra, because they are the impassioned doers and speakers, constantly in the foreground; and it is with their ears that we hear the owl and the cricket, the voices in the castle and the knocking at the gate. And still more clearly than in the veiling of the horrors the method is that of the ancients. The central complication—the contrast—is that recommended by Aristotle,[3] the *good* man doing the dreadful deed, though not unwittingly, nor quite unwillingly either. As with the ancients, again, he is under the sway of fate; for the Weird Sisters and his Lady—"burning in unquenchable desire to beare the name of a queene" [4]—together amount to that.

This, of course, is not what we ordinarily call motivation, not psychology. For both—the narrative or external motivation and the internal—there was, positively and negatively, better provision in Holinshed—not only the "juste quarell (as he took the matter)" but also "the feeble and slouthfull administration of Duncane," [5] no treachery or violation of the laws of hospitality in the killing, and the just and efficient rule (for ten years) in the sequel.[6] *La carrière ouverte aux talents,* and Macbeth had the justification of Napoleon, of Cromwell. But not Shakespeare's Macbeth.

Nor is this what we call drama, either, as it is ordinarily practiced today. It is as in Aristotle,—situation first and motivation or psychology afterwards, if at all. The effect is emotional, with which psychology or even simple narrative coherence often considerably interferes. To Schiller's neglect of careful motivation, and in a day of psychology and philosophy both, Goethe even attributes his superiority on the stage.[7] Shakespeare sometimes neglects it because it can be counted upon as familiar; sometimes, as with Hamlet's feigning of lunacy and Lear's dividing of the kingdom, because, the motive in the old play not being a good one, it is better that it should be omitted or only hinted at; but in Macbeth the omission is for a positive purpose, and the contravention of psychological probability is so as well. Here, as generally in Shakespeare, *Coriolanus* being only a partial exception, character is not its own destiny, the action is not exclusively derived from it. For Shakespeare "a human being" is *not,* as in Galsworthy's words or as in his own and his fellows' practice, "the best plot there is." To his minor characters the words better apply. The hero's conduct, at the heart of the action, is often not in keeping with his essential nature but in contrast with it.

Manifestly, and, if not forthwith, certainly upon a moment's consideration, by all the motives prompting or circumstances attending the murder of Duncan that have been omitted, the big, sharply outlined, highly emotional contrast in the situation of a good man doing the deed of horror would be broken or obscured. If Macbeth had been thwarted or (to use Holinshed's word) "defrauded," as having, at this juncture, a better title to the throne than Malcolm, or had thought himself better fitted to rule; or, again, if Duncan had not borne his faculties so meek and been so clear in his great office, as in the tragedy but not the chronicle he is; why, then, Macbeth's conduct in killing him would have been more reasonable and more psychologically in keeping, to be sure, but less terrible, less truly tragic. Even if Duncan had been less affectionate and generous, less admiring and confiding, still the hero's conduct would have been less truly tragic! There is positive need of "the deep damnation of his taking off." For the tragedy is of the brave and honorable man suddenly and squarely—fatally, too—turned against the moral order. Sir Arthur compares him to Satan about to engage in the temptation: "Evil, be thou my good." Or "Fair is foul and foul is fair," as the Weird Sisters have it, which Macbeth on his first appearance echoes—

So foul and fair a day I have not seen.

And that situation, no question, is a contrast big and sharp enough.

Sir Arthur does not, indeed, pause to take notice how unpsychological the change here is. Others besides fallen archangels have so turned about, but evil they do not continue to call evil. Macbeth so does. He has scarcely a word of ambition beforehand, not a word of delight in the power when attained. As Mr. Firkins and even Mr. Bradley have noticed, it is the deterrents that he dwells upon, not the incentives; it is the spectral bloody dagger that he sees, not a glittering crown; it is "withered murder" that he follows to the chamber, not the call to sovereign sway and masterdom. In horror he commits the crime, even as he is to remember it. There is no satisfaction but only torment in the thought of it. The conscience in him, before and after, is that of a good man, not that of the man who can do such wickedness;

first the voice of God, then either that or else—"accuser of man-kind"!—the devil's.[8] It is Macbeth himself that considers the "deep damnation," and neither before nor after does he deceive himself, as the good turning to wickedness necessarily do. But the contrast is kept clear and distinct; and the emotional effect —that the whole world has acknowledged.

If, on the other hand, Shakespeare had kept to history, to reality and psychology! If he had followed Holinshed—made more of Macbeth's grievances, dilated on Duncan's unfitness and his own fitness to rule, without bringing on his head the blood of an old man, asleep, his benefactor and guest! If he had dwelt on reasons for committing instead of not committing the crime! And if afterwards he had expressed the psychologically natural or appropriate opinions upon his own conduct, excusing or pal-liating it, perhaps even justifying it! If in short Macbeth (and his Lady, too, who invokes the powers of evil at the outset and is tormented by conscience at the end) had acted more like the human beings we know of; why, then we should have had de-cidedly less of contrast and excitement, of imaginative and emo-tional power generated and discharged, of poetry and drama.

2

The treatment of the material in *Othello*, probably an earlier play, is somewhat the same. In Cinthio there is no warrant for introducing the supernatural; but in Shakespeare's hands the villain takes the place of Fate—of the Weird Sisters and the Lady —and more completely than is usual in the tragedy of the Renaissance. He is a devil in the flesh, as Booth played him, as Coleridge and Lamb implied, and George Woodberry, J. J. Chap-man, Lytton Strachey, John Palmer, not to mention others, have put it explicitly.[9] Iago himself practically acknowledges it in the soliloquies—"Hell and night," "Divinity of hell! when devils will the blackest sins put on"—and on that point apparently he and Othello at the end are agreed:

> If that thou beest a devil, I cannot kill thee—
> [*wounds* IAGO]
> I bleed, sir, but not kill'd.

Before that, to be sure, the Ancient is misapprehended by everybody; yet as Fate, as master of the show, he is holding nearly all the strings of the action in hand, and leading both heroine and hero to destruction. In the victim now, not the victimizer, is the great change; but from good to evil only under a complete delusion—"be thou my good" he neither says nor thinks, and the prince of villains himself has no need to say it. For again, as in *Macbeth,* the motives are dispensed with. The Ensign of the *novella* is deprived of the internal incentives to his wickedness, and the Moor relieved of the traits which might have provoked or somewhat warranted it.

As Professor Wolfgang Keller notices, the villainy is "better motived" in the source. That is, more plausibly, more realistically. Not a devil in the flesh, a "black angel," as Mr. Chapman calls him, Cinthio's Ensign is still of "the most depraved nature in the world" (*della più scelerata natura che mai fosse huomo del mondo*). But as such he has provocation enough. He is a rejected suitor, and really suspects the Captain (Shakespeare's Cassio) of being the favored one. Against both him and the lady he has a grudge; his love for her is turned to the "bitterest hate"; whereas in the tragedy his love for Desdemona and her intrigue with Cassio are, like Cassio's and Othello's with Emilia, pretexts and afterthoughts. There he has need of these. His genuine reason for resentment is against Othello, but only for promoting Cassio above him, and against Cassio (incidentally) for being promoted. In soliloquy, as always in drama, the truth will out. "I hate the Moor," he mutters,

> *And it is thought* abroad that 'twixt my sheets
> He has done my office.

And the next moment the pretext is made still plainer: "I know not if't be true, but I for mere suspicion in that kind will do as if for surety." [10]

So the Ensign is deprived of his motive as much as the Thane of Glamis—as much as Richard III of his, which was ambition, or as Goneril and Regan of theirs, which was envy,[11]—but without an external Fate to relieve him of the burden of his iniquity. He carries it indeed, like the Weird Sisters, lightly enough; and the Aristotelian contrast of the good man doing the deed of horror is presented in his victim, who, however, unlike Macbeth, is guilty only of a mistake in judgment—the *hamartia*—and is far from uttering Satan's cry. Othello never loses our sympathy, as Macbeth, despite the poignant presentation of his sufferings, cannot but in some measure do.

What is almost quite as important to the emotional effect—to the steep tragic contrast—as the apparently unmitigated wickedness of Iago, is, as in the Caledonian tragedy, the nature of the victim and the circumstances of the crime. As we have seen, Shakespeare's Moor has changed places with his wife in the villain's enmity. Love turned to hatred is too ambiguous and appealing a passion—it is that, moreover, into which the Moor himself is precipitated, and, as Strachey observes, the villain's must not be anything of a parallel. For the contrast, again, it must not be. Moreover, though Cinthio's Moor is given some noble and attractive traits, especially at the outset, Shakespeare's is both there and throughout on a far higher level of intelligence and feeling. He is not a stupid dupe or a vulgarly vindictive cuckold. He is not the man to call the informer in to do the killing, or the concealing of it afterwards. For his own safety, Shakespeare's, unlike Cinthio's Moor, shows no concern. Nor is there, for that matter, the slightest evidence in his conduct or his utterance, nor in the woman's either, of the love Iago suspects between him and Emilia—no more than there is in Iago's own conduct or utterance, indeed, of his own love for Desdemona—though of late there has been a fairly prominent critic to say there is.[12] That would be like thinking, with some Germans, that Hamlet had betrayed Ophelia, for which, to be sure, there is a little evidence, though far from enough; or with some Frenchmen, that Lady Macbeth, as, reenacting in memory the deed of blood, she whispers, "to bed, to bed! there's knocking at the gate . . . to bed, to bed, to bed," she, having enticed her husband, is now for rewarding him. On the contrary, the black man is made the grandest and noblest of Shakespeare's lovers; and it is only through Iago's overwhelming reputation for honesty and sagacity, the impenetrableness of his mask together with the potency of his seductive arts, that he is led astray and succumbs. For the highest tragic effect it is the great and good man that succumbs. Like other supreme artists, Shakespeare has here created his own world, which holds together. Like Corneille (*les grands sujets de la tragédie doivent toujours aller au delà du vraisemblable*) Goethe holds that *in den höheren Regionen des künstlerischen Verfahrens, hat der Künstler ein freieres Spiel, und er darf sogar zu Fiktionen schreiten.*[13] This Shakespeare boldly does. No one else sees through Iago, including his own wife; so Othello, for not seeing, is no gull or dupe. In the matter of the Ancient's cleverness in maneuver and also of his success in hypocrisy the English is a little indebted to the Italian writer; but the Ensign's wife does see through him and only for fear of him holds her tongue.

3

In both *Macbeth* and *Othello*, then, it is the whole situation that is mainly important, not the character; it is the reciprocal matter of motivation (whether present or missing), of defects or qualities in both victim and victimizer together. Here lies the chief point of the present discussion. What if Shakespeare's Macbeth and Duncan had been like Holinshed's, or like Henry IV and Richard II, or like Cromwell and Charles I? And as I have elsewhere said, "How the scope and stature of Iago's wickedness (and of Othello's virtue) would be limited by any adequate grudge!"[14] How they would be also by a credulous or suspicious nature—a predisposition or a psychology—in the hero! Against that Shakespeare has guarded not only by Iago's impregnable reputation and by his all-prevailing arts but also by Othello's own reputation for capability and for virtue. (A world of reputation and circumstance here, not of motive!) Before the temptation begins, as in *Macbeth*, but much more fully and felicitously, the Moor has not only in his own right but through the admiration of everybody (and here even of the villain been firmly established in our good opinion and our sympathies. So with Desdemona, too, and she is not deceitful or supersubtle as Mr. Shaw would have her, not enough so "to strengthen the case for Othello's jealousy"; the dramatic preparations are emotional, not analytical and psychological, primarily for the situation, not the character. And both women, Emilia at the last and Desdemona once the action is well started, are shocked at the discoveries

they make in their husbands. But she is justified, when hers gives
signs of jealousy, in being unable to believe it; "not easily jealous"
he himself says (where a Shakespearean hero, or his best friend,
is expected to know and everything comes to light) at the end.
Even Iago, hearing that Othello is angry, exclaims,

> and is he angry?
> Something of moment, then. I will go meet him.
> There's matter in't indeed, if he be angry.

And in the fourth act, when the jealous rage is fully upon him,
Lodovico, newly come from Venice, is moved to wonder and to
grief.

> Is this the nature
> Whom passion could not shake? whose solid virtue
> The shot of accident nor dart of chance
> Could neither graze nor pierce?

"He is much chang'd," Iago coolly, and still not superfluously,
replies. So he is, until, in the last scene, by Emilia's disclosures
and Iago's self-betraying resentment, he recovers something of
his old stately and generous self.

Macbeth too is changed, but for once and all. Othello had suffered from an overpowering delusion, and has just now, he thinks,
performed an act of justice. Macbeth, not deluded, has come
under the dominion of evil, his "eternal jewel given to the common enemy of man." Neither change is probable. In neither is
there much of what can be called psychology. In life neither person would really have done what he did. In both tragedy and
comedy, however, that is not exactly what is to be expected: for
a Henry IV, a Cromwell, we should turn to history, not the stage.
What is expected is what from life we do not get—enlargement,
excitement, another world, not a copy of this. And that airy
edifice, an imaginative structure, is the emotionally consistent
story or situation as a whole,—the conduct of characters both
active and passive, perhaps also a motiving both external and
internal, but in any case an interplay of relations or circumstances
as important as the motives themselves; not to mention the appor-
tionment of emphasis or relief whether in the framework or the
expression, the poetry that informs both, and the individuality

of the speech, which, real, though poetical, leads one to accept and delight in the improbable things said or done. "It is when their minds (those of the audience) are preoccupied with his personality," says Dr. Bridges of Macbeth, "that the actions follow as unquestionable realities." [15] Not merely, that is, when the actions proceed from the character; and the convincing quality of the speech is only a participating element in the consistent overpowering imaginative and emotional effect of the whole.

4

"In tragedy and comedy both," I have said elsewhere, "life must be, as it has ever been, piled on life, or we have visited the theater in vain." It is not primarily to present characters in their convincing reality that Shakespeare and the Greeks have written, nor in an action strictly and wholly of their doing, but to set them in a state of high commotion, and thus to move and elevate the audience in turn. And here I fall back upon the authority of Mr. Santayana, a philosopher (but also a poet and critic) who, without my knowledge until of late,[16] expressed, though from a different point of view, similar opinions before me:

> Aristotle was justified in making the plot the chief element in fiction; for it is by virtue of the plot that the characters live, or, rather, that we live in them, and by virtue of the plot accordingly that our soul rises to the imaginative activity by which we tend at once to escape from the personal life and to realise its ideal. . . .

And as the eminent critic proceeds, he maintains that poetry is not

> at its best when it depicts a further possible experience, but when it initiates us, by feigning something which as an experience is impossible, into the meaning of the experience which we have actually had.

And that is partly because "in the theater," as the producer Mr. Robert Edmond Jones has assured us, "the actual thing is never the exciting thing. Unless life is turned into art on the stage it stops being alive and goes dead." [17] It is by the excitement that the meaning is brought home to us. And that is true, as in the next chapter we shall see, even without a stage or without poetry, as in Dickens, who, according to Chesterton, "could only make his characters probable if he was allowed to make them impossible."

NOTES

1. *Boswell-Stone's Holinshed* (1896), p. 25. Sir Arthur's quotation, preceding, is curtailed: "for that Duncane did what in him lay to defraud him of all maner of title and claime, which he might, in time to come, pretend unto the crowne."

2. *Harper's* (November, 1906), p. 818. Touched on in the preceding chapter and in note 10 there.

3. *Poetics, cap.* 13, 14.

4. *Boswell-Stone's Holinshed* (1896), p. 25.

5. *Ibid.,* p. 32. Cf. p. 20: "At length, Macbeth speaking much against the kings softnes and overmuch slacknesse in punishing offenders." . . .

6. *Ibid.,* p. 32: "he set his whole intention to maintaine justice and to punish all enormities and abuses which had chanced," etc.; "made manie holesome laws and statutes for the publike weale."

7. Eckermann (Castle), I, 400.

8. Cf. below, chap. XVI.

9. For their opinions see my *Shakespeare and Other Masters,* pp. 233, 238, 243-44.

10. Cf. *Shakespeare and Other Masters,* pp. 236-38, for the way that his suspicions become convictions.

11. In the old *King Leir,* envy of Cordelia's beauty, cf. E. E. Kellett, *Suggestions* (1923), p. 38. For Richard, cf. Brandl, *Shakespeare* (1937), p. 120.

12. It is of course not enough to urge the probabilities upon us —that a healthy and vigorous soldier of the time would lead "a *man's* life," and that Emilia was none too good for taking up with him. As I have repeatedly reminded my readers, no character in fiction has a private life, beyond the reach of the writer, which a character in a biography or history, on the other hand, has, not being the writer's own creation. And in Shakespearean drama, as in the ancient or the classical French, none has the

"past" or the "love life" that is more readily expected, and so more easily suggested, today. Cf. chap. VIII, above.

13. Eckermann, April 18, 1827.—I hope Corneille here does not go beyond the endurable.

14. *Shakespeare and Other Masters*, p. 245.

15. *The Influence of the Audience on Shakespeare's Drama*.

16. *Poetry and Religion* (1900). Cf. my *Shakespeare and Other Masters*, p. 369. The passage here quoted is as in the *Works* (Scribner, N. Y., 1936) ii.

17. *The Dramatic Imagination* (1941), p. 82 (quoted by W. W. Lawrence, *Modern Language Review*, October, 1942, p. 424).

Robert B. Heilman

WIT AND WITCHCRAFT:
AN APPROACH TO *OTHELLO*

THE CRITIC who proposes a reading of *Othello* may hope for it
that it will appear at least to illuminate some of the parts and at
most to contribute to the understanding of the sum of the parts.
If *Othello* is not the most complex of the tragedies, the problem
of its over-all form is still a large one, and he who aspires to a
full account of the creative relationship of all the parts [1] must
be content if he seems generally to be moving in the right direction. The theory of the whole that proceeds from an examination
of the parts will at best be a distant cousin of the drama; such
wit as the critic may have can but follow the witchcraft of the
dramatist (to take Iago's words out of context) from afar. But
the cousin may help identify the drama, the wit tell how the
witchcraft has gone. At the same time the critic, whatever he
imparts, must at many points duplicate and parallel his predecessors while essaying to be himself; so he runs the double risk of
not encompassing the novelty which will absolve him of the suspicion of merely repeating what oft was thought, or of falling
into innovations which in other quarters will seem dubious because such things were never thought.

The parts which make up the whole are numerous and diverse.

From *The Sewanee Review*, Vol. 64, No. 1, Winter 1956, copyright 1956 by the University of the South, pp. 1-4, 8-10 and *Arizona
Quarterly*, Spring 1956, pp. 5-16. Reprinted by permission of the
author and the editors, with new transitional material supplied by the
author. The ideas in this essay are among those developed by Mr.
Heilman in *Magic in the Web: Action and Language in Othello*, copyright 1956 by the University of Kentucky Press; used with permission.

Othello is a part. Iago is a part. Iago's deception of Roderigo is a part. Iago's remarks on reputation, Desdemona's incredulity at the sexual misbehavior of wives, Emilia's revulsion against Iago, Cassio's drunken babbling are parts. All recognitions and reversals, all thoughts and feelings of characters are parts. The night-time in which most of the major actions occur is a part. Iago's use of *honesty* is a part. All the uses of *honesty* are a part. All the metaphors of medicine and disease, the images from army life, the language of light and dark are parts.

The point is to keep the idea of the part flexible and inclusive, as a step toward adequate freedom in the description of structure. A view of the parts begotten of a preoccupation with gross anatomy will yield a coarse and constricted account of structure. On the other hand, compiling an unlimited serial list of parts would be futile. The main thing is to be aware of a part in all its relational possibilities.[2] Othello's farewell to arms (3.3.348ff.) is relevant to the specific situation of the moment, to Othello's personality generally, to Shakespeare's conception of the modes of response to disaster possible to human beings. Emilia's picking up the handkerchief helps advance the action by contributing to Iago's deception of Othello, but it is also relevant to her character and to Shakespeare's conception of the modes of wifely devotion and marital relationship (not to mention its relations by contrast with actions of Desdemona and Bianca and of Emilia herself later). The theories of sex which Iago advances to Roderigo are relevant to his purpose of controlling Roderigo, to his modes of thought generally, and to Shakespeare's awareness of the whole realm of philosophies of love.

For working criticism, the broad categories of the parts whose relatedness is to be observed are two: plot and poetry. We might again borrow Iago's words for metaphor and speak of the wit and witchcraft of the dramatist: the conscious designing and articulating; and the mysterious endowing of many parts—especially the poetic language—with dramatic value and meaning far in excess of the minimal logical requirements of the occasion: the magic in the web. This is less a theory of composition than an effort to suggest different aspects of the play that are only theoretically separable. Let us put it another way. If love is what *Othello* is "about," *Othello* is not only a play about love but a

poem about love.[3] It has parts which interact in the mode of
"pure" drama—people having such and such an effect on each
other, irrespective of whether they communicate in verse, prose
or pantomime; it also has parts which interact in the manner of
a poem. Again, this is a theoretical separation: the characters
have such and such an effect by means of the words they speak;
and conversely, an analysis of the words they speak involves the
student regularly in a consideration of the "action" and interaction of the speakers. Yet when the dramatist has his characters
speak in poetic language, he vastly complicates their communication with each other and with us. Figure, rhythm, poetic order do
not merely make "more vivid" or "heighten" a literal prose statement that is otherwise unchanged; they constitute a fundamentally different statement by the introduction of the nuance,
overtone, feeling, association, implication, and extension characteristic of them; in other words, by subtly carrying us beyond
the finiteness, one-dimensionalism, and contextual restrictions of
the pure statement determined only by the strict logical requirements of the immediate situation. When Othello summons Desdemona and dismisses Emilia, "Leave procreants alone . . . ;
/Cough or cry hem if anybody come./ Your mystery, your mystery! . . ." (4.2.28-30), he not only dismisses Emilia, accuses
Desdemona of infidelity, and betrays his own insane bitterness,
but he converts the marriage into a brothel arrangement in
which all three are involved, and by so doing establishes imaginative lines of connection with the role of Bianca and particularly with the Iago philosophy of sexual conduct. If we take all
the lines of one character out of context and consider them as
a unit, we have always a useful body of information; but if, when
we study Iago's lines, we find that he consistently describes himself in images of hunting and trapping, we learn not only his
plans of action but something of his attitude to occasions, to his
victims, and to himself; and beyond that there is fixed for us an
image of evil—one of those by which the drama interprets the
human situation. When Othello says he threw away a "pearl,"
we recall that Brabantio, in acceding to Desdemona's departure,
called her "jewel"; when Desdemona says she would rather have
lost her purse than the handkerchief, we recall that Iago, who
has stolen the handkerchief, has spoken of stealing a purse; we

spontaneously make these connections, and, even if we go no further, our reading has brought forth linkings that cannot be expunged; but we often do go further, and seek out the formal order that is exemplified in these images that leap out of their own contexts and carry our imaginations into other parts of the play.[4] When to these we add many other instances in which poetic language, functioning doubly or triply, takes us beyond specific moments of action into others and on into general areas of character, feeling, and thought, we find that we have an immensely complicated verbal structure with which we must come to terms—the "poem about love," as I have called it. We are trying to describe what Traversi called "a new kind of dramatic unity." [5]

In pursuit of this dramatic unity we must inevitably take account of one notable characteristic of Shakespeare's verbal drama—its repetitiveness of images and likewise of abstract words. After Emilia has three times incredulously asked, "My husband?" Othello demands, "What needs this iterance, woman?" (5.2.150). We all must play Othello to Shakespeare's Emilia: "iterance" forces itself upon us as a critical problem. The dramatist cannot conspicuously repeat words and rely upon figures of the same class (e.g., clothes, military life) without catching our eye and raising a question about what goes on. We are hardly likely to attribute this recurrency to the artist's carelessness or failing resourcefulness or to stop at description—an inert lexicon of repetitions. When editors devotedly multiply cross references to dictional or rhetorical echoes and anticipations, they act, one assumes, more from a sense of relationship than from a delight in coincidence. Speaking of *Antony and Cleopatra*, Professor Clemen uses a phrase that is valid for other plays: "this symbolical meaning of certain sequences of imagery." [6] As Paul Goodman puts it, Shakespeare's "profusion of images is so handled through a long play that it forms a systematic structure and is part of the plot." He elaborates on

a method that is characteristically Shakespearean: this is to present a line of thought by an independent development of the system of imagery. Put formally: when several characters independently and throughout the play employ the same system of images, the diction becomes an independent part of the plot implying a thought, action, etc., whatever is the principle of the system. For it is not in character for different characters to use the same images.[7]

I suspect that it *may* be "in character for different characters to use the same images," which can be a device for suggesting similarities or even contrasts among them; or if the images belong dominantly to one character in one part of the play, and to another in another part, the change may be an important mark of dramatic progression, as when the almost pre-emptive use of animal imagery passes in mid-play from Iago to Othello. But beyond all its possible uses in characterization, recurrent diction has still other functions. Goodman's phrase "independent development" is the key. For though speeches are in one sense not separable from the characters, in another sense they do become disengaged from particular speakers and enter the general verbal fund of the play. (The more rich and profuse the language, the more this is likely to be true, just as the more rich and powerful the literary work, the more likely it is to become disengaged from its own times, however much these times may be needed for exegetic purposes, and to enter the general timeless fund of literary possessions.) Reiterative language is particularly prone to acquire a continuity of its own and to become "an independent part of the plot" [8] whose effect we can attempt to gauge. It may create "mood" or "atmosphere": the pervasiveness of images of injury, pain, and torture in *Othello* has a very strong impact that is not wholly determined by who uses the images. But most of all the "system of imagery" introduces thoughts, ideas, themes —elements of the meaning that is the author's final organization of all his materials.[9]

II

Before coming directly to the forming of the love-theme that differentiates *Othello* from other Shakespeare plays that utilize the same theme, I turn arbitrarily to Iago to inspect a distinguishing mark of his of which the relevance to thematic form in the play will appear a little later. When Iago with unperceived scoffing reminds Roderigo, who is drawn with merciless attraction to the unreachable Desdemona, that love effects an unwonted nobility in men, he states a doctrine which he "knows" is true but in which he may not "believe." Ennoblement by love is a real possibility in men, but Iago has to view it with bitterness and to try to undermine it. With his spontaneous antipathy to spiritual achievement, he must in principle deny the mysterious transformation of personality; instinctively he is the observer of all these habits that suggest infinite corruptibility as the comprehensive human truth. He is the believer in shrewd observation and in corruption in whose credo, which is not altogether unique, man is a union of lusting, folly, and plotting.

Good sense, hard sense, common sense, no nonsense, rationality—all these terms, we may suppose, are ones which Iago might consider as defining his perspective. As he plays against Othello with his game of honest and loving friend, he uses words that put him on that side of the fence. First he can't tell Othello his "thoughts" (about Cassio) because of his "manhood, honesty," or *"wisdom"* [10] (3.3.153-54); a little later he finds *"reason"* to tell them (193). Othello considers him *"wise"* (4.1.75). While privately Iago may deny his love and kid his honesty, he takes his brains seriously. "Thus do I ever make my *fool* my purse," he boasts; to spend time with Roderigo otherwise, "Mine own gain'd *knowledge* should profane" (1.3.389-90). Othello is to be treated like an *ass* (1.3.408; 2.1. 318). Iago applies the term *fool* successively to Roderigo (2.3.53), Cassio (2.3.359), Desdemona (4.1.186), and Emilia (4.2.148), and condescends to fools "credulous" and "gross" (3.3.404; 4.1.46). His view of himself as the clearheaded manipulator of gulls is significantly unchallenged despite the barrage of derogatory rhetoric eventually aimed at him. He remains the "smart man," apt in "deals," scornful of "suckers."

It is more fun for the smart man if his victim thinks he is using *his* head with especial acuteness. Early in the big deception scene (3.3.93ff.) on which all the subsequent action turns, Iago urges Othello "that your *wisdom* yet" should "take no notice" of Iago's "unsure observance" (148-151); later he repeats, "Nay, but be *wise*" (432). The idea that he is being sharp goes to Othello's head; he resolves to be *"cunning* in my patience" (4.1.91), and he queries erring Desdemona, "Are you *wise*?" (4.1.245). With his new wisdom he murders his unwise wife, and Emilia tells him what he has become: "O *gull!* O *dolt!* / As *ignorant* as dirt! . . . O thou *dull* Moor, . . . what should such a *fool* / Do with so good a wife?" (5.2.163-234). How does Iago try to stop this confessional outburst which will ruin him? By commanding Emilia, "Be *wise,* and get you home" (223). Here he cannot induce that wisdom that serves his own end; the sharp-eyed engineer of folly in others now by necessity collapses into senseless abuse and violence. But Othello's reproach to himself, "O fool! fool! fool!" (323), inadequate a self-judgment as it is, acknowledges Emilia's indictment and, inadvertently, the success of Iago's plot to make him "egregiously an ass." After all this, Othello's "lov'd not wisely" is unconsciously an understatement.

Making a fool of someone else is an aesthetic demonstration of intellectual superiority. It is implicitly partial, temporary; a comic episode after which life goes on. Let this exploit in self-aggrandizement expand with the full pressure of passion, and the attack becomes an ultimate one against sanity: Iago's design to put Othello "into a jealousy so strong / That judgment cannot cure," driving him "even to madness" (2.1.310-11, 320). It is the extreme revenge possible to the man of "reason," a chaos that logically extends and completes the other modes of chaos which Iago instinctively seeks, in a variety of ways, at all stages of the action. Twice again he speaks of Othello's madness as a likelihood or as a formal objective (4.1.56, 101), and his program works well enough to make Lodovico inquire about Othello's mental soundness (4.1.280) and to make Othello express a doubt about his own sanity (5.2.111). Madness spreads: Emilia fears lest Desdemona "run mad" (3.3.317), Othello cries to her that he is "glad to see you mad" (4.1.250), and she in turn fears his "fury" (4.2.32). But the planned madness eventually recoils upon its creator: "What, are you mad?" is Iago's response when Emilia tells the truth about what he has done (5.2.194).

Such points in the auxiliary theme of madness (a slender anticipation of what will be done in *Lear*) mark the course of rational Iago. Insofar as he identifies rationality and wisdom with his own purposes, he is close enough to Everyman; but he is sharply individualized, and at the same time made the representative of a recognizable human class, when the drama reveals that his purposes require the irrationalizing of life for everyone else. Of the insights that create Iago, none is deeper than the recognition that a cool rationality may itself bring about or serve the irrational. Though Brabantio, awakened by the nocturnal outcries in front of his house, thinks that Iago has "lost" his "wits" and that Roderigo comes "in madness" (1.1.92, 98), their universal technique of matching half-truths to latent fears makes him give up his sane conclusions and accept their distorted history of what has happened to Desdemona, so much so that he then attributes "a judgment maim'd and most imperfect" (1.3.99), i. e., failure of mind, to anyone who takes a different view of the situation. Here Iago simply has to make Brabantio as irrational as possible; shortly he has to curb Roderigo's irrationality, or rather, to convert it from a less to a more serviceable form, from suicidal despair to the sexual pursuit of Desdemona. Now for the first step in this conversation Iago utilizes the traditional argument of the "authority of . . . our wills" and of "one scale of reason to poise another of sensuality"; "But we have reason to cool our raging motions, our carnal stings, our unbitted lusts; . . ." (1.3.329-36). If in one sense this is the devil talking Scripture, in another it is Iago paying tribute to a faculty that he values deeply. He is the self-conscious possessor of brain-power. But reason has many functions, and the critical utility of this passage is that it points to the distinction between the ostensible and the real functions that Iago assigns to reason. In no way does he press Roderigo really to apply reason to his emotional ailment, to diagnose it and moderate and perhaps cure it; on the contrary he assures him that his cause "hath . . . reason" (373) and encourages him to found his hopes on Desdemona's sharing in a universal unregeneracy which Iago quite evidently believes is subject to rational control by no one. But more than that we see that Iago has not the slightest thought of using reason to "cool" his own "raging motions," "carnal stings," and "unbitted lusts": reason is rather the agent of his unbitted lusts and of the raging motions of his hate. It is in their behalf that he reasons with Roderigo; his reason is instrumental, serving his own unreason by playing upon Roderigo's. When he mentions the rumor that his wife Emilia has been unfaithful with Othello, he hurries on to say, "I know not if't be true" (394); rather he intends to act on "mere suspicion," just to make sure. His mind is used not to determine the truth but to convert into action a feeling not founded in truth. This is a basic Shakespearian definition of evil: the sharp mind in the service of uncriticized passion. And the final irony, as Shakespeare sees it, is that the owner of the sharp mind is eventually destroyed by the passion his mind serves.

We see the innermost mechanism of this rational instrument when the Iago-Roderigo relationship comes to its last phase. Like several of the major characters, Roderigo is able at times to assess his own headwork: once he almost resolves to give up the lecherous pursuit of Desdemona and to return to Venice with "a little more wit" (2.3.374); he is angrily aware that he has "foolishly suffer'd" and he suspects that he is "fopp'd" (4.2.182, 197). Iago retorts by praising Roderigo for both his brains (". . . your suspicion is not without *wit* and *judgment*") and his moral quality (214-19). The recurrent irony for Roderigo is that he cannot rely on his own good sense but falls back instead on Iago's version of what is good sense for him. Here comes the payoff. When once again Iago asserts that there is a way of sleeping with Desdemona, Roderigo's reply is, "Well, what is it? Is it within *reason* and compass?" (223-4). Is it "reasonably practical"? No other question, no other issue of sanction or value. How many philosophic frills are being got rid of, and how far down to positive bedrock this is getting, appears when Iago reveals the program: kill Cassio. Roderigo is still shockable. Iago soothes him, "Come, stand not amaz'd . . ." (245), and offers a cure for "amazement": "I will show you such a necessity in his death that you shall think yourself bound to put it on him" (245-6). To this promise of logical demonstration Roderigo responds in the same key: "I will hear further *reason* for this" (251). Iago makes good his promise, "And you shall be satisfied" (252), for when Roderigo is finally lying in wait to kill Cassio, he sums up the rationale of the project:

> I have no great devotion to the deed,
> And yet he hath given me satisfying *reasons*.
> *'Tis but a man gone.*   (5.1.8-10)

Despite his moral hesitancy, Roderigo has found "satisfying reasons" for committing murder and thinking it a way to Desdemona's bed. In this climax of persuasion to evil, Iago's "reason" mediates between his own uncontrollable irrational drives and those of Roderigo. The rational serving one irrationality and appearing to serve another while playing selfishly upon it: this sums up, and sums up archetypally, the fundamental operating methods of the Iago way of life.

"'Tis but a man gone" is pure Iago thought. It does away with every value or imperative or speculation that "man" or the death of man traditionally evokes, and it makes "a man" simply a neutral instance of a category, a statistical item, an object that can be acted on without moral responsibility. The philosophy "'Tis but a man gone" (of which there are contemporary manifestations in whole political systems, in demagogic practices of our own, in some methods of business and advertising and even abstract thought, in propaganda) is consistent with Iago's reductive contention, which he develops at length, that love is no more than unstable sexual appetite; his declaration that "there is more sense" in a "bodily wound" than in "reputation," which he says is a chimera; his skepticism about "honour," which he implies is unreal because unseen; and even, in a slightly different way, with his contempt for Cassio's theoretical knowledge, "Mere prattle, without practice" (1.1.26). Theory of any kind may open the door to values that transcend the immediately utilitarian. "Iago's is a pragmatic world, and his imagery finds its authority in social usage," as Arthur Sewell has said. Iago says tacitly, "Let's get down to facts," that is, the tangible and the visible. (Seen from a slightly different perspective, he has affiliations with the anti-metaphysical thinker, the extremist in semantics, the constitutional debunker.)

III

Reason as an ally of evil is a subject to which Shakespeare keeps returning, as if fascinated, but in different thematic forms as he explores different counter-forces. In *Macbeth* the rational effort to minimize the killings done for ambition's sake runs finally into the force of conscience. In *Lear*, rationalized self-seeking is counterbalanced by all the fidelities implied in *pietas*. And in *Othello*? Although Iago, as we saw, does not take seriously the ennobling power of love, he does not fail to let us know what he does take seriously. When, in his fake oath of loyalty to "wrong'd Othello," he vows "The execution of his wit, hands, heart" (3.3.466), Iago's words give a clue to his truth: his heart is his malice, his hands literally wound Cassio and kill Roderigo, and his wit is the genius that creates all the strategy. How it enters into the dialectic of structure, or the thematic form, is made clear in one of Iago's promises to Roderigo that he shall have Desdemona: "if sanctimony and a frail vow betwixt an erring barbarian and a supersubtle Venetian be not too hard for my wits and all the tribe of hell, thou shalt enjoy her" (1.3.362-6). "Tribe of hell" is somewhat rhetorical; the real antagonist is "my wits"—set against the rival power of love, which he cannot tolerate. But even beyond Iago's own conscious battle, his brains against a vow of love, there is a symbolic conflict in the heart of the drama. And for this symbolic conflict Iago, again assuaging the pain of Roderigo, gives us a name by the words he chooses:

Thou know'st we work by wit, and not by witchcraft;
And wit depends on dilatory time. (2.3.378-9)

Wit and *witchcraft:* in this antithesis is the symbolic structure, or the thematic form, of *Othello*. By *witchcraft*, of course, Iago means conjuring and spells to induce desired actions and states of being. But as a whole the play dramatically develops another meaning of *witchcraft* and forces upon us an awareness of that meaning: *witchcraft* is a metaphor for love. The "magic in the web" of the handkerchief, as Othello calls it (3.4.69), extends into the fiber of the whole drama. Love is a magic bringer of harmony between those who are widely different (Othello and Desdemona), and it can be a magic transformer of personality; its ultimate power is fittingly marked by the miracle of Desdemona's voice speaking from beyond life, pronouncing forgiveness to the Othello who has murdered her (5.2.124-5). Such events lie outside the realm of "wit"—of the reason, cunning, and wisdom on which Iago rests—and this wit must be hostile to them. Wit must always strive to conquer witchcraft, and there is an obvious sense in which it should conquer; but there is another sense in which, though it try, it should not and cannot succeed; that, we may say, is what *Othello* is "about." Whatever disasters it causes, wit fails in the end: it cuts itself off in a demonic silence before death (Iago's "last words" are "I will never speak word"—5.2.304), while witchcraft—love—speaks after death (Desdemona's last farewell).

Between the poles of wit and witchcraft, all the major characters in the play find their orientation. Emilia looks at a good deal of life through the Iago wit, but yields to the love for Desdemona which transforms her into a sacrificial figure. Under the influence of the Iago wit, Cassio, acting through Desdemona's friendly love, tries to high-pressure Othello into a charity (a revocation of his dismissal) that could come only spontaneously. Roderigo falls under the witchcraft of love, but, instead of letting it take effect as it might, to bring him death or renunciation, chooses Iago's wit game and plays for what he cannot have. Emilia and Desdemona, dying, are not creatures of wit: what we have called witchcraft has led them to a trans-rational achievement of spirit.

The conflict of Desdemona and Iago for Othello can be called the conflict of love and hate, or the conflict of two different potentialities in the soul where both reside. It may also be called the conflict of wit and witchcraft for Othello. Though Othello seems to be all the naivete of Everyman, and Iago to be all his calculatingness and slyness, Othello gives himself more to wit than to witchcraft because he and Iago, though in different degrees, have much in common—a histrionic bent, an inadequate selfhood that crops up in self-pity and an eye for slights and injuries, an uncriticized instinct to soothe one's own feelings by punishing others (with an air of moral propriety), the need to possess in one's own terms or destroy, an incapacity for love that is the other side of self-love. All this is in another realm from that of witchcraft. When Othello decides to follow Iago and be "wise" and "cunning," he adopts a new code: he will "see" the facts, get the "evidence," "prove" his case against Desdemona, and execute "justice" upon her. This is the program of "wit." Now this is not only utterly inappropriate to the occasion on which, under Iago's tutelage, Othello elects to use it, nor is it simply one of several possible errors; rather he adopts an attitude or belief or style which is the direct antithesis of another mode of thought and feeling which is open to him. He makes that particular wrong choice which is the logical opposite of the right choice open to him. He essays to reason when reason is not relevant: he substitutes a disastrous wit for a saving witchcraft. He could reject Iago's "proof" against Desdemona "by an affirmation of faith," as Winifred Nowottny has put it, "which is beyond reason, by the act of choosing to believe in Desdemona." Othello, the prime beneficiary of witchcraft, might win all its gifts had he the faith that would open him to its action; but he is short on faith, is seduced by wit (the two actions are simply two faces of the same experience), and ruined. He knew the first miracle of love, the thing given without claim, but cut himself off from the greater miracle, the transformation of self into a giver. His final failure is that, though he comes to recognize that he has been witless, he is never capacious enough in spirit to know how fully he has failed or how much he has thrown away. He never sees the full Desdemona witchcraft.

In the light of Desdemona's spiritual wealth—the unfailing love that continues into forgiveness of her murderer—we can understand Iago as a spiritual have-not. Like the have-not in the realm of things who in a materially oriented culture suffers from envy and malice, the spiritual have-not lives in characteristic vices that Shakespeare has analyzed with many-angled perception. The analogy between the material and the spiritual have-not is confirmed by a line in *Lear*, Edmund's "Let me . . . have lands by wit," and by Iago's own addiction to actual theft (of Roderigo's gifts meant for Desdemona). If the analogy fails at one point—that the achievement of spiritual wealth depends on the individual and cannot be essentially helped by external accidents or blocked by external obstacles—that failure only underscores the failure of the spiritual have-not. His modes of action are exhaustively canvassed in Shakespeare's plot and in the poetry of the play. Wit is Iago's instrument to compensate for what he does not have. He perversely hates and yet lusts after what he does not have (Desdemona as a person, and as a symbol of love), and he undertakes to disparage it, minimize it, debunk it, and destroy it. Rule-or-ruin becomes rule-by-ruining. He must fashion the world after his own image: "And knowing what I am, I know what she shall be" (4.1.74). So it pleases him to trap (he repeatedly uses the language of hunting and trapping) those who are unlike himself, by proclaiming virtues which he does not possess ("honest Iago," the friend of all), confusing the appearance of things seeming to act in one way (as light-bringer and physician during the two nocturnal brawls which he stirs up) while acting in another (making things "dark," wounding and killing). Noisiness and vulgarity of style become him, though as a skilled actor he can simulate the amiable, contained, and discreet adviser and consoler. His most far-reaching method is to seduce others philosophically—to woo them from assumptions in which their salvation might lie (faith in the spiritual quality of others), to baser assumptions that will destroy them (their freedom to act in the light of the accepted unregeneracy of all about them). Iago the moral agent is akin to Iago the philosopher: there is a common element in stealing purses, stealing good names, and stealing ideas needed for survival.

In sociological terms we might allegorize Iago as the criminal type, in political as the self-seeking divisive force or the patriot-eer or the power-seeker who will pay any price, in cultural as the mass-mind, in psychological as all the impulses that lead to despair of human possibility, in moral as envy or hate or spiritual hardness (versions of pride), in mythical as The Enemy—the universal destroyer of ultimate values. Before all these, he is simply a human being, the apparent friend and lover of everybody. We think of these diverse tentative formulations only because he is so variously and richly set before us as the final outcome when certain potentialities of Everyman are freed to develop fully. There is no single way into this extraordinary characterization. As the spiritual have-not, Iago is universal, that is, many things at once, and of many times at once. He is our contemporary, and the special instances of his temper and style —as distinct from the Iagoism to which all men are liable—will be clear to whoever is alert to Shakespeare's abundant formulations. Seen in a limited and stereotyped form, he is the villain of all melodrama. He is Elizabethan—as Envy or Machiavel. And to go further back still, we see in how many parts of Dante's *Inferno* he might appear. He could be placed among the angry and violent. But his truer place is down among those who act in fraud and malice—the lowest category of sinner who on earth had least of spiritual substance and relied most on wit. Here we might put him on a higher level with the panders, but again it is when we reach the lower level that he is summoned more strongly, not once but by group after group: the hypocrites, the thieves, the evil counselors, the sowers of dissension, and, at the very bottom of the eighth circle, the impersonators and false witnesses. Finally, in the ninth and last circle, "damn'd beneath all depth in hell," come the treacherous. And here at last we go beyond time into our timeless myths of evil.

By an extraordinary composition of character Shakespeare has made Iago, literally or symbolically, share in all these modes of evil. And in Iago he has dramatized Dante's summary analysis: "For where the instrument of the mind is joined to evil will and potency, men can make no defense against it." But he has also dramatized the hidden springs of evil action, the urgency and passion and immediacy of it. He contemplates, too, the evildoer's "potency" and man's defenselessness: but these he interprets tragically by making them, not absolute, but partly dependent on the flaws or desire of the victims themselves. In the *Othello* world, Iago, seductive as he is, is not an inevitable teacher. Whoever would, could learn from Desdemona. He would have the choice of wit or witchcraft.

NOTES

1. One who is committed to a detailed study of the parts might seize protectively on Edward A. Armstrong's observation, "There is a strange psychological bias which tempts those interested in large issues to belittle detailed work," in *Shakespeare's Imagination* (London, 1946), p. 125n. Cf. G. Wilson Knight's preface to the 4th edition of *The Wheel of Fire* (London: Methuen, 1949), pp. vi-vii. In *Flaming Minister* (Durham: Duke University Press, 1953), G. R. Elliott makes a detailed commentary on individual passages and on their relationships.

2. Cf. L. C. Knights, *Explorations* (New York: Stewart, 1947), p. 31.

3. Cf. E. E. Stoll's phrase, "a tragedy which is also a poem, in which the parts 'mutually support and explain each other' . . ." This is in *Shakespeare and Other Masters* (Cambridge: Harvard University Press, 1940), p. 219. In *Poetry and Drama* (Cambridge: Harvard University Press, 1951), p. 43, T. S. Eliot speaks of the "perfection of verse drama, which would be a design of human action and of words, such as to present at once the two aspects of dramatic and musical order."

4. For numerous examples of images which link separated passages, see W. H. Clemen, *The Development of Shakespeare's Imagery* (Cambridge: Harvard University Press, 1951). Clemen makes a telling comment on the general sense of the interrelatedness of all parts which is created by the imagery (p. 224).

5. D. A. Traversi, *Approach to Shakespeare* (London, 1938), p. 14; and see his whole first chapter. Of *Othello* he says, "Plot and imagery, in fact, are fused as never before" (p. 86). Cf. his "Othello," *The Wind and the Rain*, vi (1950), 268-9. On the importance of the language spoken, the "wording," there are some relevant comments by E. E. Stoll in *Poets and Playwrights* (Minneapolis: University of Minnesota Press, 1930), pp. 5ff., 128.

6. Page 162.

7. *The Structure of Literature* (Chicago: University of Chicago Press, 1954), pp. 17, 64.

8. One might speak of an image-system as an inner organism—a part of the whole that could not exist without the whole and yet an entity having parts that function with respect to each other. This would be "a verbal drama" as distinct from "verbal drama" generally. As a created thing it does not "just happen"; nor yet, I believe, is it deliberately blue-printed and executed. One may surmise: a certain image or kind of image "comes up" for a speaker on a certain occasion; then it is felt consciously or semi-consciously to have some relevance to the import of the whole; and it continues to be used (with the varying degrees of consciousness presumably characteristic of the creative process) as a way of exploring character or mood or theme.

9. Cf. Price, *Construction in Shakespeare* (Michigan, 1951),

pp. 24 and 35ff., and George Rylands, "Shakespeare's Poetic Energy," *Proceedings of the British Academy*, XXXVII (1951), 99-119. Note his statement that the "repetition of a word in diverse contexts throughout the play, with its correlatives and associations, often gives the clue to the poetic thought, the *dianoia,* which informs the whole" (p. 102).

10. All italics are my own.

Arthur Sewell

TRAGEDY AND THE "KINGDOM OF ENDS"

THERE IS, I believe, a logical connexion—I will not say, development—discernible in the three great tragedies, in terms of which
Shakespeare is seen to treat this debate between that which is
temporal and that which is metaphysical, in three different
modes. One mode was to set side by side in the play, separate
from each other, secular society—as it is apprehended in the
comedies and, perhaps, the histories but seen now as "immoral"
—and a single human soul. This is done in *Othello*. A second
mode was to follow the single human soul into the darkness,
where reality and morality are cancelled, and where the soul
seeks but never finds identity in the dark recesses of his own
being. This is done in *Macbeth*. A final and supreme mode was
to see that world in which the hero seeks identity as wholly involved with the life of society, and to move for a moment towards the vision of a kind of identity which comes to men when
they are members of each other. This is done in *King Lear*.

In the opening scenes of *Othello* the sense of society is strongly
emphasized. Othello lives and loves in a society as particularized,
as concrete, as the society depicted in *The Merchant of Venice*.
It is much the same kind of society, too; its values and behaviours
are of the same sort, they belong to the same Venice. But they
are no longer seen *from within,* but from without, and hence
differently. They themselves come up now for judgement. It is
a society, indeed, which has also something in common with the
society of *Measure for Measure*. Natural man is similarly at odds
with social order, and there is a licence in men's conduct which

From *Character & Society in Shakespeare*, 1951, pp. 91-121. Reprinted by permission of Oxford University Press, Inc.

social disapproval barely contains and privily condones. It is this sense of a particular and restricted society which gives to *Othello* a general quality different from that of *Macbeth* or *King Lear*; something not so grand, something less universal in its range. In *Othello* we are aware of a human community closely contained within its own meannesses, hypocrisies, and greeds. Part of the tragedy consists in the reduction of the large spirit of Othello to the petty dimensions of the society in which he moves.

Professor Wilson Knight has suggested that one of the notable things about this play is the separateness of the "worlds" in which the major characters live. And superficially, perhaps, it looks as though Iago's world is quite opaque to Desdemona's and Desdemona's to Othello's. But only superficially. Surely Desdemona and Iago belong to the same world, to the same Venice. Desdemona is not less truly Brabantio's daughter than Roderigo is Iago's dupe. I think she has been imagined as a citizen of that world. This does not mean that she must be full citizen as perhaps Iago is. It means, rather, that her world implies Iago's world and Iago's hers.

For there is little relation between Othello's valuation of fidelity and hers. She takes her valuation from that very same world in which Iago has turned cynic. His cynicism is the natural corollary of her innocence, and they belong to the same level of human being. Her innocence has, indeed, as little true spiritual value—it has a like charm—as Eve's before the Fall.

There is, however, a significant separateness of "worlds" in *Othello*; it is the separateness of Othello's world from that to which all the other characters equally belong. In an earlier section I pointed out the difference between Othello's world and Iago's. It must now be suggested that Iago's world is the world of Venice, to which all the Venetians were born and in which they were imagined. It is more than that. It is society as Shakespeare now presented it. The central recommendation of society, so conceived, is cynically summed up in Iago's "Put money in thy purse." It is a world in which soldiers compete for office and prestige. It is a world in which, as Emilia well knows, men will do each other's offices in the women's beds. It is a world in which lust flaunts its finery and is not abashed. It is a world, indeed, from which spirit has been drained, and all is measured by use and entertainment and position. It is a kingdom of means, not ends.

We do not judge this society by any standard to which any actual society might attain. We do not set against it an ideal society towards which an actual society might asymptotically move. In judging the society in this Venice, we make a judgement on the very nature of all society whatsoever. We see that this society is, in fact, representative of society in general; and that society in general sets up use against value, expediency against integrity, prestige against principle, behaviour against moral being. In *Othello,* two worlds are set in opposition: the world set in time and inhabited by the Venetians; the world of the spirit, in terms of which we apprehend Othello. For this reason, in the bulk of the play, these Venetians are seen by Shakespeare from the outside, they are seen as they behave; whereas Othello is seen from within, he is seen as he is.

Othello is, in one respect, an extremely simple play, for the conflict between "value" and "use" is set out in its most extreme terms. Othello, in his deepest spirit, knows very little of use; Iago nothing of value. Othello's thought and feeling at the beginning of the play are free from the pressures of temporal things; they have a purity and spontaneity which remind us of an early innocence. There is a sense, indeed, in which Othello is at first imagined as without original sin, and self-regarding impulses in him are not yet touched with guilt, but—so undivided is he from the world he makes for himself—these very impulses are transmuted and (to speak in Christian terms) of themselves turn God-ward. They are naturally innocent.

In *Othello,* indeed, is re-enacted the Fall of Man; and Othello himself has that superiority of spiritual being over Desdemona which Adam had over Eve. Iago is the Tempter, but in conspiracy with him is all Venice and all the Venetians. They very aptly make that world within which fallen man confined himself. Othello is brought by Iago—and, perhaps in another way, by Desdemona—to indulge himself, to surrender himself to self-regarding impulses which are all infected and diseased by the meaner expectations and vanities which society may breed in our flesh. He becomes subject to the very itches of the flesh, and jealousy degrades his love so that it becomes no more than lust. As to Adam, so to Othello, "Chaos is come again." Hoodwinked by Iago, he leaves the true domain of value and comes down, shedding all the bravery of his spirit, into Iago's world, where value is unknown; into Desdemona's world, where (except through him as by Eve through Adam) value has never yet been known.

Chaos comes indeed to Othello. But what comes after? What vision does "character" fulfil at the end of the play?

Perhaps the first observation we must make, in answering this question, is that in the closing scene Othello becomes very much aware of his audience. Even if it is wrong to accuse him of "cheering himself up," it is at least true that he appears to be "setting himself right"; and in the process of "setting himself right" he seems to lose something of the distinction he once had and the authority he once exercised amongst the Venetians. Iago's work, in a measure, has been successful, and Othello has lost both innocence and grace. He seeks to restore the proper love of himself by recalling what he has been in the past; and to do this is to come down to the level of the Venetians. And, of course, he fails.

But perhaps that is the wrong way to speak of the matter. After Othello has discovered his fatal error—and perhaps even before—there is a change in the mode in which his character is presented. Shakespeare seems no longer to "dart himself forth." He seems, indeed, to have ceased altogether that kind of charac-ter-creation of which I have spoken earlier in this essay—when, in language, a human soul seeks identity in his encounter with the universe. Othello now seeks no such identity. Shakespeare pre-sents him; and Othello no longer seems to be fashioning his identity and settling his vision from moment to moment in words. He is as he is presented. The settlement he is making now is with society, not with the universe. The provenance of the images and their reinforcement are now to be found in social and secular experiences and assessments. Rhetoric now persuades, and no longer reveals. Vision is of a different kind and employs another mode, a more oblique mode, of character-presentation. Shakespeare, we may say, is now outside Othello's spirit and the presentation is now third-personal. He shows forth Othello to the audience in a certain light. And this light is secular light, plain social daylight. Othello is fallen man, indeed, but Shakespeare—all metaphysical consideration now put aside—exhibits him, even excuses him, to the social judgement—as though he would say: He has done the state some service, and that is something. He has shown valour in war, and, but for being tried intolerably, he has shown loyalty in love. Some pre-eminence amongst men he must be judged to have had—pre-eminence amongst men.

It was, I have said, Iago's filthy function to bring Othello down to the level of the Venetians. So well does he succeed that at the end of the play it is the social judgement that comes into its own again. Society, we may suppose, is not absolutely represented in Iago. Valour and devoted love are values which society must respect, if it would continue itself. But something has vanished like a dream—the glory and the grandeur of the universe to which we had once thought that Othello had belonged. The tale of fallen man is complete, and, for my part, I find here as yet no hint of regeneration or redemption.

Not one of the central images in *Macbeth* is regulative; not one steadies us for life in society. And this can be said of no other of Shakespeare's plays. In *Othello* we are continually reminded in Cassio, in Iago, even in Othello himself by image and idea of a world of social obligation and expectation. In *King Lear* order in society is apprehended with the same actuality as the threat of chaos, whether in society or the individual. It is true that in *Othello* the accepted, the external, world is hard and harsh with cynicism and the test of use, but we never lose the sense of the actuality of that world. And in *Lear* the animal imagery is balanced and criticized by the images of clothes. Bestial individualism is set against the needs and imperatives of life in civilized society. But in *Macbeth* we are never so steadied by inescapable reminders from the actual world, and we lose the sense of that ethical and political order which is expressed in social institutions.

It was inevitable, then, that at least one of the central images should be the image of blood, for blood is the symbol both of life and death, the principle of energy within. It has deep significance in sacrifice and sacrament. The pulse of the blood sets

the rhythm of our beings, and its movement records and expresses every chance and change of the spirit. Both joy and horror
affect it; and the dry skin or the parched lips are only secondary
appearances of these affections of the blood. There could be no
other image which so strikingly marked that moment in the development of Shakespeare's vision in which, with all its implications, he saw and imagined the workings of the human spirit
absolutely from within.

The image recurs time and again in *Macbeth*. Duncan's first
words are:

> What bloody man is that?

Lady Macbeth calls upon the spirits "that tend our mortal
thoughts":

> Make thick my blood.

She bids her husband

> smear
> The sleepy grooms with blood.

But Macbeth looks at his hangman's hands and cries out:

> Will all great Neptune's ocean wash the blood
> Clean from my hand?

Lennox cries of the murdered grooms:

> Their hands and faces were all badged with blood,

and of Duncan it is said:

> His silver skin lac'd with his golden blood.

During the banquet scene Macbeth speaks much of blood:

> Blood hath been shed ere now.
> It will have blood; they say, blood will have blood.
> I am in blood
> Stepp'd in so far that, should I wade no more,
> Returning were as tedious as go o'er.

And, towards the end, Lady Macbeth walks in her sleep, making as though she would wash her hands;

> Yet who would have thought the old man to have had so much blood in him?
> Here's the smell of blood still.

With the evocation of these images the social sense has nothing to do.

Similarly there are many images of night and sleep. These again are not regulative or descriptive; they evoke in us the very act of annihilating real and solid things, of making blurred the outlines of objects, of mantling the surfaces with darkness. Lady Macbeth calls on night in her opening soliloquy:

> Come, thick night,
> And pall me in the dunnest smoke of hell,
> That my keen knife see not the wound it makes,
> Nor heaven peep through the blanket of the dark,
> To cry, "Hold, hold."

At night reality loses its noted order;

> The night has been unruly; where we lay,
> Our chimneys were blown down.
>   . . . the obscure bird
> Clamour'd the livelong night.

The murder of Duncan is done near midnight. Throughout the third act of the play we expect the night.

> Come, seeling night,
> Scarf up the tender eye of pitiful day;
> And with thy bloody and invisible hand
> Cancel and tear to pieces that great bond
> Which keeps me pale! Light thickens; and the crow
> Makes wing to the rooky wood;
> Good things of day begin to droop and drowse
> While night's black agents to their preys do rouse.

Before night comes, but with night in the air, Banquo is murdered;

> The west yet glimmers with some streaks of day.

And something of the common experience of nightfall is reported in the words of the first murderer:

> Now spurs the lated traveller apace
> To gain the timely inn.

When the guests have left the banquet-hall, Macbeth asks:

> What is the night?

And Lady Macbeth tells him:

> Almost at odds with morning, which is which.

The witches belong to the night; they are "secret, black and midnight hags." And it is at night, fearfully, that Lady Macbeth walks in her sleep.

I find it difficult to set down the significance of the images of sleep. In sleep the spirit returns to its elemental resting-place and in a natural rhythm the energies are given pause. In sleep, too, reality is suspended and its demands on us are for the time being quiet. But there may be, too, a sleep which is no sleep but a waking, when the spirit is troubled, and wayward impulses find speech and chance expression. Sleep of this kind is a twilight kingdom, in which we dwell with things half-real. The images of sleep, then, in *Macbeth*, have not a simple but a complex significance. They are an expression of the half-wish to cancel reality; they show within the very anarchy of energy a nostalgia for rest. They represent that ultimate abrogation of the external world in which either the untroubled heart is at rest or else the troubled spirit stirs and mutters and is afraid.

For Macbeth there is to be no more the sweetness of sleep;

> Methought I heard a voice cry, "Sleep no more!
> Macbeth doth murder sleep!"

And this sleep is "innocent," it is a

> Sleep that knits up the ravell'd sleave of care,
> The death of each day's life, sore labour's bath,
> Balm of hurt minds, great nature's second course,
> Chief nourisher in life's feast.

Duncan knows such a sleep in death;

> Wake Duncan with thy knocking! I would thou couldst.
> > Duncan is in his grave:
> After life's fitful fever he sleeps well.

At the end of the banquet scene Lady Macbeth says to her husband:

> You lack the season of all natures, sleep.

And Macbeth replies:

> Come, we'll to sleep.

We remember all this of sleep when Macbeth asks of the doctor,

> Canst thou not minister to a mind diseased,
> Pluck from the memory a rooted sorrow,
> Raze out the written troubles of the brain,
> And with some sweet oblivious antidote
> Cleanse the stuff'd bosom of that perilous stuff
> Which weighs upon the heart?

Terror and unrest come, too, with these images of sleep, as though in sleep this perilous stuff may have at its mercy the deeps of the spirit and all the mind. Banquo first mentions this helplessness in sleep, when he says:

> And yet I would not sleep; merciful powers,
> Restrain in me the cursed thoughts that nature
> Gives way to in repose!

The grooms must have been disturbed by dreams, when one laughed in his sleep and one cried "Murder!" After the murder, Macbeth will risk anything rather than

> > sleep
> In the affliction of these terrible dreams
> That shake us nightly.

Lady Macbeth in "a most fast sleep" rises from her bed, throws her nightgown upon her, takes forth paper, writes upon it, reads it, afterwards seals it, and again returns to bed.

Nothing in the play is what it seems; nothing belongs to its own "law of kinde." In *Macbeth*, "fair is foul and foul is fair"; pleasantly-sited castles are the settings for dreadful murder;

> by the clock, 'tis day,
> And yet dark night strangles the travelling lamp;

a man may be not of woman born; and Birnam Wood can come to Dunsinane.

This leads me to mention the emphasis laid in the play on phantasmal experience, on illusion, on half-appearance. The energy of inner imagining seems very often to be too much for solid reality; and the world of Macbeth becomes a world of shadows, of visitations from a space other than this. The eye conjures beings out of the very air; and things real dissolve into unreality. Neither the eye nor the ear can be wholly believed and all assurance is lost.

Banquo asks of the witches:

> I' the name of truth,
> Are ye fantastical, or that indeed
> Which outwardly ye show?

And when they have vanished he says:

> The earth hath bubbles, as the water has,
> And these are of them. Whither are they vanished?

Macbeth gives him his answer:

> Into the air; and what seemed corporeal melted
> As breath into the wind.

Certainly the dagger which Macbeth sees before he goes in to murder Duncan is "fantastical." When he would clutch it, he clutches empty air. He has it and he has it not. It is "a dagger of the mind, a false creation," and yet it is in form as "palpable" as that which now he draws. In the "dagger" soliloquy, the images of sleep and the images of dreams are joined with fantastical imaginings—and with night:

> Now o'er the one half world
> Nature seems dead, and wicked dreams abuse

> The curtained sleep; witchcraft celebrates
> Pale Hecate's offerings, and withered murder,
> Alarum'd by his sentinel, the wolf,
> Whose howl's his watch, thus with his stealthy pace,
> With Tarquin's ravishing strides, towards his design,
> Moves like a ghost.

What has all this to do with character? In the first place, we can surely say that what goes on in Macbeth's mind when he fears that he will sleep no more, when he knows that "blood will have blood," when Nature in half the world seems dead to him, is just as revealing, though differently, as the practical question which he puts to himself: Shall I kill a king? We can say more: we can say that killing a king would be a small and merely public matter, were it not that to kill a king involves Macbeth in less palpable encounters, which find their mimesis in the poetry. To kill a king was the first act—and what followed may be thought of as a catalogue of crimes, but, more truly, is apprehended as an ever closer encounter with darkness.

Early in the play Macbeth is in some doubt: he hesitates on the very brink of action. The theme of his soliloquy, "If it were done, &c.," is the theme of "judgement here," something that has to do not with moral conscience, but with the fear of consequences. This fear has puzzled a large number of critics in the past, and if we inquire, What is it Macbeth really fears? we shall be hard put to it to find an answer. One would not suppose that he fears physical punishment. By his own hypothesis he does not fear death. What then? The answer is that he fears nothing in particular. He fears that unknown chain of consequences which (once we think of them) may make us tremble before any act whatsoever. The fear phrases itself but does not define itself for Macbeth as a judgement, as the return of the poisoned chalice to his own lips. But the fear is, in fact, something fundamental and more deeply rooted in the general condition of man; it is the fear, or the distrust, or the moral uncertainty, which attaches itself to any act whatsoever. It is precisely the same fear which prevented Hamlet from killing the king. It is the Either/Or of our human being.

But in *Macbeth* the matter is a little different. The play is not

a play about doubt or indecision; it is a play about those ineluc-
table processes which follow decision. It is not irrelevant to point
out here that Shakespeare deliberately distorted the historical
facts. The historical Macbeth reigned well, as far as we know, for
ten years after the murder. Our Macbeth is from the moment
of the act an exile from the daylight. We can be sure, then, that
Shakespeare, as by way of supreme experiment, takes as the
hypothesis of his play an extreme case of a man's delivery of himself, through action, to darkness, to chaos. Macbeth, as a tragic
hero, is a man with a capacity, one might almost say a taste, for
damnation. This capacity, as Mr. Eliot once pointed out, is not
so very different from a capacity for salvation. *Macbeth* is a terrible play because its business is to give us some notion of what
that damnation is which a man embraces when he is, indeed,
man enough for it.

Whereas in *Othello* we witness the Fall of Man, in *Macbeth*
we have a study (not, as Mr. Stewart would have us suppose,
of a man) of Fallen Man; Man, who, because he is fallen, cannot reject the discipline of daylight without involving himself in
utter darkness. And how vision reveals itself in *Macbeth* may be
conveniently illustrated from the two main soliloquies in the
play, one at the beginning, the other at the end. In the soliloquy
just mentioned, when Macbeth hesitates before the act, order
(the order of civil institutions and decent hospitalities) is still
actual for him. He remembers that Duncan is his king, his kins-
man, and his guest. In the same speech he remembers "virtue"
and "angels" and "heaven's cherubin"; and although I do not
think these argue a Christian "philosophy" in the play, they do at
least indicate that Macbeth is not yet committed to the darkness. Something still tells him that "institutions are necessary,"
and, although he does not say so, necessary perhaps to salvation.
Towards the end of the play—the hypothesis has worked itself
out—all sense of actuality and order is lost. Life has become "a
tale told by an idiot, full of sound and fury, signifying nothing."

But vision does not rest there, for while Shakespeare may not
here affirm Divine Order, he certainly could not accept a godless
existentialism. This is as far as vision, discovering itself in and
through Macbeth, could go; but now it changes its mode, as it
does at the end of *Othello*. In these last moments Macbeth, not

perhaps for himself but for us, is brought back to the daylight world. Social order, daylight order, reasserts itself. He himself admits that the juggling fiends have paltered with him in a double sense, and, as he confesses this, he opens his eyes to the world and to his audience. He becomes a man once again behaving in the presence of men, and that is how Shakespeare represents him. One social virtue he can still exhibit, not redeeming him, but giving him distinction and pre-eminence—the virtue of courage, however desperately called upon. His vision no longer matters, except in so far as we judge it and find it wanting. But his courage matters, for men should be brave. And yet, in a sense, it is wrong to say that his vision no longer matters: for through it we have been brought to the edge of nothingness and dissolution. And it is as men who have been so near that edge that we hear at last the mention of "measure, time, and place."

King Lear is the play in which Shakespeare returns once again to see man as a human soul, not in opposition to society, not rejecting society, but finding in society the sphere of fulfilment. Order is now seen, for the first time, and perhaps imperfectly, "not merely negative, but creative and liberating." It is a vision of society very different from that discovered in *Othello*. In *Othello* we cannot suppose that society is ever moral or good. Othello and Iago die, but future Othellos will find themselves betrayed in Venice, and future Iagos will still prey upon its profligates. In *King Lear* the conflict is no longer apprehended as a conflict between the individual and society; the conflict is now within society itself. Disorder in the human soul is both the agent and the product of disorder in society. Social order is the condition, as it is the resultant, of sweet and affirmative being, without which man relapses into a beastly and self-destructive individualism.

The play gives an impression of towns and villages and castles, on which the barren moor and the wild marshland are ever ready to encroach. Outside the walls lies the realm of brutishness, of animals and roots, of standing pools and naked madmen. Certain of the characters become exiles from comfort, from decent living, from politeness. Lear, in the wind and the rain and the thunder, and in the hovel, is such an exile. So is Edgar, in the rags of Tom o'Bedlam. So are the fool and, afterwards, the blind Gloucester. The beastly life is very close, near neighbour to civilized man; and man has not much to do to resume the life of the beast.

He has only to cast off his clothes—for in this symbolism Shakespeare dramatically anticipates Carylye. Clothes alone divide men from the animals:

> Is man no more than this? Consider him well. Thou owest the worm no silk, the beast no hide, the sheep no wool, the cat no perfume. Ha! here's three on's are sophisticated! Thou art the thing itself: unaccommodated man is no more but such a poor, bare, forked animal as thou art: Off, off, you lendings! Come, unbutton here.

And when Lear flings off his clothes we may remember his words to Regan earlier in the play:

> O, reason not the need: our basest beggars
> Are in the poorest thing superfluous:
> Allow not nature more than nature needs,
> Man's life is cheap as beast's: thou art a lady;
> If only to go warm were gorgeous,
> Why, nature needs not what thou gorgeous wear'st,
> Which scarcely keeps thee warm.

Brutish nature is made actual for us in the frequent mention of animals, especially those who prey upon each other. And disorder in humanity is symbolized in rank and wayward weeds which seem ever to encroach on the cultivated field.

The imagery of clothes—and many other things in the play— reinforce the notion that in society "institutions are necessary"; and character in the play is certainly conceived in terms of social rank and function, as well as in terms of the family. We expect trouble, indeed, when at the beginning of the play we learn that Lear intends to continue rank without function, has subscribed his power, and confined it merely to "exhibition," and would manage those "authorities" which he has given away. The bastardy of Edmund ("there was good sport at his making") has such results that we see a "fault," where a woman has "a son for her cradle ere she [has] a husband for her bed." Ironically enough, it is an insistence on the rightness and reasonableness of institutions which gives some point to the sisters' complaint that Lear's hundred retainers are intolerably more than "nature" needs. There is nothing in the play to cast suspicion upon the rightness of external order—there is much in the play to make us feel that without it we are lost, to affirm that not discipline, but indiscipline destroys. But there is also much to support the view that even discipline will destroy where it is not involved in self-discipline and in love.

King Lear—this is a large claim to make—is the only one of Shakespeare's plays in which personal relationship is treated as an end and not as a means; the only play in which personal relationships seem to determine character rather than to have an effect upon character. It is not merely that, say, in *Hamlet* the relationships between Hamlet and his mother and Hamlet and Ophelia are subsidiary in the major vision of the play; it is rather that what these characters are, and especially Hamlet, in his personal relationships, is important and enriches the vision, but the relationship in itself plays no necessary part in that vision and is incidental to it.* We may think that Ophelia's kind of love is a betrayal and that Hamlet's spirit is the more embittered: but what concerns us is not that Hamlet should have loved Ophelia but that by love he should be so embittered. In *King Lear*, however, all the characters are conceived—and this is central to the vision—in their relationships with other people, in their relationships with each other, and society is a vital complex of such relationships. In *King Lear*, then, not only is individual character differently conceived, but also living society itself.

The question is one of priority, not psychological but imaginative. In *Hamlet* (to continue the example) the nature of personal relationship is dependent on the nature of the characters: in *King Lear*, in a large measure, the nature of the character is revealed in the personal relationship. In *Hamlet* relationship and character are separable: in *King Lear* they are wholly bound up with each other. So it is that in *King Lear* personal relationships are the field of character-fulfilment.

* Family relationships are not the same, of course, as personal relationships.

None other of Shakespeare's plays contains such moving and dramatic references to personal loyalty and love. This play opens with the grand and, perhaps, grotesque announcement of the major theme in Lear's demand that his daughters shall declare their love. I do not find this opening difficult to accept; it is a bold enlargement of that morbidity which can poison affection, when affection gives nothing and asks everything. Lear's need to be told is matched by the two elder daughters' readiness in the telling; and it is seen, not wholly but in part, for what it is, in Cordelia's inability to tell. There follow immediately many variations of the theme; for Burgundy personal relationship is a matter of use, whereas to the King of France it is a matter of value. Kent is loyal, Goneril and Regan whisper together because, for a while, their interests are in common. The King of France finds words for the theme, when he says:

> Love is not love
> When it is mingled with regards that stand
> Aloof from the entire point.

More subtly and more movingly, Cordelia's conduct quickens and illuminates the vision; for her love, which cannot speak, has some regards—she cannot help it—which stand "aloof from the *entire* point." She is to blame, although she can do no other, for keeping herself blameless.

There is no need to rehearse the way in which Shakespeare deepens and develops this vision in the creation of his characters in *King Lear*. One or two of the minor characters catch a vivid if momentary life from it. I think of the servant who bids Cornwall hold his hand:

> I have served you ever since I was a child,
> But better service have I never done you
> Than now to bid you hold.

Or of the old man who brings the blinded Gloucester to Edgar:

> O my good lord!
> I have been your tenant, and your father's tenant,
> These fourscore years.

Such a man sweetens and fortifies institutions with loyalty and service. Loyalty is found in Oswald, too—and in Kent. Lear himself—although this is too large a matter to do more than hint at—insists on his hundred followers, but comes to the moment when he bids the fool go first into the hovel; thinks of "poor naked wretches"; will make a little society of affection in prison with Cordelia; thanks a gentleman for undoing his button. And is not something darker suggested, related to this same vision, when the two sisters both desire Edmund?

> Yet Edmund was belov'd;
> The one the other poison'd for my sake
> And after slew herself.

The weeds, after all, spring from the same soil as the "sustaining corn."

Personal relationships, however, are conceived in two ways—in loyalty and consideration which are owed according merely to the "bond," and in that going out of oneself which makes of love and loyalty something more than is demanded by the bond. So, in the first Act, Lear does a terrible thing to Cordelia; he inhibits in her that love which has no need of a bond. So we apprehend that moral behaviours are inseparably bound up with each other, hers with his, for it is Lear who puts Cordelia in the position of relying merely on the bond. In similar fashion, Kent's honesty shows a loyalty something more than his commitment—and this honesty has in it a bluntness something more than the mere requirement of its occasion. There is, indeed, throughout the play a deep sense of the evil that must mix with goodness—and of the "reason" that may mix with evil; and Shakespeare makes it clear that the admixture of good with evil, of evil with "reason," is both proof and product of the fact that, morally, we are members of each other. There is, indeed, in *King Lear*, a kind of irony which is not, to any important extent, to be found in any other play: the irony which lies in the contradiction between the rightness of what is said and the wrongness of its being said by that particular character, or in that particular situation, or in that particular manner. Lear is old, and his age is full of changes, but his daughters should not say so. There is no reply—no reply but "Nothing"—to Lear's request that Cordelia should outdo her sis-

ters in protestation of her love; but Cordelia should not make
that reply. Kent should warn the king, but loyalty asks for more
mannerly phrasing. The vision that is discovered in character in
the early part of the play is that vision which sees, in all its com-
plexities, the play in conduct of mere "reason" and "rightness," at
odds with that other play of something more than "reason,"
something more than "rightness." So much is this the theme of
the first Act that we may risk the judgement that this is what the
play is about. Nature, we are to learn, needs more than reason
gives.

Except for the King of France, the first Act shows all the other
characters—this is the manner in which they were conceived—
determining their conduct and their speech either by self-regarding "reason" or by a sense of "rightness" which has in it something of self-regard. At any rate, conduct in them is determined,
in one way or another, according merely to the need or the letter,
and, because of this, has in it an admixture of evil and necessary
imperfection. Whether the regard for self be "proper" or "improper," at the beginning of the play the impulse in conduct is
almost universally self-regarding, or has in it something self-
regarding as a presiding element. Something in self, something
inhibitory in the conduct of another combining with something
in self, prevents a "going out" of the self. Even where the spirit
is generous, it is forced to seek refuge in "reason," in the letter,
and is thereby frustrated and impoverished. At the end of the
play, however, conduct—again in one way or another—becomes
something more than "reason" needs. There is, for example, a
kind of generosity, a certain "going out" of the self, in Goneril,
when she says, "I have been worth the whistle." There is, in
this, release from the self, and much more than "reason" needs.
So, too, in Edmund's "Yet Edmund was belov'd"; and it is significant that this is followed immediately by something very
much like remorse for others. Edmund—and Goneril, too, for that
matter—shows himself for a moment as man enough to be
damned. When Lear thinks of the "poor naked wretches," there
is a most subtle play on all these themes—for such compassion in
him has been in the past more than reason has seemed to need
and is now a "going out" of himself; and yet in this compassion
there is a higher reason, which shows the heavens "more just."

Reason and compassion come together at last, when Kent says of the king:

> Vex not his ghost: O! let him pass; he hates him
> That would upon the rack of this rough world
> Stretch him out longer.

And, a little later:

> I have a journey, sir, shortly to go;
> My master calls me, I must not say no.

The movement of the play seems to be from conduct (and character) in which reason is governed by self-regard, to conduct (and character) in which reason is transformed by compassion. In an image, this compassion becomes a healing and medicinal balm. So the third servant says of Gloucester:

> I'll fetch some flax and whites of eggs
> To apply to his bleeding face.

And Cordelia of her father:

> O my dear father! Restoration hang
> Thy medicine on my lips, and let this kiss
> Repair those violent harms that my two sisters
> Have in thy reverence made!

That was one way of representing compassion.

"Institutions are necessary," but they are administered by men, and, necessary though they are, they are no guarantee against viciousness and evil. Lear, in his madness, has a terrible picture of what may lie beneath the façade of social and political institutions, and for a moment we have a vision of all society itself, in its forms and customs, rotten and hypocritical. It is a picture of society in which institutions are all false-seeming, and justice itself is so perverted that it lends itself as a disguise to those very ills on which it passes judgement. The image of clothes is still used by Shakespeare:

> Through tatter'd clothes small vices do appear;
> Robes and furred gowns hide all.

Here is society, as Lear in his madness sees it, without grace, without sweetness. The law conceals what it cannot prevent, and, by stealth, luxury goes to it, pell-mell. As we envisage such a society, we have a physical nausea, which makes us wish, like Lear, "an ounce of civet" to sweeten our imaginations. We have raised the stone and seen the maggots. Shakespeare never gave us a clearer clue—and there is another in that travesty of justice as Lear arraigns the joint-stools in the hovel—to the vision of the play from which the characters draw their identities.

But it is not a merely secular society in which these characters are conceived to have their being. Nor, on the other hand, do I think it can be said (even through allegory) to be a society understood in terms of Christian theology. Nevertheless, to put the matter quite simply, we certainly get the impression in the play that the characters are imagined not only as members of each other but also as members of a Nature which is active both within themselves and throughout the circumambient universe. Man is nowhere so certainly exhibited as a member of all organic creation and of the elemental powers. Man's membership of society is more than legal, is more than political, because it is subtended in a wider membership, in which plants and animals, the wind and the thunder, are also included. And is it too extravagant to suggest that this natural universe is, in the earlier part of the play, peopled not only by men but also by beings of a primitive pagan belief—by Hecate, by Apollo, by Jupiter, by "the gods"; and that the dominion of these beings is, in the action of the play, superseded? Is it, indeed, too extravagant to suggest that in the play we have a veritable change in dispensation? That, at any rate, is the impression given as the imagery changes and one store of images gives way to another. What the final dispensation is, however, it is difficult to determine, for Shakespeare seems not to specify it. The most we can say is that, like the promise of rain in Mr. T. S. Eliot's *The Waste Land,* there are moments and images towards the end of *King Lear* which give promise of grace and benediction.

It is hard, then, to understand how *King Lear* can ever have been taken to be "the most Senecan of all Shakespeare's tragedies." Even Mr. Eliot, while seeking to suggest that there is "much less and much more" than Senecan Stoicism in the play, agrees that "there is [in it] a tone of Senecan fatalism; *fatis agimur*." I should have thought that of all Shakespeare's tragedies this statement is least true of *King Lear*. It cannot be argued, surely, that we are to take as true for the whole play Gloucester's statement:

> As flies to wanton boys, are we to the gods:
> They kill us for their sport.

The characters seem to me to be self-active and responsible, and even the idea that "ripeness is all" is scarcely resignation as Seneca might have understood it. What might be mistaken for resignation is, indeed, something very different, and not at all Senecan; I mean the humility which manifests itself unmistakably in Lear, in Edgar, in Albany, at the end of the play. Goneril's "I have been worth the whistle" and Edmund's "Yet Edmund was belov'd" have in them something of the element which Mr. Eliot has called "cheering oneself up"; but they are more than that. Moreover, these utterances come too late, in a moment too desperate, for them to be dismissed merely as the speech of Pride. Not Pride, indeed, but Humility, which is the "reverse" of the stoical attitude, is the most memorable principle at the end of the play; but we could never have known what this Humility was, had we not learned also something about Pride. True humility, moreover, goes hand in hand with compassion, and so it is in the closing scenes of *King Lear*. Does not the play look forward to Dostoievsky, rather than back to Seneca?

In general, the tragic hero is conceived as pursuing a settlement not only with secular society but also with his universe. Settlement with society is not enough; for he must also find for himself an identity which, while giving him mastery over his temporal problems, justifies that mastery with a more than temporal sanction. The nature of his settlement with his universe is determined in the pursuit of settlement itself. In this sense it is true to say that Shakespeare had no "philosophy." It is no prefabricated universe with which the hero seeks to find accommodation; it is no prefabricated universe which at his peril and cost he ignores. The Christian categories never preside over the vision, although, naturally enough, the vision is impregnated with Christian sentiment. Tragedy finds its origin not in a Christian idea of imperfection but in "Renaissance anarchism."

Only through grace, perhaps, if at all, can man find blessedness; and Shakespearian tragedy is tragedy simply because in it Fallen Man seeks to find rehabilitation in "infiniteness"—but without grace. The tragedy is in the failure, and perhaps the failure is general to the case of Man. The tragic character (and in this there is no Senecan "cheering oneself up") will not resign himself to confinement in the secular world; but he has no certitude of status in a world more absolute. We cannot judge the tragic character in terms of our temporal moralities; neither can we schematize those mysteries of redemption which might at last exempt him from such judgements. He believes that he belongs to this world and he believes that he does not. He would jump the life to come—and yet he dare not. He comes to know that "the readiness is all," but that same ripeness, which releases him from the importunities of this world, discovers for him no other. Shakespearian tragedy is the product of the change in men's minds—the Renaissance change—by which men came to feel themselves separate from God; by which, indeed, the idea of God receded from men's habitual certitudes and became no more and often less than an intellectual construction, a merely credible hypothesis, a Being remote and not certainly just or beneficent, perhaps the Enemy. In a world where anarchism was of recent development and men had not yet resigned themselves to a disabling opportunism man's perennial hunger for metaphysical being prompted Shakespeare to create supreme drama out of the question, How shall man find the intersection between that which is in time and that which is out of time? Or, to put the matter simply, and I do not think too simply, What shall we do to be saved?

John F. Danby

THE FOOL AND HANDY-DANDY

I PROPOSE in this chapter to isolate one aspect of the Fool. The aim is to see how far Shakespeare's larger theme—the theme of man and his society, of the two Natures and Janus-like Reason—is reflected in the shivered mirror of the Fool's verse.

The manner of that verse is gnomic and elliptic. It is an ideal idiom for twisting broken fragments into unexpected patterns. On one side it might originate in the medieval nonsense poem. The sixteenth century popular ballad still kept this alive in such scraps and oddments as the Fool sings. On the other it comes down through Shakespeare's own period of Gobbo-like confusion-mongering. It ends, in *King Lear*, as the sort of thing Blake might have taken as a model for his own octosyllables. It is not a carefree or a happy verse, for all its capering and jauntiness. It is taut with anxiety and bafflement, with distress and bitterness. It is abrupt and bewildered. It can juggle with fragments of the two Natures and the two Reasons, and then shrug off the whole business with hideous flippancy. Pain distorts the Fool's grimace, but the pain might equally mask compassion or contempt.

A passage from the Fool's first scene in the play provides a fair example of his normal idiom:

Lear:
> When were you wont to be so full of songs, sirrah?

Fool:
> I have used it nuncle, e'er since thou mad'st thy
> daughters thy mothers, for when thou gav'st them

From *Shakespeare's Doctrine of Nature: A Study of King Lear,* 1949, pp. 102-113. Reprinted by permission of Faber & Faber Limited.

> the rod, and put'st down thy own breeches,
> Then they for sudden joy did weep,
> And I for sorrow sung,
> That such a King should play bo-peep,
> And go the fools among.
> Prithee nuncle keep a schoolmaster that can teach
> thy fool to lie, I would fain learn to lie.

Lear:

> An you lie, sirrah, we'll have you whipped.
>
> (I, iv.)

We might note first that the Fool is under a compulsion to tell the truth, so that what he says has professional reliability. Second, the popular ballad material incorporated into his part is not chosen at random: it matches his own manner, and throws new light on what he has to say. Thirdly, very often his speeches deliberately re-state what has already been given expression in the play elsewhere. "Thou mad'st thy daughters thy mothers," for example, repeats Goneril's outburst of the scene before:

> Idle old man
> That still would manage those authorities
> That he hath given away, now by my life,
> Old fools are babes again, and must be us'd
> With checks as flatteries, when they are seen abus'd.
>
> (I, iii.)

Each of these points is a commonplace of criticism: their combined force is sufficient warrant for treating the whole of the Fool's lines as serious and homogeneous utterance. His statements have as much weight, for interpretation, as those of anyone in the play.

The most significant aspect of the Fool's verse is also illustrated in the passage. This is his habit of translating everything into handy-dandy. (Cp. "When a man is over-lusty at legs, then he shall wear wooden nether-stocks.")

He sees everything as a see-saw. Whichever end of the see-saw anyone chooses, the Fool's job is to be counterweight. The King himself is an instance of this universal handy-dandy. He has made his daughters his mothers. Instead of wielding the rod, he receives correction himself. Instead of remaining a ruler on the throne he has become an irresponsible child playing bo-beep. Handy-dandy is a psychological law, too:

> Then they for sudden joy did weep
> And I for sorrow sung.

The ballad lines, apart from the *King Lear* context, are merely Launcelot Gobbo silliness. In the *King Lear* context, however, they develop characteristic overtones. There is first the obvious common-sense meaning: excessive joy can make one weep, and hysterical sorrow will sometimes sing. But this in itself shows how the mind rocks perpetually between extremes, with no fixed centre of measure or control. Furthermore there is the meaning that comes from the deliberate switching of the tears and the song. The daughters have stolen the Fool's tears; he is left to sing their song. It might be a profound hypocrisy on the daughters' part—the kind of hypocrisy that steals the good man's weapons and leaves him with none but those the hypocrite has discarded. (This, of course, is Cordelia's plight when she must be dumb because the hypocrites have already made truth seem like a lie.) Hypocrisy can always seize the initiative, put truth in this false position and leave it paralysed and immobile; hypocrisy can force even truth to seem a collaborator. The Fool appears to be as callous as the sisters, they are no more cruel than he. The Fool can see it all happening, and knows exactly how it works. But his knowledge leaves him no better off. It is all an inevitable and miserable handy-dandy.

A striking thing about the Fool is that while his heart makes him belong to the Lear-party, and while his loyalty to Lear himself is unshakeable, his head can only represent to him that meaning for Reason which belongs to the party of Edmund and the Sisters. He is aware of the two common senses in the debate between Goneril and Albany. But his constant recommendation to the King and his following is a counsel of self-interest. Here is his advice to Kent:

> Let go thy hold, when a great wheel runs down a hill, lest it breaks thy neck with following. But the great one that goes upward, let him draw thee after: when a wise man

gives thee better council give me mine again: I would have
none but Knaves follow it since a Fool gives it:

> That Sir, which serves and seeks for gain,
>   And follows but for form;
> Will pack, when it begins to rain,
>   And leave thee in the storm,
> But I will tarry, the Fool will stay,
>   And let the wise man fly:
> The Knave turns Fool that runs away,
>   The Fool no Knave perdy.

                     (II, ii.)

It is usual to claim that in instances such as this the Fool is submitting the loyalty of Lear's following to a test. He gives advice
which he knows will not be taken by the disinterested; he is a
hypocrite in a benevolent sense. This view, I think, makes the
Fool less ambiguous than he really is. As I see him, he really does
believe that to follow Lear to disaster is foolishness. Absolute
loyalty is irrational, and the Fool never suggests that there is a
supernatural sanction for such irrationality. Folly is an alternative to knavery, certainly. But that does not make it a virtue. The
third term that would rescue him from the counterbalancing
negatives is simply missing. Handy-dandy works on the ethical
level, too. It is this which separates the Fool from Albany whom
Goneril calls a "moral fool." The Fool can see no sense in the
foolish morality Albany would urge his wife to pursue. On the
other hand, Goneril's alternative is no more acceptable. The Fool
is quite clear on the point that such common sense as hers (such
wisdom) is mere knavishness. Wiseman has come to mean for
him, as for Bunyan later, worldly-wiseman. Unlike Bunyan the
Fool does not see the wiseman as a candidate for damnation.

    Handy-dandy operates in society, too. The "great wheel" runs
down the hill and another is drawn upward by its very descent.
It is tempting to see behind this image some new device of
haulage machinery. (Massinger's image for the great man and
his satellites was the great wheel of a mill that makes the lesser
wheels go round. In Chapman the wheels are those of a spit.)
The wheel is probably, however, the wheel of Fortune. Either
way a strong sense pervades the lines of the individual's weakness

in the authoritarian setting for human action. The Great Man himself is as insecure as the small man. The tilted plane of society makes tug and scamble inevitable. Under such conditions the panic of save-your-own-skin will be the prevailing mood.

The Fool holds up to Lear a model of cautionary excellence. It is the hypocrite, the canny capitalist, and the self-denying puritan combined:

> Mark it, nuncle;
> Have more than thou showest,
> Speak less than thou knowest,
> Lend less than thou owest,
> Ride more than thou goest,
> Learn more than thou trowest,
> Set less than thou throwest;
> Leave thy drink and thy whore,
> And keep in a door,
> And thou shalt have more,
> Than two tens to a score.
>
> (I, iv.)

Goneril has already charged Lear with the vices of the old regime, riotous "Epicurism and Lust"—the excess of those impulses which, in the mean, are sociability, comradeship, free self-expression, and love. The Fool prescribes the complementary vices of the new dispensation: a riot of acquisitiveness, self-protection, suspicion.

Again, it is impossible to say that the advice is meant only as irony. The model proposed is certainly mean and contemptible, an inversion of the grand image of the King in the scheme of natural theology. It is not one that would be freely espoused if other alternatives were open. However, the Fool doubts whether any alternative does lie open, apart from the permanent alternative of Folly.

We are tempted to think of the Fool as being on the side of some social Utopia, until we see handy-dandy applied to this, too:

> When priests are more in word, than matter;
> When brewers mar their malt with water;

> When nobles are their tailors' tutors,
> No heretics burned, but wenches' suitors;
> When every case in Law, is right;
> No squire in debt, nor no poor knight;
> When slanders do not live in tongues;
> Nor cutpurses come not to throngs;
> When usurers tell their gold i' th' field,
> And bawds, and whores, do churches build,
> Then shall the Realm of Albion,
> Come to great confusion;
> Then comes the time, who lives to see't,
> That going shall be us'd with feet.
> This prophecy Merlin shall make, for I live
>   before his time.

                                             (III, ii.)

The first four lines describe the actual state of present corruption. The next four switch without warning to the coming Utopia. The two lines following manage to mix both together:

> When usurers tell their gold i' th' field,
> And bawds, and whores, do churches build.

We can read this either as total conversion or as utter unregeneracy. The confusion is completed by the last four lines. The Golden Age to come will entail the overthrow of Albion, and the last stage will return us to the point from which we start:

> Then comes the time, who lives to see't,
> That going shall be us'd with feet.

There is little hope of enlisting the Fool as a social reformer.

Handy-dandy is even applied to Time: "This prophecy," the Fool explains, "Merlin shall make; for I live before his time." Direction and purpose in history itself are lost. The motion from past to future becomes that of a wheel again.

The wheel is the key to much of the Fool's imagery. The great wheel running up and down the hill is a double wheel-image—a wheel running round in a circle. We used the image of the see-saw to explain the working of the Fool's opposites. A suspended wheel is an endless series of see-saws. The old man and

the babe, the moralist and the knave, the wise man and the fool
—these are opposites diametrically counterpoised, and then (since
the wheel always comes full circle) identified. The mechanism
is shown at work in the individual, in society, in the pattern of
the moral world, and in history itself. Man is caught in a con-
traption that bears him up and down, carries him round and
round, continually.

Edmund and the Sisters see society as a competition; and
Goneril says it is safer to fear than to trust too far. In this competitiveness there is a certain combative courage, and for them
fear is an offensive-defensive of caution. Man even as an animal
still retains a kind of dignity. He is King of the Beasts. The Fool
sees this competitiveness and fear in a different light. "He that
has a house to put's head in," he remarks, "has a good head-
piece." Or, another occasion:

Fool:
>Canst tell why an oyster makes his shell?

Lear:
>No.

Fool:
>Nor I neither; but I can tell why a snail has a house.

Lear:
>Why?

Fool:
>Why, to put's head in, not to give it away to his
>daughters and leave his horns without a case.

(i, v.)

Here he makes the fear, timidity, and the creatures nearest to
man in this general respect the close oyster and the fearful snail.
Self-interest does not only lead to an aggressive outgoing among
one's fellows. It leads also to a self-protective shrinkage within
one's shell. Man is a poor, cowering, threatened creature, and will
do well to look after himself as best he can.

The shell and the sheltering creature symbolize for the Fool
man in the carapace of his society. The compelling factor in the
image is the suggestion of the external threat. Man must defend
himself in such an environment. His mean shifts are a necessity
imposed on him by the sub-humanity of the surrounding uni-

verse, a universe constantly threatening to crush the shell men have built for themselves. It is this same sub-humanity (sensed by Kent, as well as by the Fool, as lying behind the Thunder) which amply sanctions man's inhumanity to man. Not all can be equally warm or sheltered. Those like Poor Tom who are pushed outside must blame themselves only—and the elements.

The Fool, like Hobbes, knows that "the passion to be reckoned upon is fear." Fear throbs as a motive through his human world, and beats down from the non-human world of the heavens. It is this underlying feeling which explains the Fool's sincerest piece of advice to the suffering King he accompanies over the heath. It is an example of compassion working to the same effect as cruelty: an unconscious handy-dandy. He is alone with Lear on the heath; the storm is still raging; the King has just called on the "all-shaking thunder" to

> Strike flat the thick rotundity o' th' world,
> Crack Nature's moulds, all germens spill at once
> That makes ingrateful man.
>
> (III, ii.)

The Fool says:

> O nuncle, Court holy-water in a dry house, is better than this rain water out o' door. Good nuncle, in, ask thy daughters' blessing; here's a night pities neither wise men, nor fools.
>
> (III, iii.)

The heath tests the breaking-points of the human beings wandering over it. This is the Fool's, and a nadir of negated humanity is reached. "Court holy-water" is the sycophancy and corruption of the time-servers that fawn on power. Under the threat of Thunder the Fool's opposition collapses. He will abjectly consent even to playing the hypocritical knave. He urges the king to accept the worst terms society can offer, the blessing of pelican daughters:

> The Knave turns Fool that runs away.

This is an ultimate bankruptcy. And it is the intellect's sincere advice. There is neither bitterness nor irony, only moral panic.

We are invited back with Lear into the corrupt world we were glad to have quitted—invited to stand by the same fire with Lady Brach, and stink.

The corrupt world is the final clue to the meaning of the Fool. He is not of tragic scope. He affirms the dignity of man neither as animal nor angelic reason. Nor has he the ennobling weakness of compassion. He remains a figure of pathos because he is so helpless—helplessly immobilized by a handy-dandy of opposites neither of which he can choose. Nor will he admit of any third ground, the possibility that knavishness might not be an ulti-mate, that wisdom might be redeemable, that society might be capable of re-birth. He does not survive his own grim laughter, and disappears for that reason. He could not survive, without metamorphosis, in the same context as Cordelia. He is fast in the sickening stasis of his handy-dandy.

His summary of the human situation is as follows:

> He that has a house to put's head in, has a good head-piece:
> > The codpiece that will house,
> > Before the head has any;
> > The head, and he shall louse:
> > So beggars marry many.
> > The man that makes his toe,
> > What he his heart should make,
> > Shall of a corn cry woe,
> > And turn his sleep to wake.
>
> For there never yet was fair woman, but she made mouths in a glass.
>
> (III, ii.)

This is the closest knot Shakespeare ties in the idiom he in-vented for the Fool, and is original for both manner and matter.

That the imagery should be both social and sexual is not chance prurience. The idea of sexual love in Shakespeare's time was approaching the end of an interesting career. It had been a relation under which to figure the ideal destiny of man, both as a person and a social agent. In Spenser, for example, love is the consummation of the whole course of virtue in man. It may be that wherever love is more than casual mating it inevitably serves as an allegory of the marriage of the individual to truth. Throughout the Elizabethan period (and in Petrarch and Dante) this liaison seems certainly to have been well established. By 1600 optimism had reached its term (maybe a nemesis for Elizabeth's over-stimulation of the cult of Gloriana). In the Shakespearean breakdown of confidence, extending to most of the human values, love was also involved. *King Lear* reflects moods that are not only anti-authoritarian, and anti-social, but also anti-sexual. Love is left with none of the Spenserian glamour (except in relation to Cordelia) and the revulsion is expressed crudely—as by Lear in his mad speeches, and by the Fool here.

The codpiece is part of the gallant's costume, and also, quite simply, the phallus. The first four lines thus describe how improvident lechering leads to disease, and how this begins a vicious circle: because the head, too (shrewd prudence and cautious provision against all the potential threats of life) becomes lousy. Once the process has started it is increasingly difficult to stop it. This is the explanation of the paradox concerning the Beggarman and his long train of doxies. He "marries" so many because he is poor (the result of an initial imprudence), and not vice versa. The four lines give a kind of condensed Rake's Progress, and the career of proud gallant becoming Abram man conforms to the mechanism of the wheel. This central idea in the lines is repeated, of course, in Poor Tom—the courtier whose vices had just been those that set the wheel turning and who becomes a naked Bedlamite.

The next four lines fuse the images of Beggarman and Courtier after another fashion. The "toe" can belong to either: it might be the Courtier's pinched in his over-tight shoes, or the Beggarman's that has burst through his boot. A sexual symbolism, paralleling "codpiece," accompanies the social reference. The toe is also (*pace* Freud) the phallus.—I take the lines to mean: "The man—rich or poor—who makes his 'toe' the centre of all his hopes, aspirations, and satisfactions, sacrificing, if he be a courtier, all real human feeling to vanity, or, if he be a beggar, squandering his emotional means in slovenly lust—this man, the composite social creature, will suffer the inevitable pain consequent on his perversity: pangs of guilty remorse that will never let him rest. Thus both extremes in society, acting in opposite

ways from opposite motives, come together in the same state—
a state of self-torment."

Handy-dandy is doubly exerted in these lines. First, one half
of society is neatly folded over the other. The quatrains seem at
first sight to be referring only to one, but are in fact applicable
to the other, too. The effect is to argue, seemingly, that haves
and have-nots are in an identical plight. Secondly, through the
intertwining of the social and sexual in the same image, the public world of community and the private world of personal emotional life are shown to interlock.

Yet a third handy-dandy remains to be noted. The poem is
about the strife between head and heart, both of them sinning
and sinned against. The first quatrain illustrates a sin against
the head: lust flouts prudence, and the unregulated instinct after
one's kind leads to disaster. The second depicts a sin against
the heart: either by the vain courtier (cultivating the externals
instead of attending to the inward things of the spirit) or
through the coney-catching beggarman (exposing and parading
his ill-shodness, yet not revealing the design and deceit in his
breast). Head and heart, like courtier and beggarman are equally
badly off. Neither is a reliable guide. Both are mutually con-
founding. The eight lines summarize the plight of a fissured
society and of a divided man: a severance that is self-perpetuat-
ing and self-aggravating. Society and man come together only
to make each other worse. This applies to rich as well as poor.
At either end of the social scale (and it is a scale with no middle)
we see a travesty of human nature—flaunting codpiece, calloused
toe, man lacerated in head and heart, in mind and body, by
disease or conscience.

To sum up, the Fool can be regarded as the consciousness of
a split society. Like man, its creator, the society is a twin-headed
monster at strife with itself. The Fool consistently uses the
imagery of disease and perversity. Complementary ill-healths
counterbalance in perpetual handy-dandy. He sees rich man and
poor man, head and heart, sympathizes with neither, yet cannot
dissociate himself from the conditions of the strife. Harsh as the
handy-dandy world of corrupt society is, there is no escape from
it: "In, nuncle, in, and ask thy daughters' blessing."

We began by observing the unconscious handy-dandy in the

Fool's own behaviour. His head thinks with the Reason of Goneril and Regan, yet what he does is directly counter to the self-interest which for them and for him is the only thing that makes sense. His greatest bit of cruelty is wrung from him by compassion. While he counsels flight, with wiseman and knave, he will not desert the king: because he is a Fool. What he does will not square with what he says, and it is a redeeming insincerity. Wilfully and blindly he holds to the Great Wheel going downhill.

The Fool, I think, stands for the unillumined head—the intellect—as Lear is the soul, and Cordelia the spirit. He can discern in his cold light the alternatives between which he cannot choose. The sort of thing he could desire he will not admit to exist. It would be too good to be true. Nature in him is an arrest of motion. His head will not allow him to descend the scale with Edmund and the Sisters, and yet it shows no sign of rushing into the natural theology of Lear and Cordelia. The Fool is incapable of Goneril's wickedness, of Lear's error and his subsequent growth, of Cordelia's faultless integration. He prefers, however, to walk in a darkness he cannot fathom rather than stay in the light of such reason as he cannot abide. The head would betray him back to Goneril's hearth, with Lady Brach. But for reasons neither he nor the head knows he follows Lear over the heath.

Mark Van Doren

ANTONY AND CLEOPATRA

IF *Antony and Cleopatra* was written first among the three
tragedies in which Shakespeare returned to Plutarch for his
source, the writing of it involved the removal of his imagination
to a distance that almost staggers measurement. The poet of
King Lear and *Macbeth* now works freely under a great dome of
lighted sky which knows no clouds except an occasional illusory
and indistinct one, and which feels no wind beyond the soft one
of its own effortless breathing. The world of *Antony and Cleopatra* is so immense that time yawns in it; and this is not because
time is going to die as it did in *Macbeth* but because it luxuriates
in a sense of perfect and endless health. The mandragora that
Cleopatra wants to drink so that she may "sleep out this great
gap of time" (I, v, 5) while Antony is away needs scarcely to
be drunk in a universe already drugged with a knowledge of its
own size. It is all the world that Plutarch knew or that Shakespeare knows as he writes: the Mediterranean world where
opulent Africa lies across a gleaming sea from Spain, Italy, and
Greece, and where innumerable kingdoms stretch eastward to
the horizon. Nor is there terror in such distances. Men are at
home in "the wide arch of the rang'd empire," and call each other
naturally the most glorious names: "triple pillar of the world,"
"demi-Atlas of this earth," "senators alone of this great world,"
"world-sharers," "universal landlord," "sole sir o' the world."
There is no terror because there is so much light. When Iras says

> the bright day is done,
> And we are for the dark,
>
> (v, ii, 193-4)

she is bidding good-by to an afternoon which has been long with life; and the dark for which she is destined seems somehow to have no blackness in it, for the same reason that when Cleopatra utters her command:

> Darkling stand
> The varying shore o' the world
>
> (iv, xv, 10-11)

we cannot imagine that any cliff or headland has ceased to be luminous even though the sun has burned the great sphere it moves in. Light plays on everything with undiscouraged luxury: on land, on rivers, on islands, and on the sea. We are never far away from the limpid and life-giving element of water, which, rather than forming like dew as it did in *A Midsummer Night's Dream*, now spreads a rich iridescent film over the whole of a vast daylight existence. There is of course the sea, and Antony is one who with his sword

> Quarter'd the world, and o'er green Neptune's back
> With ships made cities.
>
> (iv, xiv, 58-9)

But there is also the Nile, whose "slime and ooze," creative of "flies and gnats" as well as crocodiles, we are kept no less conscious of than we are kept conscious of flowing streams wherein "tawny-finn'd fishes" play, where swan's-down feathers float at full of tide, and from which rise swifts and mallards. It is a world of languid and abundant life which cannot surprise us with news that swallows have built their nests in Cleopatra's sails (iv, xii, 3-4), or that the river of Cydnus fell in love with her barge as it burned on its water.

> The oars were silver,
> Which to the tune of flutes kept stroke, and made
> The water which they beat to follow faster,
> As amorous of their strokes.
>
> (ii, ii, 199-202)

At night, since night must be, there is nevertheless the moon, whose fleeting terrene visits keep Italy and Egypt flooded with yellow light. And day by day again there is certain to be music— "moody food," says Cleopatra (II, v, 1-2), "of us that trade in love." But it is not music played in a chamber, like the music of *Twelfth Night,* or on the lawn of a great lady's estate as in *The Merchant of Venice.* It has the dome of the world to fill, so that it plays "far off" while Cleopatra fishes (II, v, 11), and runs both through the air and underground when

> the god Hercules, whom Antony loved,
> Now leaves him.
>
> (IV, iii, 16-17)

Such a world needs a special style, and the play triumphantly provides it. The units of this style, curiously enough, are very brief. Nothing is drawn out as with too little thought we might have expected it to be. The action is broken into as many as forty-two scenes; our attention is constantly shifted from one to another portion of the single scene which is the earth. And so with the speech, the characteristic unit of which is almost breathlessly short. There are no rolls of rhetoric, no attempts to loop the universe with language. This universe is too large to be rendered in anything but fragments, too much alive in its own right to care for extended compliment and discourse. It can be handled only by a process of constantly reassembling its many small parts—moving them about in an always flexible mosaic. For the world of *Antony and Cleopatra* shows its strength in nothing so much as its flexibility. Any part, examined closely, yields the whole, just as any speech, once it is made, escapes into some far altitude of the air without exactly losing itself; in the long run it will count. The action expresses itself in many ripples, like a resting sea. The climate in which Antony and Cleopatra so completely love each other permits them the luxury of little phrases, as if with their breath it panted the tale of its own endless well-being. Accommodating itself to its heroine, it utters itself with a refined sensuousness, opening its lips and pronouncing delicious words in which the light sounds of i, short a, s, st, l, and ing predominate.

          By the fire
That quickens Nilus' slime, I go from hence
Thy soldier, servant.

                              (I, iii, 68-70)

          This common body,
Like to a vagabond flag upon the stream,
Goes to and back, lackeying the varying tide,
To rot itself with motion.

                              (I, iv, 44-7)

          Think on me,
That am with Phoebus' amorous pinches black,
And wrinkled deep in time?

                              (I, v, 27-9)

How much unlike art thou Mark Antony!
Yet, coming from him, that great medicine hath
With his tinct gilded thee.

                              (I, v, 35-7)

By Isis, I will give thee bloody teeth.

                              (I, v, 70)

          She
In the habiliments of the goddess Isis
That day appear'd.

                              (III, vi, 16-8)

That which is now a horse, even with a thought
The rack dislimns, and makes it indistinct,
As water is in water.

                              (IV, xiv, 9-11)

With thy sharp teeth this knot intrinsicate
Of life at once untie.

                              (V, ii, 307-8)

This is an aspic's trail; and these fig-leaves
Have slime upon them, such as the aspic leaves
Upon the caves of Nile.

                              (V, ii, 354-6)

The speech of any person in the play is likely to spill itself in agreeable gasps, as if it came through gills; and the blank-verse line of the earlier dramas has almost lost its form in the fluid element that surrounds it.

> Let Rome in Tiber melt, and the wide arcn
> Of the rang'd empire fall! Here is my space.
> Kingdoms are clay; our dungy earth alike
> Feeds beast as man; the nobleness of life
> Is to do thus, when such a mutual pair
> And such a twain can do 't.
>
> (I, i, 33-8)

> Nay, pray you, seek no colour for your going,
> But bid farewell, and go. When you sued staying,
> Then was the time for words; no going then;
> Eternity was in our lips and eyes,
> Bliss in our brows' bent; none our parts so poor,
> But was a race of heaven. They are so still,
> Or thou, the greatest soldier of the world,
> Art turn'd the greatest liar.
>
> (I, iii, 32-9)

> My salad days,
> When I was green in judgement; cold in blood,
> To say as I said then! But, come, away;
> Get me ink and paper.
> He shall have every day a several greeting,
> Or I'll unpeople Egypt.
>
> (I, v, 73-8)

> I will o'ertake thee, Cleopatra, and
> Weep for my pardon. So it must be, for now
> All length is torture; since the torch is out,
> Lie down, and stray no farther. Now all labour
> Mars what it does; yea, very force entangles
> Itself with strength.
>
> (IV, xiv, 44-9)

Such a style suits lovers who make up as quickly as they have quarreled; the anger of Antony and Cleopatra has a short memory, and pardons succeed curses with little shift of accent.

> Courteous lord, one word.
> Sir, you and I must part, but that's not it;
> Sir, you and I have lov'd, but there's not it;
> That you know well. Something it is I would,—
> O, my oblivion is a very Antony,
> And I am all forgotten.
>
> (I, iii, 86-91)

That will do for Cleopatra's text after any altercation; and Antony, who played with half the bulk of the world as he pleased and had superfluous kings for messengers, can humble himself as briefly:

> Fall not a tear, I say; one of them rates
> All that is won and lost. Give me a kiss.
> Even this repays me.
>
> (III, xi, 69-71)

Their misunderstandings are waves which there are other waves to check, just as the bits of acting they practice on each other are chopped short because they know that neither can be deceived.

Cleopatra.	Good now, play one scene
	Of excellent dissembling; and let it look
	Like perfect honour.
Antony.	You'll heat my blood. No more.
Cleopatra.	You can do better yet; but this is meetly.
Antony.	Now, by my sword,—
Cleopatra.	And target.—Still he mends;
	But this is not the best.

(I, iii, 78-83)

This banter is from a queen who is herself a consummate actress, and she knows Antony knows it. Once she fails to see through him, but that is when he is acting for men only and she does not catch the style. As he opens an old vein of oratory and contrives tremulos for the benefit of certain servitors on the eve of battle (IV, ii) she appeals to Enobarbus who is standing by: "What means this?" Enobarbus puts her off by saying that it is

an odd trick of sorrow; Antony is affected by thoughts of the
next day. But as the instrument plays on she asks again: "What
does he mean?" And Enobarbus, who knows his master even
better than she knows her lover, has to confess: "To make his
followers weep." It is mere wanton art, an expert's oratory. There
is of course a final quarrel and a final attempt at deception, for
the play is a tragedy and Cleopatra will not be able to undo her
subterfuge of the monument (IV, xiii-xv). Yet even there the
established style will prevail, and modify the tragedy. And long
before that it will have subdued every item of the action to the
tone of it own unique refinement. The drunkenness of the gen-
erals on board Pompey's galley (II, vii) is as little gross as the
love of Antony and Cleopatra is voluptuous. As wine makes the
world-sharers witty, and steeps their senses at last in "soft and
delicate Lethe," so love turns the lead of Antony and Cleopatra
into gold. Pompey credits the Queen with sultry powers that
keep the brain of her lover fuming, but the love we see is light
with jest and mellow with amusement. This is because Cleopatra is really queen of her world. When Enobarbus pays her his
famous tribute:

> Age cannot wither her, nor custom stale
> Her infinite variety. . . . She makes hungry
> Where most she satisfies, for vilest things
> Become themselves in her,
>
> (II, ii, 240-44)

he is placing her in that world which the style of the play is
forever creating: a world which is ancient yet not stale, com-
placent yet still hungry, and as becoming in its vileness as it is
cultivated in its virtues. Its infinite variety is a quality of its air,
its land, its water, its animals, its clouds, its language, and its
people. All are the creation of a style whose imponderable atoms
are ever in graceful dance, no sooner combining to produce
forms than separating to dissolve them. The next question is
whether action is possible in such an atmosphere, and if so,
what kind of action.

In one sense *Antony and Cleopatra* is actionless. A world is
lost, but it is so well lost that it seems not to have been lost

at all; its immensity was not disturbed. The peculiar greatness of this poetry defeats any conceivable dramatic end. Line for line it is perhaps the richest poetry Shakespeare wrote, but the reward it reaps is paradoxical: it builds a universe in which nothing can happen, or at any rate one in which the conflicts and crises of persons cannot be of the first importance. This explains, if it is granted that the gods ordained some sort of greatness for the play, the nakedness of its verbal intensity. The writing has to be wonderful because it is not supported by anything that Aristotle would have called a plot. And it is wonderful. Merely as expression it has that final force which permits many of its passages to stand alone, without the need of a context to recommend them. If they gain from being read in place, the place is an atmosphere rather than an action. The intensity of Hamlet, Othello, Lear, and Macbeth was derived from their respective predicaments; the intensity of Antony and Cleopatra seems to be generated in themselves, and in the poet who is writing their speeches. This will tend to be true of all the plays to come. Shakespeare's last plays contain his richest writing but they are not his best plays. Though Timon, Pericles, Imogen, and Leontes are not surpassed by any of Shakespeare's poets, their stories leave them at a disadvantage. If the disadvantage is less conspicuous in the case of *Antony and Cleopatra,* the reason may be that its poetry has come as near as poetry can come to the performing of miracles: the play has lifted itself by its language. This appears most regularly in the passages of praise which glisten everywhere as others like them will glisten through the later dramas. The final poet in Shakespeare is content to be lyrical. Praise becomes with him an occupation in itself. The explanation may be that he now has things to say about humanity which must be said directly; or that he cannot find, in the stories available to him, persons to match his thought; or that his dramatic energies have declined. Whatever the explanation, his lyre labors continually at the task of praise, and labors with regal result. Consider Lepidus on Antony:

> I must not think there are
> Evils enow to darken all his goodness.
> His faults in him seem as the spots of heaven,

More fiery by night's blackness; hereditary,
Rather than purchas'd; what he cannot change,
Than what he chooses.

(i, iv, 10-15)

Or Euphronius on Antony:

Such as I am, I come from Antony.
I was of late as petty to his ends
As is the morn-dew on the myrtle-leaf
To his grand sea.

(iii, xii, 7-10)

Or Caesar on Antony:

The breaking of so great a thing should make
A greater crack. The round world
Should have shook lions into civil streets,
And citizens to their dens. The death of Antony
Is not a single doom; in the name lay
A moiety of the world.

(v, i, 14-9)

Or Cleopatra on Antony:

O, see, my women,
The crown o' the earth doth melt. My lord!
O, wither'd is the garland of the war,
The soldier's pole is fall'n! Young boys and girls
Are level now with men; the odds is gone,
And there is nothing left remarkable
Beneath the visiting moon.

(iv, xv, 62-8)

Or Cleopatra on Antony again—and this would seem to be the
goal in the play toward which both panegyric and poetry had
been striving, for there is no better speech in Shakespeare:

His legs bestrid the ocean; his rear'd arm
Crested the world; his voice was propertied
As all the tuned spheres, and that to friends;

> But when he meant to quail and shake the orb,
> He was as rattling thunder. For his bounty,
> There was no winter in 't; an autumn 't was
> That grew the more by reaping. His delights
> Were dolphin-like, they show'd his back above
> The element they liv'd in. In his livery
> Walk'd crowns and crownets; realms and islands were
> As plates dropp'd from his pocket.
>
> (v, ii, 83-92)

In another sense *Antony and Cleopatra* has all the action it desires and deserves. There is as much drama in the deaths of its hero and heroine as there can be in the deaths of two persons who lived, at least while we knew them, without illusion; or lived, it may be more accurate to say, in the full light of accepted illusion. Change is a fairy toy for Theseus in *A Midsummer Night's Dream,* and for Macbeth it is a growing terror. For Antony and Cleopatra it is what must be expected, and they have seen so much of it that more cannot surprise them. The changeableness of life is the only thing that does not change; they know this, and to that extent cannot be touched. Their love has been too thoroughly tested to be shaken now. It is founded on its own fact, and on the humorous knowledge they have of each other. Shakespeare put their case perfectly in his 138th sonnet:

> When my love swears that she is made of truth,
> I do believe her, though I know she lies. . . .
> O, love's best habit is in seeming trust,
> And age in love loves not to have years told.

Yet not quite perfectly, either. Each knows the other to be a liar, and ultimately does not care if this is so; but one of their pastimes is telling their years. Their days are past the best, and they know this as well as Enobarbus knows that Antony is an old lion (III, xiii, 95), or as well as Caesar knows, or thinks he knows that his rival is an old ruffian (IV, i, 4). Antony's remark that gray in both of them has something mingled with their younger brown (IV, viii, 19-20) is only a courteous reference to the white hairs he elsewhere takes to himself (III, xi, 13). And Cleopatra is content with the boast:

> Though age from folly could not give me freedom,
> It does from childishness.
>
> (I, iii, 57-8)

As lovers go, then, they are old. That is why they can do without illusion—or, better still, why they know what to do with it. They prefer each other's untruth to any truth that has yet to be tried. This does not make them easy material for tragedy. It makes them indeed the most intractable material of all; for tragedy works with delusions, and they have none. They would seem to have been cut out for comedy, and indeed there is much comedy here. Only a supreme effort at writing keeps the play on its tragic keel. And even then it must do without the sense in any line that death is terrible. Tragedy counts, both in its hero and in us, upon the fear of death for its great effects. But these lovers, far from fearing death, embrace it as a third lover. Enobarbus says of Cleopatra: "I do think there is mettle in Death, which commits some loving act upon her, she hath such a celerity in dying" (I, ii, 147-9). He is satirical, and refers to the actress who puts on shows of death in order to hold her lord. But his intelligence has penetrated to the symbol which Antony no less than she will employ to express an ultimate passion. "I'll make Death love me," swears Antony as he prepares for battle (III, xiii, 193), and as he falls on his sword he elaborates the image:

> I will be
> A bridegroom in my death, and run into 't
> As to a lover's bed.
>
> (IV, xiv, 99-101)

Cleopatra, however, gives it its most sophisticated form:

> The stroke of death is as a lover's pinch,
> Which hurts, and is desir'd.
>
> (V, ii, 298-9)

Antony is a great man, but his dimensions do not express themselves in drama. The play, such as it is, pauses while his praise is sung by Lepidus, by Euphronius, by Caesar, and again and again by Cleopatra. He deserves that such things should be said of him, but we must not expect to see them exemplified in act. They are often negative things: there are not enough evils to darken his goodness, his death is not a single doom, nothing is left remarkable since he is gone, his bounty had no winter in it. And there is a further negative:

> Who tells me true, though in his tale lie death,
> I hear him as he flatter'd. . . .
> Speak to me home, mince not the general tongue.
>
> (I, ii, 102-9)

He does not trade in untruths. We learn much from such negatives, but we learn it directly, through lyric statement while the action rests. His delights were dolphin-like, they show'd his back above the element they liv'd in—the movement there goes on outside our practical vision, in a remote kingdom by the sea of metaphor. Nothing more interesting was ever said about any man, but it has to be said, it cannot be shown. Antony is finally ineffable, and Shakespeare has the tact to let him tower alone. Bounty, as the first half of *Timon of Athens* proves, is not a dramatic virtue; nor is there any attempt in this play to make it seem one, though the suicide of Enobarbus (IV, vi) states it powerfully, and Cleopatra's encomium is majestic in its range. The virtues of Antony cannot be dramatized because they are one virtue and its name is magnanimity. Actor though he is and orator though he has been, at his best he shows his back above the element he lives in. He can be moved to anger, jealousy, and pride, he can laugh within a minute after he has raged, he can be a man of forty moods; yet our last vision is of one whose spirit has grown stationary. For all his shrewdness Enobarbus does not see what has happened. He speaks of "a diminution in our captain's brain" (III, xiii, 198), but he is wholly wrong. There has been an expansion, not a contraction. Great as is the world of Roman thoughts, and Caesar reveals the limit of that greatness, Antony has found a greater world—one whose soft sky is of infinite size, and one where thoughts melt into one another as water does in water. A soothsayer warns Antony to keep space between himself and Caesar (II, iii, 23), but the space is already there. The discomfort Antony feels in Caesar's presence is based on more than political rivalry between an old lion and a young fox; it is based on an inability to tell Caesar or any other man why Egypt is so attractive. The reason is Egypt's air, which cannot be felt until it is withdrawn; when it must be found and breathed again, for a full breath cannot be taken in any other. Antony grows until he occupies the whole of Egypt's and Cleopatra's air. And his final act of occupation is his death—which, if it withdraws him from us, leaves us an exact equivalent in the greatness of that air.

Cleopatra's dimensions express themselves on the other hand with an excess of drama—in many little plays rather than in one that is round and single. She comes at us in waves, each of which breaks before it reaches us, but the total number of which is great and beautiful. She is fickle, she is spoiled—

> Pity me, Charmian,
> But do not speak to me—
> (II, v, 118-19)

she is vain, she is cowardly, she is incorrigibly unserious; yet she is a queen "whom everything becomes" (I, i, 49). Antony says that, and he means it even of one who is "cunning past man's thought"; her cunning becomes her too, and the holy priests bless her when she is riggish (II, ii, 244-5). For her variety is infinite; she perfectly expresses the elasticity of Egypt's air. Antony's immobility measures its amount, but its quality can be fingered only in her. She is mercury, she is changeable silk, she is a serpent of old Nile whose movements are too many to count. The messenger's description of Octavia is nicely calculated for the woman to whom it is delivered:

> She creeps;
> Her motion and her station are as one;
> She shows a body rather than a life,
> A statue than a breather.
> (III, iii, 21-4)

Cleopatra is not like that; she is a breather, and her life is still more fascinating than her body. It is her life that makes her love so interesting. "There's beggary in the love that can be reckon'd" (I, i, 15)—Antony has learned this from her, and from the boundless air of Egypt. She teaches him even while she tortures him; that is why he can forgive her the long, ghastly effort to die which her lie about the monument imposes upon him (IV, xiv). His pleasure in her alternates with pain, and in fact the play deals more with the pain than it does with the pleasure. But between the lines we read that he could have endured as much again from one whose behavior has never been what Octavia's is, "holy, cold, and still" (II, vi, 131). Cleopatra is too seldom at rest to be easily understood; we shall never be sure, any more than Antony would have been sure, what her intentions were with respect to the treasure she withheld from Caesar (v, ii, 138-92), and whether her decision to die was inspired by loathing for Roman triumphs or by love for the "husband" to whom death would bring her. When the basket of asps arrives she announces to her people:

> My resolution's plac'd, and I have nothing
> Of woman in me; now from head to foot
> I am marble-constant; now the fleeting moon
> No planet is of mine.

(v, ii, 238-41)

Yet her demeanor in dying has no marble in it. She is still all mercury and lightness, all silk and down. "I have immortal longings in me" is said with a smile at the expense of the rural fellow who has just gone out wishing her joy of the worm and insisting that its bite is "immortal"; she must have on her robe and crown before she feels the loving pinch of death; when Iras precedes her in death she pretends to worry lest Antony's first kiss in heaven be wasted on another woman; she saves enough breath to call Caesar "ass unpolicied," and spends the last of it in likening the immortal worm to a baby at her breast. Charmian, surviving her a moment, echoes "ass unpolicied" with "lass unparallel'd," and bothers to straighten her mistress's crown before she dies. The scene is great and final, yet nothing in it seems to be serious; and the conversation between Caesar and his train when they come in concerns a spectacle that is pretty rather than painful.

> She looks like sleep,
> As she would catch another Antony
> In her strong toil of grace.
>   (v, ii, 349-51)

The strength of Cleopatra has never appeared more clearly than in the charm with which she yields herself to death. Her greatness cannot be distinguished from her littleness, as water may not be defined in water.

Oscar James Campbell

CORIOLANUS

In *Coriolanus* we have Shakespeare's second and more successful experiment in tragical satire. The structure which in *Timon of Athens* was bare and almost crude has here become a suitable form in which to cast the Roman aristocrat's story. Yet the construction of this last of Shakespeare's tragedies has been almost universally deplored. Critics, realizing that its pattern is very different from the one which the poet employed in his great tragedies, have agreed to brand it as inept. A. C. Bradley, for example, believes that the author's unintentional departure from his usual practice accounts for the failure of the play to produce a sound tragic effect.[1] This usually acute critic did not allow for the fact that Shakespeare, at this time a thoroughly experienced dramatist, might have deliberately experimented with new dramatic structures.

It is natural enough to judge *Coriolanus* by the standards of conventional tragedy; in the first Folio it is entitled *The Tragedy of Coriolanus*. Bernard Shaw was one of the first to see that the play was not a tragedy at all. He solves the problem of *Coriolanus* by propounding a witty paradox. "It is," he asserts, "the greatest of Shakespeare's comedies." This perverse statement suggests the proper approach to the play. Shakespeare did not attempt to give *Coriolanus* the structure of a conventional tragedy. Neither in his presentation of the central figure nor in his construction of the plot does he follow orthodox tragic principles. Instead of enlisting our sympathy for Coriolanus, he deliberately alienates it. Indeed he makes the figure partly an

From *Shakespeare's Satire*, 1943, pp. 198-216. Copyright 1943 by Oxford University Press. Reprinted by permission of the publisher.

object of scorn. Instead of ennobling Coriolanus through his fall
and death, he mocks and ridicules him to the end. In brief, he
fills the tragedy so full of the spirit of derision that the play can
be understood only if it be recognized as perhaps the most successful of Shakespeare's satiric plays.

II

Shakespeare found the materials for his play in Plutarch's *Life
of Coriolanus,* but he gave the historical events a meaning entirely his own. For Plutarch they yielded a lesson in political restraint and patriotism. As he tells the story continual war has
reduced the plebs to dire poverty. Indeed their misery is so
great that they demand a change in their constitution—the creation of new officers to be called tribunes, who are to redress
the wrongs of the people. This agitation contains a threat of
revolution. But the peril is averted because the senate is wise
enough to send to the plebs "certain of their pleasantest old
men" to discuss the grievances of the commoners. These ambassadors agree to the creation of the new officers and induce the
plebs to join with the patricians in the defense of Rome against
a foreign enemy.

Shakespeare completely changes the significance of these
events. His play opens "in the midst of a riot staged by the
mutinous masses," who are starving because of a shortage of
wheat. For their misery they blame not the drought, which is
the real cause of the famine, but their governing class, the
patricians, and, in particular, Coriolanus, the leader and mouthpiece of the aristocrats. They hate him for the contempt he has
always shown them. Coriolanus in his very first speech proves
that their charge is just, for he addresses them as:

> dissentious rogues
> That, rubbing the poor itch of your opinions,
> Make yourself scabs.
>
> (I. i. 168-70)

This unsavory figurative language is characteristic of most of
the utterances of the haughty patrician. On the occasion in
question the vituperative torrent is interrupted by a messenger

who brings Coriolanus an order to lead the Roman army against the Volscians and Aufidius their leader. Since carnage is his natural element, he responds to this call with enthusiasm. But even the heroism he summons for the battle cannot temper his fundamental brutality. When at the first onslaught of the enemy his soldiers flee in disorder, he berates them with characteristically foul speech. By insults rather than encouragement he drives his men back into the fray, where he does deeds of superhuman valor, defeats Aufidius in single combat, and brings complete victory to his army.

On his return to the capital, the populace greets him with wild acclaim and the senators at once nominate him for consul. He craves the office, but his whole nature flares into revolt against the convention which demands that he stand in the market place and beg the plebians for their votes. However, at the insistence of his dominating mother he submits to the humiliation of this electioneering. Though his appeal is filled with disdain, it seems to succeed. But after he has come through his ordeal and gone home, the tribunes persuade the crowd that he has mocked them. If they possess any self-respect, they will at once revoke their "ignorant election." This they do and drive Coriolanus into the rage which the tribunes anticipate and exploit.

When they inform him of the people's change of heart, he insults them with mounting violence, until they call in a "rabble of plebians" and precipitate a brawl. In the course of this uproar the people and their officers are driven off. Later they return to find that Coriolanus has been persuaded by his mother to allay their anger with fair speech. But his amenity does not divert them from their intention to drive him into one of his fits of uncontrollable rage. They call him traitor, and to the word he reacts as they had planned. He looses upon them a torrent of abuse. This stimulates the rabble to shout for his banishment, and in the words of Coriolanus they "whoop" him out of Rome. Through his uncontrollable rage he has been manipulated into a course of action which is to lead to his self-destruction.

Then he goes straight over to the enemy, and although he treats all the Volscians with overbearing arrogance, his military genius enables him to lead their conquering army to the very

gates of Rome. There various representative citizens meet him
with desperate pleas to spare his native city. They find him
adamant. As a last resort his mother, Volumnia, accompanied
by his wife Virgilia and his small son, is sent out to confront
him. She feels sure that she can force him to abandon his dire
purpose, for she well knows her irresistible influence upon the
man who in many respects is still her little boy. She wisely does
not ask him to rejoin the Roman forces, but merely to force
Aufidius to make peace. Coriolanus is deaf to his mother's entreaties but cannot hold out against her anger. He yields in the
flurried terror of a frightened child.

Returning to the Volscian army, Coriolanus induces Aufidius
to "frame convenient peace." By thus snatching the fruits of
complete victory from the Volscians, he wins the undying resentment of their leader, who lays a clever trap to catch and destroy
the haughty Olympian schoolboy. He knows how to stimulate
Coriolanus to one of his characteristic fits of wild anger. He uses
the same method which the tribunes had found effective, and
insults him publicly. In the presence of a crowd of confederates
he brands him as a traitor to his adopted country. The accusation
has the desired effect. Coriolanus throws into the teeth of the
Volscians his former triumphs over them and raises their resentment to the killing point. Then, though the Lords of Corioli
protest, the Volscian plebians fall upon Coriolanus and kill him.

III

From this brief resumé of the action it should be clear that
Coriolanus, like all Shakespeare's other history plays, embodies
some of the author's political ideas. Some critics, to be sure,
hesitate to attribute any definite political views to him. The
idolaters of the early nineteenth century and their modern rep-
resentatives are responsible for this transcendental attitude
toward their hero. Shakespeare, they proudly assert, was not
of an age, but of all time. Of all movements in a given era,
political squabbles are the most ephemeral. Therefore to the
idolaters an assertion that Shakespeare expressed positive political opinions even in his chronicle history plays was the rankest
heresy. A. C. Bradley expressed their view when he wrote, "I

think it extremely hazardous to ascribe to him [Shakespeare] any political feeling at all and ridiculous to pretend to any certainty on the subject." [2] This betrays a strange view of the dramatist's art. He, less than any other man of letters, dares to retire to an ivory tower, remote from the social interests of his contemporaries, in order to allow the trade winds from eternity to blow through his philosophic mind. Shakespeare based his profound studies of human motive and human passion upon a realistic appraisal of the various milieux in which his characters came to life; and of all the environments in which human beings must live, the political organization most interested Shakespeare and his contemporaries. The problems of Tudor politics obsessed them.

The usual view is that in *Coriolanus* Shakespeare expresses his contempt for the common man and his conviction that political power in the hands of the mob always brings disaster to the state.[3] More recently critics have looked at the other side of the picture and discerned in Coriolanus' conduct an exposure of the brutal methods that dictators in every age must employ to retain their absolute power.[4] Each of these apparently contradictory views is partly correct. Though Shakespeare is not in this play showing his contempt for the common man, he is nevertheless expressing his vigorous disapproval of democracy. In common with all political theorists of his age, he regarded it as the absence of all government—a form of organized disorder.[5]

But he does not lay all the blame for the social chaos on the plebs and its leaders. To his mind Coriolanus is equally guilty. He is a bad ruler. In the many volumes that the fifteenth and sixteenth centuries devoted to the education of a prince, the supreme magistrate—usually the king—is admonished to regard his subjects as his children and to be a father to them. He must sympathize with their trials and dangers and feel keenly his responsibility for their welfare. He must follow the example set by Henry V toward his soldiers in Shakespeare's play of that name. But Coriolanus acts in a manner diametrically opposed. He hates the people. On almost every occasion in which he meets them face to face he berates them and curses them vilely. Inevitably he finds them hostile and recalcitrant to his leadership —brave and efficient though it be in battle. Instead of correcting their faults, he goads them to anarchy by his hostility and violence. Coriolanus is thus as much responsible as the plebs for the political débâcle.

As a political *exemplum* the play presents a case of violent political disorder and reveals its causes. The trouble lies in the fact that no civil group performs its prescribed duties properly. As a result the divinely revealed pattern for the state is disrupted and society reels toward primal chaos. This lesson could not be clearly taught in the terms of tragedy. With its interest concentrated upon the tragic career of Coriolanus the man, an audience might easily ignore the political significance of the play. But the satiric form gave Shakespeare an opportunity to treat derisively both the crowd and Coriolanus, between whose "endless jars" the commonweal was sorely wounded. A careful analysis of the play will show how skillfully the political teaching, the central theme of every Elizabethan history play, has been fitted to the satiric form of the drama.

IV

The play opens with a picture of a mutinous mob, in this way establishing immediately the atmosphere of social turmoil which is to exercise its destructive power throughout the action and to form a natural milieu for the subversive forces in the little world of Coriolanus' passions. In the midst of the uproar Menenius appears. He is the chief of the many commentators and expositors in this play who serve as Shakespeare's mouthpiece. He performs this service with a fussy garrulity that is intended to rouse our laughter. Later in the play he explains that he is "a humorous [i.e. crotchety] patrician and one that loves a cup of hot wine with not a drop of allaying Tiber in 't . . . One that converses more with the buttock of the night than with the forehead of the morning. What I think, I utter, and spend my malice in my breath" (II. i. 51-8 *passim*). The character of this speech, particularly its unsavory metaphors, stamps Menenius as Shakespeare's variant of the now familiar buffoonish commentator. Like Carlo Buffone he says right things in the wrong way, thus giving to his comments a kind of outrageous pertinence.

His first speech to the crowd only partly reveals these characteristics. In order to persuade it to cease its revolutionary uproar, he tells the fable of the rebellion which the other members of the body once raised against the belly,

> That only like a gulf it did remain
> I' the midst o' th' body, idle and unactive,
> Still cupboarding the viand, never bearing
> Like labor with the rest.
>
> (I. i. 101-4)

But the belly replies that by sending rivers of blood to all parts of the body it serves as the source of the health and the very life of the whole organism. The belly, it appears, stands in this parable for the senators, and for Coriolanus in particular, because in Rome he and his fellow patricians exercised the functions of the king. The mutinous members of the body represent the plebians.

The audience would have regarded this figure of the belly and its functions as a speech designed to characterize Menenius—to stamp him as a garrulous old man. But they would also recognize it as a conventional way of stating a familiar principle of current political philosophy. It would seem like a page torn from almost any political primer. Because both the plebs and Coriolanus disregard the principles illustrated in Menenius' parable they bring disaster to Rome and to themselves. The people, in seeking to exercise the functions of a ruler, were permitting "the foot to partake in point of preëminence with the head." They were instituting a form of democracy which was universally regarded as a monstrous body of many heads.[5] Coriolanus himself employs this figure to describe the proletariat. As he stands outside the gate of Rome, whence he has been driven by the mob, he exclaims

> The beast
> With many heads butts me away.
>
> (IV. i. 2-3)

Elsewhere in the play he calls the plebs Hydra.[6] Through the repeated use of such familiar figurative language the author impressed his historical lesson upon his audience. No member of it could fail to recognize the drama as an exhibition of the forces

of democracy at their destructive work. The most obvious lesson
that the drama is designed to teach is, then, as follows: The people should never be allowed to exercise any of the functions
proper to a ruler. That way lies anarchy. But the career of
Coriolanus is to constitute an equally impressive warning: No
ruler must act as cruelly and brutally toward his subjects as does
this man. He is more of a slave driver than a kind father. Such a
magistrate is always an architect of social confusion.

v

A character cast to play such an admonitory role cannot be
treated like an ordinary tragic hero. And Shakespeare deals with
Coriolanus from the moment of his first appearance through the
whole course of the play to the catastrophe in a manner directly
opposite to the one he invariably adopted for his real tragic
protagonists. In the first place he endows all his true tragic
heroes with many noble traits which appear and reappear
through the play. In particular he puts into the mouths of other
characters words of praise for the hero as they knew him before
he became a slave to one of the subversive passions. Shakespeare
also puts into his hero's mouth reflective soliloquies which reveal
his struggles between good and evil, and win our sympathetic
understanding even while he is losing his battle with destiny.
Then, as his protagonist stands at the very brink of the catastrophe, the poet allows him to utter a poignant speech which recalls to the minds of the spectators the loftiness of his nature
before he had been caught in the net of his tragic fate. Finally,
after the hero's death some character who has survived the holo-
caust is likely to utter a brief encomium or a benediction upon
the soul of the dead man.

These dramatic characteristics are all clearly illustrated in the
tragedy of *Hamlet*. In this play Shakespeare finds numerous
opportunities to describe his hero's nature before it was over-
whelmed with grief and melancholy. Ophelia's lament is the most
famous of these portraits of the uncorrupted Hamlet:

> O, what a noble mind is here o'erthrown!
> The courtier's, scholar's, soldier's eye, tongue, sword,

The expectancy and rose of the fair state,
The glass of fashion and the mould of form,
The observ'd of all observers—quite, quite down.

(III. i. 158-62)

The same innate gentleness shines through Hamlet's colloquies with the friends of his youth. It comes out clearly in his talks with Horatio, and only a little less appealingly in his conversations with his renegade friends Rosencrantz and Guildenstern.

But it is on the eve of his death that Shakespeare allows the best in Hamlet's nature to reveal itself in a final burst of splendor. He generously forgives Laertes. And he appeals to Horatio's loyalty in terms of idealistic friendship. Shakespeare enriches these speeches by marrying lofty thought to some of his most inspiring verbal music. Moreover Hamlet's death is followed by Horatio's benediction, in which he invokes the deepest religious emotions to add poignancy and elevation to the feelings aroused by the passing of his friend:

Good night, sweet prince,
And flights of angels sing thee to thy rest.

(V. ii. 370-71)

Coriolanus is treated in a completely different fashion. The very first comments made upon him are derogatory. The two citizens who discuss him in the opening scene are detractors. The first of them asserts that Coriolanus has served his country not from patriotic motives but only to please his mother and to flatter his own pride. The second feebly defends Coriolanus by saying, "What he cannot help in his nature, you account a vice in him." The first citizen, unimpressed by the notion that innate faults are not vices, replies, "He hath faults (with surplus) to tire in repetition." This very first expository scene presents Coriolanus' passion nakedly, stripped of all nobility. It is what Mark Van Doren calls "an animal pride—graceless, sodden, and hateful." This initial exposition is but the first of many conversations about Coriolanus, all contributing features to a disagreeable portrait.

The accumulation of derogatory comment does much to set the satiric tone of the play. "Groups of people," says Mark Van Doren, "tribunes, citizens, servants, officers laying cushions in the Capitol, travellers on the highway, the ladies of his household—are forever exchanging opinions on the subject of Coriolanus. And the individuals who share with him the bulk of our attention are here for no other purpose than to make leading remarks about him." [7] In other words the play is crowded with satiric commentators.

When two or three characters gather together, the subject of their conversation is always Coriolanus. And even his wife's friend Valeria and his mother Volumnia, in contriving what they think is praise of Coriolanus, reveal the savage results of his pride. Valeria's description of the little boy at play becomes a revelation of his father's heady violence. She says, "I saw him [the boy] run after a gilded butterfly; and when he caught it, he let it go again and after it again, and over and over he comes and up again; catch'd it again; or whether his fall enrag'd him or how 'twas, he so set his teeth and tear it! O, I warrant, how he mamock't it [tore it to shreds]" (I. iii. 66-71). Volumnia's comment on this incident —made with complete satisfaction—is "One on's father's moods." And she is right. Irascibility and anger are the emotions which Coriolanus most often displays—and properly, for they are the inevitable results of thwarted pride.

Of all the commentators Menenius is the least obvious in his hostility. That is because, being a buffoon, he inevitably draws the fire of some of the derision. Yet in his characterization of the tribunes, his unsavory metaphors arouse laughter, even while they furiously mock. Witness his vulgar description of the tribunes' attempt to act as judges: "When you are hearing a matter between party and party, if you chance to be pinch'd with the colic, you make faces like mummers, set up the bloody flag against all patience, and, in roaring for a chamber pot, dismiss, the controversy bleeding, the more entangled by your hearing . . . When you speak best unto the purpose, it is not worth the wagging of your beards; and your beards deserve not so honorable a grave as to stuff a botcher's cushion or to be entombed in an ass's packsaddle" (II. i. 81-7, 95-9). This is the buffoon at his expert best.

When this "perfect giber for the table" (and "giber" is an almost exact equivalent for our slang "wise-cracker") turns his wit upon Coriolanus, he realizes that it must combine exposition of the man's nature with his ridicule. Once while attempting to excuse his friend's violence, he says:

> His nature is too noble for the world.
> He would not flatter Neptune for his trident
> Or Jove for's power to thunder. His heart's his mouth;
> What his breast forges, that his tongue must vent,
> And being angry does forget that ever
> He heard the name of death.
>
> (III. i. 255-9)

The first line of his speech, torn from its context, has been used by many critics to prove that Coriolanus' pride is the tragic flaw in an otherwise noble nature.[8] But Menenius is speaking not of pride, but of headlong anger. Even if the old patrician had meant to say that the pride of Coriolanus was the infirmity of his noble mind, no one in an Elizabethan audience would have mistaken his opinion for Shakespeare's. By the third act even the slowest-minded spectator would have recognized Menenius as a sort of buffoon and his comments as food for laughter.

After this attempt to palliate his hero's anger, Menenius returns to his more characteristic vein of comment. Such is the tone of his description of his friend's appearance when rejecting the old man's appeal to save Rome: "He no more remembers his mother now than an eight-year-old horse. The tartness of his face sours ripe grapes. When he walks, he moves like an engine, and the ground shrinks before his treading. He is able to pierce a corslet with his eye, talk like knell and his hum a battery . . . He wants nothing of a god but eternity and a heaven to throne in" (v. iv. 14-26 *passim*). This is bitterly derisive comment, utterly inappropriate for a tragic hero on the verge of his catastrophe, but just the sort of talk best calculated to keep alert to the end of the play the satiric attitude of an unsympathetic audience.

VI

This purpose is accomplished throughout the drama in still more direct ways. Instead of revealing a rich inner nature in profound poetic soliloquies, Coriolanus exhibits over and over again his one

ruling passion—the choler which Renaissance philosophers regarded as the inevitable result of wounded pride. At every one of
his encounters with the people his rage boils at their imperti-
nence. His contempt he displays through the insults which a
"lonely dragon" or Caliban might pour upon "rank-scented" men.
When his soldiers retreat before the attack of the Volscians, he
shouts:

> All the contagion of the South light on you,
> You shames of Rome! you herd of—. Biles and plagues
> Plaster you o'er, that you may be abhorr'd
> Farther than seen, and one infect another
> Against the wind a mile! You souls of geese
> That bear the shapes of men, how have you run
> From slaves that apes would beat!
>
> (I. iv. 30-36)

For this voice we can feel only aversion. Yet its vigor and its lean
thrust form an almost perfect expression of the spirit of Juvenalian
satire. Indeed the bare poetic style of this play, lamented by most
critics, is exquisitely adapted to the author's derisive intentions.

Understanding the easy inflammability of Coriolanus, the
tribunes are able to teach the plebs just how to induce his
paroxysms of anger. When thus beside himself, he becomes their
easy victim: "Put him to choler straight," they advise,

> . . . Being once chaf'd, he cannot
> Be rein'd again to temperance; then he speaks
> What's in his heart; and that is there which looks
> With us to break his neck.
>
> (III. iii. 25-30)

By following these instructions the mob produces a rhyth-
mical recurrence of Coriolanus' grotesque rage; and this stimulated repetition of a vice or a folly is of the very essence of satire
of every sort. It turns Coriolanus into a jack-in-the-box. Every
time his self-esteem is depressed, it springs back with the same
choler-distorted face. This emotional automatism deprives his
pride and his anger of all dignity. It makes him a natural object
of derision.

Coriolanus is also his mother's puppet. Volumnia transforms him into a terrified little boy every time the two confront each other. Shakespeare may have intended her to represent an austere patrician woman of early Rome, a worthy mother of grim warriors. Yet she wins from her son not the respect of a man, but the frightened obedience of a whimpering urchin. His attitude toward her remains completely infantile.

It is Volumnia who has forced her son to become a soldier and to exult in the blood and sweat of war. Plutarch describes Coriolanus as driven to battle by an irresistible impulse of his own nature. But Shakespeare tells us that it was Volumnia, "poor hen, who clucked him to the wars and home." This barn-yard figure incidentally deprives the martial impulses of Coriolanus of every shred of dignity. As a soldier he was and remains his mother's creature. Her proud boast is the truth:

> Thy valiantness was mine, thou suck'st it from me.
>
> (III. ii. 129)

When he is at the front, she relieves her anxiety by imagining him wading in triumph through seas of carnage and blood.

Though Volumnia has also bred into her son his contempt for the people, she knows that he must placate them. She realizes that if he is ever to become consul, he must stand in the market place and humbly beg for their votes. So at first she entreats him to go through the distasteful ceremony merely to please her:

> I prithee now, sweet son, as thou hast said
> My praises made thee first a soldier, so,
> To have my praise for this, perform a part
> Thou hast not done before.
>
> (III. ii. 107-10)

But even for his mother's sake Coriolanus refuses to let his disposition be possessed by "some harlot's spirit," to turn his voice "into a pipe small as an eunuch," or to allow a "beggar's tongue make motion through his lips." His answer to her courteous pleading is a flat, "I will not do't."

Then Volumnia loses her temper and soundly scolds her son. Her burst of scorn and anger immediately brings him around, reducing him to the stature of a frightened child, ridiculously eager to pacify an irate parent:

> Pray be content [he almost whimpers];
> Mother, I am going to the market place.
> Chide me no more.
> . . . Look I am going.
>
> (III. ii. 130-32; 134)

The contrast between his arrogant attitude toward all other persons in the drama and his infantile cowering before his mother's severity is ridiculous, and is intended to be so.

His last scene with Volumnia, in which she finally dissuades him from leading the victorious Volscians into Rome, is a kind of incremental repetition of the interview just described. When neither her pathetic appeals, made as she kneels before him, nor his wife's tears divert him from his purpose, his mother again loses her temper. She rises from her knees, crying

> Come, let us go.
> This fellow had a Volscian to his mother;
> His wife is in Corioles, and his child
> Like him by chance. Yet give us our dispatch.
> I am hushed until our city be afire.
> And then I'll speak a little.
>
> (v. iii. 177-82)

The old woman's fierce indignation again cows her son. Terrified by her anger, he cries out, like a helpless little boy:

> O mother, mother!
> What have you done? . . .
>
> O my mother, mother! O!
> You have won a happy victory to Rome;
> But for your son—believe it, O, believe it!—
> Most dangerously you have with him prevail'd.
>
> (v. iii. 182-3; 185-8)

This repeated quailing before his mother deprives Coriolanus of the dignity every tragic hero must possess. He never submits to her will through conviction or a sense of duty. His surrender is never evidence of filial respect. It is always a boy's frightened submission to a domineering woman. His undeviating arrogance toward the rest of humanity thus seems to be not exaggerated self-esteem, but compensation for the fear of his mother. He never attains the mean between these two unnatural extremes of emotion, but careens wildly between them. This instability renders him at once absurd and doomed. The forebodings which seize him after his final yielding to his mother are fulfilled. They set him in the path which leads straight to his downfall.

When Coriolanus returns to the Volscian army, he finds Aufidius hostile. He has all along been jealous of the renegade Roman and now sees a chance to destroy him. Knowing how easy it is to drive Coriolanus into a fit of blind rage, he sets the stage for the undoing of his enemy in a scene which constitutes the finale of the drama. And a masterful scene it is—an admirable catastrophe for a satirically conceived tragedy. It is an almost exact replica of those in which Coriolanus has collided again and again with the Roman mob. For Aufidius knows as well as the Roman tribunes how to manipulate his foe for his sinister purpose. He stirs the commoners against his enemy by haranguing them on the subject of Coriolanus' perfidy:

> He has betrayed your business, and given up
> For certain drops of salt your city—Rome,
> (I say "your city") to his wife and mother;
> Breaking his oath and resolution like
> A twist of rotten silk; never admitting
> Counsel o' the war; but at his nurse's tears
> He whin'd and roar'd away your victory.
>
> (v. v. 91-7)

In the course of this diatribe he taunts Coriolanus with epithets like "traitor" and "boy of tears," words which drive the warrior to an almost pathological seizure of rage. Then Coriolanus, shouting insults to the crowd, stirs the Volscian populace to fury. Once aroused, they rush upon him with cries of "Tear him to pieces!—Do it presently—He killed my son!—My daughter—He killed my cousin Marcus! He killed my father." The lords of Corioli, aghast at the blood-thirstiness of the mob, try in vain to calm it. But Aufidius and his conspirators have aroused the masses to the killing point. With cries of "Kill, kill, kill, kill, kill him" they fall upon Coriolanus and murder him.

This catastrophe gives final emphasis to the satiric view of Coriolanus. His automatic response to the artfully arranged provocation has at last entrapped him to his death. His end is the direct result of an over-stimulated reflex mechanism. The catastrophe of such an automaton is not tragic. It is so completely devoid of grandeur and dignity that it awakens amusement seasoned with contempt.

VII

This derision is much less absorbing than the pity and terror provoked by a genuinely tragic denouement. For that very reason a satiric play is better suited than a tragedy to present forcefully a political exemplum. In *Coriolanus* our interest is not held by the fall of a great man destroyed by forces beyond his control. It is rather caught by the picture of social and political chaos produced both by subversive forces of democracy and by a man who is temperamentally unable to be a successful ruler. The drama, then, is a satiric representation of a slave of passion designed to teach an important political lesson.

If this is true, why has *Coriolanus* never been a popular play? The principal reason is that critics and producers have invariably regarded it as a tragedy of an orthodox but greatly inferior sort. As a tragedy it lacks, as Stoll suggests, "constructive mechanism." Neither Fate nor a villain spins the plot. Coriolanus is destroyed by what is false within his nature. Yet we do not behold the inner emotional conflict that ends in disaster. We never see the dramatic struggle taking place within his mind and spirit. Therefore his nature inevitably seems poor and shallow. More than that, all the positive qualities which he displays are offensive. The remnants of a noble pride appear darkly through a cloud of childish impatience and uncontrolled rage. Finally, his catastrophe fixes ineradicably in the minds of all who expect a tragedy an impression of Shakespeare's artistic ineptitude. Coriolanus is manipulated into a fatal crisis and he meets his end in a riot which his mad fury has precipitated. No proper tragic hero moves thus toward his end in automatic response to artfully arranged stimuli. Nor can a death which comes to a man in a wild brawl signalize any triumph of the spirit.

These are defects only if Shakespeare intended *Coriolanus* to be a tragedy of the usual sort. If he meant the play to be more satire than tragedy, most of these qualities are virtues. Shakespeare naturally avoids arousing sympathy for a man whom he wishes to deride. For this reason he fills the early scenes with trenchant speech of hostile commentators, whose business is to draw a well-rounded satiric portrait of Coriolanus. Then the author traps his victim again and again so that we may see repeatedly the writhings of his anger. Finally he artfully designs a final scene which will make his satiric intention unmistakable. The murder of Coriolanus is not the moving death of a great hero; it is the deserved result of a supreme exhibition of his folly.

The bareness of the plot of *Coriolanus* also contributes to the satiric emphasis of the drama. True to the genius of satire it keeps the minds of the spectators riveted upon the ridicule of human faults. Derision, unless associated with moral indignation, does not easily awaken aesthetic pleasure. But in *Coriolanus* ridicule has been made to serve the teaching of sound political theory and only by a few can the descriptive forces in a healthy state be strongly enough felt to moderate the discomfort which most men feel at the persistent satire of a strong man.

NOTES

1. A. C. Bradley, "Coriolanus. Second Annual Shakespeare Lecture" (1 July, 1912), Proceedings of the British Academy 1911-12, pp. 457-73. Hazelton Spencer in *The Art and Life of William Shakespeare* (1940), 346-50, takes a similar view. "In *Coriolanus*," says the critic, "he [Shakespeare] frankly takes the line of least resistance." The idea is that he simply followed mechanically the facts laid down in his source—"that is all."

2. Bradley, op. cit. p. 461.

3. George Brandes, for example, in a chapter in *William Shakespeare, a Critical Study* (New York, 1902) emphasizes the absence in *Coriolanus* of "any humane consideration for the oppressed condition of the poor" and his "physical aversion for the atmosphere of the people." M. W. MacCallum expresses the more

measured view by admitting that "Shakespeare invariably treats crowds of citizens, whether in the ancient or modern world . . . as stupid, disunited, fickle" (*Shakespeare's Roman Plays and Their Background,* London, 1910, p. 470).

4. Serge Dinamov, *Works of Shakespeare,* 4 vols. I, xix.

5. These ideas have been thoroughly presented in James E. Phillips Jr.'s *The State in Shakespeare's Greek and Roman Plays* (N. Y., 1940) *passim.*

6. William Fulbecke in his *Pandectes of the Law of Nations* (1602) cites the history of Coriolanus to confirm his contention that the people is the "beast with many heads." This example he offers as part of his evidence drawn from history to prove that democracy is contrary to natural law.

7. Mark Van Doren, *Shakespeare,* New York, 1939, p. 10.

8. John W. Draper in an article called "Shakespeare's *Coriolanus:* A Study in Renaissance Psychology," West Virginia Bulletin (Philological Studies III, Sept. 1939, pp. 22-36) develops these ideas. He believes that *Coriolanus* is a perfect illustration of the notions on this subject developed in Plutarch's *Morals,* La Primaudaye's *The French Academie,* and Thomas Adams' *Diseases of the Soul* (1616) first introduced into Shakespeare studies by Lily B. Campbell in her *Shakespeare's Tragic Heroes* (Cambridge, 1930).

G. Wilson Knight

"GREAT CREATING NATURE":
AN ESSAY ON *THE WINTER'S TALE*

The Winter's Tale presents a contrast of sinful maturity and nature-guarded youth in close association with seasonal change. But there is more to notice. Shakespeare's genius is labouring to pit his own more positive intuitions, expressed hitherto mainly through happy-ending romance and comedy, against tragedy: they are to work as redeeming forces. The idyll of Florizel and Perdita will fall naturally into place: but romance in Shakespeare regularly enjoys the support, or at least the company, of humour. In Leontes Shakespeare's tragic art has reached a new compactness and intensity; and now in our next scenes, he gives us a figure of absolute comedy, Autolycus.

Richest humour offers a recognition of some happy universal resulting from the carefree stripping away of cherished values: elsewhere [1] I have compared such "golden," or sympathetic, humour, of which Falstaff is an obvious example, with humour of the critical, moralistic, Jonsonian, sort, such as that Shakespeare touches in Malvolio. Falstaff, though utterly unmoral, yet solicits our respect, and in that recognition consists the fun. The fun itself is, moreover, in essence a lark-like thing; it will sing, or dance, and may elsewhere house itself in spring-frolic and lyrical verse, such as "It was a lover and his lass . . ." introduced by Touchstone in *As You Like It* (v. iii.). Autolycus is a blend of burly comedian and lyrical jester.

From *The Crown of Life*, 1947, '48, '52, pp. 98-128. Reprinted by permission of Methuen & Co., Ltd.

He enters singing verses redolent of spring:

> When daffodils begin to peer,
> With heigh! the doxy over the dale,
> Why, then comes in the sweet o' the year;
> For the red blood reigns in the winter's pale.
>
> (IV. ii. 1)

He is spring incarnate; carefree, unmoral, happy, and sets the note for a spring-like turn in our drama, reversing the spring and winter conclusion of Shakespeare's first comedy, *Love's Labour's Lost*. His following stanzas continue with references to country linen on the hedge (cp. *Love's Labour's Lost*, v. ii. 914), song-birds, tooth-ache, ale, the lark and jay, "summer songs for me and my aunts," hay-merriment: it is a glorious medley of inconsequential realistic rusticity. Suddenly he comments in prose:

> I have served Prince Florizel and in my time wore three-pile; but now I am out of service.
>
> (IV. ii. 13)

He interrupts himself only to drop again into song—"But shall I go mourn for that, my dear?" Like Touchstone, and Poor Tom in *King Lear*, he has seen better days, but remains happy, his thoughts slipping naturally into song. He next explains his profession of minor thief, off the high road, as "a snapper up of unconsidered trifles" (IV. ii. 26).

His play with the Clown is supremely satisfying, and far more convincing than most stage trickery (e.g. Iago's of Cassio, Roderigo and Othello). The Clown is presented as a thorough gull, though not inhumanly so, as is Sir Andrew or Roderigo. Every phrase tells. As the supposedly injured man is carefully lifted—"O! good sir, tenderly, O!" (IV. ii. 76)—his purse is being delicately manœuvred within reach; the victim's attention is meanwhile firmly directed away from the danger-zone—"I fear, sir, my shoulder blade is out" (IV. ii. 78); and, when the business is successfully accomplished, there is the delightful *double entendre*. "You ha' done me a charitable office" (IV. ii. 82). Shakespeare's last work often recalls the New Testament, and here we have, in Autolycus' account of his beating, robbery and loss of clothes, a clear parody of the parable of the Good Samaritan, the pattern being completed by the Clown's continuation, "Dost lack any money? I have a little money for thee" (iv. ii. 83), and Autolycus' hurried and anxious disclaimer, "No, good sweet sir: no, I beseech you, sir . . . Offer me no money, I pray you! that kills my heart." (iv. iii. 85). There follows Autolycus' description of himself with some rather ordinary court-satire and finally the delightful conclusion, crying out for stage-realization:

Clown.	How do you now?
Autolycus.	Sweet sir, much better than I was: I can stand and walk. I will even take my leave of you, and pace softly towards my kinsman's.
Clown.	Shall I bring thee on the way?
Autolycus.	No, good-faced sir; no, sweet sir.
Clown.	Then fare thee well: I must go buy spices for our sheep-shearing.

(iv. iii. 119)

"Softly" is spoken with an upward lilt of the voice. Autolycus is a sweet, smooth-voiced rogue. The Clown says his last speech to the audience with a broad grin on his vacant face. When he is gone, Autolycus takes one agile skip, then:

> Jog on, jog on, the footpath way
> And merrily hent the stile-a:
> A merry heart goes all the day
> Your sad tires in a mile-a.
> (iv. iii. 133)

The incident circles back to its start, enclosed in melody. It is all utterly unmoral, as unmoral as the scents of spring. This might well be called the most convincing, entertaining, and profound piece of comedy in Shakespeare. Such personal judgements are necessarily of doubtful interest, except to help point my argument that, so far from relaxing, Shakespeare's art is, on every front, advancing.

The sheep-shearing scene similarly sums up and surpasses all Shakespeare's earlier poetry of pastoral and romance. It is, however—and this is typical of our later plays—characterized by a

sharp realism. The Clown's shopping list has already built a
sense of simple cottage housekeeping and entertainment, with
a suggestion of something out-of-the-ordinary in his supposed
sister, Perdita:

> Three pound of sugar; five pound of currants; rice. What
> will this sister of mine do with rice? But my father hath
> made her mistress of the feast, and she lays it on.
>
> (IV. ii. 40)

His following reference to psalm-singing puritans sticks out awk-
wardly; more in place are the "nosegays" and "raisins o' the sun"
(IV. iii. 43-53), especially the last. Autolycus has already sung
of the "red blood" reigning after winter (IV. ii. 4), and soon our
merry-makers are to be "red with mirth" (IV. iii. 54). We are to
watch a heightening of English country festivity, touched with
Mediterranean warmth, something, to quote Keats,

> Tasting of Flora and the country green,
> Dance, and Provençal song, and sun-burnt mirth.

So we move from spring to summer, under a burning sun.

The sun has not been so honoured before.[2] We have known
the moon-silvered encounters of Romeo and Juliet and glimmering tangles of the "wood near Athens"; also the cypress shadows
of *Twelfth Night* and chequered glades of Arden; but never
before, not even in *Antony and Cleopatra*—a necessary step,
where sun-warmth was, however, felt mainly through description, the action itself searching rather for "gaudy" (III. xi. 182)
or moonlit nights—never before has the sun been so dramatically
awakened, so close to us, as here; and there is a corresponding
advance in love poetry, compassing, though with no loss of magic,
strong fertility suggestion and a new, daylight assurance:

> These your unusual weeds to each part of you
> Do give a life: no shepherdess, but Flora
> Peering in April's front. This your sheep-shearing
> Is as a meeting of the petty gods,
> And you the queen on't.
>
> (IV. iii. 1)

So speaks Prince Florizel. But Perdita's answer witnesses both her country simplicity and feminine wisdom; she fears, as does Juliet, love's rashness and insecurity. Indeed, all Shakespeare's love-heroines, following the pattern laid down by Venus' prophecy in *Venus and Adonis* (1135-64), are given tragic undertones; they have an aura of tragedy about them. Florizel's love is more confident and showy (as usual in Shakespeare), but his use of mythology, as in "Flora" above, has a new, and finely convincing, impact. He catalogues the gods who have disguised themselves for love: Jupiter as a bellowing bull, Neptune a bleating lamb and, giving highest poetic emphasis to our play's supreme deity,

> the fire-rob'd god,
> Golden Apollo, a poor humble swain
> As I seem now.
>
> (IV. iii. 29)

"O Lady Fortune," prays Perdita in a phrase reminiscent of *Pericles*, "stand you auspicious" (IV. iii. 51). Though she remains doubtful, her doubts, a mixture of shyness and hard-headed feminine realism, only make the poetry more poignant. So, too, do the many homely reminders, as in the old shepherd's reminiscences of his dead wife's busy behaviour as hostess on such festival days as this, cooking, serving, and dancing in turn, bustling about, "her face o' fire" (IV. iii. 60) with both exertion and refreshment. Now Perdita, following Thaisa at the court of Simonides (the repetition is close, both fathers similarly reminding their apparently shy daughters of their duties), is "mistress of the feast" (IV. iii. 68; cp. "queen of the feast" at *Pericles* II. iii. 17), and has to conquer her shyness.

There follows Perdita's important dialogue with Polixenes. She, rather like Ophelia in a very different context, is presenting posies according to the recipient's age and offers the two older men (Polixenes and Camillo wear white beards, IV. iii. 417) rosemary and rue, which, she says, keep their savour "all the winter long" (IV. iii. 75): notice the recurring emphasis on age and seasons. Polixenes, however (forgetting his disguise?), appears to resent being given "flowers of winter" (IV. iii. 79) and

Perdita gracefully apologizes for not having an autumnal selection:

Perdita.	Sir, the year growing ancient,
	Not yet on summer's death, nor on the birth
	Of trembling winter, the fairest flowers o' the
	season
	Are our carnations, and streak'd gillyvors,
	Which some call nature's bastards: of that kind
	Our rustic garden's baren, and I care not
	To get slips of them.
Polixenes.	Wherefore, gentle maiden,
	Do you neglect them?
Perdita.	For I have heard it said
	There is an art which in their piedness shares
	With great creating nature.
Polixenes.	Say there be;
	Yet nature is made better by no mean
	But nature makes that mean; so, over that art,
	Which you say adds to nature, is an art
	That nature makes. You see, sweet maid, we
	marry
	A gentler scion to the wildest stock,
	And make conceive a bark of baser kind
	By bud of nobler race; this is an art
	Which does mend nature, change it rather, but
	The art itself is nature.
Perdita.	So it is.
Polixenes.	Then make your garden rich in gillyvors
	And do not call them bastards.
Perdita.	I'll not put
	The dibble in earth to set one slip of them;
	No more than, were I painted, I would wish
	This youth should say, 'twere well, and only
	therefore
	Desire to breed by me. Here's flowers for you;
	Hot lavender, mints, savory, marjoram;
	The marigold, that goes to bed wi' the sun,
	And with him rises weeping: these are flowers

> Of middle summer, and I think they are given
> To men of middle age. You're very welcome.

Camillo.   I should leave grazing, were I of your flock
> And only live by gazing.

Perdita.   Out, alas!
> You'd be so lean, that blasts of January
> Would blow you through and through.

(IV. iii. 79)

Of this one could say much. Notice first, the continued emphasis on seasons at the opening and concluding lines of my quotation; the strong physical realism (recalling Hermione's defence) in Perdita's use of "breed"; and the phrase "great creating nature" (to be compared with "great nature" earlier, at II. ii. 60).

The speakers are at cross purposes, since one is referring to art, the other to artificiality, itself a difficult enough distinction. The whole question of the naturalist and transcendental antinomy is accordingly raised. The art concerned is called natural by Polixenes in that either (i) human invention can never do more than direct natural energy, or (ii) the human mind and therefore its inventions are nature-born: both meanings are probably contained. Human civilization, art and religion are clearly in one sense part of "great creating nature," and so is everything else. But Perdita takes her stand on natural simplicity, growing from the unforced integrity of her own country up-bringing, in opposition to the artificialities of, we may suggest, the court: she is horrified at dishonouring nature by human trickery. Observe that both alike reverence "great creating nature," though differing in their conclusions. No logical deduction is to be drawn; or rather, the logic is dramatic, made of opposing statements, which serve to conjure up an awareness of nature as an all-powerful presence, at once controller and exemplar. The dialogue forms accordingly a microcosm of our whole drama.

There is a certain irony, too, in Polixenes' defence of exactly the type of love-mating which Florizel and Perdita are planning for themselves. Polixenes is, perhaps, setting a trap; or may be quite unconsciously arguing against his own later behaviour. Probably the latter.

Perdita next turns to Florizel:

Perdita.   Now, my fair'st friend,
                    I would I had some flowers o' the spring that
                          might
                    Become your time of day; and yours, and yours,
                    That wear upon your virgin branches yet
                    Your maidenheads growing: O Proserpina!
                    For the flowers now that frighted thou let'st fall
                    From Dis's waggon! daffodils
                    That come before the swallow dares, and take
                    The winds of March with beauty; violets dim,
                    But sweeter than the lids of Juno's eyes
                    Or Cytherea's breath; pale prim-roses
                    That die unmarried ere they can behold
                    Bright Phoebus in his strength, a malady
                    Most incident to maids; bold oxlips and
                    The crown imperial; lilies of all kinds,
                    The flower-de-luce being one. O! these I lack
                    To make you garlands of, and my sweet friend,
                    To strew him o'er and o'er!
Florizel.   What! like a corse?
Perdita. No, like a bank for love to lie and play on;
                    Not like a corse; or if—not to be buried,
                    But quick and in mine arms. Come take your
                          flowers:
                    Methinks I play as I have seen them do
                    In Whitsun pastorals: sure this robe of mine
                    Does change my disposition.

                                                    (IV. iii. 112)

Reference to the season-myth of Proserpine is natural enough; indeed, almost an essential. You might call Perdita herself a seed sowed in winter and flowering in summer. "Take" = "charm," or "enrapture." Though Autolycus' first entry suggested spring, we are already, as the nature of our festival and these lines declare, in summer. Note the fine union, indeed identity, of myth and contemporary experience, finer than in earlier Shakespearian pastorals: Dis may be classical, but his "wagon" is as real as a wagon in Hardy. See, too, how classical legend and folk-lore coalesce in the primroses and "bright Phoebus in his strength," a phrase pointing the natural poetic association of sun-fire and mature love (as in *Antony and Cleopatra*): the sun corresponding, as it were, to physical fruition (as the moon to the more operatic business of wooing) and accordingly raising in Perdita, whose poetry is strongly impregnated with fertility-suggestion (the magic here is throughout an earth-magic, a sun-magic), a wistful aside, meant presumably for herself. Perdita's flower-poetry reaches a royal impressionism in "crown imperial" and "garland" suiting the speaker's innate, and indeed actual, royalty. The contrasting suggestion of "corse" quickly merging into a love-embrace (reminiscent of the love and death associations in *Antony and Cleopatra* and Keats) finally serves to heighten the pressure of exuberant, buoyant, life. The "Whitsun pastorals," like our earlier puritans, though perhaps historically extraneous, may be forgiven for their lively impact, serving to render the speech vivid with the poet's, and hence, somehow, our own, personal experience.

Perdita's royalty is subtly presented: her robes as mistress of the feast have, as she said, made her act and speak strangely. Florizel details each of her graces (iv. iii. 135-43), wishing her in turn to speak, to sing, to dance—as "a wave o' the sea"—for ever. He would have her every action perpetuated, the thought recalling Polixenes' recollections of himself and Leontes as "boy eternal" (i. ii. 65). Florizel has expressed a delight in the given instant of youthful grace so sacred that it somehow deserves eternal status; when she moves he would have her, in a phrase itself patterning the blend of motion and stillness it describes, "move still, still so." Watching her, he sees the universe completed, crowned, at each moment of her existence:

> Each your doing,
> So singular in each particular,
> Crowns what you are doing in the present deed,
> That all your acts are queens
>
> (iv. iii. 143)

As once before, we are reminded, this time more sharply, of Blake's "minute particulars." The royalistic tonings here and in the "crown imperial" of her own speech (iv. iii. 126) not merely

> I take thy hand; this hand,
> As soft as dove's down, and as white as it,
> Or Ethiopian's tooth, or the fann'd snow that's bolted
> By the northern blasts twice o'er.
>
> (iv. iii. 374)

As in Keats' "Bright Star" sonnet, human love is compared to the
steadfast gazing on earth, or sea, of heavenly light:

> He says he loves my daughter:
> I think so too; for never gazed the moon
> Upon the water as he'll stand and read
> As 'twere my daughter's eyes . . .
>
> (iv. iii. 171)

This (with which we should compare the similar love imagery
of *Love's Labour's Lost*, iv. iii. 27-42) parallels Leontes' picture
of Mamilius' "welkin eye" followed by fears for the "centre" (i.e.
of the earth), forming an association of emotional and universal
stability (i. ii. 137, 139); and also his later contrast and identification of "nothing" with "the world and all that's in it" and the
"covering sky" (i. ii. 293-4). The universal majesty is continually
imagined concretely as earth and sky facing each other, as in
Leontes' "plainly as heaven sees earth or earth sees heaven"
(i. ii. 315); it is the universe we actually know and see, without
the cosmic, spheral, idealizing emphasis of *Antony and Cleopatra*
and (once) *Pericles*. So Florizel, questioned by Polixenes, calls
the universe as witness to his love:

> . . . and he, and more
> Than he, or men, the earth, the heavens, and all . . .
>
> (iv. iii. 383)

Should he prove false, then

> Let nature crush the sides o' the earth together
> And mar the seeds within!
>
> (iv. iii. 491)

Though reminiscent of nature's "germens" in *King Lear* (iii. ii.
8), those "seeds" belong especially to this, as to no other, play.
The emphasis on earth's creativeness is repeated:

Not for Bohemia, nor the pomp that may
Be thereat glean'd, for all the sun sees or
The close earth wombs or the profound sea hides
In unknown fathoms, will I break my oath
To this my fair belov'd.

                                      (IV. iii. 501)

The sun, as the moon before, is thought as "seeing"; it is the "eye" of heaven of Sonnet XVIII. The sun is constantly reverenced throughout *The Winter's Tale*, either directly (as in "welkin eye" etc.) or "the fire-rob'd god, golden Apollo" (IV. iii. 29) and his oracle. Nature here is creative, majestic, something of illimitable mystery and depth ("profound sea," "unknown fathoms"); but it is never bookish. Nor is it dissolved into any system of elements. Earth, sea, sun and moon are felt rather as concrete realities of normal experience, nearer Renaissance commonsense than Dantesque or Ptolemaic harmonies, whilst housing strong classical-mythological powers.

As for Polixenes' brutal interruption, we recall Capulet, Egeus, York, Polonius, Lear: Shakespeare's fathers are normally tyrannical and Polixenes has, according to his lights, cause. His threats, excessive as Capulet's, drive home a contrast of social tyranny with rustic health, clinched by Perdita's admirable comment already noticed: there is court satire elsewhere (as at IV. ii. 94-101; IV. iii. 723-6). Of course, this contrast works within, without disrupting, the prevailing royalism: apart from the old shepherd, the country folk are mainly represented by three fools and a knave.

The pastoral interest slackens and significant passages become less dense as we become involved in the rather heavy machinery of getting everyone to Sicilia. Both Camillo's tortuous scheme and Autolycus' additions to it lack conviction, and we suffer rather as in *Hamlet* during Claudius' and Laertes' long discussion about the Norman, Lamond. There is, however, some purpose in the sagging action of *Hamlet*,[3] whereas here we seem to be confronted by plot-necessity alone. About Autolycus' lengthy fooling with the Shepherd and Clown there is, however, something to say.

The dialogue not only protracts the sagging action, but rouses discomfort, Autolycus' description of the punishments awaiting the rustics, though pictorially in tone here (involving "honey," "wasps," midday sun, flies: iv. iii. 16-25), being a trifle unpleasant. Resenting Autolycus' fall from his first entry, one is tempted to dismiss the incident as an error. Autolycus is, however, being used to elaborate the vein of court satire already suggested by Polixenes' behaviour; it is almost a parody of that behaviour. The pick-pocket pedlar, now himself disguised as "a great courtier" (iv. iii. 777), becomes absurdly superior and uses his new position to baffle the Clown precisely as Touchstone the courtier-fool baffles William. His elaborate description of torments is extremely cruel; but then the court—Polixenes' harshness fresh in our minds —is cruel.

But we can still disapprove the subordination of humour to satire; and yet this very subordination serves a further purpose concerned with the essence of humour itself. Autolycus is first a composite of spring music and delightful knavery; during the sheep-shearing festival he is a source of rather ribald entertainment and catchy song. Next, he goes off to sell his wares, and on his re-entry recounts his successful purse-picking, which now, however, wins less approval in view of our accumulated concern for the simple people on whom he battens as a dangerous parasite. He is later by chance forced to dress as a courtier and further looks like making a good thing out of the two rustics and their secret. He is advancing rapidly in the social scale; the fates assist him. As he says,

> If I had a mind to be honest, I see Fortune would
> not suffer me: she drops booties in my mouth.
> (iv. iii. 868)

He is now all out for "advancement" (iv. iii. 873). After donning courtier's clothes, his humour takes an unnecessarily cruel turn. Something similar happened with Falstaff, who, a creature of pure humour (and also robbery) in Part I of *Henry IV*, becomes less amusing in Part II where he has advanced socially, wears fine clothes, and is tainted by a courtier's ambition.[4] He is himself subscribing to the very values which we thought he scorned and our source of humour to that extent weakened. The humorous parasite cannot afford to be too successful, any more than the saint. So with Autolycus: the merry robber-tramp, as he makes his way, becomes less merry. His vices become less amusing as he indulges his lust for power; as his egotism expands, a cruel strain (compare Falstaff's attitude to his recruits and Justice Shallow) is revealed; and he is at once recognized as inferior to the society on which, as a happy-go-lucky ragamuffin, he formerly preyed for our amusement. More widely, we can say that the delicate balance of unmoral humour—and no finer examples exist than the early Falstaff and Autolycus—must be provisional only; it cannot maintain the pace, cannot survive as a challenge among the summery positives here enlisted against tragedy: Falstaff was, necessarily, rejected by Prince Hal. Moreover, just as the Falstaff of *Henry IV* becomes finally the buffoon of *The Merry Wives of Windsor,* so Autolycus' last entry, when they have all arrived in Sicilia, and the Shepherd and Clown are rich and he a recognized knave, is peculiarly revealing: we see him now bowing and scraping to his former gull.[5] Meanwhile, our humorous sympathies have passed over to the Clown, rather tipsy and talking of himself as having recently become a "gentleman born" (v. ii. 142-64), so providing a new and richly amusing variation in social comment.

The long scene (IV. iii.) accordingly has a falling movement; from exquisite pastoral and the accompanying flower-dialogue, through robust country merriment to an all but ugly humour. The romance is to survive; not so Autolycus, who is to lose dramatic dignity. No one will accuse Shakespeare of lacking humour, but it is too often forgotten that his humour works within the limits set by a prevailing "high seriousness".

Our final summing movement takes us back to Sicilia, where all the people foregather and the complications are resolved.

Leontes is a figure of accomplished repentance. From now on religious phraseology is insistent, with strong Christian tonings:

> Sir, you have done enough, and have perform'd
> A saint-like sorrow; no fault could you make
> Which you have not redeem'd; indeed, paid down
> More penitence than done trespass. At the last,

> Do as the heavens have done, forget your evil;
> With them forgive yourself.
>
> (v. i. 1)

His kingdom, as the oracle foretold, is, through his own sin, heirless (v. i. 10). The contrast in *Macbeth* between tyranny without issue and Banquo's descendants may assist our response to Leontes' punishment. Both heroes offend against creation and are accordingly themselves uncreative. Paulina stands beside him, a perpetual reminder, referring to Hermione as "she you kill'd" (v. i. 15):

> *Leontes.*   I think so. Kill'd!
> She I kill'd! I did so; but thou strik'st me
> Sorely to say I did; it is as bitter
> Upon thy tongue as in my thought. Now, good now
> Say so but seldom.
>
> (v. i. 16)

Paulina is here to personify Leontes' "thought." Cleomenes, who cannot be expected to consider her dramatic office, rebuffs her sharply; and Dion, in a speech (v. i. 24-34) loaded with regal and religious impressions ("sovereign name," "his highness," "royalty," "holy," "holier"), urges the King to marry to beget an heir. Paulina, however, demands respect to the gods' "secret purposes" and the oracle of "divine Apollo," which asserted that Leontes should remain heirless till his child was found (v. i. 35-40); and he, wishing he had always followed her counsel, agrees, while further imagining Hermione's return, in accusation. His remarriage, he says,

> Would make her sainted spirit
> Again possess her corpse and on this stage—
> Where we're offenders now—appear soul-vex'd,
> And begin, 'Why to me?'
>
> (v. i. 57)

The world of sinful men is widely conceived; but also, ever so delicately, Hermione's return is hinted. Paulina next suggests that had his dead queen "such power" (v. i. 60) of return, she would have full "cause" of anger. Were she, Paulina, the ghost, she would shriek, point to his second wife's eyes, calling out, like the ghost in *Hamlet,* "Remember mine" (v. i. 67):

> *Leontes.*   Stars, stars!
> And all eyes else dead coals.
>   (v. i. 67)

Leontes sits almost tranced, in a state of other-worldly remembrance, all but outside the temporal dimension. Paulina continues to play with the thought of Hermione's return. Leontes is not to marry

>   unless another
> As like Hermione as i her picture,
> Affront his eye.
>   (v. i. 73)

His new wife shall be, she says, older than the first:

>   She shall be such
> As, walk'd your first queen's ghost, it should take joy
> To see her in your arms.
>   (v. i. 79)

Leontes enters into the grave game, willingly agreeing not to marry till Paulina bids him, and she clinches the compact, whilst further preparing for the resurrection:

>   That
> Shall be when your first queen's again in breath;
> Never till then.
>   (v. i. 82)

Observe how carefully we are being prepared for the conclusion, our thoughts whetted, our minds subtly habituated, if not to its possibility, at least to its conceivability.

On the entry of Florizel and Perdita our most important impressions concern Perdita herself, given the usual praise accorded these later heroines: she is "the rarest of all women" (v. i. 112), a "goddess" (v. i. 131), a "paragon" (v. i. 153), or —exactly suiting our recurring impressionism of earth and sun —"the most peerless piece of earth" "that e'er the sun shone bright on" (v. i. 94). She reminds the tactless but purposeful Paulina of that "jewel of children," Mamilius (v. i. 117). She is a creature

> Would she begin a sect, might quench the zeal
> Of all professors else, make proselytes
> Of who she did but follow.
>
> (v. i. 107)

Earthly and transcendental impressions intermix in her praise. Both recur together in Leontes':

> And you, fair princess—goddess! O, alas!
> I lost a couple, that 'twixt heaven and earth
> Might thus have stood begetting wonder as
> You, gracious couple, do.
>
> (v. i. 131)

Children, planted between heaven and earth, beget "wonder," a word to be used later on for miraculous events. Children are copies of their parents:

> Your mother was most true to wedlock, prince;
> For she did print your royal father off,
> Conceiving you.
>
> (v. i. 124)

We remember Mamilius' resemblance to Leontes and Paulina's description of Leontes' baby daughter. Children are nature's miracles, and these two as welcome "as is the spring to the earth" (v. i. 151). So Leontes prays that "the blessed gods" may "purge all infection from our air" whilst their stay lasts (v. i. 168), a phrase harking back to the description of Delphos, intimations of a transfigured nature matching our sense of a transfigured humanity. Man is, at his royal best, almost divine:

> You have a holy father,
> A graceful gentleman; against whose person,
> So sacred as it is, I have done sin.
> For which the heavens, taking angry note
> Have left me issueless . . .
>
> (v. i. 170)

The supreme punishment here, especially for a king, is to be left without natural issue; Florizel, however, lives, to render his father "bless'd" (v. i. 174). Through the royalistic convention the poetry touches some truth concerning man, his high worth in the creative chain, his ultimate stature, that outdistances political concepts.

This semi-divine essence is also dependent on the creative love-faith of the young pair. Disaster dogs them. After surviving "dreadful Neptune" (v. i. 154), they hear of Polixenes' pursuit. But, though "Heaven set spies" (v. i. 203) on them; though the "stars," in another typical image, will first "kiss the valleys" (v. i. 206) before they be united; indeed, though Fortune appear as a "visible enemy" (v. i. 216), their love is to remain firm. As Leontes gazes on Perdita, the stern Paulina remarks that his eye "hath too much youth in't" (v. i. 225), and reminds him of Hermione. "I thought of her," he answers, softly, "even in these looks I made" (v. i. 227).

Leontes' reunion with his daughter is presented indirectly by the gentlemen's conversation: it has already been dramatized in *Pericles* and our present dramatic emphasis is to fall on Hermione's resurrection. These gentlemen converse in a prose of courtly formality, leaving poetry to return in full contrast later. The scene is preparatory to the greater miracle and its style well-considered, introducing us lightly and at a distance to those deep emotions which we are soon to feel with so powerful a subjective sympathy. It strikes a realistic and contemporary note, using the well-known trick of laying solid foundations before an unbelievable event: we are being habituated to impossible reunions. Moreover, the slightly ornate decorum leads on to the formal, ritualistic, quality of the later climax. There is emphasis, as one expects, on Perdita's innate and actual royalty "above her breeding" (v. ii. 41) and a comparison of earlier events to "an old tale" (v. ii. 30, 67; cp. v. iii. 117). The description, plastic rather than dramatic, serves to create a *sub specie aeternitatis* effect, and so further prepare us for the statue-scene:

> . . . They seemed almost, with staring on one another, to tear the cases of their eyes; *there was speech in their dumb-*

> *ness, language in their very gesture;* they looked as they had
> heard of *a world ransomed, or one destroyed:* a notable
> passion of *wonder* appeared in them; but the wisest be-
> holder, that knew no more but seeing, could not say if the
> importance were *joy or sorrow;* but in the extremity of the
> one it must needs be. (v. ii. 12)

My italicized phrases are important. With the first compare
the Poet's comment on a painting in *Timon of Athens:* "To the
dumbness of the gesture one might interpret . . ." (I. i. 34):
see also *Cymbeline,* II. iv. 83-5. The watchers are, to quote
Milton, made "marble with too much conceiving"; made to
share the frozen immobility of art. Leontes' reaction to Hermione's statue is to be similar. Next, notice the apocalyptic suggestion of "ransomed" and "destroyed": is the miracle a transfiguration of nature or wholly transcendental? Certainly it strikes
"wonder." Last, observe the indecisive reference to "joy" and
"sorrow," which recurs again in description of Paulina:

> But O! the noble combat that 'twixt joy and sorrow was
> fought in Paulina. She had one eye declined for the loss
> of her husband, another elevated that the oracle was ful-
> filled. (v. i. 80)

Exactly such a blend of joy and sorrow is to characterize our
final scene. Though we are pointed to "the dignity of this act"
performed by kings and princes (v. ii. 88), it is all carried
lightly, the dialogue following on with courtly fluency:

> One of the prettiest touches of all, and that which angled
> for mine eyes—caught the water though not the fish—was
> when at the relation of the queen's death, with the manner
> how she came to it . . . (v. ii. 91)

And yet the easy, almost bantering, manner can, without losing
its identity, handle the most solemn emotions justly, as in the
account of Leontes' confession:

> Who was most marble there changed colour; some
> swounded, all sorrowed; if all the world could have seen
> it, the woe had been universal. (v. i. 100)

As in "ransom'd" and "redeem'd" earlier, the drama is, as it were, on the edge of something "universal": we watch more than a particular incident.

Now this dialogue has been leading us on very carefully to its own little climax, directly preparatory to the play's conclusion:

> No; the princess hearing of her mother's statue, which is in the keeping of Paulina—a piece many years in doing, and now newly performed by that rare Italian master, Julio Romano; who, had he himself *eternity* and could put *breath* into his work, would beguile *Nature* of her custom, so perfectly he is her ape: he so near to Hermione hath done Hermione that they say one would speak to her and stand in hope of answer: thither with all greediness of affection are they gone, and there they intend to sup. (v. ii. 105)

For the general thought of art imitating nature's human handiwork, compare the "nature's journeymen" of Hamlet's address to the Players (*Hamlet*, III. ii. 38). Here the statue is already associated with "eternity," regarded as the creative origin; [6] "breath" is to be important again. The implications of "eternity" are semi-transcendental in attempt to define that unmotivated power behind the mystery of free generation in nature and in art; indeed, implicit in freedom itself. The Gentlemen next refer to the statue as "some great matter" already suspected from Paulina's continual visits to the "removed house" where it stands (v. ii. 117-20). We are made thoroughly expectant, attuned to a consciousness where "every wink of an eye some new grace will be born" (v. ii. 124); a queer phrase whose courtly ease points the miracle of creation in time—there was a mysticism within Renaissance courtliness, as Castiglione's book indicates—whilst recalling the apocalyptic phrase in the New Testament about men being changed "in the twinkling of an eye."

Both through Paulina's dialogue with Leontes in v. i. and the Gentlemen's conversation we have been prepared for the resurrection. But there are earlier hints, not yet observed. At Hermione's death, Paulina asserted:

> If you can bring
> Tincture or lustre in her lip, her eye,

> *Heat outwardly or breath within,* I'll serve you
> As I would do the gods.

(III. ii. 205)

A warm physical realism is regularly here felt as essential to resurrection. Paulina is suggesting that it would need a Cerimon, in Christian thought Christ, to work the miracle: the possibility at least was thus early suggested. Later Florizel referred to just such superhuman power when, after calling vast nature and all men as witness, he swore:

> That, were I crown'd the most imperial monarch,
> Thereof most worthy, were I the fairest youth
> That ever made eye swerve, *had force and knowledge*
> *More than was ever man's,* I would not prize them
> Without her love.

(IV. iii. 385)

This close association of royalty ("crowned," "imperial," "monarch") with superhuman strength and wisdom may assist our interpretations elsewhere of Shakespeare's later royalism, whose spirituality (to use a dangerously ambiguous word) was forecast in Romeo's and Cleopatra's dreams of immortal, and therefore *imperial,* love (*Romeo and Juliet,* v. i. 9; *Antony and Cleopatra,* v. ii. 76-100). The king is, at the limit, a concept of superman status. Florizel later addresses Camillo in similar style:

> How, Camillo,
> May this, almost a miracle, be done?
> That I may call thee something more than man,
> And after that trust to thee.

(IV. iii. 546)

Another clear reminiscence of Cerimon, with suggestions of some greater than human magic; white magic.

Now, as the resurrection draws near, we are prepared for it by Perdita's restoration. St. Paul once seems, perhaps justly, to consider resurrection as no more remarkable than birth (see *Romans,* IV. 17 in Dr. Moffatt's translation).[7] Certainly here the safeguarding of Perdita is considered scarcely less wonderful than the resurrection of the dead. That the child should be found, says Paulina,

> Is all as monstrous to our *human reason*
> As my Antigonus to break his grave
> And come again to me.
>
> (v. i. 41)

Yet she is restored, as the Gentlemen recount, and human reason accordingly negated. Scattered throughout are dim fore-shadowings of the miraculous. Nevertheless, death looms large enough still, in poetry's despite: Paulina sees to that. When a gentleman praises Perdita she remarks:

> O Hermione!
> As every present time doth boast itself
> Above a better gone, so must thy grave
> Give way to what's seen now.
>
> (v. i. 95)

The temporal order demands that the past slip away, that it lose reality; the more visible present always seems *superior*. Paulina resents this; and her remark may be aligned with both our early lines on boyhood never dreaming of any future other than to be "boy eternal" (i. ii. 65) and Florizel's desire to have Perdita's every act in turn—speaking, dancing, etc.—perpetu-ated. All these are strivings after eternity. Paulina, moreover, here suggests that the gentleman concerned, who seems to be a poet, is himself at fault: his verse, which "flow'd with her [i.e. Hermione's] beauty once," is now "shrewdly ebb'd" (v. i. 102). The complaint is, not that Hermione has gone, but that the gentleman has failed in some sense to keep level. Death is accordingly less an objective reality than a failure of the sub-ject to keep abreast of life. This may seem to turn an obvious thought into meaningless metaphysics, but the lines, in their context, can scarcely be ignored. Throughout *Troilus and Cressida* (especially at iii. iii. 145-84, an expansion of Paulina's comment) Shakespeare's thoughts on time are highly abstruse (see my essay in *The Wheel of Fire*); so are they in the Sonnets. Wrongly used time is as intrinsic to the structure of *Macbeth* as is "eternity" to that of *Antony and Cleopatra* (see my essays on both plays in *The Imperial Theme*). As so often in great poetry, the philosophical subtlety exists within or behind a speech, or plot, of surface realism and simplicity. Now *The Winter's Tale* is hammering on the threshold of some extraordinary truth related to both "nature" and "eternity." Hence its emphasis on the seasons, birth and childhood, the continual moulding of new miracles on the pattern of the old; hence, too, the desire expressed for youthful excellence perpetuated and eternal; the thought of Perdita's every action as a "crowned" thing, a "queen," in its own eternal right (IV. iii. 145-6); and also of art as improving or distorting nature, in the flower-dialogue, in Julio Romano's uncanny, eternity-imitating, skill. And yet no metaphysics, no natural philosophy or art, satisfy the demand that the lost thing, in all its nature-born warmth, be preserved; that it, not only its descendant, shall live; that death be revealed as a sin-born illusion; that eternity be flesh and blood.

The action moves to the house of the "grave and good Paulina" (v. iii. 1). The scene is her "chapel," recalling the chapel of death at III. ii. 240, where Leontes last saw Hermione's dead body. Paulina shows them the statue, which excels anything "the hand of man hath done" (v. iii. 17); and they are quickly struck with—again the word—"wonder" (v. iii. 22). Leontes gazes; recognizes Hermione's "natural posture" (v. iii. 23); asks her to chide him, yet remembers how she was tender "as infancy and grace" (v. iii. 27):

> O! thus she stood,
> Even with such life of majesty—warm life
> As now it coldly stands—when first I woo'd her.
> I am asham'd: does not the stone rebuke me
> For being more stone than it? O, royal piece!
>
> (v. iii. 34)

Sweet though it be, it remains cold and withdrawn, like Keats' Grecian Urn. Yet its "majesty" exerts a strangely potent "magic" (v. iii. 39) before which Perdita kneels almost in "superstition" (v. iii. 43). Leontes' grief is so great that Camillo reminds him how "sixteen winters" and "so many summers" should by now alternately have blown and dried his soul clean of "sorrow"; why should that prove more persistent than short-lived "joy"?

(v. iii. 49-53). Leontes remains still, his soul pierced (v. iii. 34) by remembrance. Paulina, however, speaks realistically of the statue as art, saying how its colour is not dry yet (v. iii. 47); half apologizing for the way it moves him, her phrase "for the stone is mine" (v. iii. 58) re-emphasizing her peculiar office. She offers to draw the curtain, fearing lest Leontes' "fancy may think anon it moves" (v. iii. 61). The excitement generated, already intense, reaches new impact and definition in Paulina's sharp ringing utterance on "moves."

But Leontes remains quiet, fixed, in an other-worldly consciousness, a living death not to be disturbed, yet trembling with expectance:

> Let be, let be!
> Would I were dead, but that, methinks, already—
> What was he that did make it?
>
> (v. iii. 61)

A universe of meaning is hinted by that one word "already" and the subsequent, tantalizing, break. Now the statue seems no longer cold:

> See, my lord,
> Would you not deem it breath'd, and that those veins
> Did verily bear blood?
>
> (v. iii. 63)

As the revelation slowly matures, it is as though Leontes' own grief and love were gradually infusing the thing before him with life. He, under Paulina, is labouring, even now, that it may live. The more visionary, paradisal, personal wonder of Pericles (who alone hears the spheral music) becomes here a crucial conflict, an *agon*, in which many persons share; dream is being forced into actuality. "Masterly done," answers Polixenes, taking us back to common-sense, and yet again noting that "the very life seems warm upon her lip" (v. iii. 65). We are poised between motion and stillness, life and art:

> The fixure of her eye has motion in't,
> As we are mock'd with art.
>
> (v. iii. 67)

The contrast drives deep, recalling the balancing of art and nature in Perdita's dialogue with Polixenes; and, too, the imaging of the living Marina as "crown'd Truth" or monumental Patience (*Pericles*, v. i, 124, 140). Paulina reiterates her offer to draw the curtain lest Leontes be so far "transported" (cp. III. ii. 159; a word strongly toned in Shakespeare with magical suggestion) that he actually think it "lives"—thus recharging the scene with an impossible expectation. To which Leontes replies:

> No settled senses of the world can match
> The pleasure of that madness. Let't alone.
>
> (v. iii. 72)

He would stand here, spell-bound, forever; forever gazing on this sphinx-like boundary between art and life.

Paulina, having functioned throughout as the Oracle's implement, becomes now its priestess. Her swift changes key the scene to an extraordinary pitch, as she hints at new marvels:

> I am sorry, sir, I have thus far stirr'd you: but
> I could afflict you further.
>
> (v. iii. 74)

She has long caused, and still causes, Leontes to suffer poignantly; and yet his suffering has undergone a subtle change, for now this very "affliction has a taste as sweet as any cordial comfort" (v. iii. 76). Already (at v. ii. 20 and 81, and v. iii. 51-3) we have found joy and sorrow in partnership, as, too, in the description of Cordelia's grief (*King Lear*, iv. iii. 17-26). So Leontes endures a pain of ineffable sweetness as the mystery unfolds:

> Still, methinks,
> There is an air comes from her: what fine chisel
> Could ever yet cut breath?
>
> (v. iii. 77)

However highly we value the eternity phrased by art (as in Yeats' "monuments of unaging intellect" in *Sailing to Byzantium* [8] and Keats' *Grecian Urn*), yet there is a frontier beyond which it and all corresponding philosophies fail: they lack one

thing, breath. With a fine pungency of phrase, more humanly
relevant than Othello's "I know not where is that Promethean
heat . . ." (*Othello*, v. ii. 12), a whole world of human idealism
is dismissed. The supreme moments of earlier tragedy—Othello
before the "monumental alabaster" (v. ii. 5) of the sleeping
Desdemona, Romeo in Capel's monument, Juliet and Cleopatra
blending sleep and death—are implicit in Leontes' experience;
more, their validity is at stake, as he murmurs, "Let no man
mock me" (v. iii. 79), stepping forward for an embrace; as old
Lear, reunited with Cordelia, "a spirit in bliss," says "Do not
laugh at me" (*King Lear*, IV. vii. 68); as Pericles fears lest his
reunion with Marina be merely such a dream as "mocks" man's
grief (*Pericles*, v. i. 144, 164). Those, and other, supreme
moments of pathos are here re-enacted to a stronger purpose.
Leontes strides forward; is prevented by Paulina; we are
brought up against a *cul-de-sac*. But Paulina herself immediately
releases new impetus as she cries, her voice quivering with
the Sibylline power she wields:

> Either forbear,
> Quit presently the chapel, or resolve you
> For more amazement. If you can behold it,
> I'll make the statue move indeed, descend,
> And take you by the hand; but then you'll think—
> Which I protest against—I am assisted
> By wicked powers.
>
> (v. iii. 85)

The "chapel" setting is necessary, for we attend the resurrection
of a supposedly buried person; the solemnity is at least half
funereal. Much is involved in the phrase "wicked powers": we
watch no act of necromancy. The "magic" (v. ii. 39), if magic
it be, is a white magic; shall we say, a natural magic; the living
opposite of the Ghost in *Hamlet* hideously breaking his tomb's
"ponderous and marble jaws" (I. iv. 50). The difference is that
between Prospero's powers in *The Tempest* and those of Marlowe's Faustus or of the Weird Sisters in *Macbeth*. The distinction in Shakespeare's day was important and further driven
home by Paulina's:

> It is requir'd
> You do awake your faith. Then, all stands still;
> Or those that think it is unlawful business
> I am about, let them depart.
>
> (v. iii. 94)

The key-word "faith" enlists New Testament associations, but
to it Paulina adds a potency more purely Shakespearian: music.
Shakespeare's use of music, throughout his main antagonist to
tempestuous tragedy, reaches a newly urgent precision at
Cerimon's restoration of Thaisa and Pericles' reunion with
Marina. Here it functions as the specifically releasing agent:

> *Paulina.*   Music, awake her: strike! (*Music sounds*)
> 'Tis time; descend; be stone no more; approach;
> Strike all that look upon with marvel. Come;
> I'll fill your grave up: stir, nay, come away;
> Bequeath to death your numbness, for from him
> Dear life redeems you. You perceive she stirs:
> (<i>Hermione comes down</i>)
> Start not; her actions shall be holy as
> You hear my spell is lawful: do not shun her
> Until you see her die again, for then
> You kill her double. Nay, present your hand:
> When she was young you woo'd her; now in age
> Is she become the suitor?
> *Leontes.*   O! she's warm.
> If this be magic, let it be an art
> Lawful as eating.
>
> (v. iii. 98)

"Redeems" (cp. "ransomed" at v. ii. 16), "holy" and "lawful"
continue earlier emphases. The concreteness of "fill your grave
up" has analogies in Shelley's *Witch of Atlas* (LXIX-LXXI) and the
empty sepulchre of the New Testament. Such resurrections are
imaged as a re-infusing of the dead body with life. Hermione's
restoration not only has nothing to do with black magic; it is not
even transcendental. It exists in warm human actuality (cp.
Pericles, v. i. 154): hence our earlier emphases on warmth and
breath; and now on "eating" too. It is, indeed, part after all of

"great creating nature"; no more, and no less; merely another miracle from the great power, the master-artist of creation, call it what you will, nature or eternity, Apollo or—as in the New Testament—"the living God."

The poet carefully refuses to elucidate the mystery on the plane of plot-realism. When Polixenes wonders where Hermione "has liv'd" or "how stol'n from the dead," Paulina merely observes that she *is* living, and that this truth, if reported rather than experienced, would "be hooted at like an old tale" (v. iii. 114-17; cp. "like an old tale" at v. ii. 30, 67). Perdita's assistance is needed to unloose Hermione's speech; whereupon she speaks, invoking the gods' "sacred vials" of blessing on her daughter and referring to the Oracle (v. iii. 121-8). Leontes further drives home our enigma by remarking that Paulina has found his wife, though "how is to be question'd"; for, he says,

> I saw her
> As I thought, dead, and have in vain said many
> A prayer upon her grave.

> (v. iii. 139)

We are not, in fact, to search for answers on this plane at all: the poet himself does not know them.[9] Certainly our plot- realism is maintained: Paulina reminds us that her husband is gone; and we may remember Mamilius. It is the same in *Pericles*. The subsidiary persons are no longer, as persons, important: the perfunctory marrying of Paulina and Camillo to round off the ritual might otherwise be a serious blemish.

The truth shadowed, or revealed, is only to be known, if at all, within the subjective personality, the "I" not easily linked into an objective argument. It is precisely this mysterious "I" in the audience that the more important persons of drama, and in especial tragedy, regularly objectify. Now within the "I" rest all those indefinables and irrationalities of free-will and guilt, of unconditioned and therefore appallingly responsible action with which *The Winter's Tale* is throughout deeply concerned; as in Leontes' unmotivated sin for which he is nevertheless in some sense responsible; with his following loss of free-will, selling himself in bondage to dark powers, and a consequent

enduring and infliction of tyranny. The outward effects are suspicion, knowledge of evil and violent blame; with a final spreading and miserable knowledge of death ("There was a man
dwelt by a churchyard"—ii. i. 28), leading on, with Paulina's
assistance, to repentance. Time is throughout present as a
backward-flowing thing, swallowing and engulfing; we are sunk
deep in the consciousness of dead facts, causes, death. Now
over against all this stands the creative consciousness, existing
not in present-past but present-future, and with a sense of causation not behind but ahead, the ever-flowing in of the new and
unconditioned, from future to present: this is the consciousness
of freedom, in which "every wink of an eye some new grace
will be born" (v. ii. 124). Hence our poetry plays queer tricks
with time, as in the "boy eternal" passage where consciousness is
confined to "to-day" and "to-morrow": in Florizel's dreams of
immediate perfection eternalized; in thought of "eternity"
(which includes the future, being over-dimensional to the time-
stream) as the creative origin; and in Paulina's annoyance at the
poet-gentleman's ready submission to time the destroyer. Freedom is creation, and therefore art; and hence our emphases on
art, in the flower-dialogue, in notice of Julio Romano's skill, in
the statue-scene; and here we approach a vital problem. It is
precisely the creative spirit in man, the unmotivated and forward
"I," that binds him to "great creating Nature," the "great nature"
by whose laws the child is "freed and enfranchised" from the
womb (ii. ii. 60-61): he is one with that nature, in so far as he
is free. Our drama works therefore to show Leontes, under the
tutelage of the Oracle, as painfully working himself from the
bondage of sin and remorse into the freedom of nature, with
the aptly-named Paulina as conscience, guide, and priestess. The
resurrection is not performed until (i) Leontes' repentance is
complete and (ii) creation is satisfied by the return of Perdita,
who is needed for Hermione's full release. Religion, art, procreation, and nature (in "warmth," "breath" and "eating") are all
contributory to the conclusion, which is shown as no easy release,
but rather a gradual revelation, corresponding to Pericles' reunion with Marina, under terrific dramatic pressure and fraught
with an excitement with which the watcher's "I" is, by most
careful technique, forced into a close subjective identity, so that

the immortality revealed is less concept than experience. Nor is it just a reversal of tragedy; rather tragedy is contained, assimilated, transmuted; every phrase of the resurrection scene is soaked in tragic feeling, and the accompanying joy less an antithesis to sorrow than its final flowering. The depths of the "I," which are tragic, are being integrated with the objective delight which is nature's joy. The philosophy of Wordsworth is forecast; for he, too, knew Leontes' abysmal "nothing"; he too suffered some hideous disillusion, in part evil; he too laboured slowly for reintegration with nature; and, finally, he too saw man's true state in terms of creation and miracle. The response, in both Wordsworth and Shakespeare, is a reverential wonder at knowledge of Life where Death was throned.[10]

The Winter's Tale may seem a rambling, perhaps an untidy, play; its anachronisms are vivid, its geography disturbing. And yet Shakespeare offers nothing greater in tragic psychology, humour, pastoral, romance, and that which tops them all and is, except for *Pericles*, new. The unity of thought is more exact than appears: it was Sicily, at first sight ill-suited to the sombre scenes here staged, that gave us the myth of Proserpine or Persephone. The more profound passages are perhaps rather evidence of what is beating behind or within the creative genius at work than wholly successful ways of printing purpose on an average audience's, or an average reader's, mind; but the passages are there, and so is the purpose, though to Shakespeare it need not have been defined outside his drama. That drama, however, by its very enigma, its unsolved and yet uncompromising statement, throws up—as in small compass did the little flower-dialogue too —a vague, numinous, sense of mighty powers, working through both the natural order and man's religious consciousness, that preserve, in spite of all appearance, the good. Orthodox tradition is used, but it does not direct; a pagan naturalism is used too. The Bible has been an influence; so have classical myth and Renaissance pastoral; [11] but the greatest influence was Life itself, that creating and protecting deity whose superhuman presence and powers the drama labours to define.

NOTES

1. In writing of Byron in *The Burning Oracle*.

2. The heavy emphasis in *Love's Labour's Lost* remains throughout imagistic, in the manner of the Sonnets. This early play does much to define both the positive end of Shakespeare's work and the reasons for its postponement. See my remarks in *The Shakespearian Tempest*.

3. For a discussion of this "sagging action" see "Hamlet Reconsidered" in the enlarged (1949) edition of *The Wheel of Fire*.

4. This contrast has been well exposed by Professor J. Dover Wilson in *The Fortunes of Falstaff*. It is, however, there one strand only in a richer, satiric, design, with Falstaff becoming more forceful as he loses humour.

5. There is a deplorable stage tradition that Autolycus should again, in this late scene, start picking the purses of the Shepherd and Clown. The comedian will, of course, get his laughs; but for Shakespeare's opinion of such "pitiful ambition" see Hamlet's address to the Players (iii. ii. 50).

6. Compare the use of "eternity" as the home of divinity in close association with power at *Coriolanus*, v. iv. 26.

7. It must, however, be noted that the birth here concerned seems to be one of an abnormal, semi-miraculous, sort; but the Pauline doctrine of resurrection holds strong fertility suggestion elsewhere, as in the great passage on immortality at 1 *Corinthians*, xv, where the dead body is compared to a grain of wheat buried in earth.

8. A yet more relevant comparison with Yeats might adduce his drama *Resurrection*. Compare also the statue-interest of Ibsen's last play.

9. Note that Shakespeare here purposely drives the miraculous to a limit not touched in *Pericles*. For a full discussion of the metaphysical implications of the immortality dramatized in *The Winter's Tale* and other such works I must refer the reader to Chapter x of *The Christian Renaissance*.

10. We find a closely equivalent sense of the miraculous in the early scenes of *All's Well that Ends Well*, where Helena's mysterious art is clearly comparable with Cerimon's, and the style of speech continually takes on a rhymed formality similar to that in

Pericles. Lafeu's excellent comment might be read as a text for *The Winter's Tale:*

> They say miracles are past; and we have our philosophical persons, to make modern and familiar things supernatural and causeless. Hence is it that we make trifles of terrors, ensconcing ourselves into seeming knowledge, when we should submit ourselves to an unknown fear. (II. iii. 1.)

Helena's success is "the rarest argument of wonder that hath shot out in our latter times"; the "showing of a heavenly effect in an earthly actor"; "in a most weak and debile minister, great power, great transcendance" (II, iii. 8, 28, 40). See also the many thoughts earlier on science, nature, death, "inspired merit," "skill infinite" and divine action at II. i. 102-89; with hint of a medicine "able to breathe life into a stone" (II. i. 76). The relation of *All's Well that Ends Well* to the Final Plays deserves more attention than can be accorded it here. See also *As You Like It* (with Rosalind as magician), v. ii. 65-9.

11. And, it would seem, Greek drama too, especially Sophocles', wherein a tyrant is punished like Leontes by the sudden loss of his son (*Antigone*) and a child exposed like Perdita (*Oedipus*).

Theodore Spencer

SHAKESPEARE AND THE NATURE OF MAN:
THE TEMPEST

The Tempest is a play with so many layers of meaning that no single interpretation can do it justice. Yet if, as our discussion of Shakespeare draws to a close, we come back to our starting point, and think of *The Tempest* not only in terms of the difference between appearance and reality, but also in terms of the three levels in Nature's hierarchy—the animal, the human and the intellectual—which were the bases of Shakespeare's view of man, we may have a central framework from which further and broader interpretations may radiate. For in this last of his complete plays, as in those he wrote at the beginning of his career, Shakespeare uses, however unconsciously, the common body of psychological assumption that was given him by his time.

And yet, like everything else in the last plays, that assumption is transfigured and transformed; it is presented in a different climate of reality from its presentation in the tragedies, and there is less need for either the background of kingship—the hierarchy of the state—or the background and hierarchy of the cosmos; the individual human life itself, in its finest manifestations, is enough. At the heart of *The Tempest* there is an incantation which accepts things as they are, a tone which has forgotten tragedy, an order melted at the edges into a new unity of acceptance and wonder.

The action of the play takes place on a deliberately unidentifiable island, the kind of place where transfiguration is possible.

> The isle is full of noises,
> Sounds and sweet airs, that give delight, and hurt not.
> Sometimes a thousand twangling instruments
> Will hum about mine ears; and sometimes voices,
> Will make me sleep again.
>
> (iii, 2, 147)

In such a place, it is fitting that the animal level should be presented half-symbolically, through Caliban. We are no longer in the climate of tragedy, where human beings themselves are seen as animals, like the Spartan dog Iago or the wolfish daughters of Lear. The "beast Caliban," as Prospero calls him, is a thing "not honor'd with human shape (1, 2, 283)"; he is set apart—as it were, abstracted, from human nature. Unlike human beings he is unimprovable; he cannot be tamed by reason, he is

> A devil, a born devil, on whose nature
> Nurture can never stick; on whom my pains,
> Humanely taken, are all lost, quite lost.
>
> (IV, 1, 188)

And it is characteristic of him that he should take Stephano, the lowest available specimen of human nature, for a god.

The human beings on the island are a various crew, perhaps almost deliberately chosen to present as wide a range as possible. Stephano and Trinculo are associated with Caliban; Alonzo and Sebastian are selfish schemers, though royal; there is the good Gonzalo, and there is Ferdinand, who, excellent young man as he is, must still pass through some difficulties before he marries Miranda, who is to him the "wonder" of the island, and like the other heroines of the last plays, is a symbol of humanity at its best. All these people, with the exception of Miranda, go through some kind of punishment or purgation. The low characters are merely punished, they get be-fouled and be-labored, as is appropriate—they are incapable of purgation. But the courtly figures, Alonzo, Antonio and Sebastian, lose their human faculties for a time, to emerge purified as rational beings. As we know, the

theme of purgation occurs earlier in Shakespeare, especially in
Lear, but Lear loses his reason through a human agency, through
filial ingratitude. Alonzo and Sebastian are purged through a
superhuman agency, through magic. They enter the charmed
circle made by Prospero (v, 1, 55) and once there, their reason,
their specifically human faculty, is temporarily taken away, as
—in such very different circumstances—Lear's reason was taken
away. Their brains are useless, "boiled" within their skull;
"ignorant fumes . . . mantle their clearer reason," until finally

> their understanding
> Begins to swell, and the approaching tide
> Will shortly fill the reasonable shores
> That now lie foul and muddy.
>
> (v, 1, 79)

As soon as he comes to himself, Alonzo resigns the dukedom,
entreating Prospero to pardon his wrongs. Then Miranda and
Ferdinand are discovered, and it is on a regenerated humanity
that Miranda looks when she exclaims:

> How beauteous mankind is! O brave new world,
> That has such people in't!

Prospero—until he drowns his book—is clearly on a level above
that of ordinary human nature. Yet though we may recognize him
as a symbol of the third, the intellectual, level, Shakespeare's
presentation of him is so shimmering with overtones and implications, that to think of him merely as a representative of pure
intellect is an obvious falsification. Nevertheless we may say that
his use of magic is a way of making his superiority dramatically
effective, and the elves and demi-puppets that have been his
agents were considered in certain contemporary circles of thought
to be creatures above man in the hierarchy of Nature, between
men and angels.[1] Prospero's command of them obviously involves
a more than human power. Yet Prospero gives up this power,
and returns to the human level again. I do not agree with those
critics who say that Prospero, at the end of the play, "finds himself immeasurably nearer than before to the impassivity of the
gods." "His theurgical operations," says Mr. Curry, "have accom-

plished their purpose. He wishes now to take the final step and to consummate the assimilation of his soul to the gods. And this step is to be accomplished through prayer." [2]

But this is clearly a misinterpretation of Shakespeare's meaning. Prospero adjures his magic not to become like the gods, but to return to humanity:

> I will discase me, and myself present,
> As I was sometime Milan.

He compares (v, 1, 170) Alonzo's "content" at his rediscovery of Ferdinand to his own content at being restored to his dukedom, and in fact much of the point of the play is lost if we do not see Prospero returning to worldly responsibility. He must be restored to his position in the state, as he must be restored to his position as a human being. In a sense his temporary control of the spirit world has also been a purgation; he has come to the conclusion that, though he can wreak supernatural havoc on his enemies,

> the rarer action is
> In virtue than in vengeance,

and, his domination of the spirits having been outside the limits of human nature, his wisdom makes him return to his rightful place as a governor of himself, and as a governor, through his dukedom, of other human beings as well. Prospero, on his enchanted island, has been like a god, controlling the world of nature and the elements:

> I have bedimm'd
> The noontide sun, call'd forth the mutinous winds,
> And 'twixt the green sea and the azur'd vault
> Set roaring war: to the dread-rattling thunder
> Have I given fire and rifted Jove's stout oak
> With his own bolt: the strong-bas'd promontory
> Have I made shake; and by the spurs pluck'd up
> The pine and cedar: graves at my command
> Have wak'd their sleepers, op'd, and let them forth
> By my so potent art.
>
> (v, 1, 41)

But he abjures his magic, and having "required Some heavenly music" so that the courtiers may be restored to their senses—in Shakespeare's theater the music would have come from above, from the musicians' gallery under the "heavens," which were painted with the stars—he breaks his staff and plans to drown his book of magic "deeper than did ever plummet sound." In the company of his fellow men, Prospero returns to Milan.

This is Shakespeare's conclusion, the conclusion of the dramatist, some of whose most normal and likeable characters—Berowne, Hotspur, Mercutio—had been, from the beginning, men with a strong sense of everyday reality. There is something of these men in Prospero, though Prospero is of course infinitely wiser than they are, since he has surveyed everything, and has risen to a control of the supernatural before returning to the normal human life which they exemplified so much more naïvely than he. But in one way they are closer to Prospero, to Shakespeare's final vision of man's nature, than the wracked and tortured heroes of the great tragedies. For those heroes were split by an internal conflict, a conflict that was expressed in terms of the conflict about man's nature that was so deeply embedded in the consciousness of the age: whereas in Prospero there is no conflict; in his control of his world, internal conflict has no place.

And yet the view of man's nature that is so profoundly and movingly illustrated in the great tragic heroes has, after all, a relation to the view of life that is illustrated by *The Tempest*. Evil does exist—in the plotting of the courtiers, in the untameable animal nature of Caliban. And it may not be too far-fetched to see, in the very different ways by which Hamlet, Othello, Lear and Macbeth become, at the end of the action, resigned to the situations in which they find themselves, some relation to the theme of acceptance and reconciliation which is dominant in *The Tempest*.

Theirs, however, was a tragic reconciliation, and though it ennobles our conception of their characters, it does not redeem the evil in man's nature which has brought about their downfall. In *The Tempest* the evil *is* redeemed. Here, as in all the last plays, there is a re-birth, a return to life, a heightened, almost symbolic, awareness of the beauty of normal humanity after it has been purged of evil—a blessed reality under the evil appearance. It is not merely a literal reality; the mountains and waters, the human beings, have changed since Shakespeare first looked at them in the early 1590's. The tragic period has intervened; the conflict has given the assurance a richer and deeper meaning. But the literal reality is there just the same, in a garland of flowers, in a harmony of music, as the basis for the acceptance and the vision.

NOTES

1. See W. C. Curry, *Shakespeare's Philosophical Patterns*, Baton Rouge, 1937, p. 194.

2. *Op. cit.*, p. 196. In support of this view, Mr. Curry, like Mr. Middleton Murry, interprets Prospero's epilogue in religious terms:

> Now I want
> Spirits to enforce, art to enchant;
> And my ending is despair,
> Unless I be reliev'd by prayer,
> Which pierces so that it assaults
> Mercy itself and frees all faults.
> As you from crimes would pardon'd be,
> Let your indulgence set me free.

But the prayer is obviously merely a prayer to the audience. It is conventional for an actor to step half out of character in an epilogue, and that is what Prospero is doing here. His "prayer" consists of the last two lines, and has no metaphysical connotations.

Edward Hubler

THE ECONOMY OF THE CLOSED HEART

THERE IS no idea to which Shakespeare returns more often than the doctrine taught by the parable of the talents. It is referred to and expounded at length in the dialogue of the plays. It is often a major dramatic theme. In the sonnets it is no less prominent than in the plays. In both it is glanced at on innumerable occasions, when, most often, it is taken as correlative to an idea of more immediate importance. None of Shakespeare's ideas is more fixed or serves more often as a measure of character. The idea is, of course, the concept of man's stewardship referred to in the discussion of plenitude. Shakespeare's use of it in connection with propagation will indicate to modern readers the pervasiveness of his belief in it. In the very first sonnet the young man was told that he consumed himself in not giving himself, and in the fourth he was warned that "Nature's bequest gives nothing, but doth lend." The point invariably made is that we hold our possessions in trust, that we are the stewards and not the owners of our excellence. It is our function to employ our excellence to the best of our ability. Conversely, the man who simply preserves what he is entrusted with is regarded as the "wicked and slothful servant" of the parable, who said "I was afraid, and went, and hid thy talent in the earth: lo, there thou hast that is thine." Shakespeare states his view of the matter at the opening of *Measure for Measure:*

From *The Sense of Shakespeare's Sonnets,* 1952, pp. 95-6, 100-109. Copyright 1952 by Princeton University Press. Reprinted by permission of the publisher.

> Thyself and thy belongings
> Are not thine own so proper, as to waste
> Thyself upon thy virtues, they on thee.
> Heaven doth with us as we with torches do,
> Not light them for themselves; for if our virtues
> Did not go forth of us, 'twere all alike
> As if we had them not. Spirits are not finely touch'd
> But to fine issues, nor Nature never lends
> The smallest scruple of her excellence,
> But, like a thrifty goddess, she determines
> Herself the glory of a creditor,
> Both thanks and use.
>
> (I. i. 30-41)

In this instance the idea is allied to another of his most pervasive convictions—the belief that a virtue cannot finally be said to exist until it has expressed itself in action. Of that, more later. These ideas are among the *données* of Shakespeare's thought. When they are not made explicit, their values are always assumed . . .

In our time there was once a youth of one-and-twenty whose approach to emotion was simpler than Shakespeare's. He listened to his elders, and in due time he found that his experience squared with what he had been told. One day he had heard a wise man say that

> "The heart out of the bosom
> Was never given in vain;
> 'Tis paid with sighs a plenty
> And sold for endless rue."
> And I am two-and-twenty,
> And oh, 'tis true, 'tis true.[1]

In this poem the hurt of the open heart is observed in isolation and with a sentimentality nicely appropriate to twenty-two. Or perhaps the pain had not been isolated; it may be that it had subsumed all the other aspects of the experience. In either case it is what a well-lettered young man of melancholy spirit is supposed to feel, and it is what this particular young man had been taught to feel. It will serve as a contrast to Shakespeare's way of apprehending the same thing. In the Housman poem the view of the

situation is simplicity itself: the heart gives itself in vain. It does
not heed the wise men, and it learns that they were right. If we
were to go beyond the poem we could only suppose that the
young man should have listened to his elders in the first place.
In Shakespeare's view the open heart must give itself away in
order to maintain its existence. It is confronted with a perpetual
dilemma: it can know of its being only through self-loss. The
alternative is to conserve itself until it has withered away. Both
courses of action are illustrated in the plays; both are observed in
the sonnets with an acuteness Shakespeare was never to exceed.

Shakespeare noticed the obverse sides of things. Although the
sonnets proclaim his affection for the young man and his indulgence of him, they also disclose the attitudes which Shakespeare
takes to both the affection and the indulgence. He forgives a
trespass, and then, in the thirty-fifth sonnet, he apologizes for the
presumption of forgiveness, for, in his words, "excusing thy sins
more than thy sins are." We should notice that the forgiveness
also involves a certain debasement on the poet's part: "Myself
corrupting, salving thy amiss." Nor does he view simply his desire to change himself. In the one hundred and eleventh sonnet
he regrets the fate which has made him a man of the theatre,
which

. . . did not better for my life provide
Than public means which public manners breeds.

And although he assures the friend that he will do anything to
wipe away this stain, he realizes that the cleansing in itself is a
kind of stain. There would be a need for a "double penance"—to
remove the stain and "to correct correction." Protesting on another occasion (Sonnet 112) that he does not care what the
opinion of critic or flatterer may be, provided he has the good
opinion of his friend, he comments, "In so profound abysm I
throw all care." It is the recognition of the obverse of one of his
most firmly held tenets. The recognition does not destroy the belief; there is, as with Hamlet, the coexistent questioning of the
value of the thing in which he believes. When the sonnets are
aware that the friend's faults constitute a threat to the friendship,
there is the recurrent accompaniment of ironic self-consciousness,
arising, it appears, from a knowledge of the waywardness with

which affection, in order to maintain its being in an imperfect world, bestows itself with imperfect cause. It must, at times, debase its currency in order to exist. The alternative to this dilemma is the economy of the closed heart.

The closed heart may be poor, but it is at ease. Those men are most content who, though they inspire affection in others, have no need of it themselves. They are the men "in hue, all hues in their controlling." They have the power to hurt, but they are not hurt. Their happiness is the ignorance of their incompleteness.

> They that have power to hurt and will do none,
> That do not do the thing they most do show,
> Who, moving others, are themselves as stone,
> Unmoved, cold, and to temptation slow;
> They rightly do inherit heaven's graces
> And husband nature's riches from expense;
> They are the lords and owners of their faces,
> Others but stewards of their excellence.
> The summer's flower is to the summer sweet,
> Though to itself it only live and die,
> But if that flower with base infection meet,
> The basest weed outbraves his dignity;
> For sweetest things turn sourest by their deeds;
> Lilies that fester smell far worse than weeds.
>
> (Sonnet 94)

Everything about the poem invites comment, from the private force of the opening phrases to the last line, which, one editor assures us, "is not true." The recorded conjectures about it are rich in everything that conjecture can lead to, and in recent years it has been the object of more critical analyses than any other sonnet. If we approach it in the light of Shakespeare's other works, we might find it less difficult than it appears.

A survey of Shakespeare's works will show that this sonnet employs his most familiar imagery and that the thought of the sonnet, bit by bit, is to be found everywhere. Primarily it is the articulation of the parts which puzzles. On first reading the sonnet, we shall, of course, notice the irony of the first eight lines; and everything that we find in the other works will confirm it. It is preposterous on the face of things to proclaim as the inheritors of heaven's graces those who are "as stone." It can be other than ironical only to the cynic, for even the hardhearted man thinks of himself as generous and cherishes an abstract admiration for warmth. In addition, it will be noticed that what Shakespeare says here contradicts everything that he has said elsewhere on the subject. The irony of the octave is Swiftian in both method and force. In specious terms the poet states as true that which he is well known to consider false: those men whose appearance does not square with reality, whose deeds do not fulfill their promise, who move others while remaining cold, are proclaimed the heirs to heaven's graces. They are the owners of themselves, whereas throughout Shakespeare's works self-possession in the sense of living without regard for others is intolerable.

After the stinging "Others but stewards of their excellence," there is a full stop, and the poet turns to one of his most familiar images, the flower which is still beautiful although it lives to itself alone. The analogy is obvious. In the opening sequence the flower had been the emblem of the young man "contracted to his own bright eyes." Throughout the sonnets the poet praises the flower for its beauty, which he insists is only one of its attributes, and, he also insists from time to time, not its supreme one. The beauty, he repeats, is made fairer by its odor, which in turn becomes the symbol of that which is usefully good, or of the essential nature of the flower, or of both. In some sonnets the odor, or essence, may be distilled into perfume, in which case its odor will live "pent in walls of glass" after the flower has died. In other instances the distillation of essence is a symbol of procreation. In still others the odor of the flower symbolizes moral good:

> By why thy odour matcheth not thy show,
> The soil is this, that thou dost common grow.
>
> (Sonnet 69)

And,

> O, how much more doth beauty beauteous seem
> By that sweet ornament which truth doth give!
> The rose looks fair, but fairer we it deem
> For that sweet odour which doth in it live . . . .
>
> (Sonnet 54)

In the sonnet under discussion, the flower living to itself, and having therefore failed to fulfill its function, is incomplete, though it still has physical beauty; but if it should meet with infection (that is, if the expression of its function should be perverted), its odor (that is, its essence, its soul, its human utility as expressed in the deeds of the young man and the perfume of the flower) becomes worse than that of weeds, worse, that is, than that from which nothing was expected.

"They that have power to hurt" is both a great poem and an imperfect one. There is neither weakness nor relaxation. It should be noticed that the failure is not, as is often the case, one of fitting the matter to the form. There is neither tacking on nor repetition of matter to fill out the prescribed length. It is rather that the unity is marred by a change in tone, though not in intensity, at the close of the octave, and that the cohesion of parts depends upon a context of ideas which are not sufficiently explicit in the poem, though they ought to be familiar to all readers of Shakespeare.

I do not want to appear to consider the poem clearer than it is. The first line is tauntingly obscure, and an understanding of the poem cannot proceed without an interpretation of it. However, it seems reasonable to resolve the enigma of "power to hurt" by reference to what follows and to other works of Shakespeare. This I have tried to do. The meaning of "do none" is apparent if we take it to be clarified by expansion in line two. It was sometimes Shakespeare's hasty way to say a thing obscurely and then to clarify it by repetition, as in *King Lear*:

> *Regan:*   I have hope
>   You less know how to value her desert
>   Than she to scant her duty.
> *Lear:*   Say, how is that?
> *Regan:* I cannot think my sister in the least would fail her
>   obligation.
>
> (II.4.140-44.)

We may take it that the meaning of "do none" is restated in the line that follows: "That do not do the thing they most do show." This is quite clear, and its meaning is made specific in the next line: "Who, moving others, are themselves as stone." The "power

to hurt" is, then, the power to move others by imposing on their
unreciprocated loyalty, and "do none" is the condition of not
doing what the loyal friend, because of his loyalty, had taken for
granted. When Emilia discovers the murder of Desdemona and
is threatened by Othello, she replies,

> Thou hast not half the power to do me harm
> As I have to be hurt.
>
> (v.2.162.)

Her power to be hurt resides, of course, in her loyalty to Desdemona. As for the "base infection," there is no knowing what it
specifically was, or what it threatened to be, for it is referred to
conditionally in the poem and may have been apprehended rather
than actual. But it is clear from the importance attached to it that
it refers to some offence of the spirit, a denial of something
Shakespeare held essential to decent humanity. "Perhaps," Re-
becca West speculates,[2] "the sin against the Holy Ghost is to
deal with people as though they were things." In any case it is
clear from many of the sonnets that the quality in the young
man which most disturbed Shakespeare was the prudence of the
closed heart.

What of the persons in the plays who were the lords and
owners of their faces? Rosencranz and Guildenstern of course;
they were the essence of prudent self-interest. Macbeth tried to
be, and failed; he was too full of the milk of human kindness.
That he failed was his misfortune on the prudential level; on the
tragic level it is his glory. Lear and Gloucester were, at the beginning of the play; but their story is their growth in wisdom
and warmth. We will look in vain for the type among the heroes,
for they are heroes in proportion to their divergence from the
type. What of the villains? Well, Edmund is almost a clear case,
but he escapes the category by the pleasure he took in being
loved. The only major character is Iago, and he, toward the end
of the play, becomes the emblem of evil. The purest instance is
Northumberland, Hotspur's father, who is motivated by "advised
respects" throughout *Richard II* and remains unchanged throughout the two parts of *Henry IV*. He sends his son to death in a vain
attempt to secure his own position and later, when still another
rebellion is failing, he writes to his fellow rebels letters of "cold

intent" announcing his retirement to Scotland. It is his whole character. As Shakespeare conceived the story of *Richard II,* it required an intermediary, a representative of Bolingbroke on whom the onus of usurpation would fall, allowing Bolingbroke a measure of integrity. And for this purpose, the creation of a despicable character, he found that the embodiment of the closed heart was what was needed. Later, when even the lesser characters are not so single, the villains are less purely villainous than Northumberland; but to the end a large measure of his soul is the hallmark of their villainy. Shakespeare had feared from the beginning of the sonnets that the young man was cold and self-contained, but it was not until the story was well advanced that the characteristic was clearly recognized, named, and condemned.

All this is far from a simple matter. It involves elements to which few readers will assign precisely the same values. It is further complicated by the young man's being something of a patron of literature in an age of fulsome deference to patrons. Doubtless this contributed to the poet's attitude, but criticism has already made too much of that. A mercenary motive will always be understood, and criticism may seize upon it without the appearance of naïveté. Though this is of great use in simplifying the critic's task, the critic who finds that the author of *King Lear* was primarily an opportunist will also find that his criticism discloses little but himself.

The finest poetry in the sonnets has for its subject the complicated friendship for the young man. It seems to me that this friendship had historical reality, and also that the historicity is not a primary matter. Whether it derives from real or imagined events, the poet's subject matter is his thoughts, emotions, and convictions; and they find expression in poetry through the poet's use of his tradition. Among the relevant aspects of the poet's personality at work here is Shakespeare's gregariousness. It seems that it was with him as with Socrates, who remarked in *Lysis* that while there were many things for which he had no violent desire, he had a passion for friends. This attitude is explicit in the sonnets and implicit in all of Shakespeare's works, as it is in Montaigne's. It would seem to have been in Shakespeare before he read Montaigne, but the priority doesn't matter. A poet adopts an idea because it awakens something in him, because he finds it true, or serviceably so in a germinal way.

Are there not times when even the mature poet is looking for his own thoughts and feelings in those of his fellow writers? And since the thoughts and feelings of an important writer are normally in a state of becoming—sometimes through conscious seeking, sometimes through assimilation, as a seed absorbs its nurture from the earth—we cannot often know what is his and what belongs to his tradition, or that, indeed, they are not the same thing. Granville-Barker has remarked that Shakespeare's writing doubtless taught him as much about people as living among them; that is, his writing required a doubling back on his own experience in order to understand it more fully. As a consequence the literary recreation of an experience may endow the poem with faculties which obscure the germinal experience even to the writer's fellow participants in it.

Like the other ideas common to the sonnets, Shakespeare's ideas of friendship recur throughout his works with a persistence which, for some, will indicate his belief and sketch an aspect of his character. Such readers will say, "Here Shakespeare speaks for himself." And even though they are right, they cannot always hope to convince others of a different persuasion of a matter so individually perceived. They would do better to observe that in by far the greatest number of recurrences the dramatist is setting forth an idea intended, as the dramatic context discloses, to arouse the admiration and sympathy of the audience, and that when the same idea is stated for the same purpose in varying contexts, it becomes apparent that the dramatist holds the idea to be one to which normal humanity will respond with warmth. The sensible man will conclude that it is only a small step from this to the belief that the dramatist responded to the idea in the same way, and that, in fact, he discloses his sympathies in the notions he takes for granted. But we shall do well to remember that the disclosure of such sympathies and thoughts sketches the dramatist's and poet's spiritual biography, or if we prefer a lesser phrase, his poetic personality. The reader cannot proceed from this to the facts of the poet's daily life; not, that is, without some external documentation. Yet what we can learn of Shakespeare from his works, stripped of particulars as it is, is not altogether a dusty answer. Of our friends and neighbors we want to know the facts, for association on the practical level of daily living requires judgments which had better have a factual basis. But of an acquaintance of long ago it is better to know that he had a capacity for loyalty and devotion, and a passion strong enough at times to deny the loyalty, than to know where and when he first encountered his mistress or what her name was. We may know Shakespeare essentially without a bill of particulars, and we may be excused for supposing that, granted the necessity of partial knowledge, we have the best.

It may be that the idea of friendship in the sonnets is an idealization, a purified recreation of the poet's experience, and that it has only a partial or intermittent coincidence with his daily life. Or it may be that Shakespeare came at last to find the idea embodied in a living presence, as Hamlet, knowing an ideal of friendship, found it embodied in Horatio, and henceforth bore them both in his heart's core. We cannot know. We know only that in the sonnets we have a sketch of a troubled friendship in which the poet believes at times that the friend conforms to the ideal, wants at other times to believe it, and fears sometimes that belief is vain.

NOTES

1. From *A Shropshire Lad* by A. E. Housman. Copyright, 1924, by Henry Holt & Company. By permission of the publishers.
2. Quoted by Donald Stauffer in *The New York Times Book Review*, December 14, 1947.

GALAXY BOOKS FOR THE DISCRIMINATING READER

ABRAMS, MEYER H., ed. ENGLISH ROMANTIC POETS   GB35
AQUINAS, ST. THOMAS PHILOSOPHICAL TEXTS
       selected and translated by THOMAS GILBY   GB29
BARKER, ERNEST REFLECTIONS ON GOVERNMENT   GB15
BERLIN, ISAIAH KARL MARX   GB25
BOWRA, C. M. ANCIENT GREEK LITERATURE   GB30
BRUUN, GEOFFREY NINETEENTH-CENTURY EUROPEAN CIVILIZATION   GB36
CLARK, GEORGE EARLY MODERN EUROPE   GB37
CLARK, GEORGE THE SEVENTEENTH CENTURY   GB47
CLIFFORD, JAMES L., ed. EIGHTEENTH-CENTURY ENGLISH LITERATURE   GB23
COCHRANE, CHARLES NORRIS CHRISTIANITY AND CLASSICAL CULTURE   GB7
COLLINGWOOD, R. G. THE IDEA OF HISTORY   GB1
COLLINGWOOD, R. G. THE IDEA OF NATURE   GB31
COLLINGWOOD, R. G. THE PRINCIPLES OF ART   GB11
CRUICKSHANK, JOHN ALBERT CAMUS AND THE LITERATURE OF REVOLT   GB43
DEAN, LEONARD, ed. SHAKESPEARE   GB46
DIXON, W. MACNEILE THE HUMAN SITUATION   GB12
EVANS-WENTZ, W. Y., ed. THE TIBETAN BOOK OF THE DEAD   GB39
FEIDELSON AND BRODTKORB, eds. INTERPRETATIONS OF AMERICAN LITERATURE   GB26
GEROULD, GORDON HALL THE BALLAD OF TRADITION   GB8
GOETHE, JOHANN GOETHE'S FAUST *translated by* LOUIS MACNEICE   GB45
GRIERSON, HERBERT, ed. METAPHYSICAL LYRICS AND POEMS OF THE
       SEVENTEENTH CENTURY   GB19
HALSBAND, ROBERT THE LIFE OF LADY MARY WORTLEY MONTAGU   GB44
HEILER, FRIEDRICH PRAYER *translated by* SAMUEL MCCOMB   GB16
HERKLOTS, H. G. G. HOW OUR BIBLE CAME TO US   GB4
HIGHET, GILBERT THE CLASSICAL TRADITION   GB5
HIGHET, GILBERT JUVENAL THE SATIRIST   GB48
HOMER THE ODYSSEY OF HOMER *translated by* T. E. SHAW   GB2
KIERKEGAARD, SØREN CHRISTIAN DISCOURSES   GB49
LEWIS, C. S. THE ALLEGORY OF LOVE   GB17
MALINOWSKI, BRONISLAW A SCIENTIFIC THEORY OF CULTURE   GB40
MATTHIESSEN, F. O. THE ACHIEVEMENT OF T. S. ELIOT, *third edition*   GB22
MILLS, C. WRIGHT THE POWER ELITE   GB20
MILLS, C. WRIGHT WHITE COLLAR   GB3
MULLER, HERBERT J. THE USES OF THE PAST   GB9
MURRAY, GILBERT THE RISE OF THE GREEK EPIC   GB41
OTTO, RUDOLF THE IDEA OF THE HOLY   GB14
RADHAKRISHNAN, S. EASTERN RELIGIONS AND WESTERN THOUGHT   GB27
ROBERTS, DAVID E. EXISTENTIALISM AND RELIGIOUS BELIEF
       edited by ROGER HAZELTON   GB28
ROSTOVTZEFF, M. ROME   GB42
RUSSELL, BERTRAND THE PROBLEMS OF PHILOSOPHY   GB21
RUSSELL, BERTRAND RELIGION AND SCIENCE   GB50
SHAPIRO, HARRY L., ed. MAN, CULTURE, AND SOCIETY   GB32
THUCYDIDES THE HISTORY OF THE PELOPONNESIAN WAR
       edited and translated by RICHARD LIVINGSTONE   GB33
TILLICH, PAUL LOVE, POWER AND JUSTICE   GB38
TURBERVILLE, A. S. ENGLISH MEN AND MANNERS IN THE EIGHTEENTH CENTURY   GB10
WAGENKNECHT, EDWARD, ed. CHAUCER   GB24
WEBER, MAX FROM MAX WEBER: ESSAYS IN SOCIOLOGY
       edited and translated by H. H. GERTH AND C. WRIGHT MILLS   GB13
WEDGWOOD, C. V. SEVENTEENTH-CENTURY ENGLISH LITERATURE   GB51
WHITEHEAD, ALFRED NORTH AN INTRODUCTION TO MATHEMATICS   GB18
WOODWARD, C. VANN THE STRANGE CAREER OF JIM CROW   GB6
WRIGHT, AUSTIN, ed. VICTORIAN LITERATURE   GB52
YOUNG, J. Z. DOUBT AND CERTAINTY IN SCIENCE   GB34